GREEN ARROW

VOLUME 3

THE TRIAL OF OLIVER QUEEN

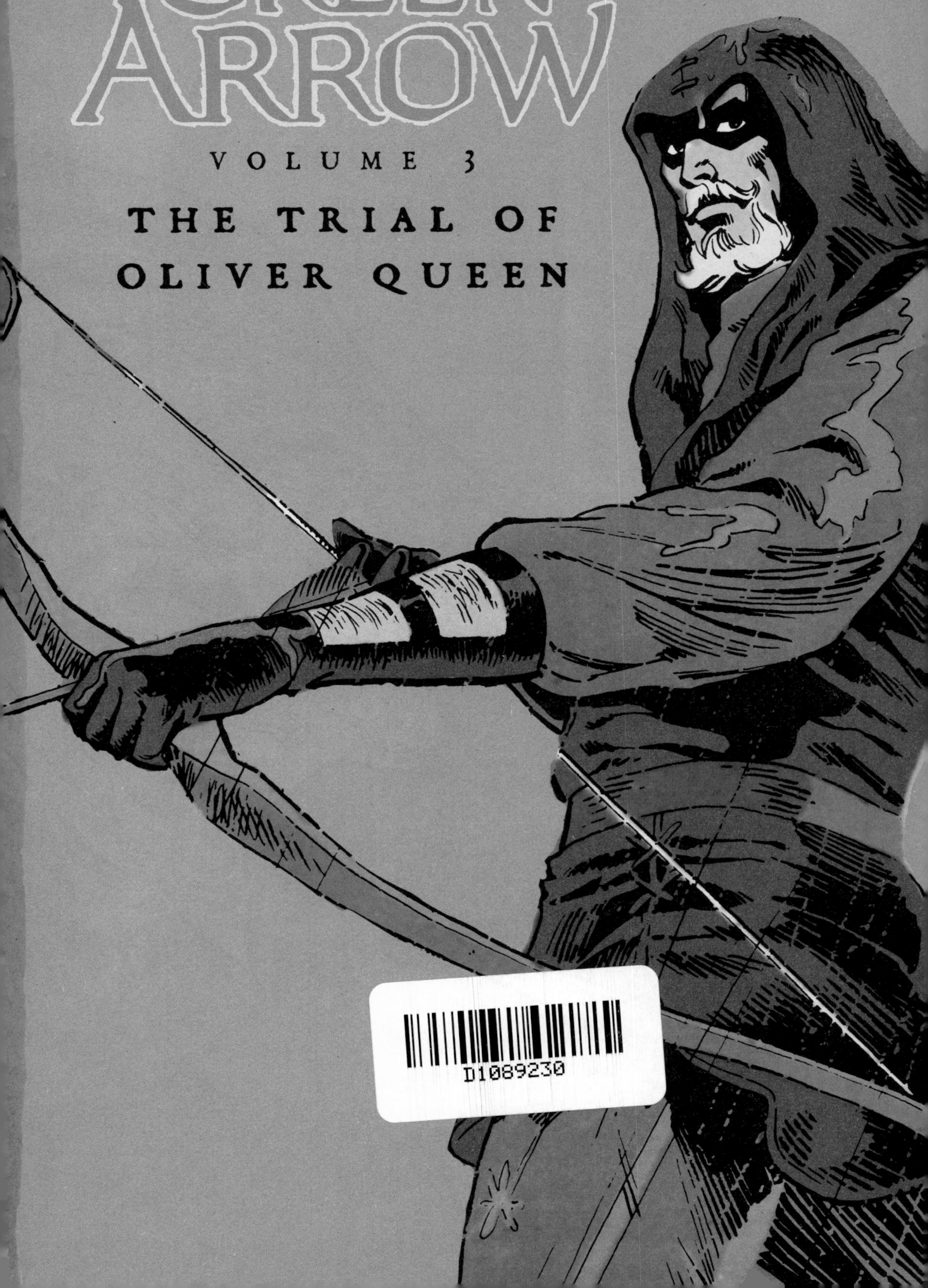

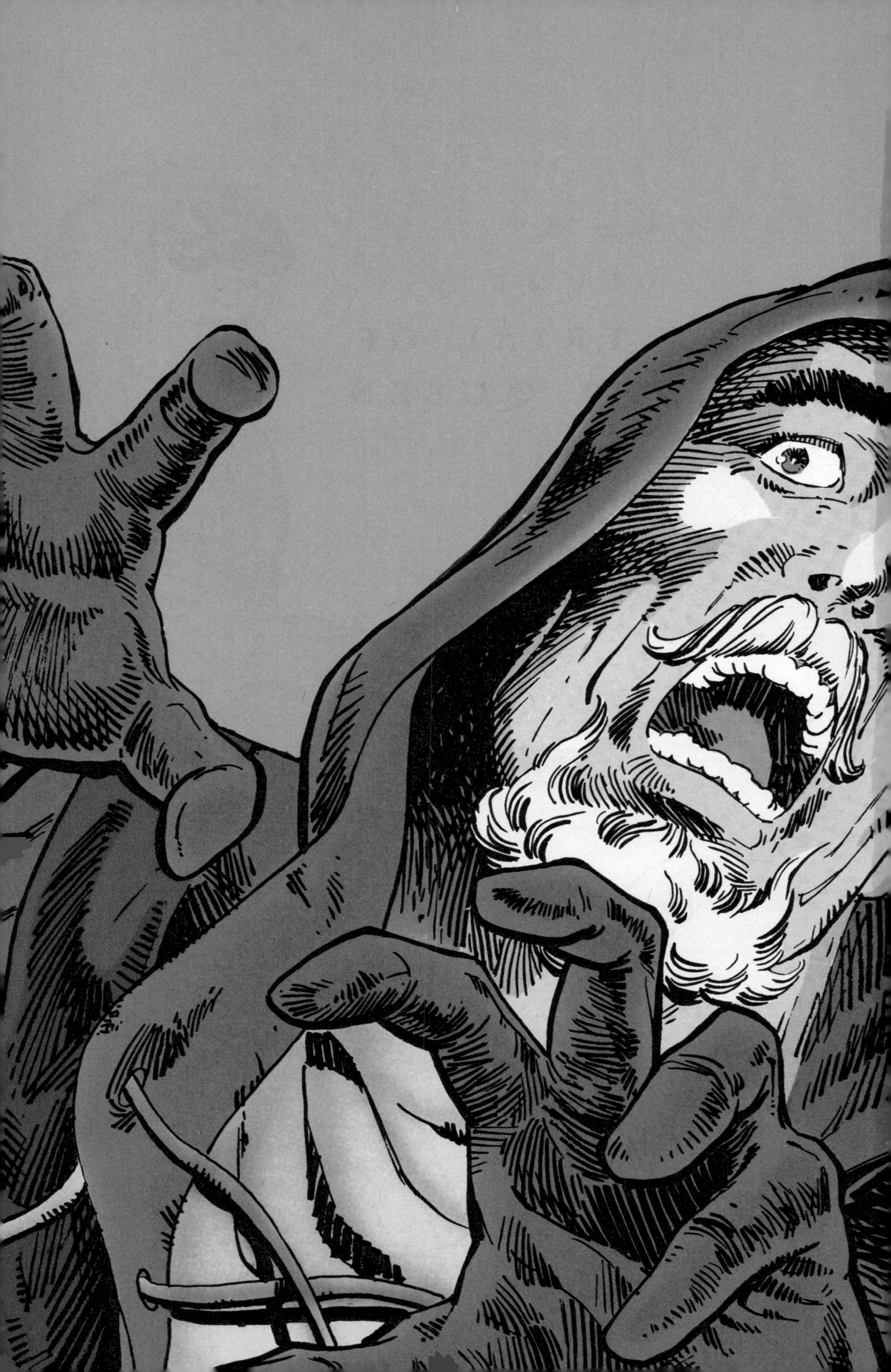

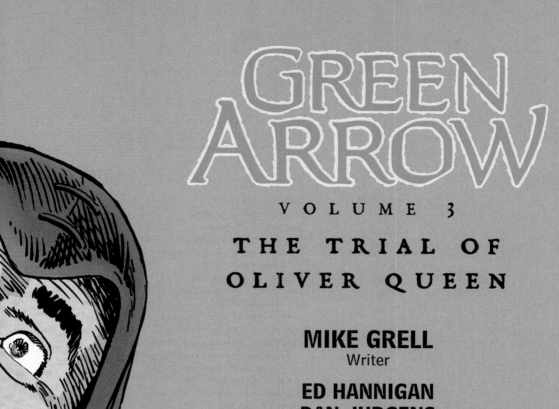

GREEN ARROW

VOLUME 3

THE TRIAL OF OLIVER QUEEN

MIKE GRELL
Writer

ED HANNIGAN
DAN JURGENS
DICK GIORDANO
FRANK MCLAUGHLIN
Artists

JULIA LACQUEMENT
Colorist

JOHN COSTANZA
Letterer

ED HANNIGAN
DICK GIORDANO
Cover Art

ED HANNIGAN
DAN JURGENS
DICK GIORDANO
Original Series Covers

Mike Gold Editor – Original Series
Brian Augustyn Associate Editor – Original Series
Scott Nybakken Editor
Robbin Brosterman Design Director – Books
Damian Ryland Publication Design

Bob Harras Senior VP – Editor-in-Chief, DC Comics

Diane Nelson President
Dan DiDio and Jim Lee Co-Publishers
Geoff Johns Chief Creative Officer
Amit Desai Senior VP – Marketing & Franchise Management
Amy Genkins Senior VP – Business & Legal Affairs
Nairi Gardiner Senior VP – Finance
Jeff Boison VP – Publishing Planning
Mark Chiarello VP – Art Direction & Design
John Cunningham VP – Marketing
Terri Cunningham VP – Editorial Administration
Larry Ganem VP – Talent Relations & Services
Alison Gill Senior VP – Manufacturing & Operations
Hank Kanalz Senior VP – Vertigo & Integrated Publishing
Jay Kogan VP – Business & Legal Affairs, Publishing
Jack Mahan VP – Business Affairs, Talent
Nick Napolitano VP – Manufacturing Administration
Sue Pohja VP – Book Sales
Fred Ruiz VP – Manufacturing Operations
Courtney Simmons Senior VP – Publicity
Bob Wayne Senior VP – Sales

GREEN ARROW VOL. 3: THE TRIAL OF OLIVER QUEEN

DC Comics
4000 Warner Blvd., Burbank, CA 91522
A Warner Bros. Entertainment Company.
Printed by RR Donnelley, Owensville, MO, USA. 5/1/15. First Printing.
ISBN: 978-1-4012-5523-7

Library of Congress Cataloging-in-Publication Data

Grell, Mike.
  Green Arrow. Volume 3, The Trial of Oliver Queen / Mike Grell,
Ed Hannigan.
     pages cm
  ISBN 978-1-4012-5523-7 (paperback)
  1. Graphic novels. I. Hannigan, Edward, illustrator. II. Title. III. Title:
The Trial of Oliver Queen.
  PN6728.G725G76 2014
  741.5'973—dc23
                                    2014015085

TABLE OF CONTENTS

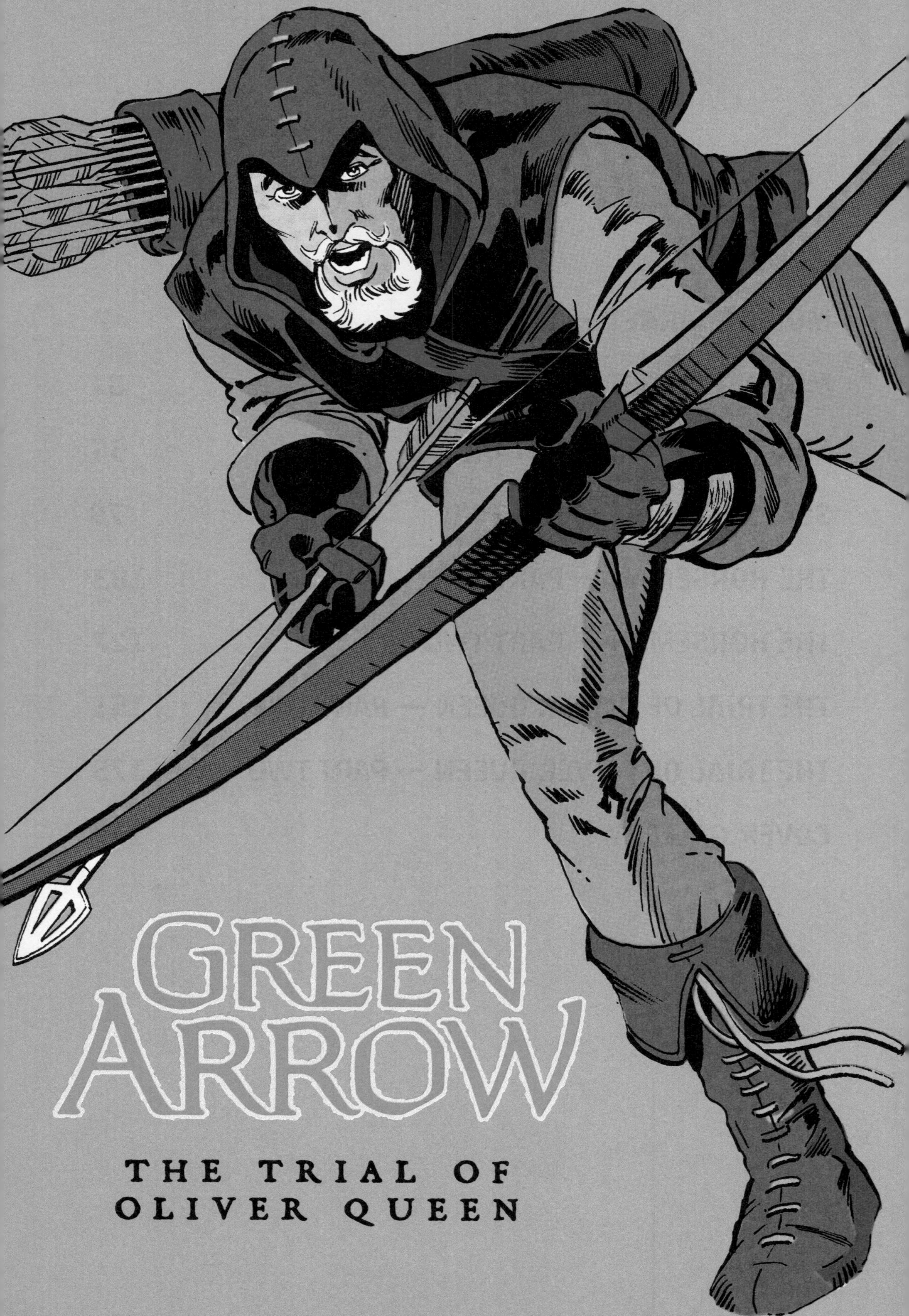

GREEN ARROW

THE TRIAL OF OLIVER QUEEN

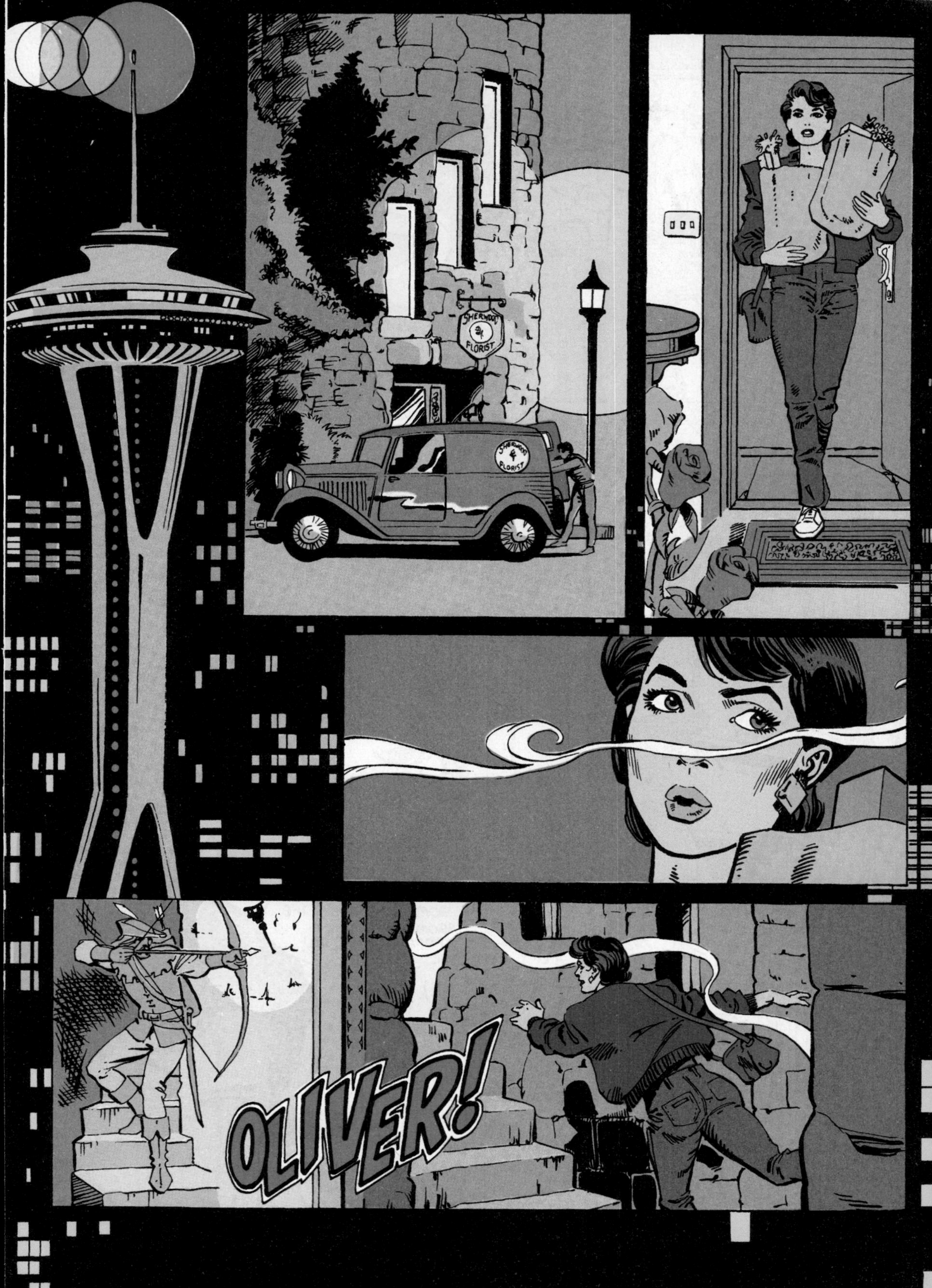

SHERWOOD FLORIST
SHERWOOD FLORIST
OLIVER!

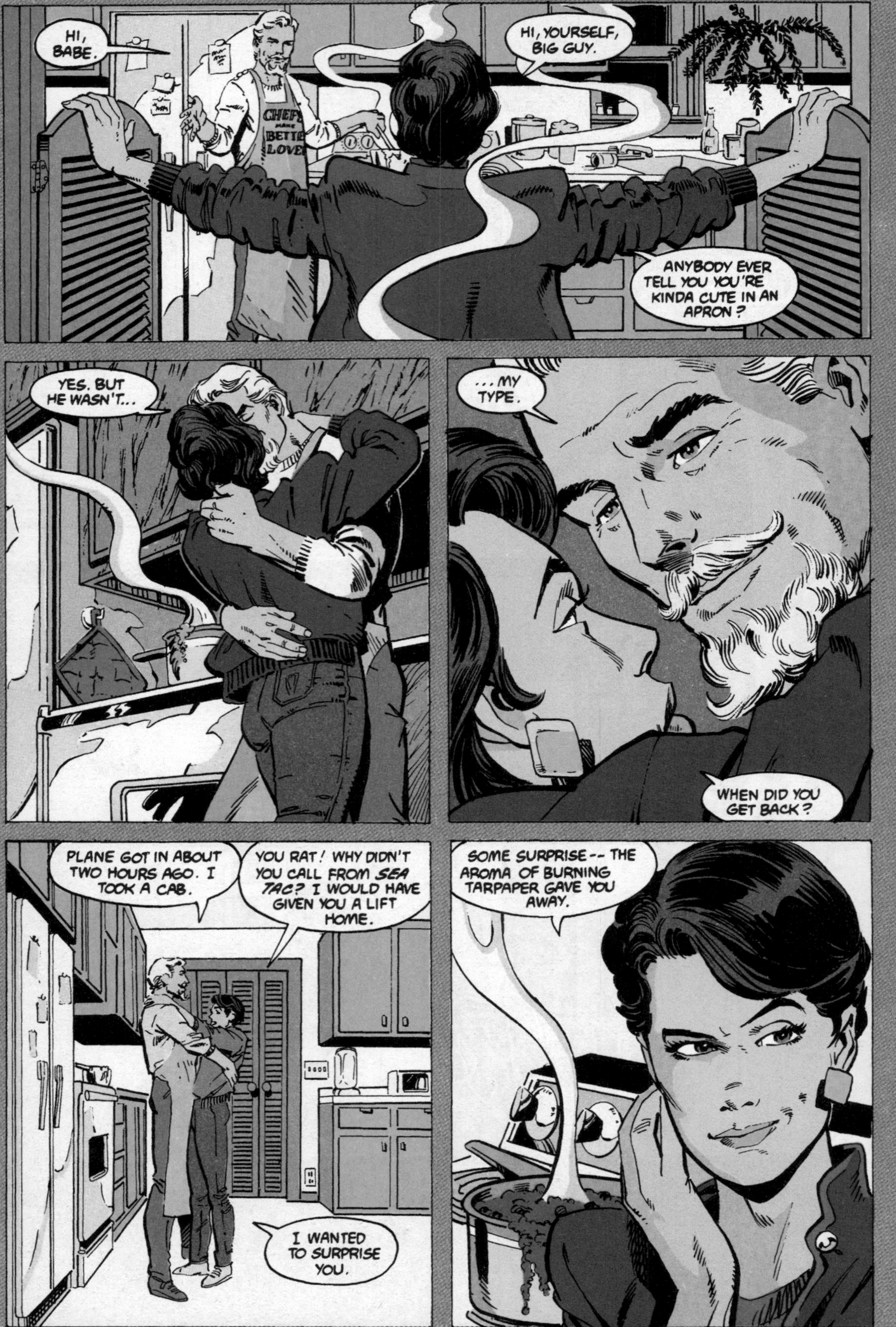
HI, BABE.
HI, YOURSELF, BIG GUY.
ANYBODY EVER TELL YOU YOU'RE KINDA CUTE IN AN APRON?
YES. BUT HE WASN'T...
...MY TYPE.
WHEN DID YOU GET BACK?
PLANE GOT IN ABOUT TWO HOURS AGO. I TOOK A CAB.
YOU RAT! WHY DIDN'T YOU CALL FROM *SEA TAC?* I WOULD HAVE GIVEN YOU A LIFT HOME.
I WANTED TO SURPRISE YOU.
SOME SURPRISE-- THE AROMA OF BURNING TARPAPER GAVE YOU AWAY.

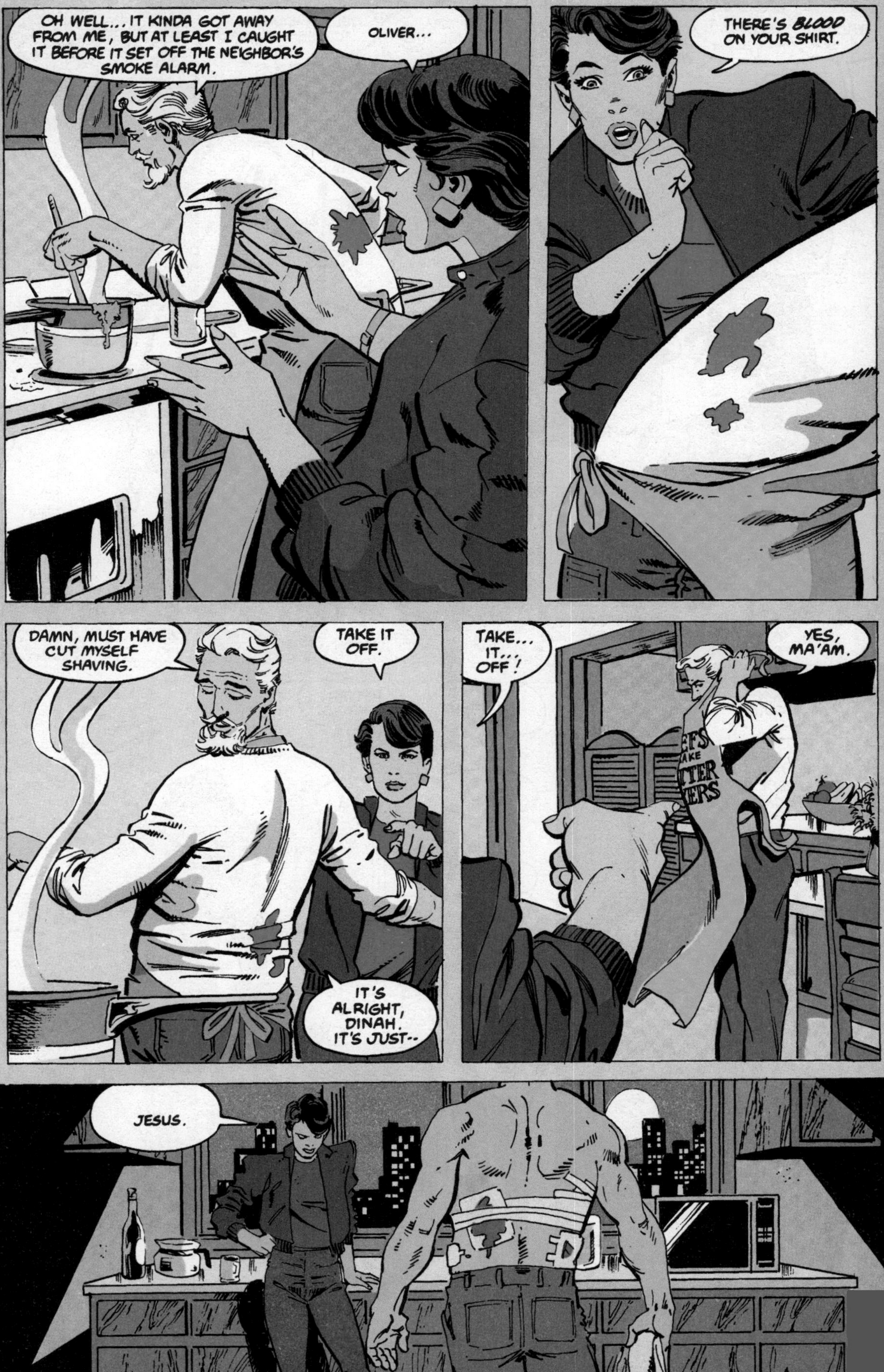
OH WELL... IT KINDA GOT AWAY FROM ME, BUT AT LEAST I CAUGHT IT BEFORE IT SET OFF THE NEIGHBOR'S SMOKE ALARM.
OLIVER...
THERE'S BLOOD ON YOUR SHIRT.
DAMN, MUST HAVE CUT MYSELF SHAVING.
TAKE IT OFF.
IT'S ALRIGHT, DINAH. IT'S JUST--
TAKE... IT... OFF!
YES, MA'AM.
JESUS.

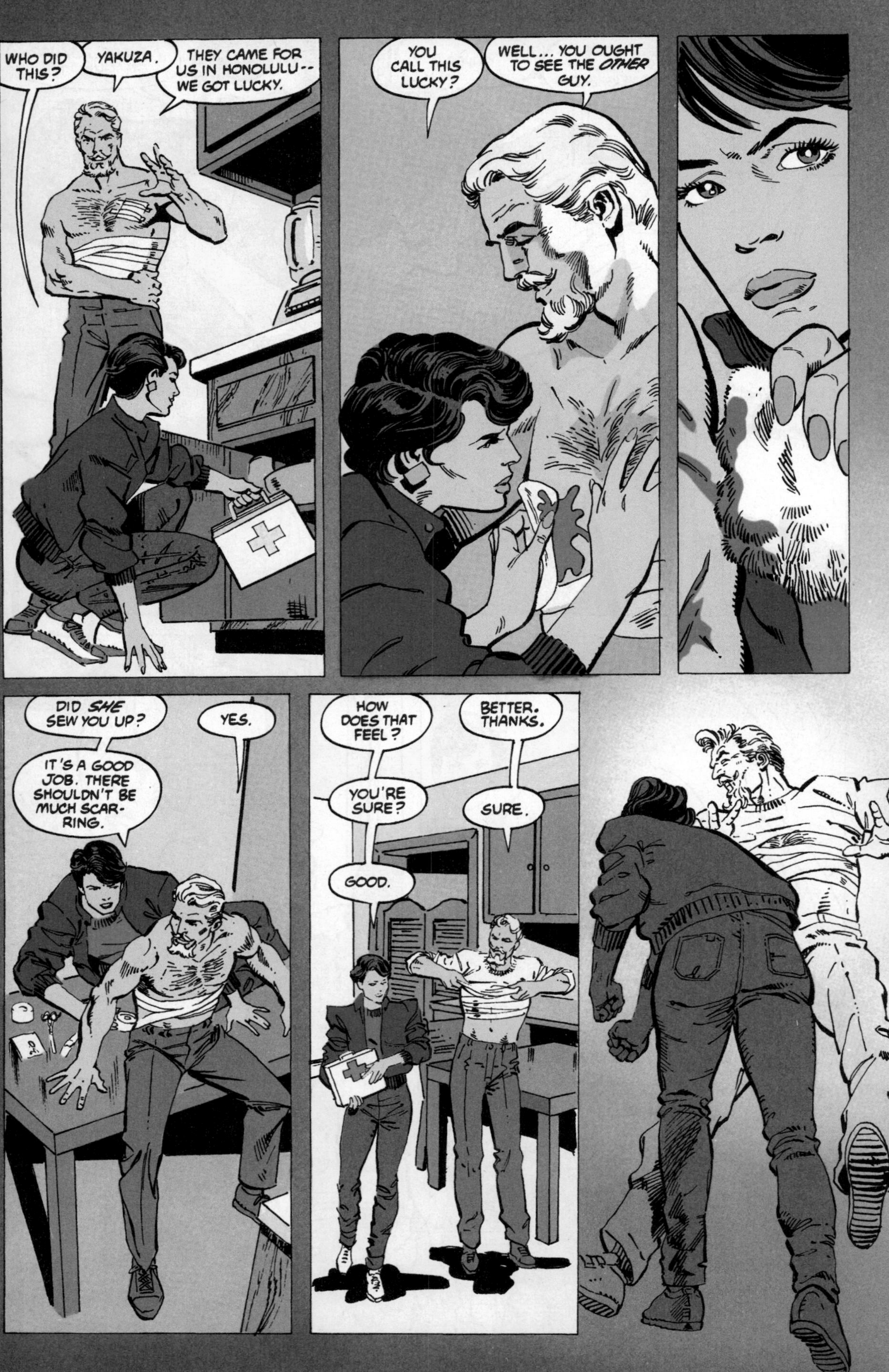
WHO DID THIS?
YAKUZA.
THEY CAME FOR US IN HONOLULU-- WE GOT LUCKY.
YOU CALL THIS LUCKY?
WELL... YOU OUGHT TO SEE THE *OTHER* GUY.
DID *SHE* SEW YOU UP?
YES.
IT'S A GOOD JOB. THERE SHOULDN'T BE MUCH SCAR-RING.
HOW DOES THAT FEEL?
BETTER. THANKS.
YOU'RE SURE?
SURE.
GOOD.

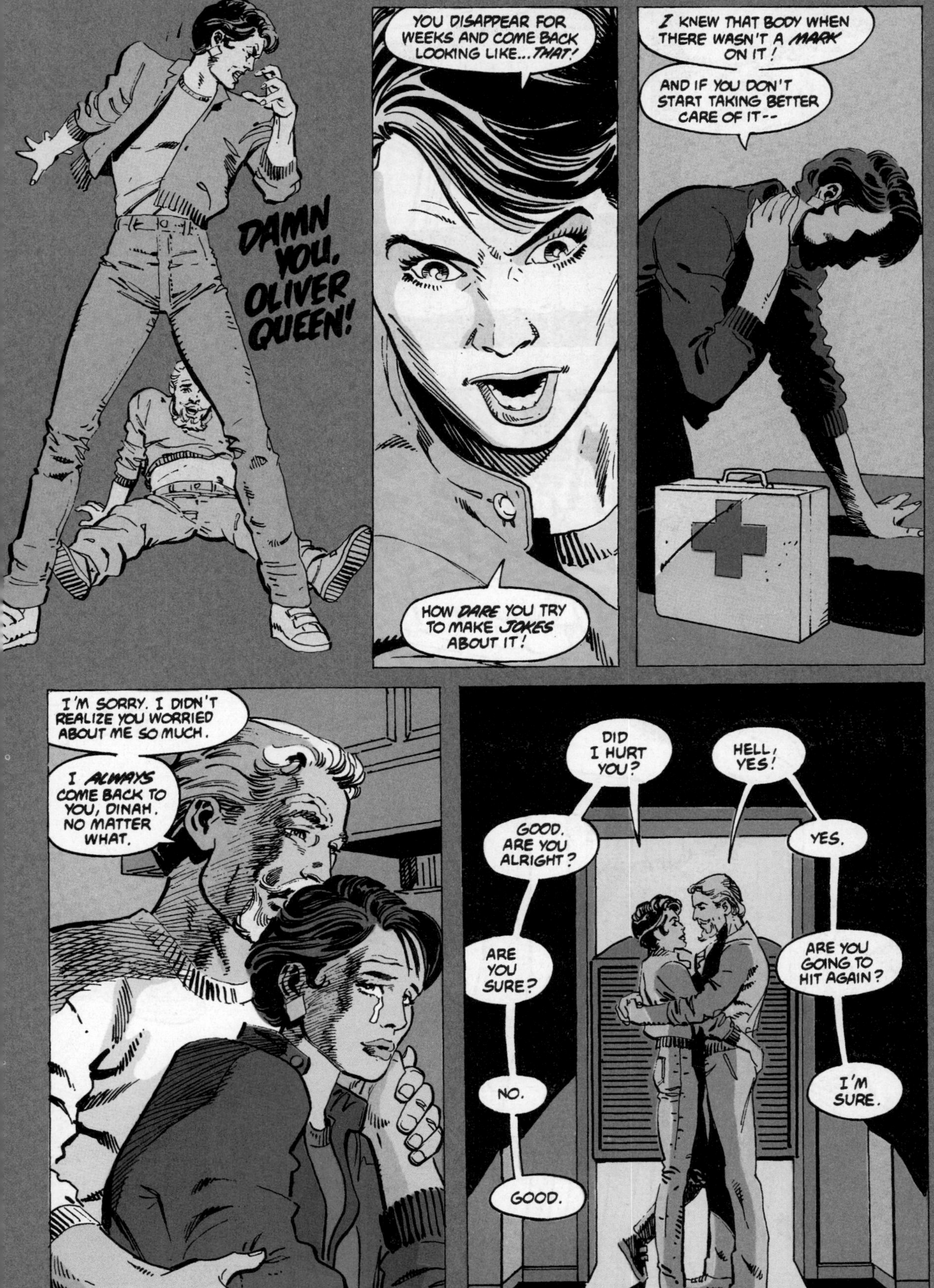
DAMN YOU, OLIVER QUEEN!
YOU DISAPPEAR FOR WEEKS AND COME BACK LOOKING LIKE... THAT!
HOW DARE YOU TRY TO MAKE JOKES ABOUT IT!
I KNEW THAT BODY WHEN THERE WASN'T A MARK ON IT!
AND IF YOU DON'T START TAKING BETTER CARE OF IT--
I'M SORRY. I DIDN'T REALIZE YOU WORRIED ABOUT ME SO MUCH.
I ALWAYS COME BACK TO YOU, DINAH. NO MATTER WHAT.
DID I HURT YOU?
HELL, YES!
GOOD. ARE YOU ALRIGHT?
YES.
ARE YOU SURE?
ARE YOU GOING TO HIT AGAIN?
NO.
I'M SURE.
GOOD.

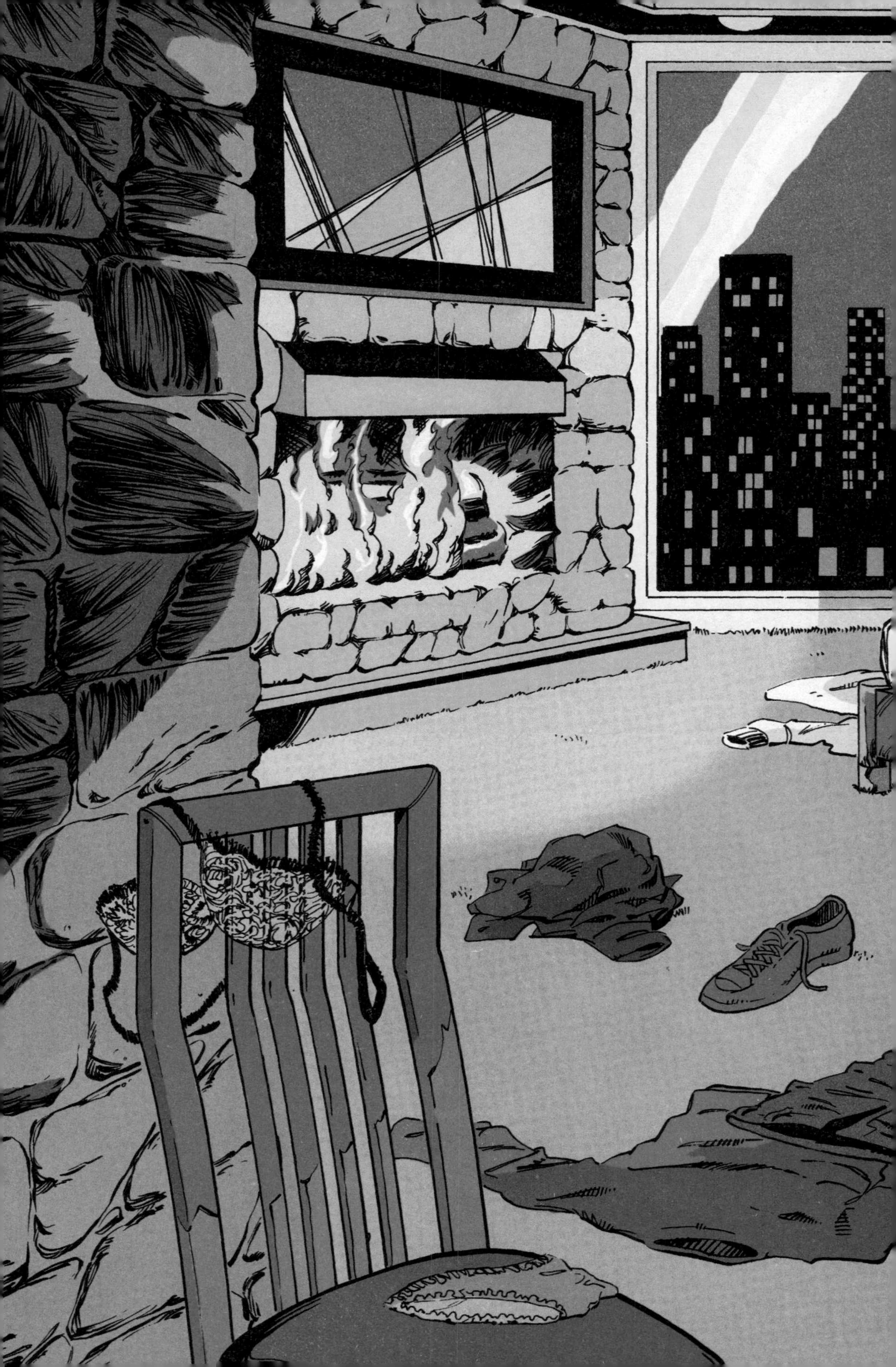

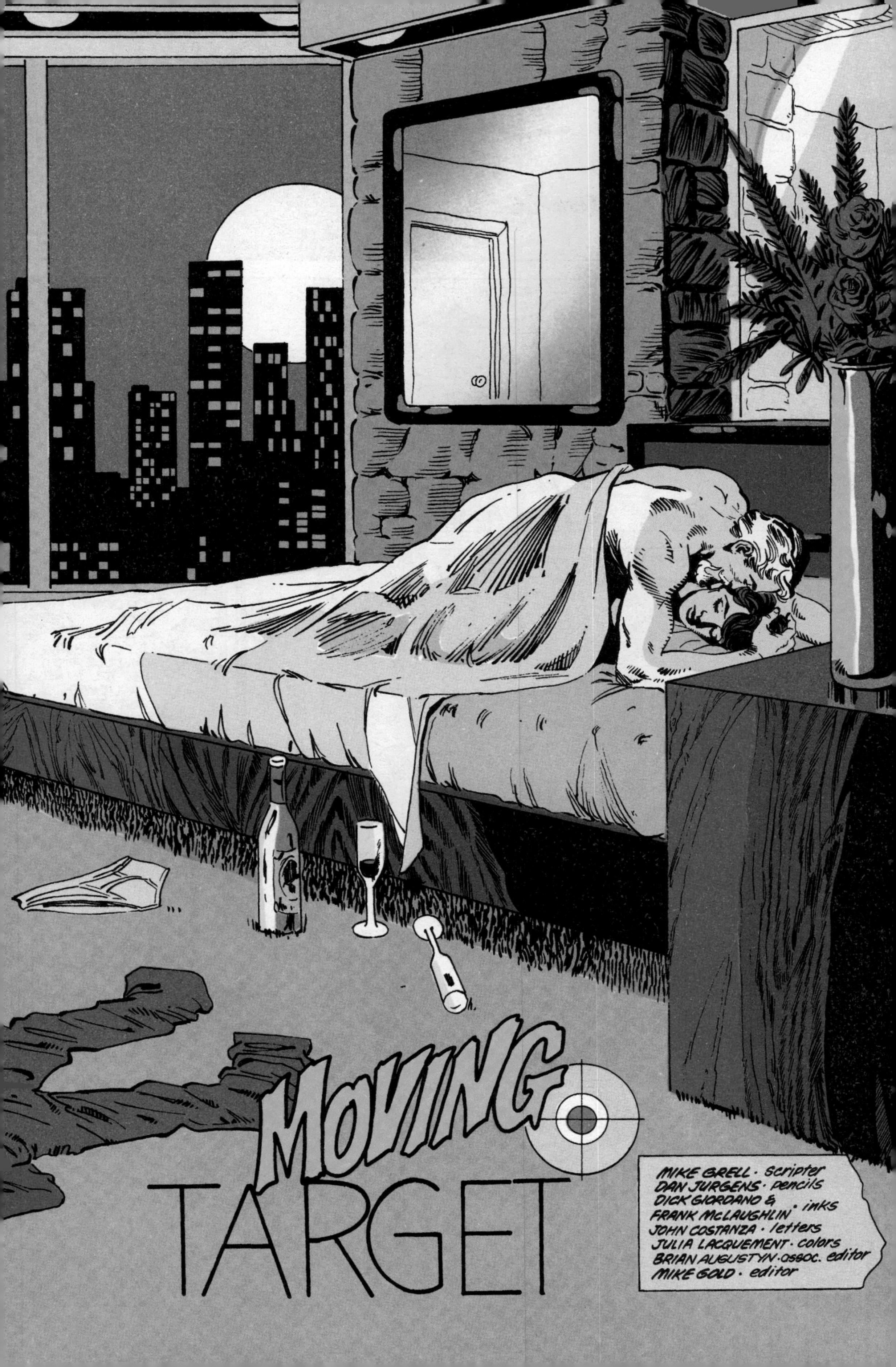

MOVING TARGET
MIKE GRELL · scripter
DAN JURGENS · pencils
DICK GIORDANO & FRANK McLAUGHLIN · inks
JOHN COSTANZA · letters
JULIA LACQUEMENT · colors
BRIAN AUGUSTYN · assoc. editor
MIKE GOLD · editor

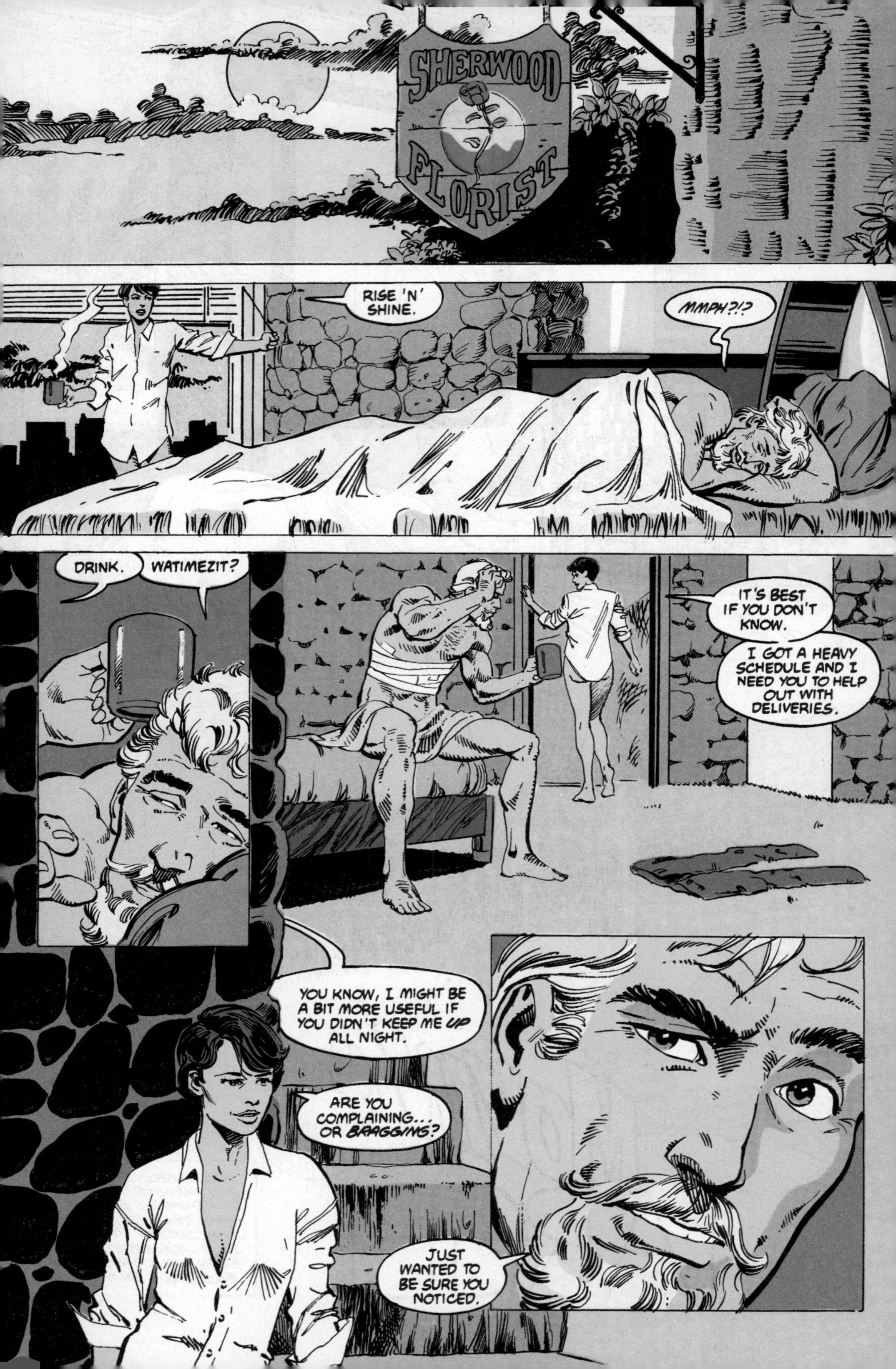
SHERWOOD FLORIST
RISE 'N' SHINE.
MMPH?!?
DRINK.
WATIMEZIT?
IT'S BEST IF YOU DON'T KNOW.
I GOT A HEAVY SCHEDULE AND I NEED YOU TO HELP OUT WITH DELIVERIES.
YOU KNOW, I MIGHT BE A BIT MORE USEFUL IF YOU DIDN'T KEEP ME UP ALL NIGHT.
ARE YOU COMPLAINING... OR BRAGGING?
JUST WANTED TO BE SURE YOU NOTICED.

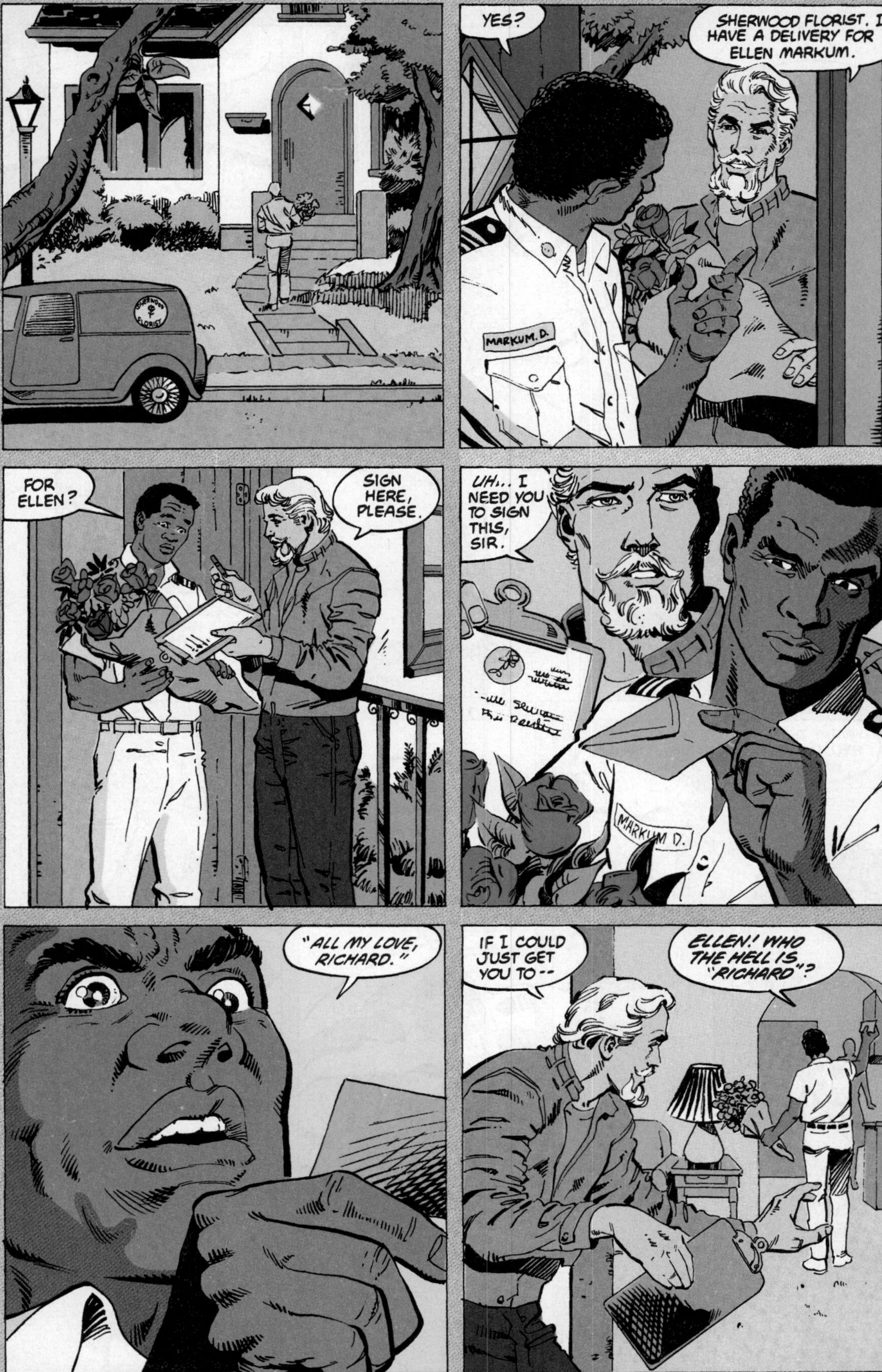
YES?
SHERWOOD FLORIST. I HAVE A DELIVERY FOR ELLEN MARKUM.
MARKUM. D.
FOR ELLEN?
SIGN HERE, PLEASE.
UH... I NEED YOU TO SIGN THIS, SIR.
MARKUM D.
"ALL MY LOVE, RICHARD."
IF I COULD JUST GET YOU TO--
ELLEN! WHO THE HELL IS "RICHARD"?

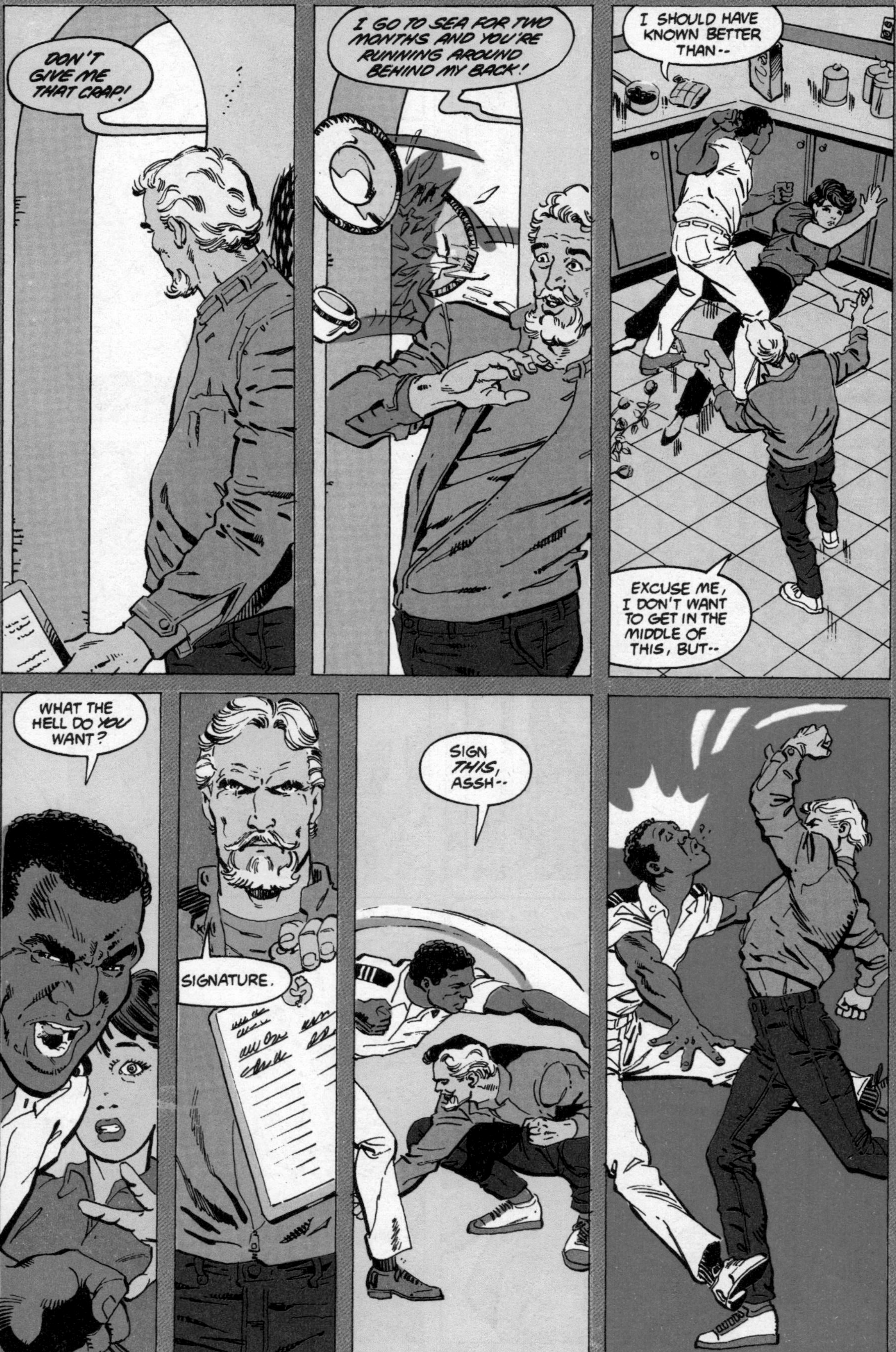
DON'T GIVE ME THAT CRAP!
I GO TO SEA FOR TWO MONTHS AND YOU'RE RUNNING AROUND BEHIND MY BACK!
I SHOULD HAVE KNOWN BETTER THAN--
EXCUSE ME, I DON'T WANT TO GET IN THE MIDDLE OF THIS, BUT--
WHAT THE HELL DO YOU WANT?
SIGNATURE.
SIGN THIS, ASSH--

THANKS, MISTER.

DAVID'S CRAZY JEALOUS. HE DOESN'T UNDER-STAND--

HEY, DON'T LOOK AT ME, LADY. I DON'T EITHER.

SIGN, PLEASE.

WELL, I APPRECIATE WHAT YOU DID.

I DIDN'T EXACTLY DO IT FOR YOU.

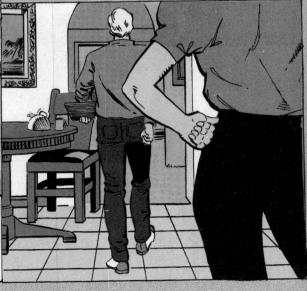

I'M NOT SURE WHAT'S GOING ON HERE, BUT IF YOU CARE ABOUT HIM YOU KNOW WHAT THE *NAVY* WOULD DO TO HIM FOR WIFE BEATING.

AT THE MOMENT, HE'S BETTER OFF LIKE HE IS.

IT MIGHT BE A GOOD IDEA IF YOU WEREN'T HOME WHEN HE WAKES UP. GIVE HIM A CHANCE TO COOL DOWN SO YOU CAN *TALK* TO HIM.

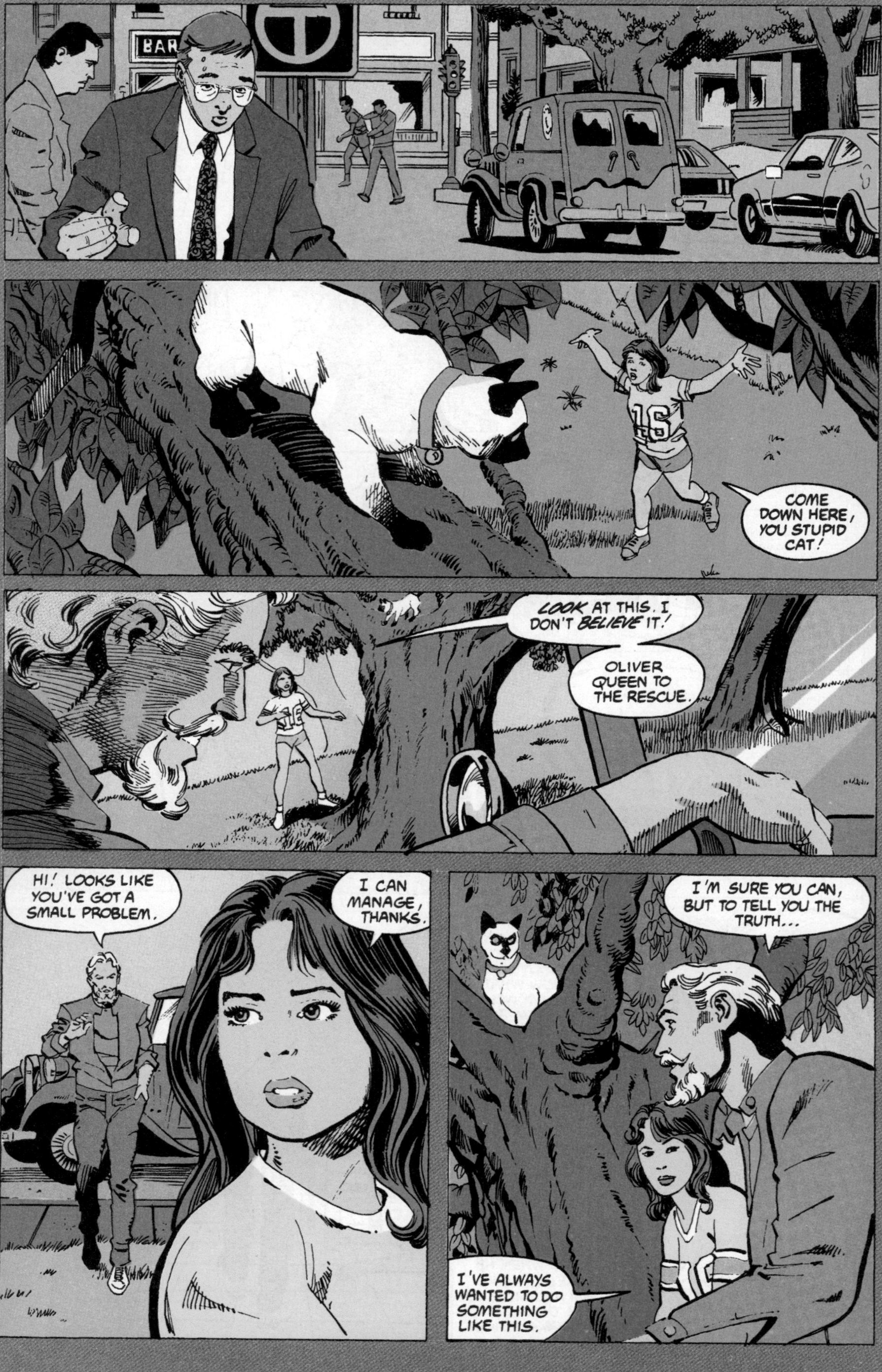
BAR
COME DOWN HERE, YOU STUPID CAT!
LOOK AT THIS. I DON'T BELIEVE IT!
OLIVER QUEEN TO THE RESCUE.
HI! LOOKS LIKE YOU'VE GOT A SMALL PROBLEM.
I CAN MANAGE, THANKS.
I'M SURE YOU CAN, BUT TO TELL YOU THE TRUTH...
I'VE ALWAYS WANTED TO DO SOMETHING LIKE THIS.

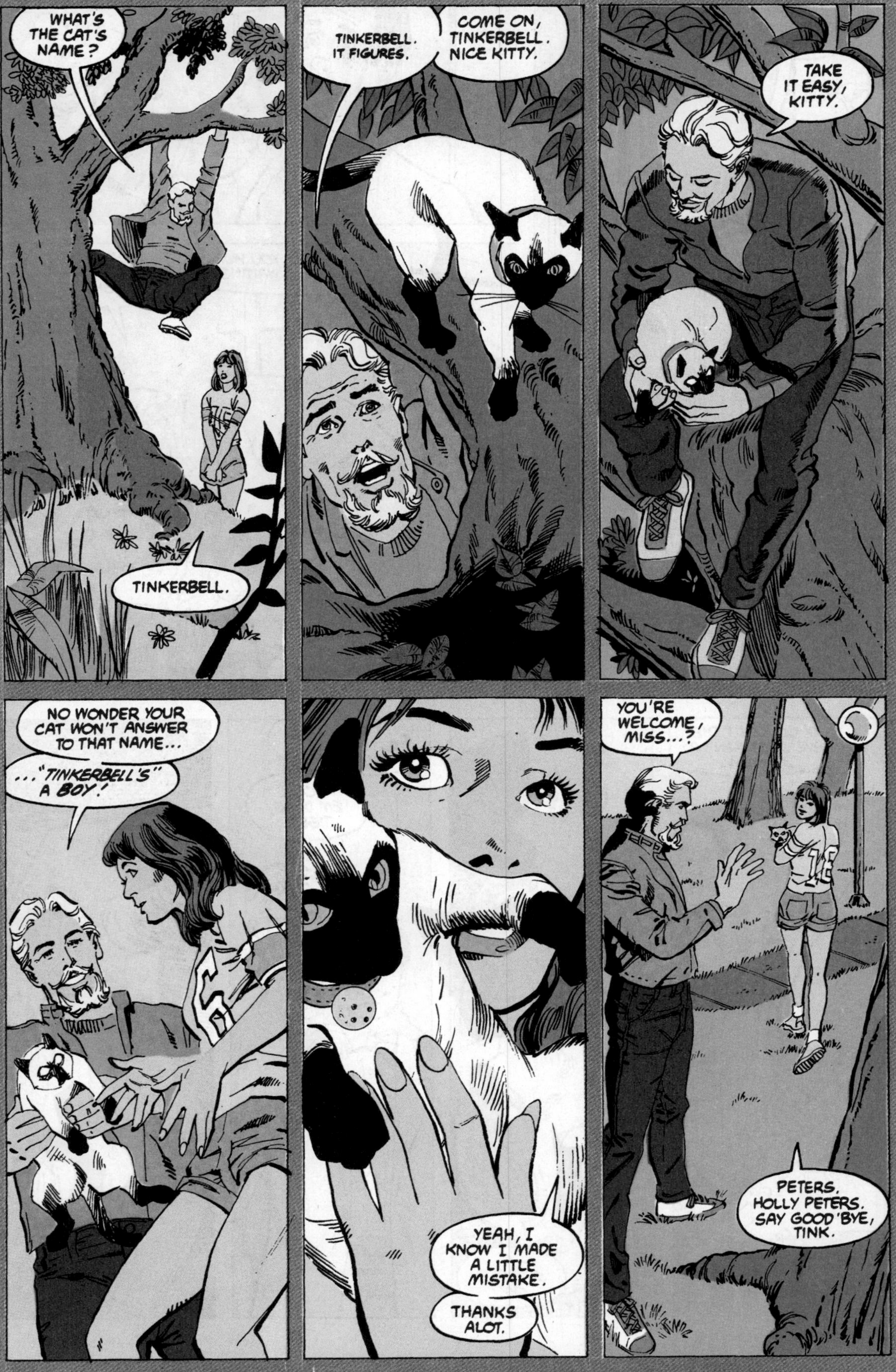
WHAT'S THE CAT'S NAME?
TINKERBELL.
TINKERBELL. IT FIGURES.
COME ON, TINKERBELL. NICE KITTY.
TAKE IT EASY, KITTY.
NO WONDER YOUR CAT WON'T ANSWER TO THAT NAME...
..."TINKERBELL'S" A BOY!
YEAH, I KNOW I MADE A LITTLE MISTAKE.
THANKS ALOT.
YOU'RE WELCOME, MISS...?
PETERS. HOLLY PETERS. SAY GOOD'BYE, TINK.

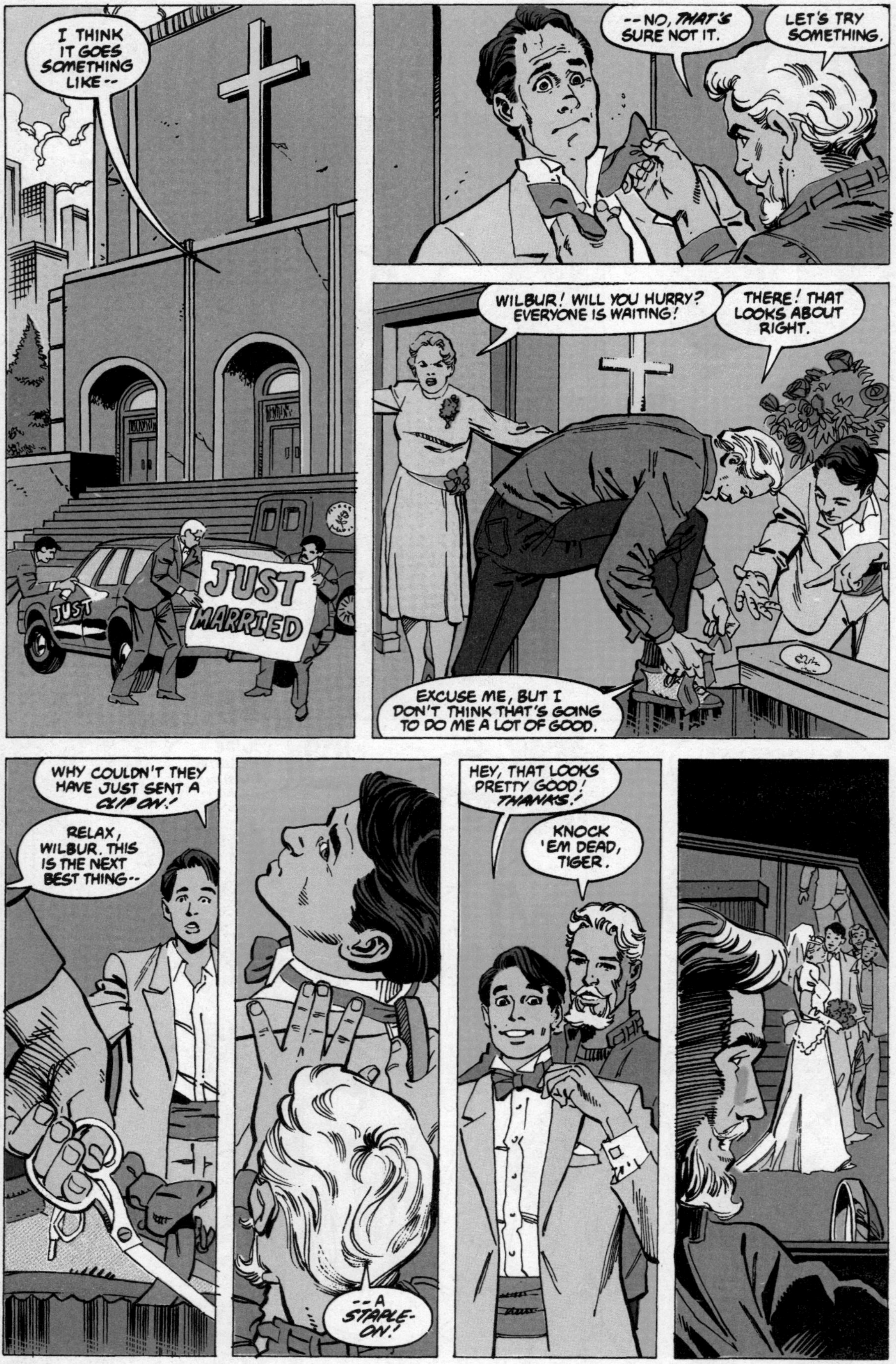
I THINK IT GOES SOMETHING LIKE--
JUST
JUST MARRIED
--NO, THAT'S SURE NOT IT.
LET'S TRY SOMETHING.
WILBUR! WILL YOU HURRY? EVERYONE IS WAITING!
THERE! THAT LOOKS ABOUT RIGHT.
EXCUSE ME, BUT I DON'T THINK THAT'S GOING TO DO ME A LOT OF GOOD.
WHY COULDN'T THEY HAVE JUST SENT A CLIP ON!
RELAX, WILBUR. THIS IS THE NEXT BEST THING--
--A STAPLE-ON!
HEY, THAT LOOKS PRETTY GOOD! THANKS!
KNOCK 'EM DEAD, TIGER.

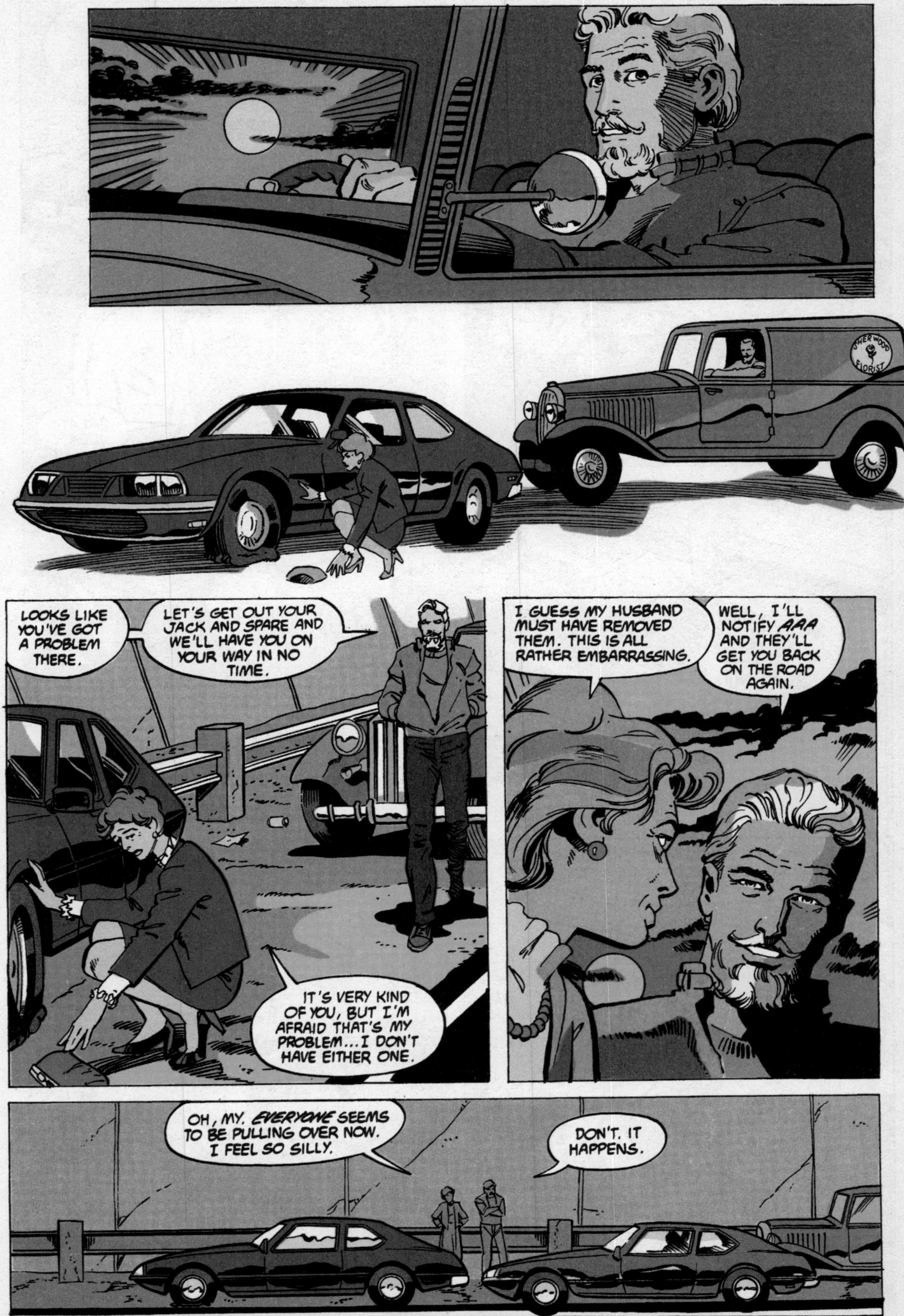
SHERWOOD FLORIST
LOOKS LIKE YOU'VE GOT A PROBLEM THERE.
LET'S GET OUT YOUR JACK AND SPARE AND WE'LL HAVE YOU ON YOUR WAY IN NO TIME.
IT'S VERY KIND OF YOU, BUT I'M AFRAID THAT'S MY PROBLEM... I DON'T HAVE EITHER ONE.
I GUESS MY HUSBAND MUST HAVE REMOVED THEM. THIS IS ALL RATHER EMBARRASSING.
WELL, I'LL NOTIFY AAA AND THEY'LL GET YOU BACK ON THE ROAD AGAIN.
OH, MY. EVERYONE SEEMS TO BE PULLING OVER NOW. I FEEL SO SILLY.
DON'T. IT HAPPENS.

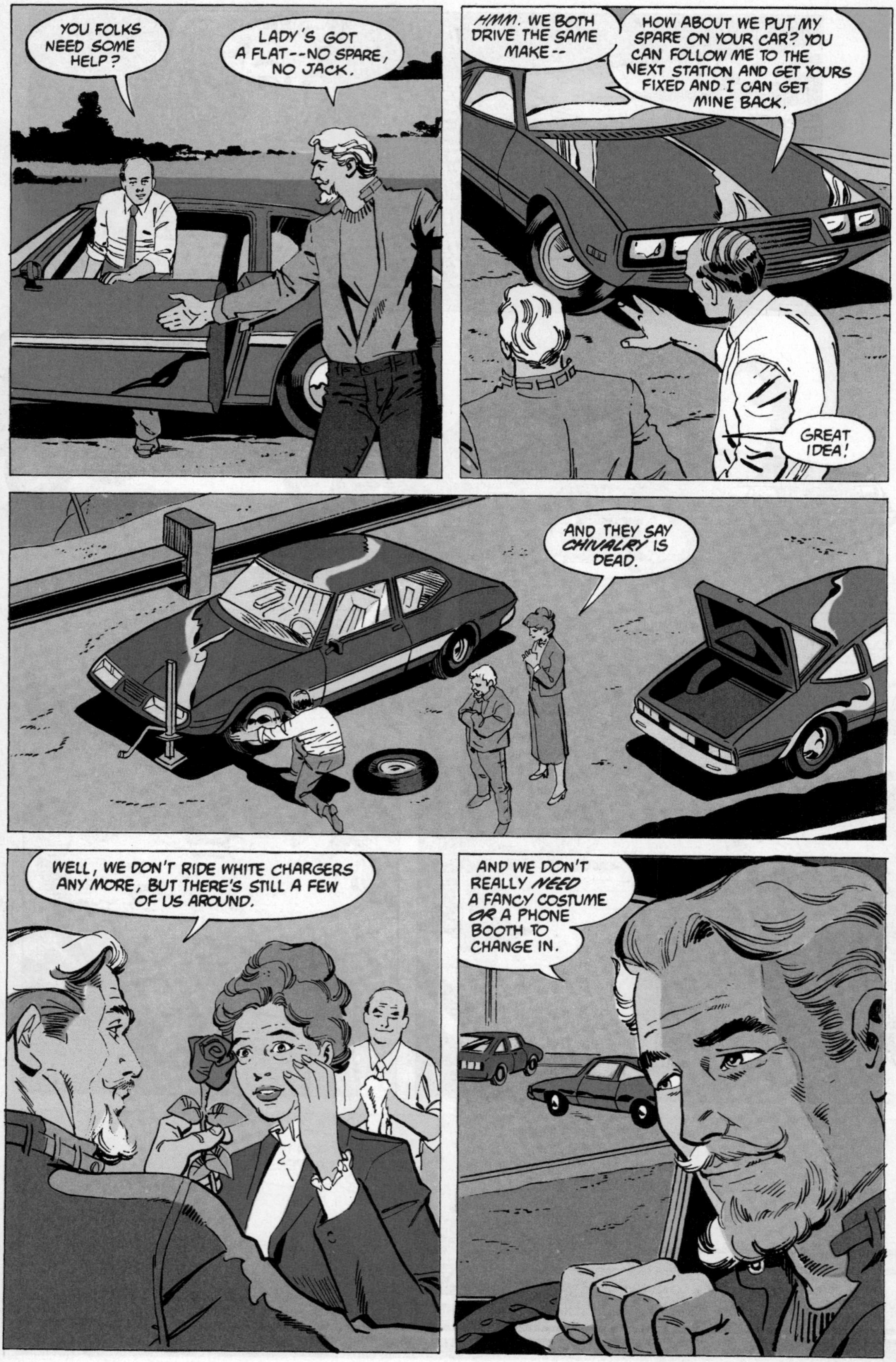
YOU FOLKS NEED SOME HELP?
LADY'S GOT A FLAT--NO SPARE, NO JACK.
HMM. WE BOTH DRIVE THE SAME MAKE--
HOW ABOUT WE PUT MY SPARE ON YOUR CAR? YOU CAN FOLLOW ME TO THE NEXT STATION AND GET YOURS FIXED AND I CAN GET MINE BACK.
GREAT IDEA!
AND THEY SAY CHIVALRY IS DEAD.
WELL, WE DON'T RIDE WHITE CHARGERS ANY MORE, BUT THERE'S STILL A FEW OF US AROUND.
AND WE DON'T REALLY NEED A FANCY COSTUME OR A PHONE BOOTH TO CHANGE IN.

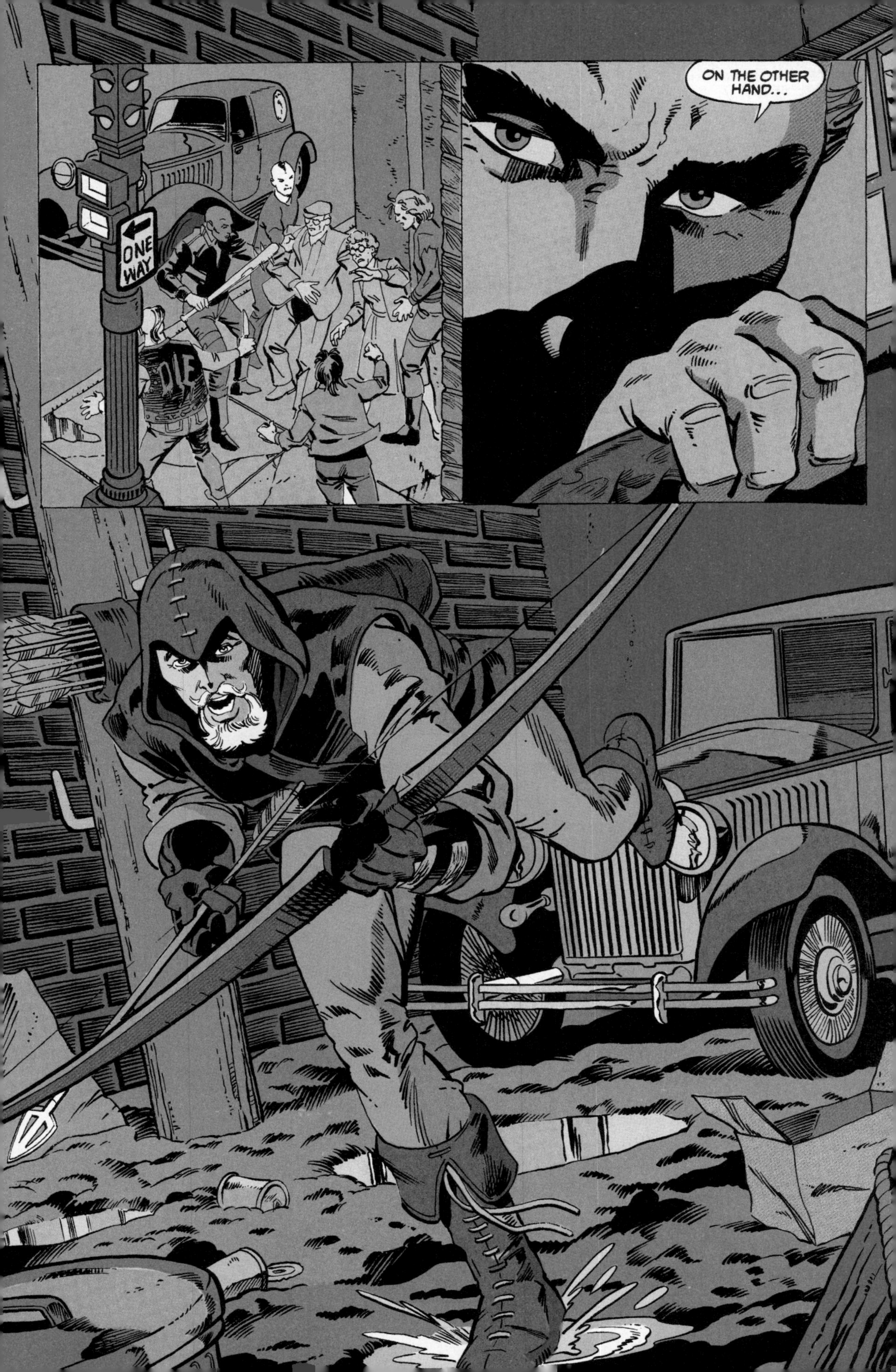
ONE WAY
DIE
ON THE OTHER HAND...

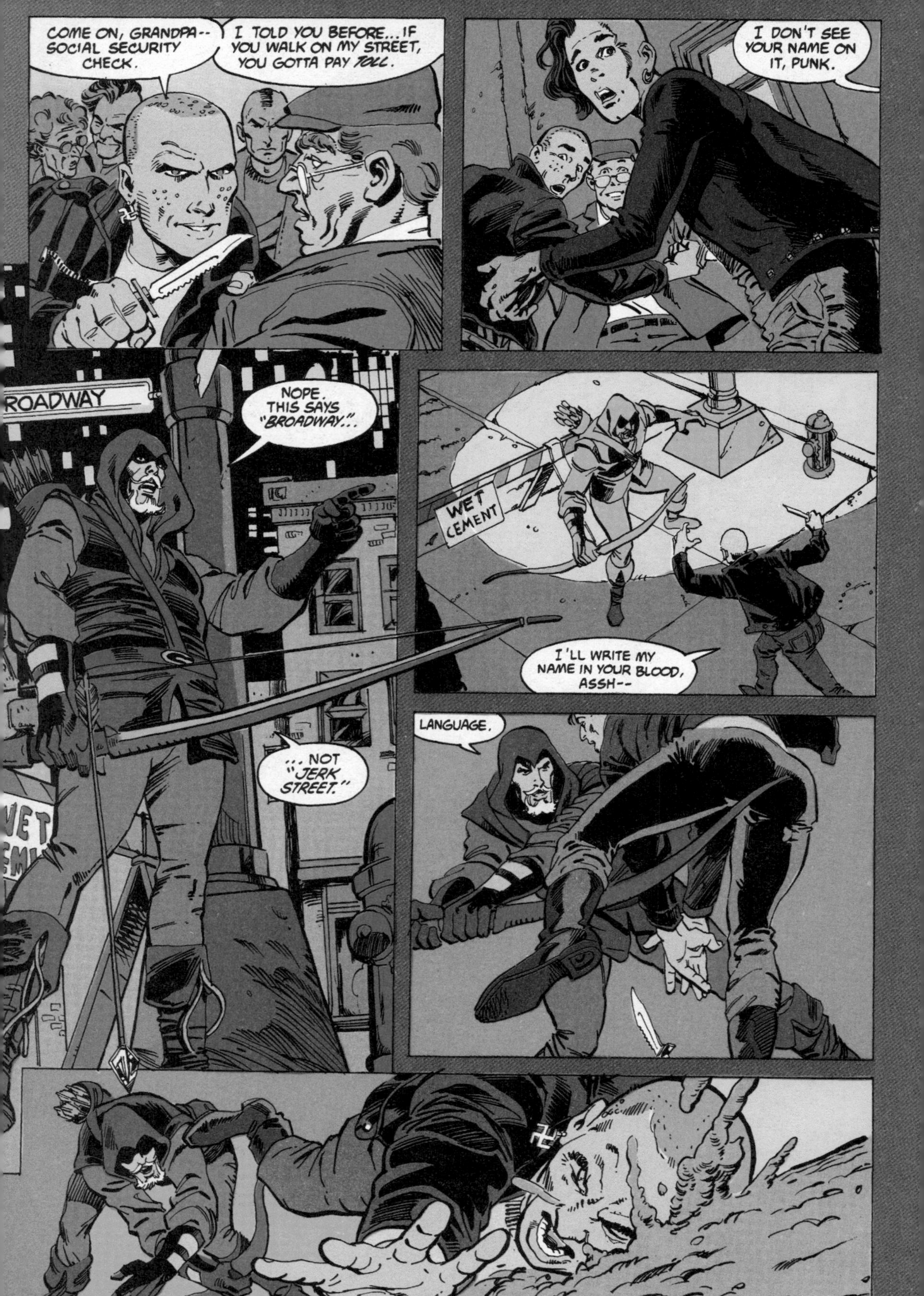

COME ON, GRANDPA-- SOCIAL SECURITY CHECK.
I TOLD YOU BEFORE... IF YOU WALK ON MY STREET, YOU GOTTA PAY TOLL.
I DON'T SEE YOUR NAME ON IT, PUNK.
BROADWAY
NOPE. THIS SAYS "BROADWAY."...
...NOT "JERK STREET."
WET CEMENT
I'LL WRITE MY NAME IN YOUR BLOOD, ASSH--
LANGUAGE.

ON THE OTHER HAND, THIS *DOES* BEAR A STRIKING RESEMBLANCE.

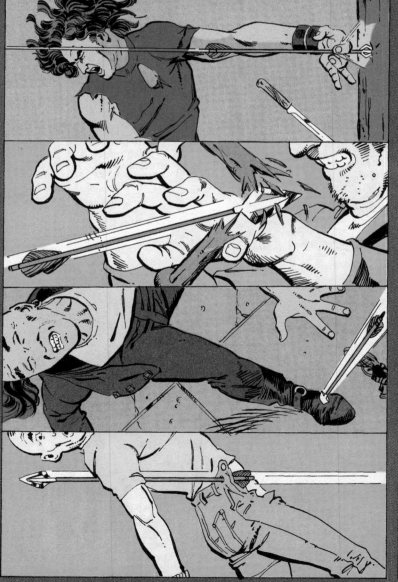

YOUR MOVE.

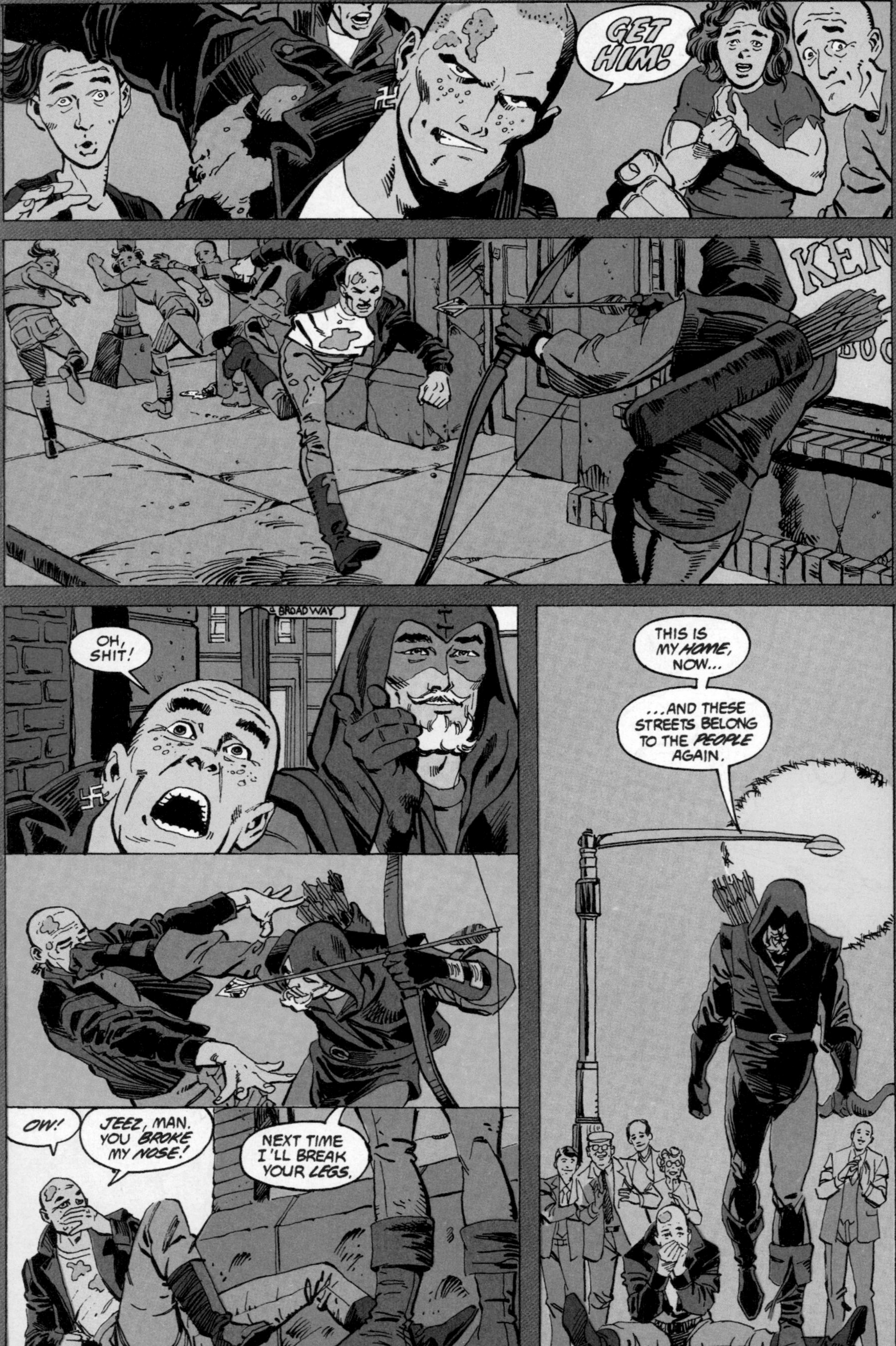
GET HIM!
OH, SHIT!
BROADWAY
THIS IS MY HOME, NOW...
...AND THESE STREETS BELONG TO THE PEOPLE AGAIN.
OW!
JEEZ, MAN. YOU BROKE MY NOSE!
NEXT TIME I'LL BREAK YOUR LEGS.

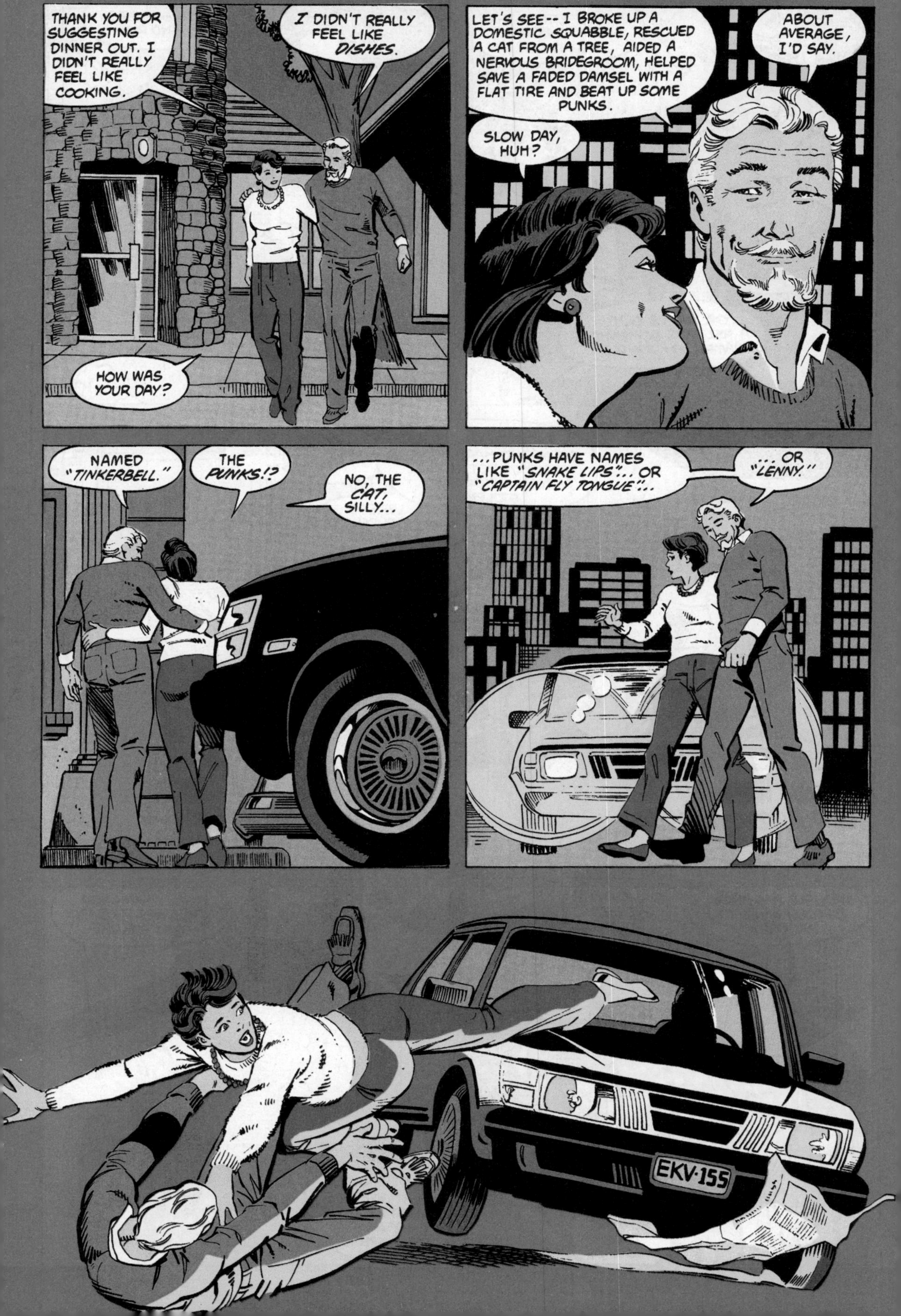
THANK YOU FOR SUGGESTING DINNER OUT. I DIDN'T REALLY FEEL LIKE COOKING.
I DIDN'T REALLY FEEL LIKE *DISHES*.
HOW WAS YOUR DAY?
LET'S SEE-- I BROKE UP A DOMESTIC SQUABBLE, RESCUED A CAT FROM A TREE, AIDED A NERVOUS BRIDEGROOM, HELPED SAVE A FADED DAMSEL WITH A FLAT TIRE AND BEAT UP SOME PUNKS.
SLOW DAY, HUH?
ABOUT AVERAGE, I'D SAY.
NAMED *"TINKERBELL."*
THE *PUNKS!?*
NO, THE *CAT*, SILLY...
...PUNKS HAVE NAMES LIKE *"SNAKE LIPS"*... OR *"CAPTAIN FLY TONGUE"*...
... OR *"LENNY."*
EKV-155

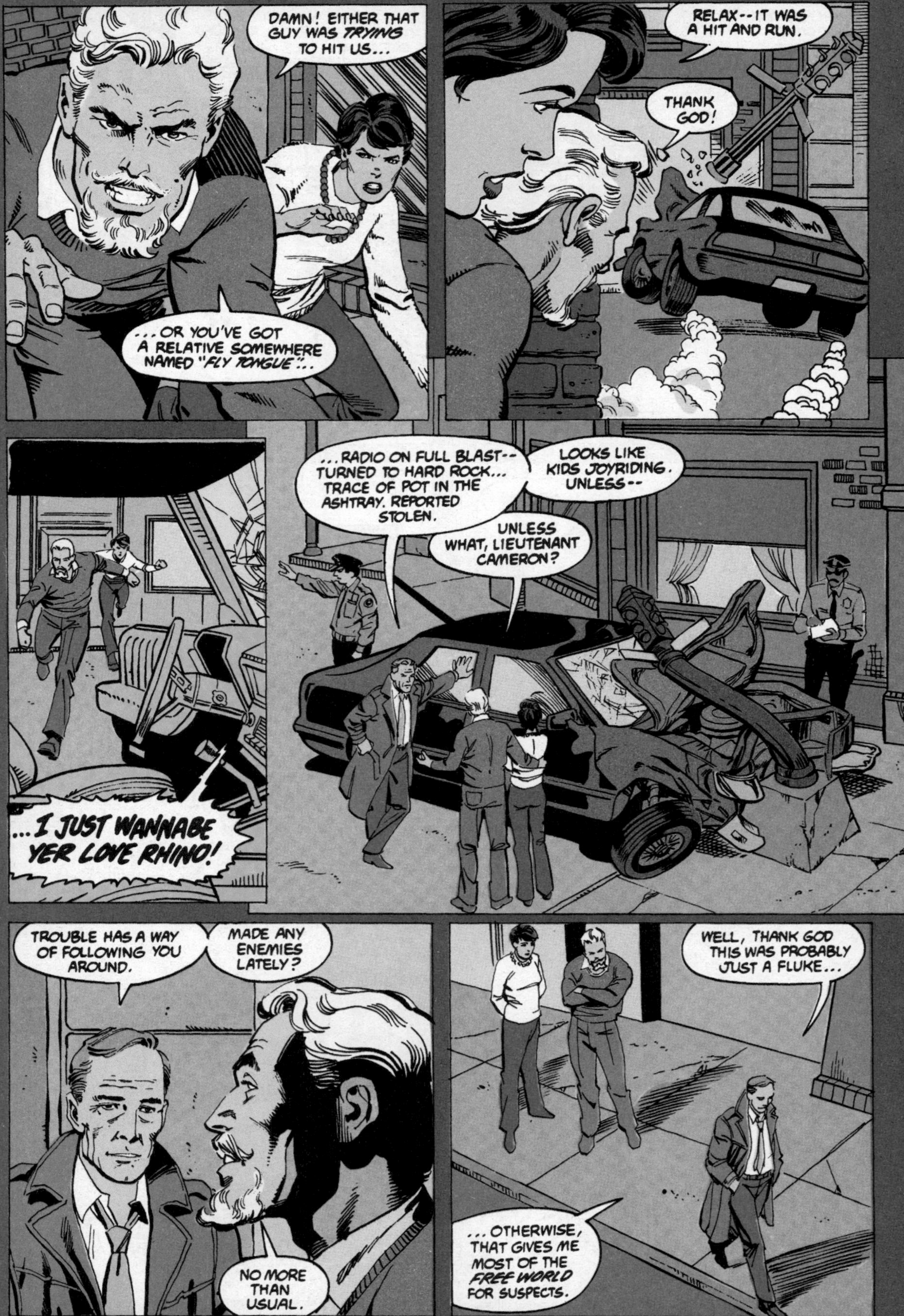
DAMN! EITHER THAT GUY WAS TRYING TO HIT US...
...OR YOU'VE GOT A RELATIVE SOMEWHERE NAMED "FLY TONGUE"...
RELAX--IT WAS A HIT AND RUN.
THANK GOD!
...I JUST WANNABE YER LOVE RHINO!
...RADIO ON FULL BLAST--TURNED TO HARD ROCK... TRACE OF POT IN THE ASHTRAY. REPORTED STOLEN.
LOOKS LIKE KIDS JOYRIDING. UNLESS--
UNLESS WHAT, LIEUTENANT CAMERON?
TROUBLE HAS A WAY OF FOLLOWING YOU AROUND.
MADE ANY ENEMIES LATELY?
NO MORE THAN USUAL.
WELL, THANK GOD THIS WAS PROBABLY JUST A FLUKE...
...OTHERWISE, THAT GIVES ME MOST OF THE FREE WORLD FOR SUSPECTS.

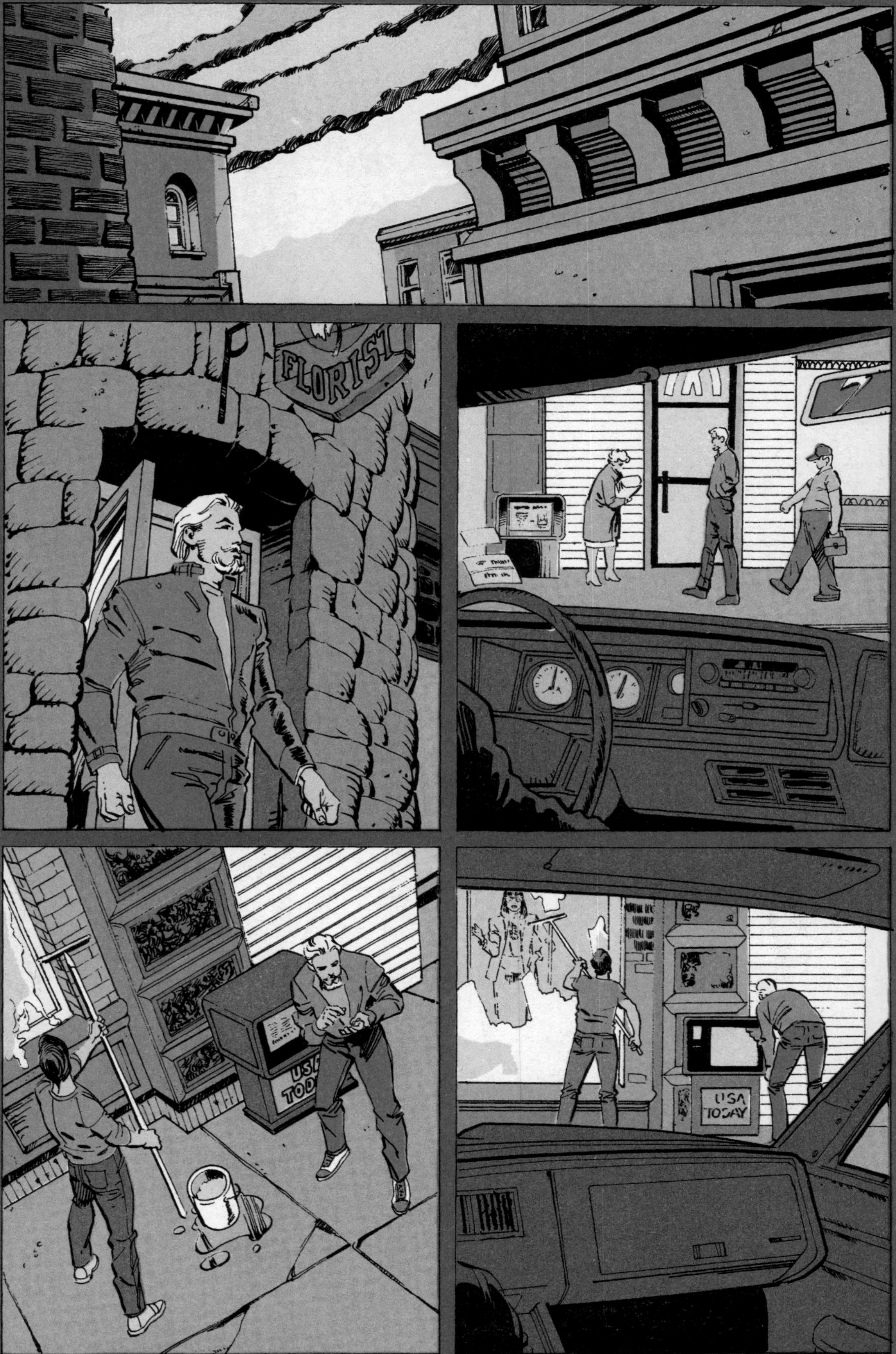
FLORIST
USA TODAY

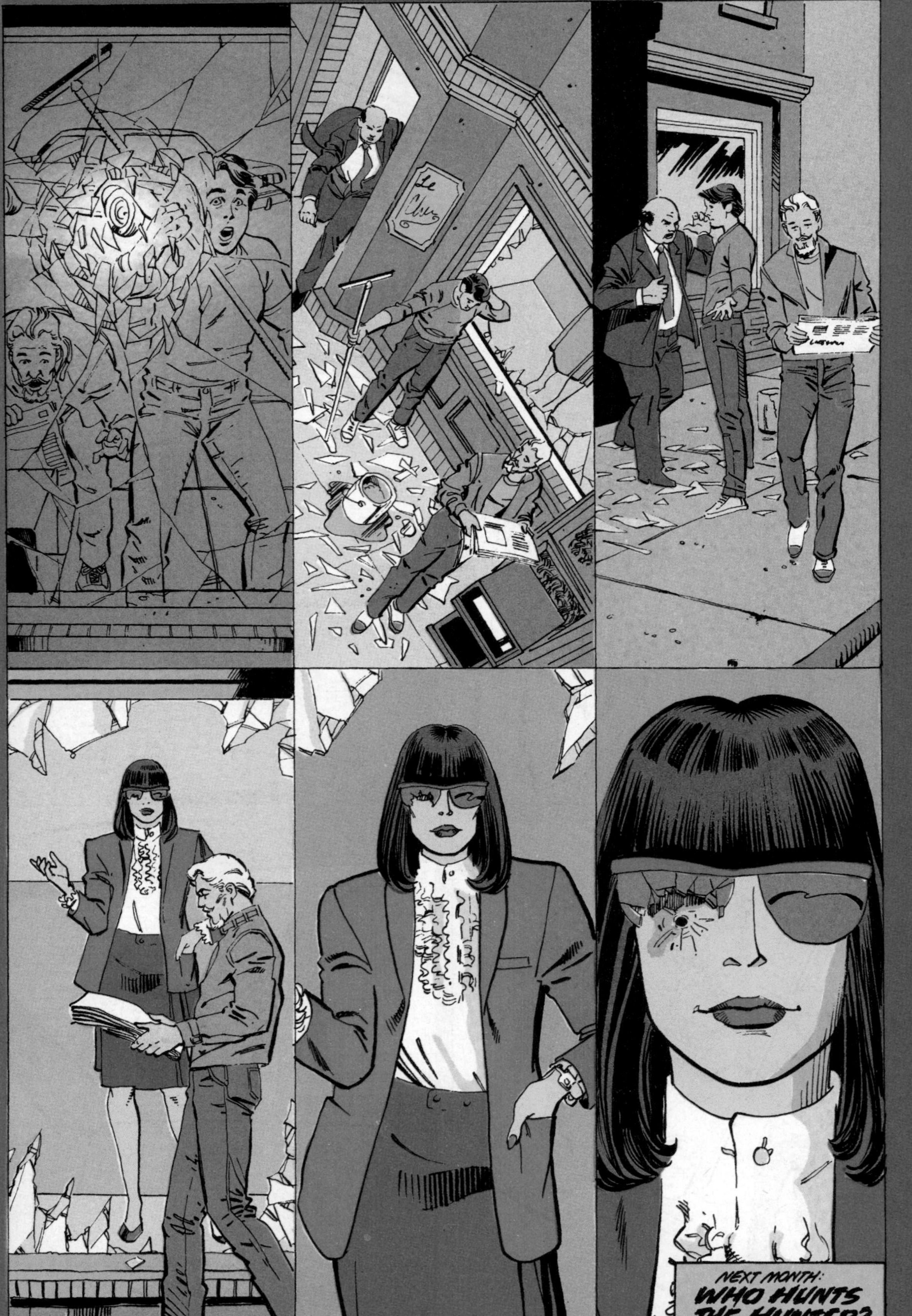
NEXT MONTH:
WHO HUNTS THE HUNTER?

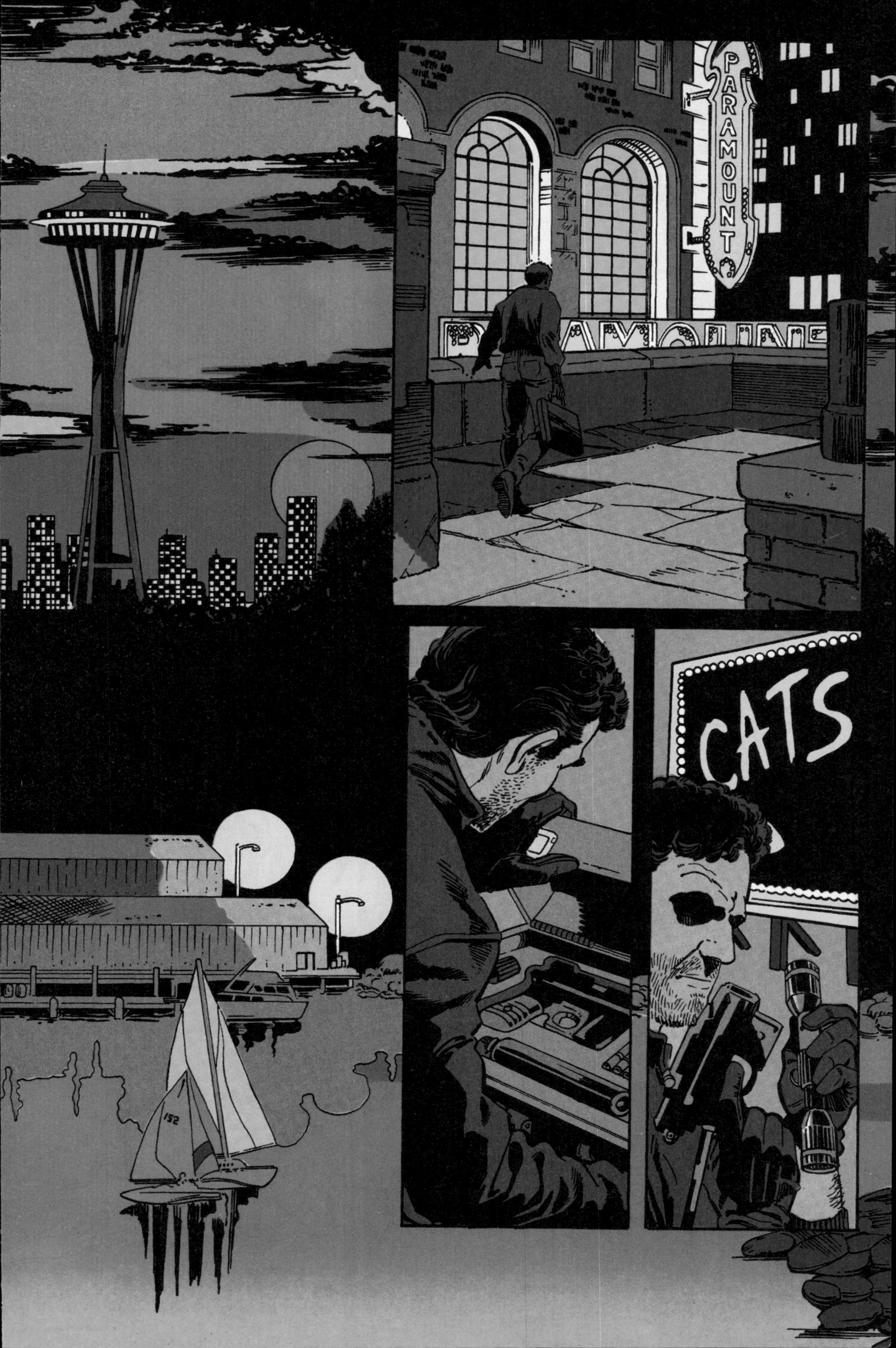
PARAMOUNT
CATS
152

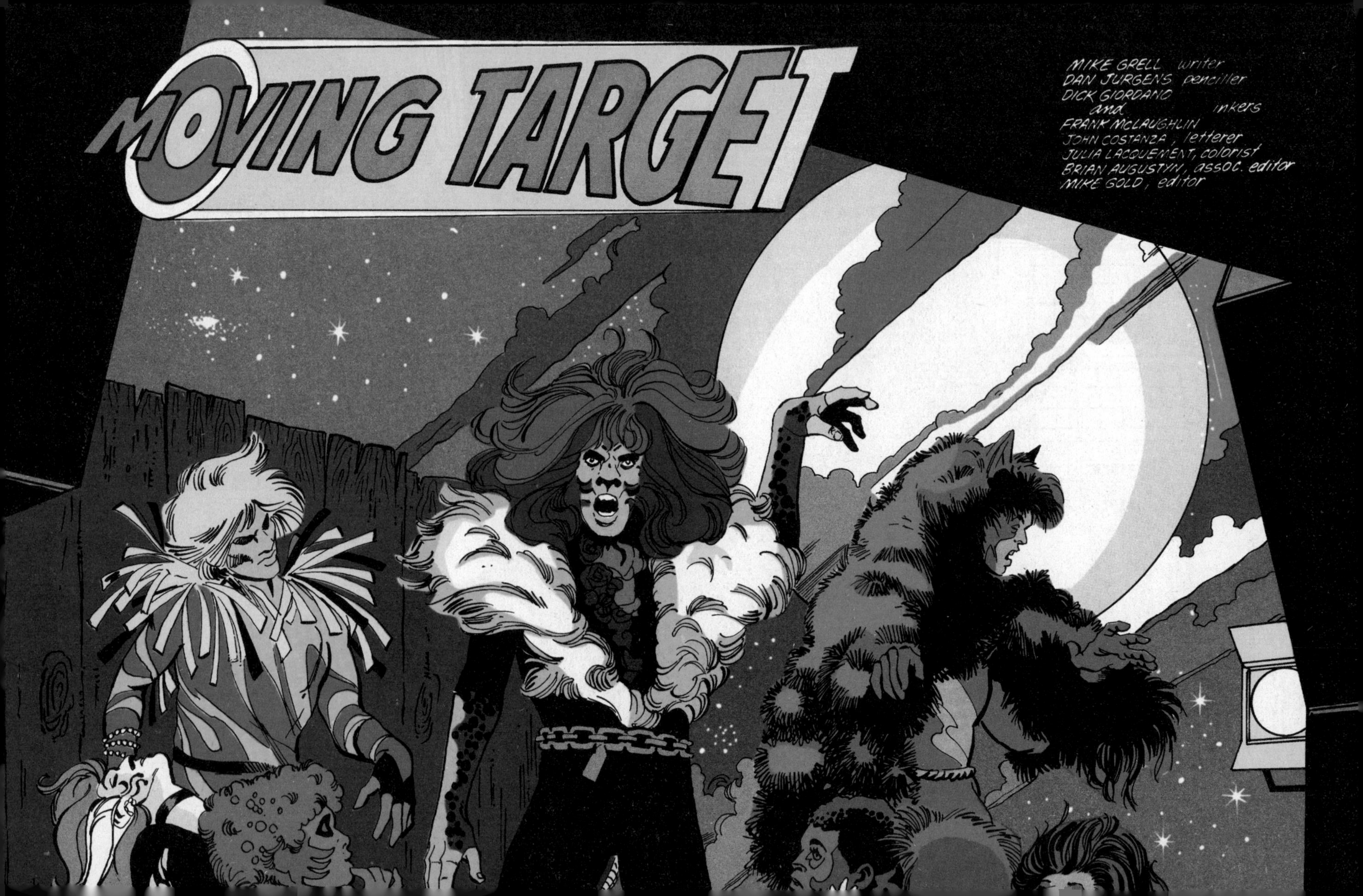
MOVING TARGET
MIKE GRELL writer
DAN JURGENS penciller
DICK GIORDANO
and inkers
FRANK McLAUGHLIN
JOHN COSTANZA, letterer
JULIA LACQUEMENT, colorist
BRIAN AUGUSTYN, assoc. editor
MIKE GOLD, editor

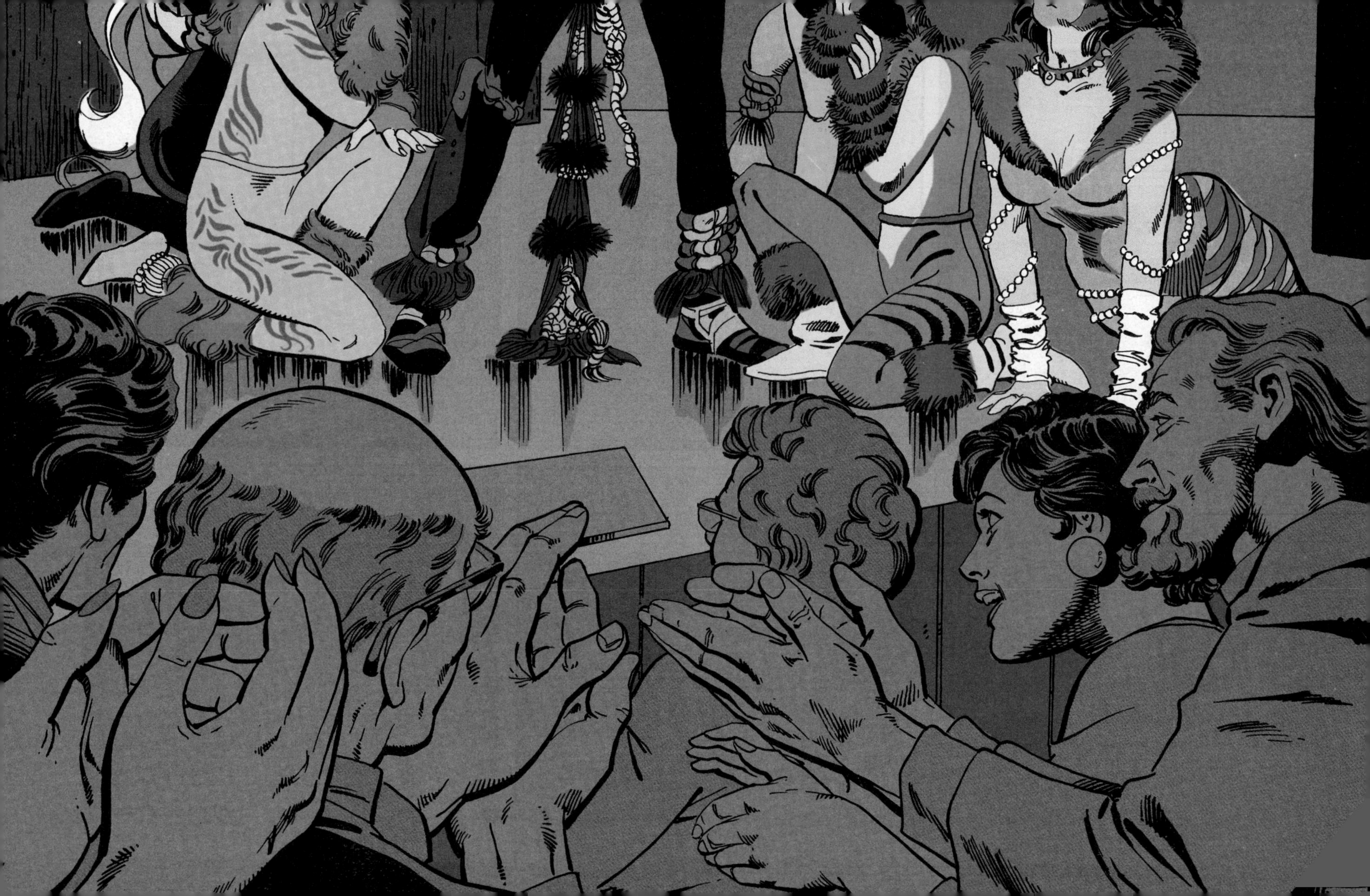

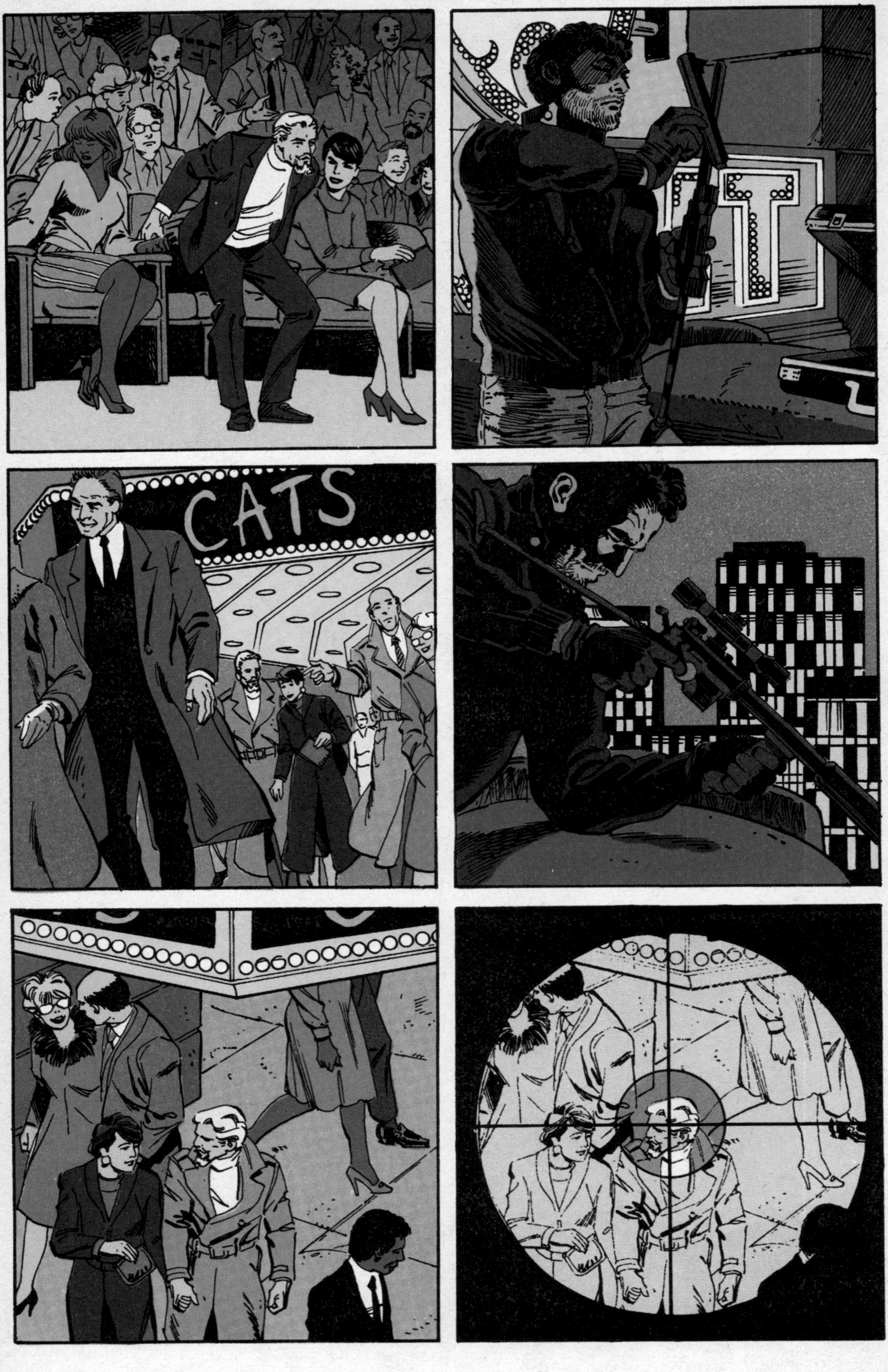
CATS

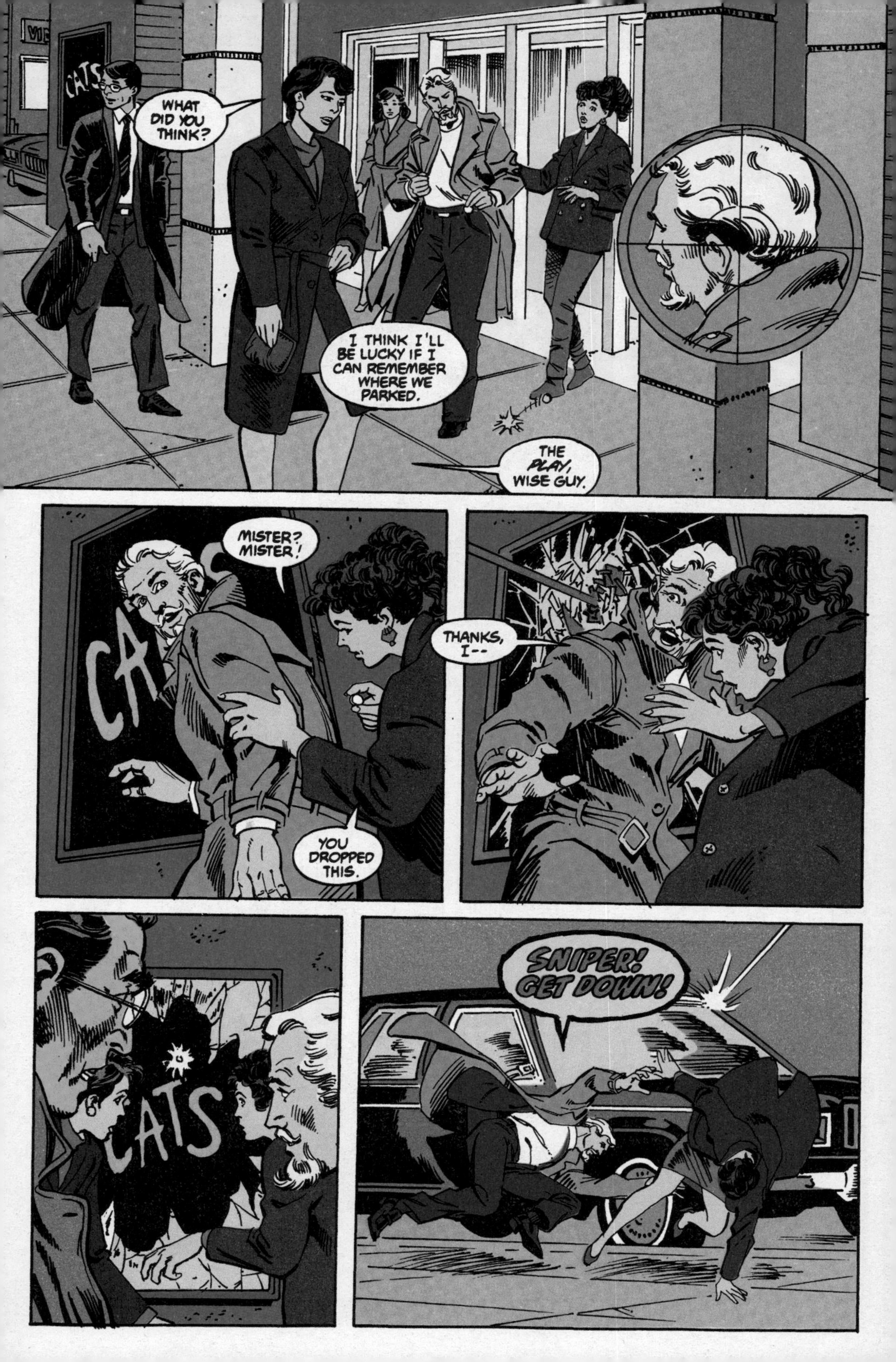
WHAT DID YOU THINK?
I THINK I'LL BE LUCKY IF I CAN REMEMBER WHERE WE PARKED.
THE PLAY, WISE GUY.
MISTER? MISTER!
YOU DROPPED THIS.
THANKS, I--
SNIPER! GET DOWN!

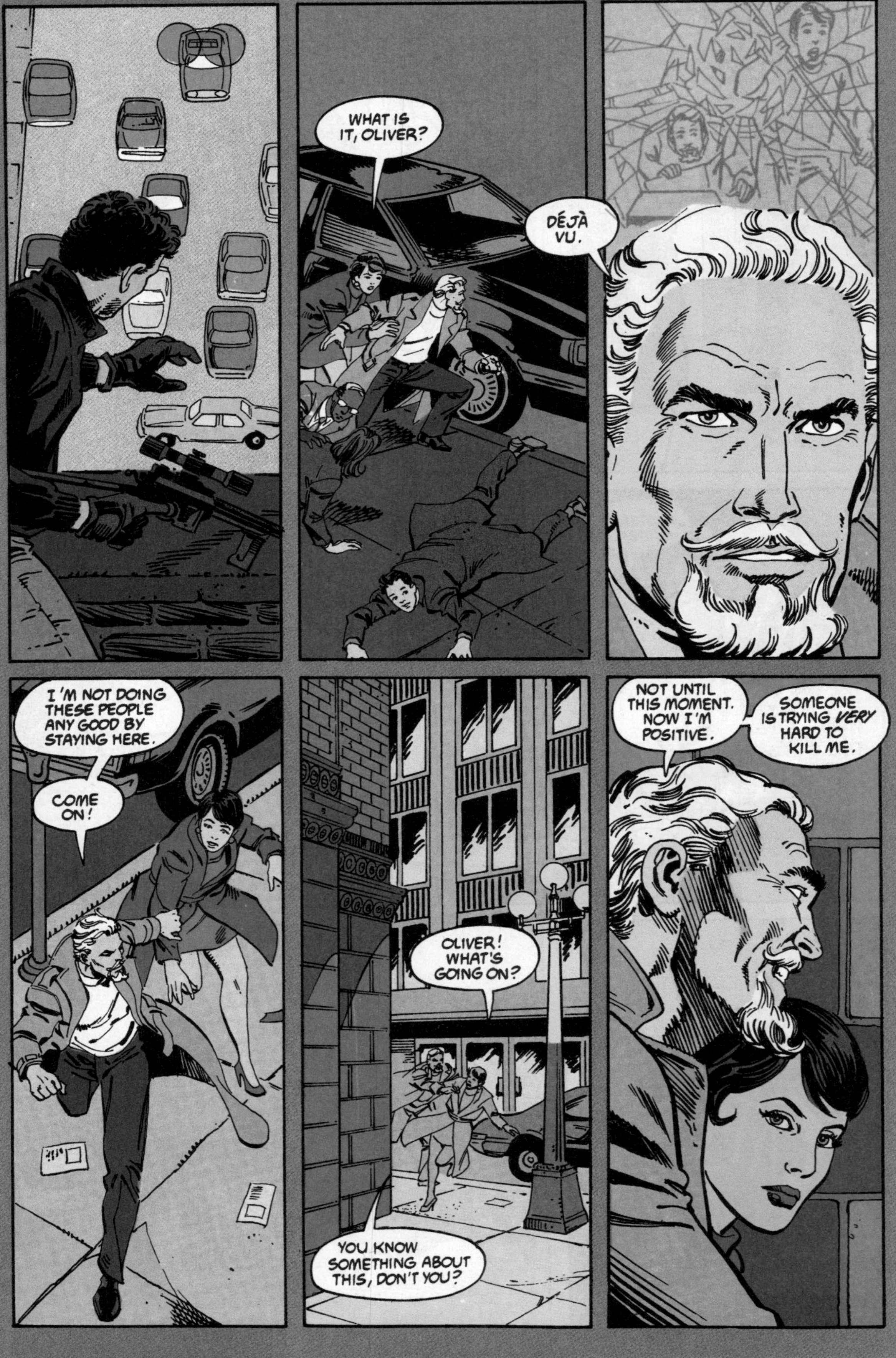
WHAT IS IT, OLIVER?
DÉJÀ VU.
I'M NOT DOING THESE PEOPLE ANY GOOD BY STAYING HERE.
COME ON!
OLIVER! WHAT'S GOING ON?
YOU KNOW SOMETHING ABOUT THIS, DON'T YOU?
NOT UNTIL THIS MOMENT. NOW I'M POSITIVE.
SOMEONE IS TRYING *VERY* HARD TO KILL ME.

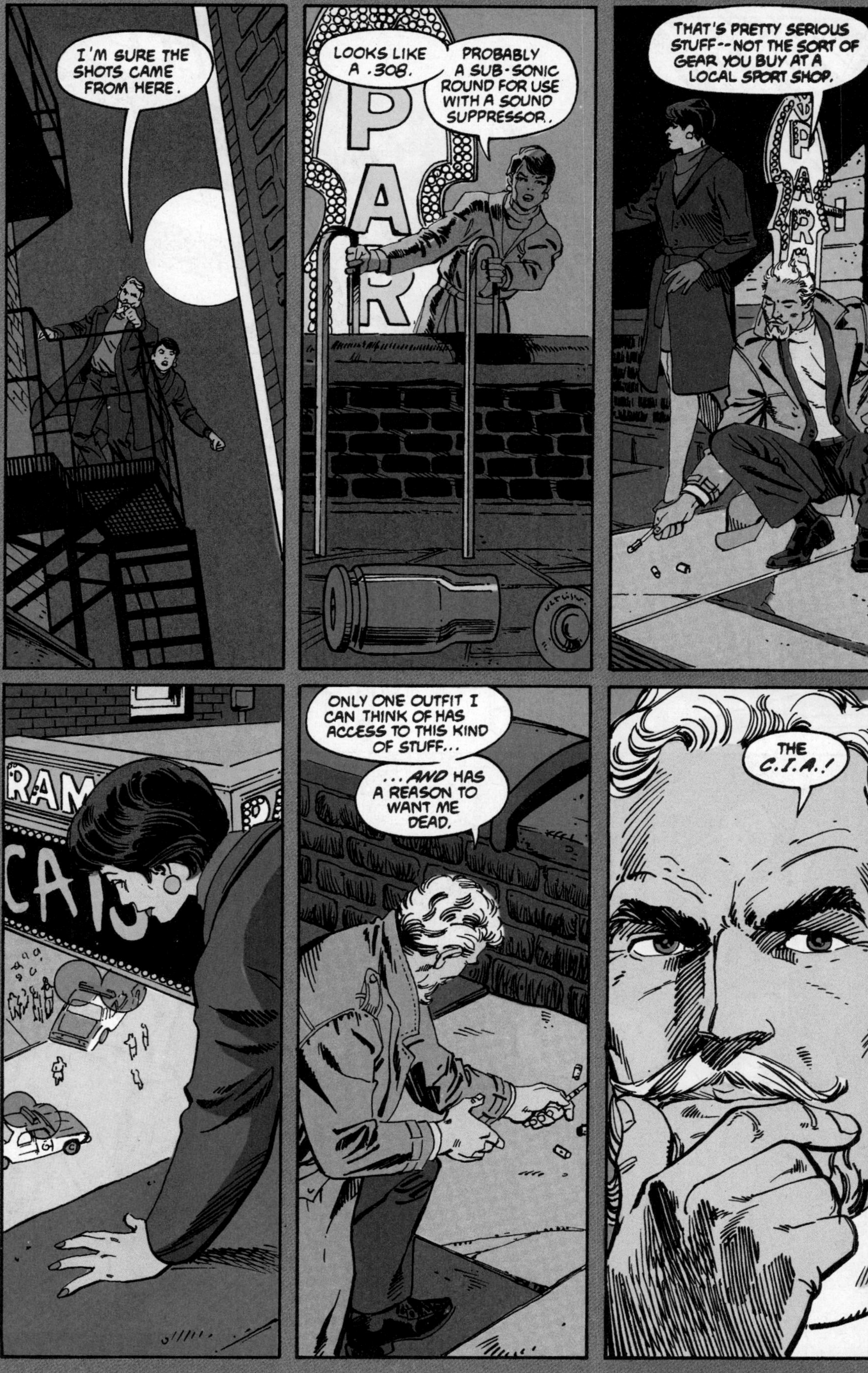
I'M SURE THE SHOTS CAME FROM HERE.
LOOKS LIKE A .308.
PROBABLY A SUB-SONIC ROUND FOR USE WITH A SOUND SUPPRESSOR.
THAT'S PRETTY SERIOUS STUFF--NOT THE SORT OF GEAR YOU BUY AT A LOCAL SPORT SHOP.
ONLY ONE OUTFIT I CAN THINK OF HAS ACCESS TO THIS KIND OF STUFF...
...AND HAS A REASON TO WANT ME DEAD.
THE C.I.A.!

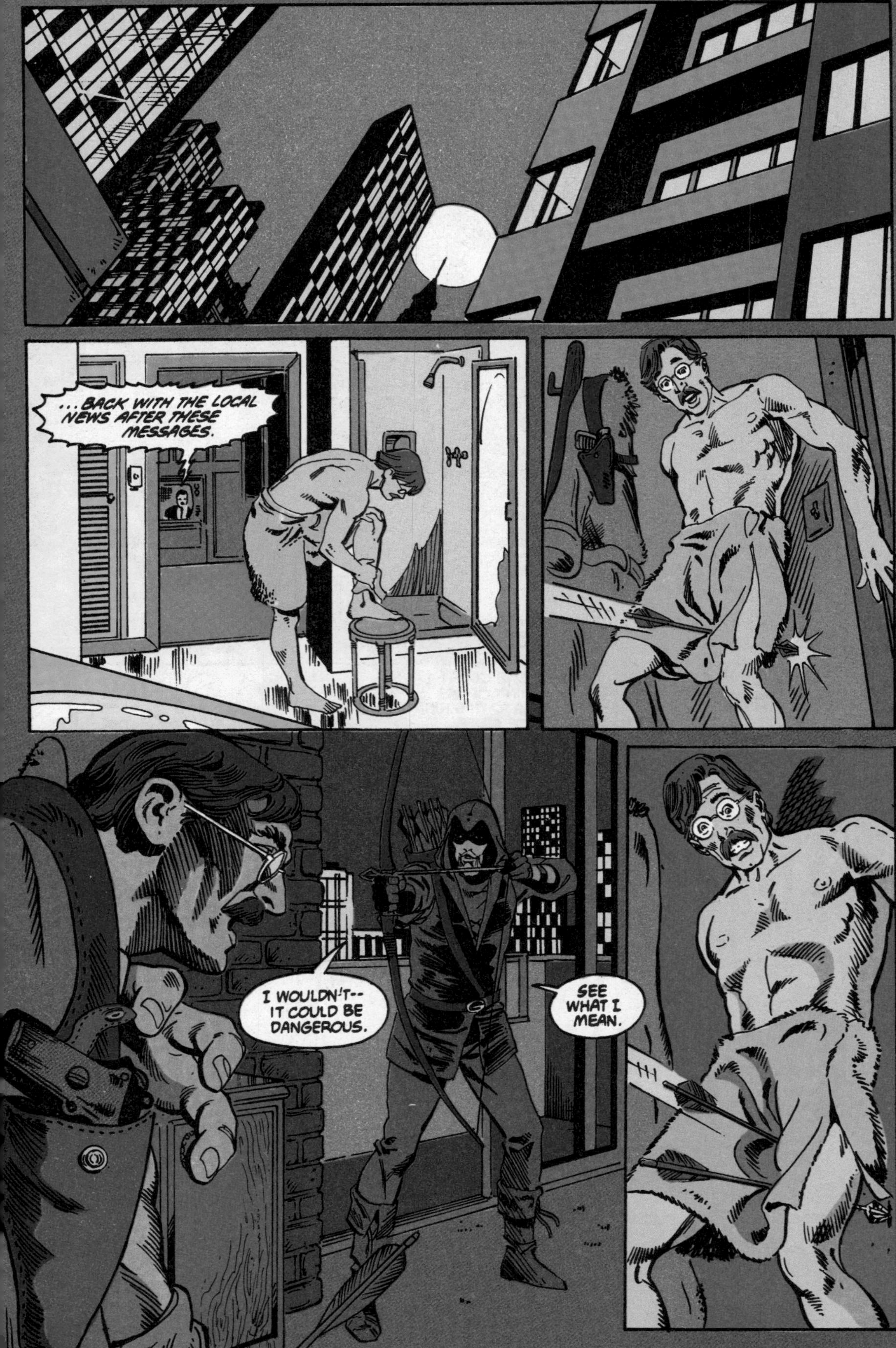

...BACK WITH THE LOCAL NEWS AFTER THESE MESSAGES.
I WOULDN'T--IT COULD BE DANGEROUS.
SEE WHAT I MEAN.

I DON'T LIKE BEING SHOT AT, FIRES.

WELL, WE'VE GOT A LOT IN COMMON, THEN... BUT IT SORT OF GOES WITH THE TERRITORY, KNOW WHAT I MEAN?

EVEN YOU CAN DIE. IT'S SIMPLE.

NEXT TIME YOU WON'T GET A WARNING SHOT.

GO BACK TO YOUR C.I.A. BOSS OSBORNE AND TELL HIM YOU'RE DROPPING THE CONTRACT.

OSBORNE?! MAYBE YOU DIDN'T HEAR, QUEEN...

--INTER-SERVICE PROFESSIONAL COURTESY, I GUESS.

THE YAKUZA GOT HIM THE SAME DAY.

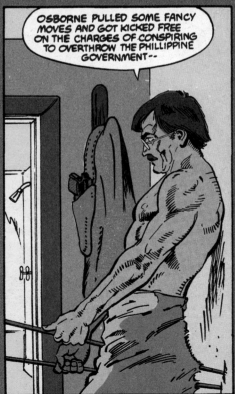

OSBORNE PULLED SOME FANCY MOVES AND GOT KICKED FREE ON THE CHARGES OF CONSPIRING TO OVERTHROW THE PHILLIPPINE GOVERNMENT--

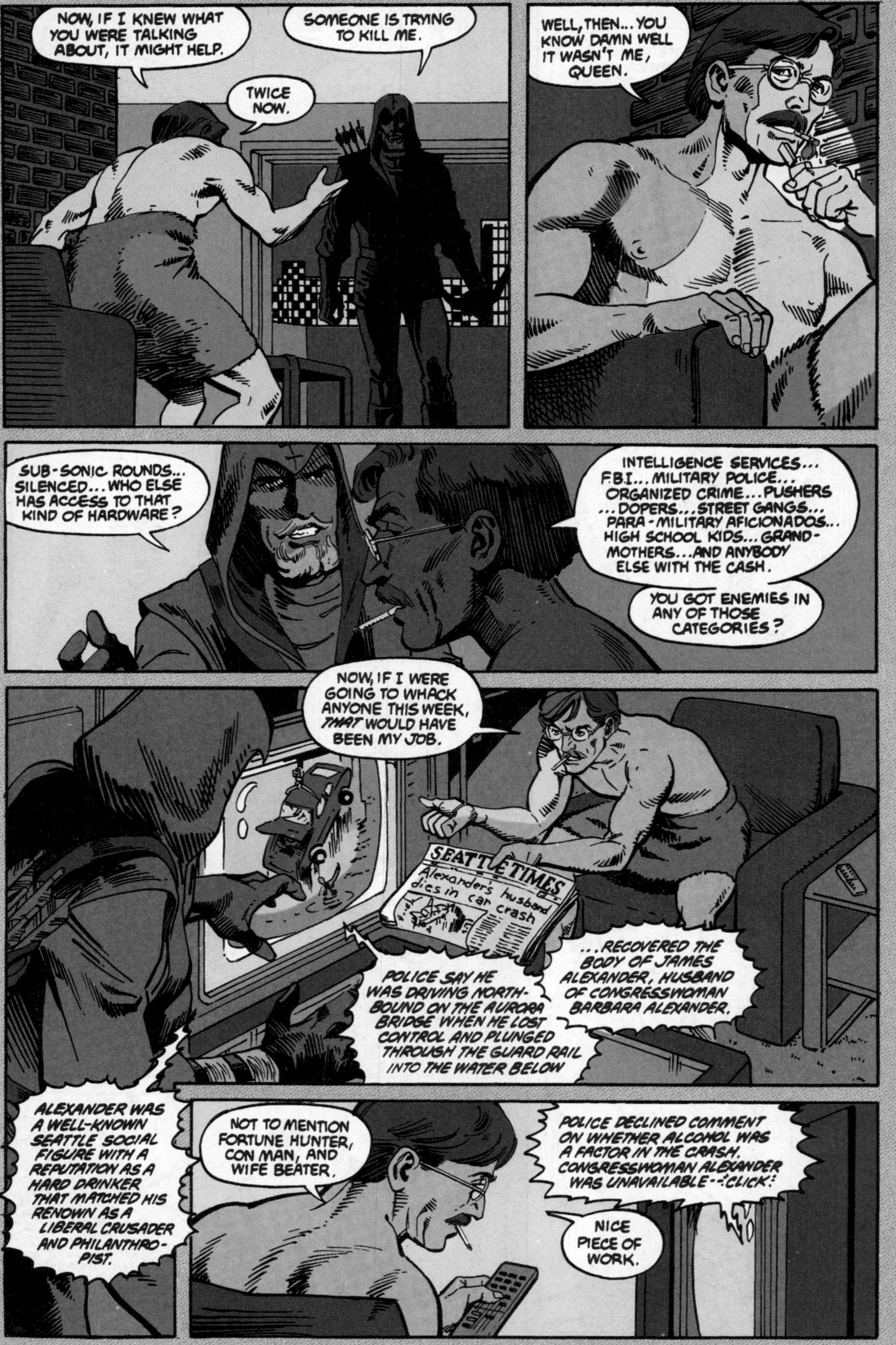
NOW, IF I KNEW WHAT YOU WERE TALKING ABOUT, IT MIGHT HELP.
SOMEONE IS TRYING TO KILL ME.
TWICE NOW.
WELL, THEN... YOU KNOW DAMN WELL IT WASN'T ME, QUEEN.
SUB-SONIC ROUNDS... SILENCED... WHO ELSE HAS ACCESS TO THAT KIND OF HARDWARE?
INTELLIGENCE SERVICES... F.B.I... MILITARY POLICE... ORGANIZED CRIME... PUSHERS ...DOPERS... STREET GANGS... PARA-MILITARY AFICIONADOS... HIGH SCHOOL KIDS... GRAND-MOTHERS... AND ANYBODY ELSE WITH THE CASH.
YOU GOT ENEMIES IN ANY OF THOSE CATEGORIES?
NOW, IF I WERE GOING TO WHACK ANYONE THIS WEEK, THAT WOULD HAVE BEEN MY JOB.
SEATTLE TIMES
Alexander's husband dies in car crash
...RECOVERED THE BODY OF JAMES ALEXANDER, HUSBAND OF CONGRESSWOMAN BARBARA ALEXANDER.
POLICE SAY HE WAS DRIVING NORTH-BOUND ON THE AURORA BRIDGE WHEN HE LOST CONTROL AND PLUNGED THROUGH THE GUARD RAIL INTO THE WATER BELOW
ALEXANDER WAS A WELL-KNOWN SEATTLE SOCIAL FIGURE WITH A REPUTATION AS A HARD DRINKER THAT MATCHED HIS RENOWN AS A LIBERAL CRUSADER AND PHILANTHRO-PIST.
NOT TO MENTION FORTUNE HUNTER, CON MAN, AND WIFE BEATER.
POLICE DECLINED COMMENT ON WHETHER ALCOHOL WAS A FACTOR IN THE CRASH. CONGRESSWOMAN ALEXANDER WAS UNAVAILABLE--:CLICK:
NICE PIECE OF WORK.

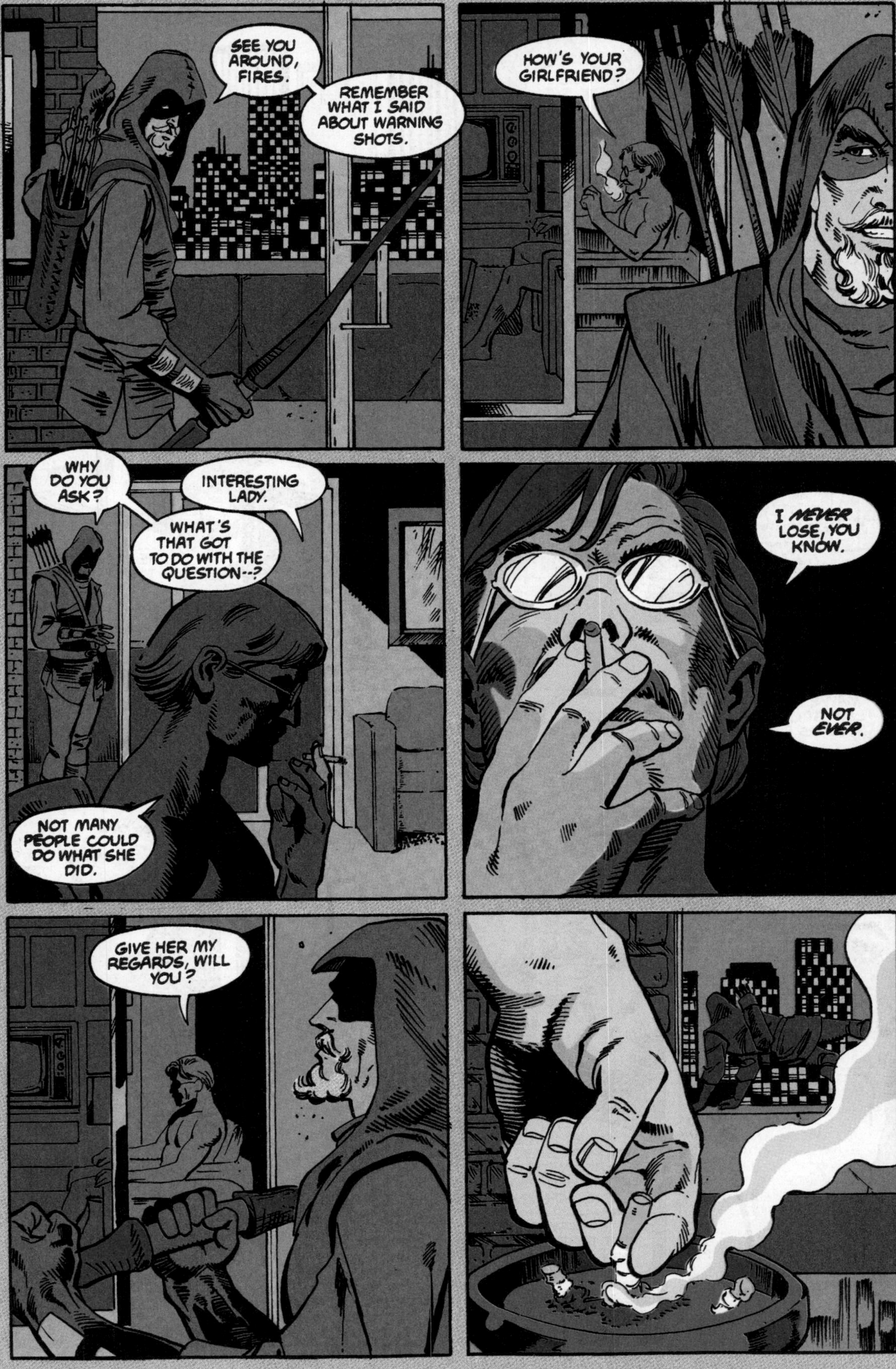
SEE YOU AROUND, FIRES.
REMEMBER WHAT I SAID ABOUT WARNING SHOTS.
HOW'S YOUR GIRLFRIEND?
WHY DO YOU ASK?
WHAT'S THAT GOT TO DO WITH THE QUESTION--?
INTERESTING LADY.
NOT MANY PEOPLE COULD DO WHAT SHE DID.
I NEVER LOSE, YOU KNOW.
NOT EVER.
GIVE HER MY REGARDS, WILL YOU?

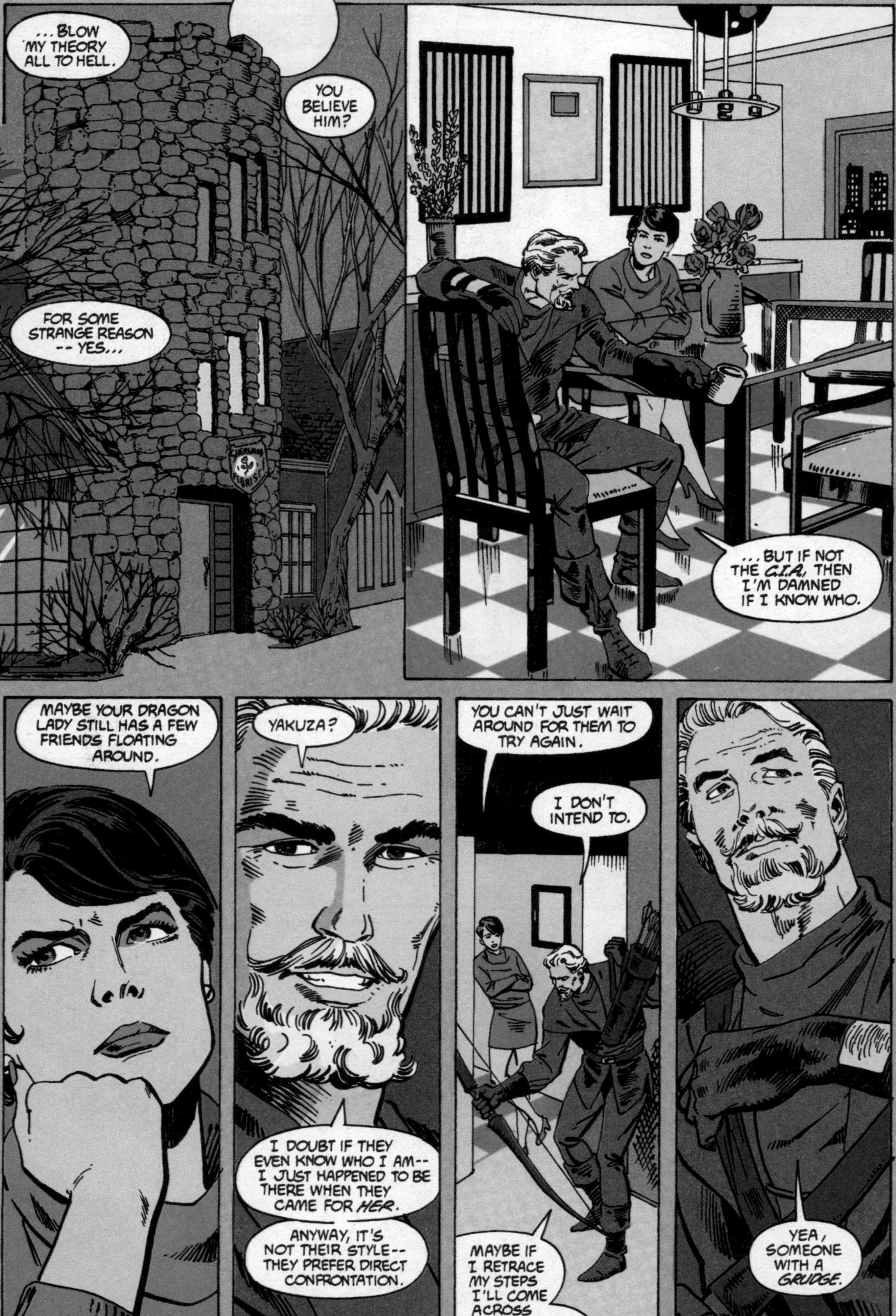
...BLOW MY THEORY ALL TO HELL.
YOU BELIEVE HIM?
FOR SOME STRANGE REASON -- YES...
...BUT IF NOT THE C.I.A. THEN I'M DAMNED IF I KNOW WHO.
MAYBE YOUR DRAGON LADY STILL HAS A FEW FRIENDS FLOATING AROUND.
YAKUZA?
I DOUBT IF THEY EVEN KNOW WHO I AM-- I JUST HAPPENED TO BE THERE WHEN THEY CAME FOR HER.
ANYWAY, IT'S NOT THEIR STYLE-- THEY PREFER DIRECT CONFRONTATION.
YOU CAN'T JUST WAIT AROUND FOR THEM TO TRY AGAIN.
I DON'T INTEND TO.
MAYBE IF I RETRACE MY STEPS I'LL COME ACROSS SOMEONE WITH A GRUDGE.
YEA, SOMEONE WITH A GRUDGE.

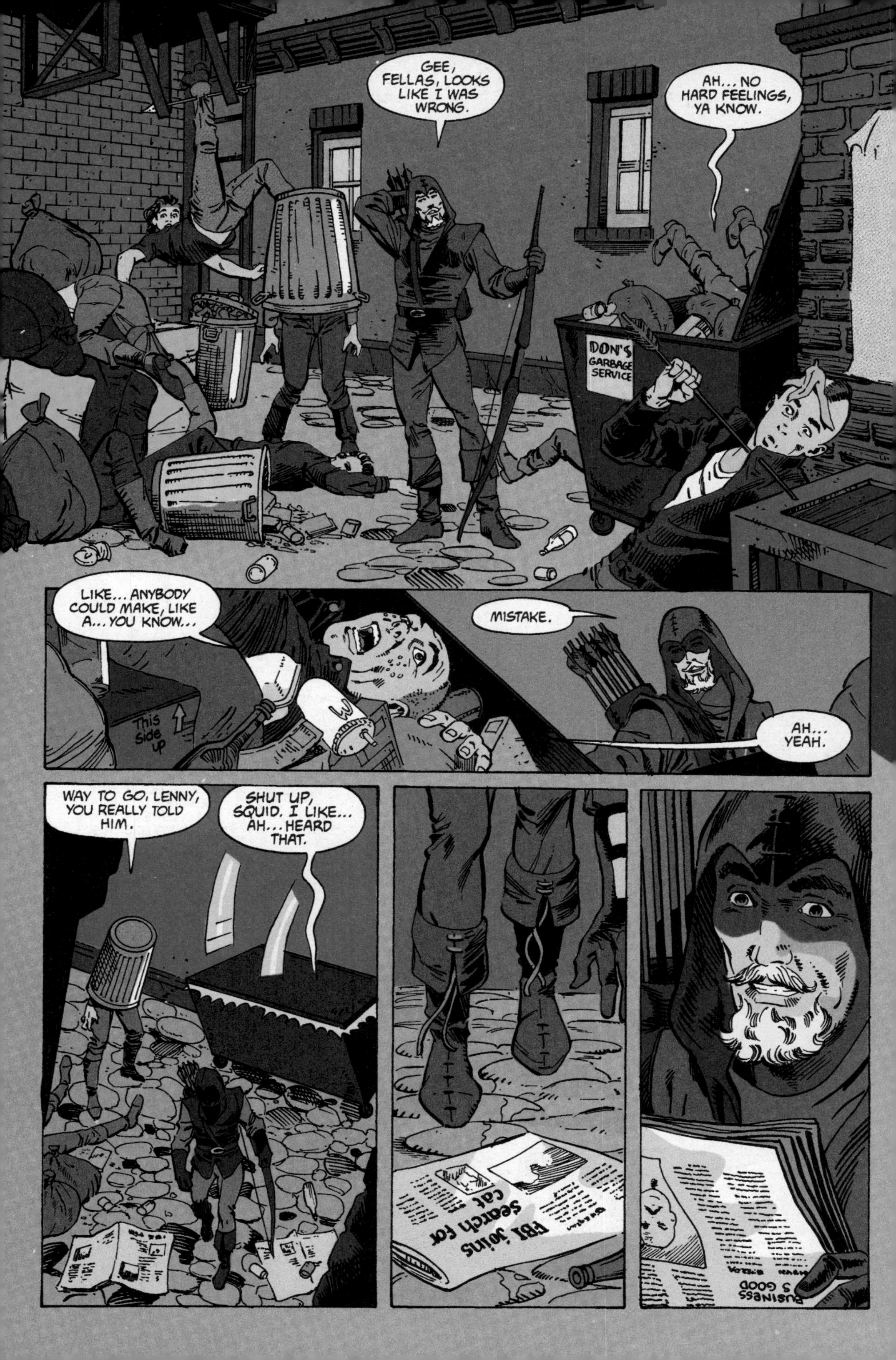
GEE, FELLAS, LOOKS LIKE I WAS WRONG.
AH... NO HARD FEELINGS, YA KNOW.
DON'S GARBAGE SERVICE
LIKE... ANYBODY COULD MAKE, LIKE A... YOU KNOW...
This side up
MISTAKE.
AH... YEAH.
WAY TO GO, LENNY, YOU REALLY TOLD HIM.
SHUT UP, SQUID. I LIKE... AH... HEARD THAT.
FBI joins search for cat
BUSINESS S GOOD

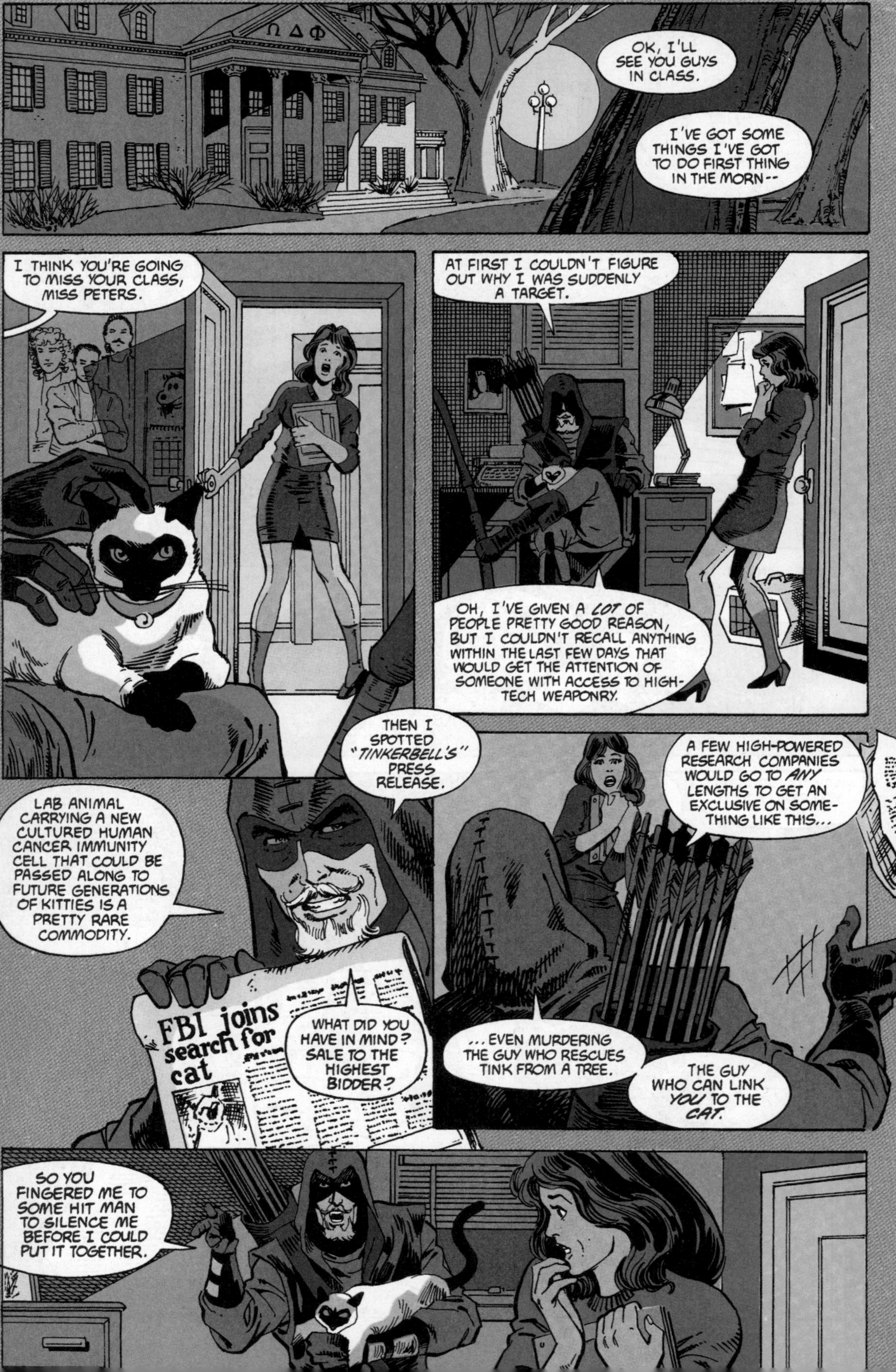
OK, I'LL SEE YOU GUYS IN CLASS.
I'VE GOT SOME THINGS I'VE GOT TO DO FIRST THING IN THE MORN--
I THINK YOU'RE GOING TO MISS YOUR CLASS, MISS PETERS.
AT FIRST I COULDN'T FIGURE OUT WHY I WAS SUDDENLY A TARGET.
OH, I'VE GIVEN A LOT OF PEOPLE PRETTY GOOD REASON, BUT I COULDN'T RECALL ANYTHING WITHIN THE LAST FEW DAYS THAT WOULD GET THE ATTENTION OF SOMEONE WITH ACCESS TO HIGH-TECH WEAPONRY.
THEN I SPOTTED "TINKERBELL'S" PRESS RELEASE.
LAB ANIMAL CARRYING A NEW CULTURED HUMAN CANCER IMMUNITY CELL THAT COULD BE PASSED ALONG TO FUTURE GENERATIONS OF KITTIES IS A PRETTY RARE COMMODITY.
FBI joins search for cat
WHAT DID YOU HAVE IN MIND? SALE TO THE HIGHEST BIDDER?
A FEW HIGH-POWERED RESEARCH COMPANIES WOULD GO TO ANY LENGTHS TO GET AN EXCLUSIVE ON SOMETHING LIKE THIS...
...EVEN MURDERING THE GUY WHO RESCUES TINK FROM A TREE.
THE GUY WHO CAN LINK YOU TO THE CAT.
SO YOU FINGERED ME TO SOME HIT MAN TO SILENCE ME BEFORE I COULD PUT IT TOGETHER.

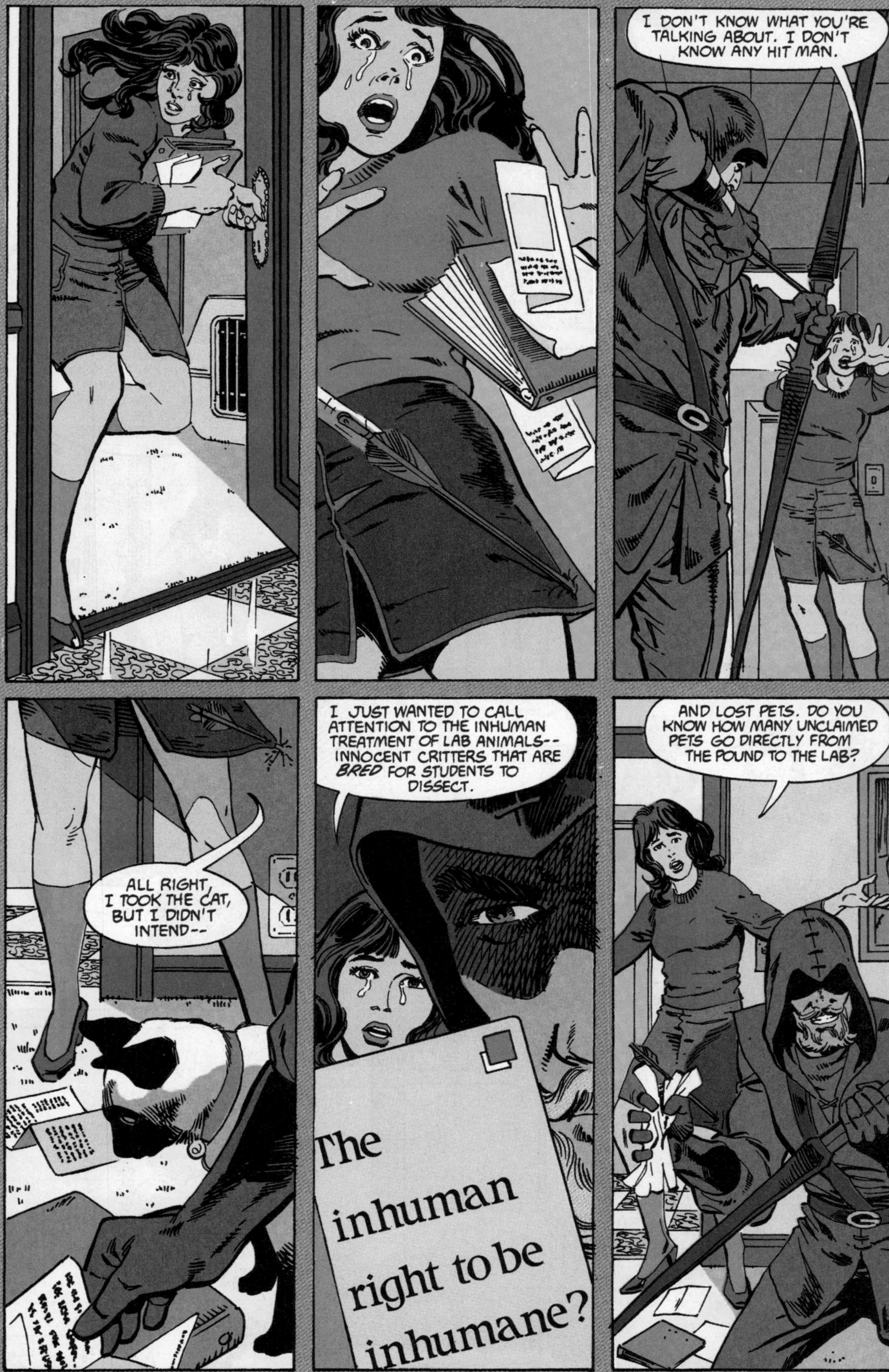
I DON'T KNOW WHAT YOU'RE TALKING ABOUT. I DON'T KNOW ANY HIT MAN.
ALL RIGHT, I TOOK THE CAT, BUT I DIDN'T INTEND--
I JUST WANTED TO CALL ATTENTION TO THE INHUMAN TREATMENT OF LAB ANIMALS-- INNOCENT CRITTERS THAT ARE *BRED* FOR STUDENTS TO DISSECT.
The inhuman right to be inhumane?
AND LOST PETS. DO YOU KNOW HOW MANY UNCLAIMED PETS GO DIRECTLY FROM THE POUND TO THE LAB?

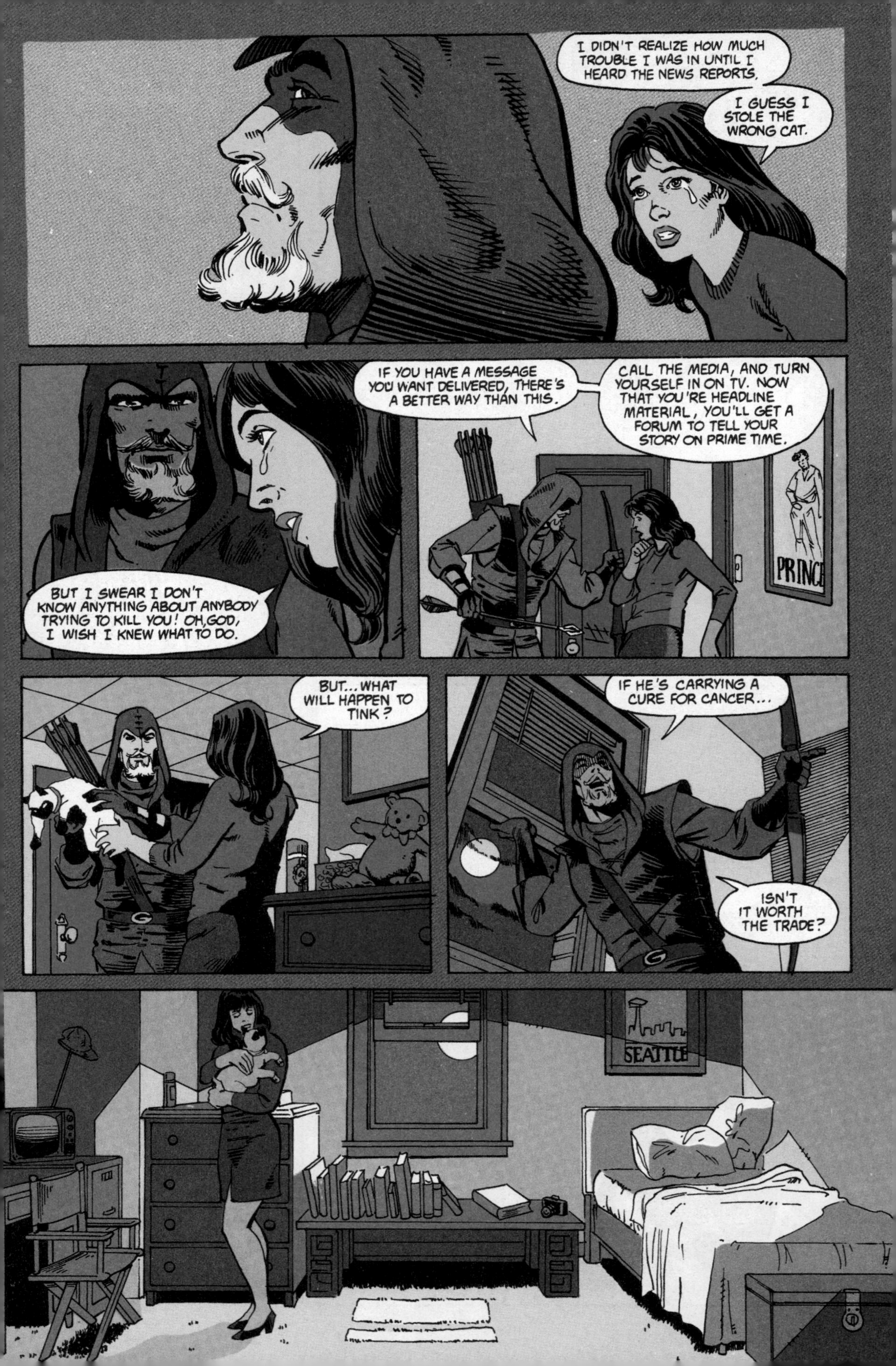
I DIDN'T REALIZE HOW MUCH TROUBLE I WAS IN UNTIL I HEARD THE NEWS REPORTS.
I GUESS I STOLE THE WRONG CAT.
BUT I SWEAR I DON'T KNOW ANYTHING ABOUT ANYBODY TRYING TO KILL YOU! OH, GOD, I WISH I KNEW WHAT TO DO.
IF YOU HAVE A MESSAGE YOU WANT DELIVERED, THERE'S A BETTER WAY THAN THIS.
CALL THE MEDIA, AND TURN YOURSELF IN ON TV. NOW THAT YOU'RE HEADLINE MATERIAL, YOU'LL GET A FORUM TO TELL YOUR STORY ON PRIME TIME.
PRINCE
BUT... WHAT WILL HAPPEN TO TINK?
IF HE'S CARRYING A CURE FOR CANCER...
ISN'T IT WORTH THE TRADE?
SEATTLE

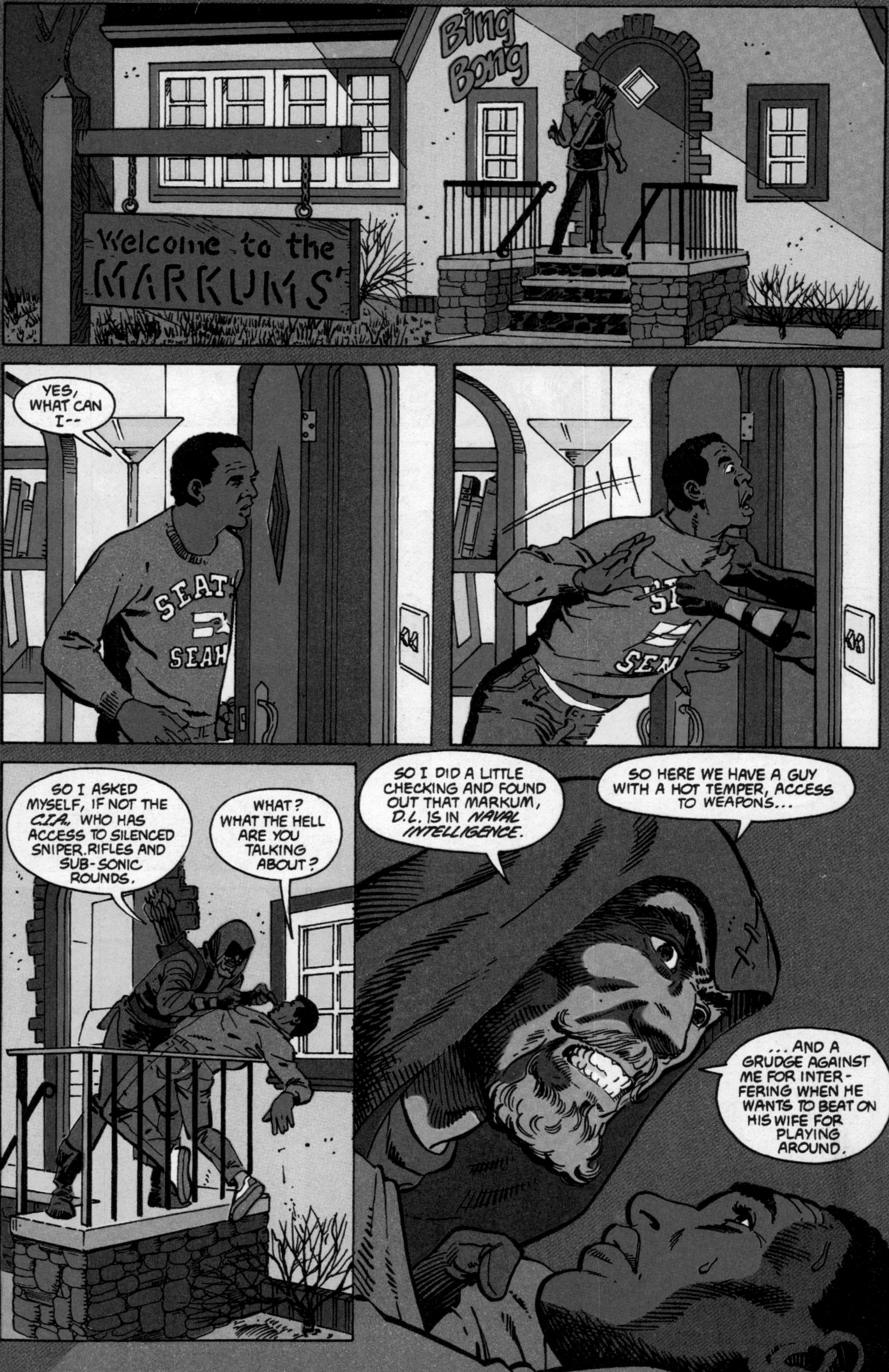
Bing Bong
Welcome to the MARKUMS'
YES, WHAT CAN I--
SEAT SEAH
SO I ASKED MYSELF, IF NOT THE C.I.A., WHO HAS ACCESS TO SILENCED SNIPER.RIFLES AND SUB-SONIC ROUNDS.
WHAT? WHAT THE HELL ARE YOU TALKING ABOUT?
SO I DID A LITTLE CHECKING AND FOUND OUT THAT MARKUM, D.L. IS IN NAVAL INTELLIGENCE.
SO HERE WE HAVE A GUY WITH A HOT TEMPER, ACCESS TO WEAPONS...
...AND A GRUDGE AGAINST ME FOR INTER-FERING WHEN HE WANTS TO BEAT ON HIS WIFE FOR PLAYING AROUND.

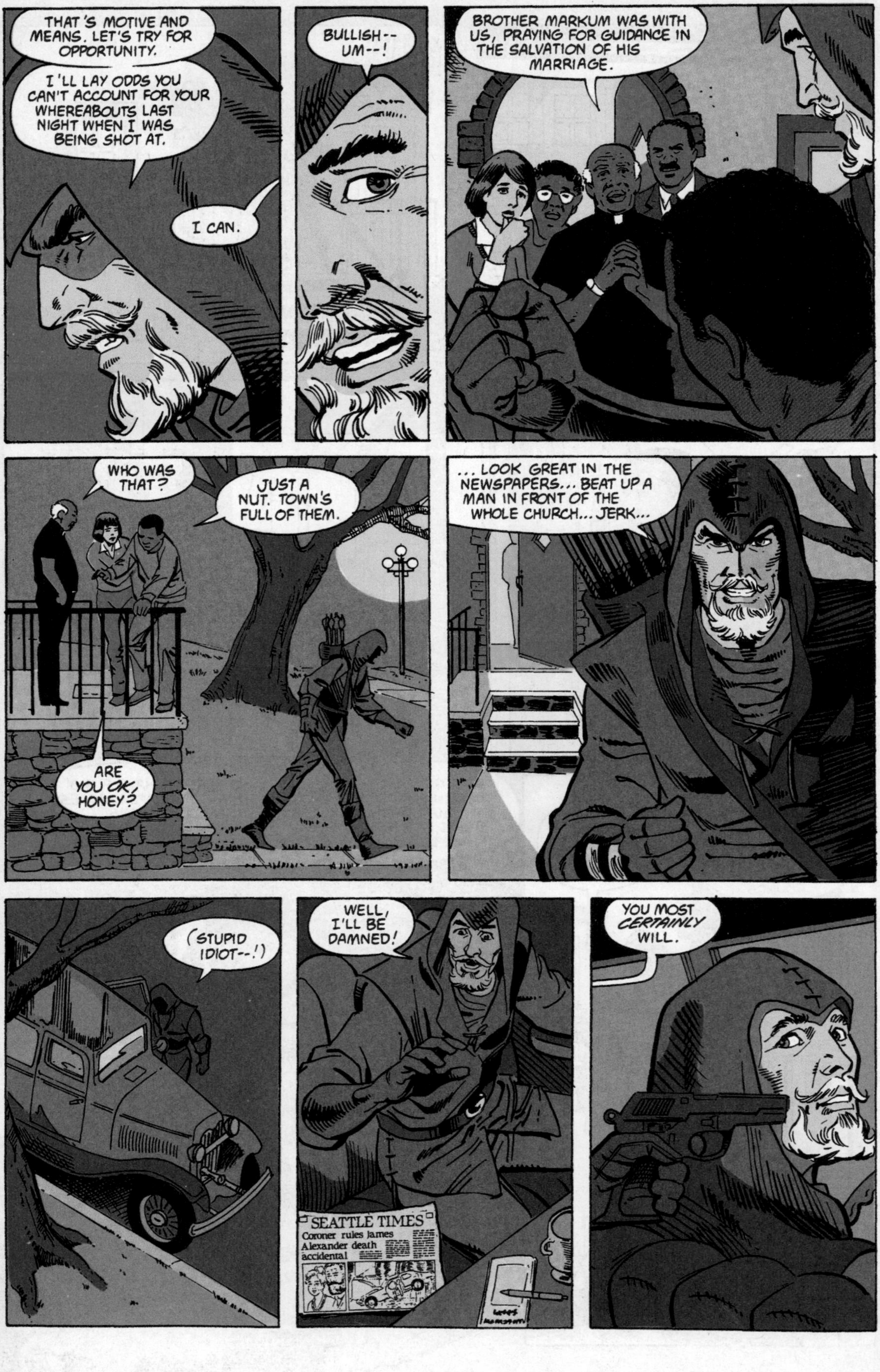
THAT'S MOTIVE AND MEANS. LET'S TRY FOR OPPORTUNITY.
I'LL LAY ODDS YOU CAN'T ACCOUNT FOR YOUR WHEREABOUTS LAST NIGHT WHEN I WAS BEING SHOT AT.
I CAN.
BULLISH-- UM--!
BROTHER MARKUM WAS WITH US, PRAYING FOR GUIDANCE IN THE SALVATION OF HIS MARRIAGE.
WHO WAS THAT?
JUST A NUT. TOWN'S FULL OF THEM.
ARE YOU OK, HONEY?
... LOOK GREAT IN THE NEWSPAPERS... BEAT UP A MAN IN FRONT OF THE WHOLE CHURCH... JERK...
(STUPID IDIOT--!)
WELL, I'LL BE DAMNED!
SEATTLE TIMES
Coroner rules James Alexander death accidental
YOU MOST CERTAINLY WILL.

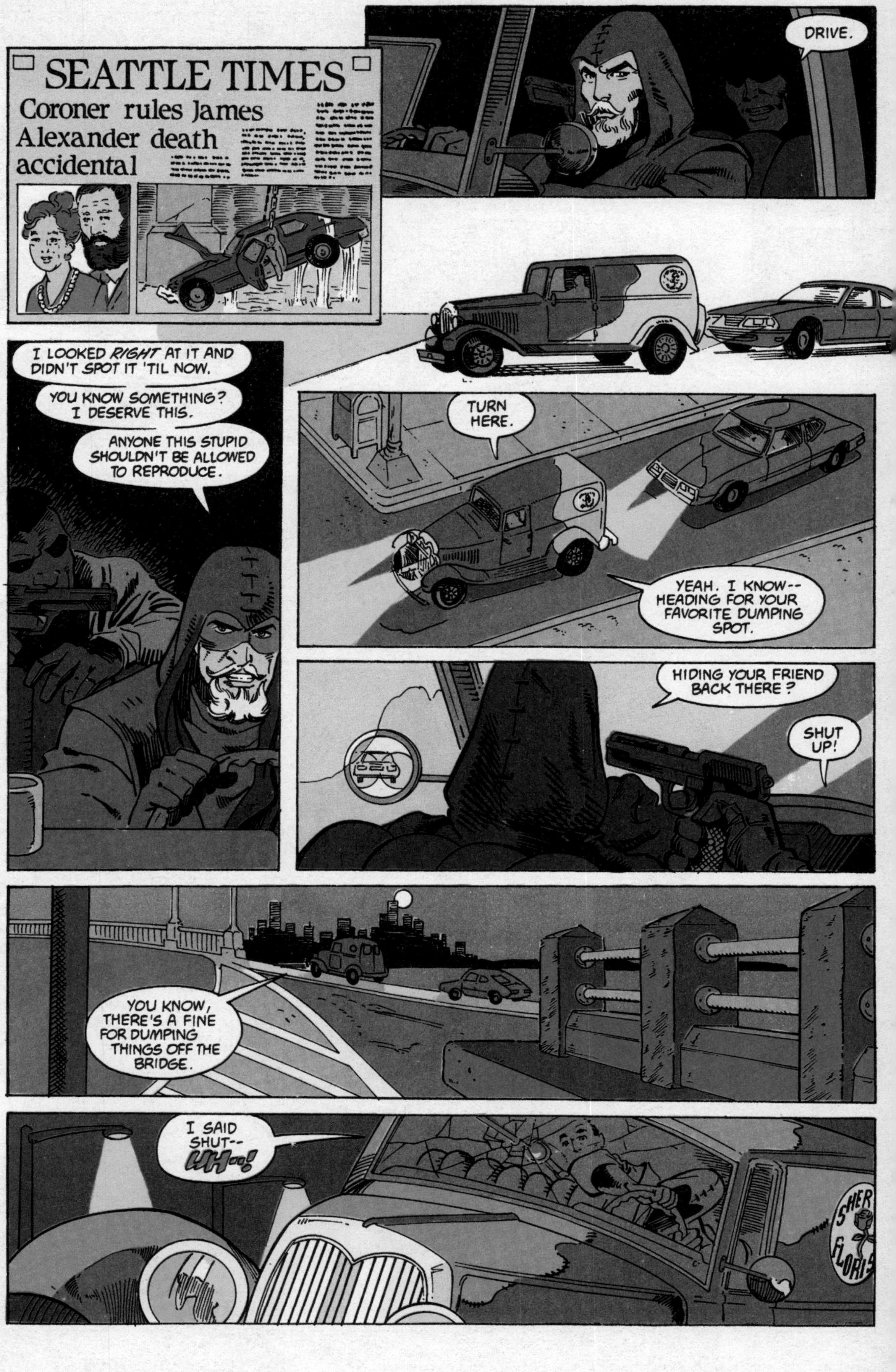
SEATTLE TIMES
Coroner rules James Alexander death accidental
DRIVE.
I LOOKED RIGHT AT IT AND DIDN'T SPOT IT 'TIL NOW.
YOU KNOW SOMETHING? I DESERVE THIS.
ANYONE THIS STUPID SHOULDN'T BE ALLOWED TO REPRODUCE.
TURN HERE.
YEAH. I KNOW-- HEADING FOR YOUR FAVORITE DUMPING SPOT.
HIDING YOUR FRIEND BACK THERE?
SHUT UP!
YOU KNOW, THERE'S A FINE FOR DUMPING THINGS OFF THE BRIDGE.
I SAID SHUT-- UH--!

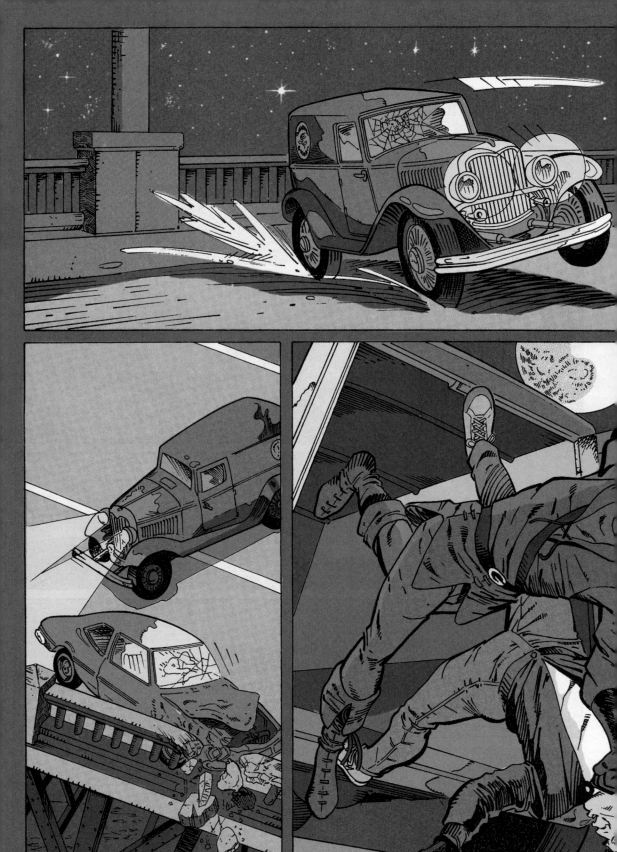

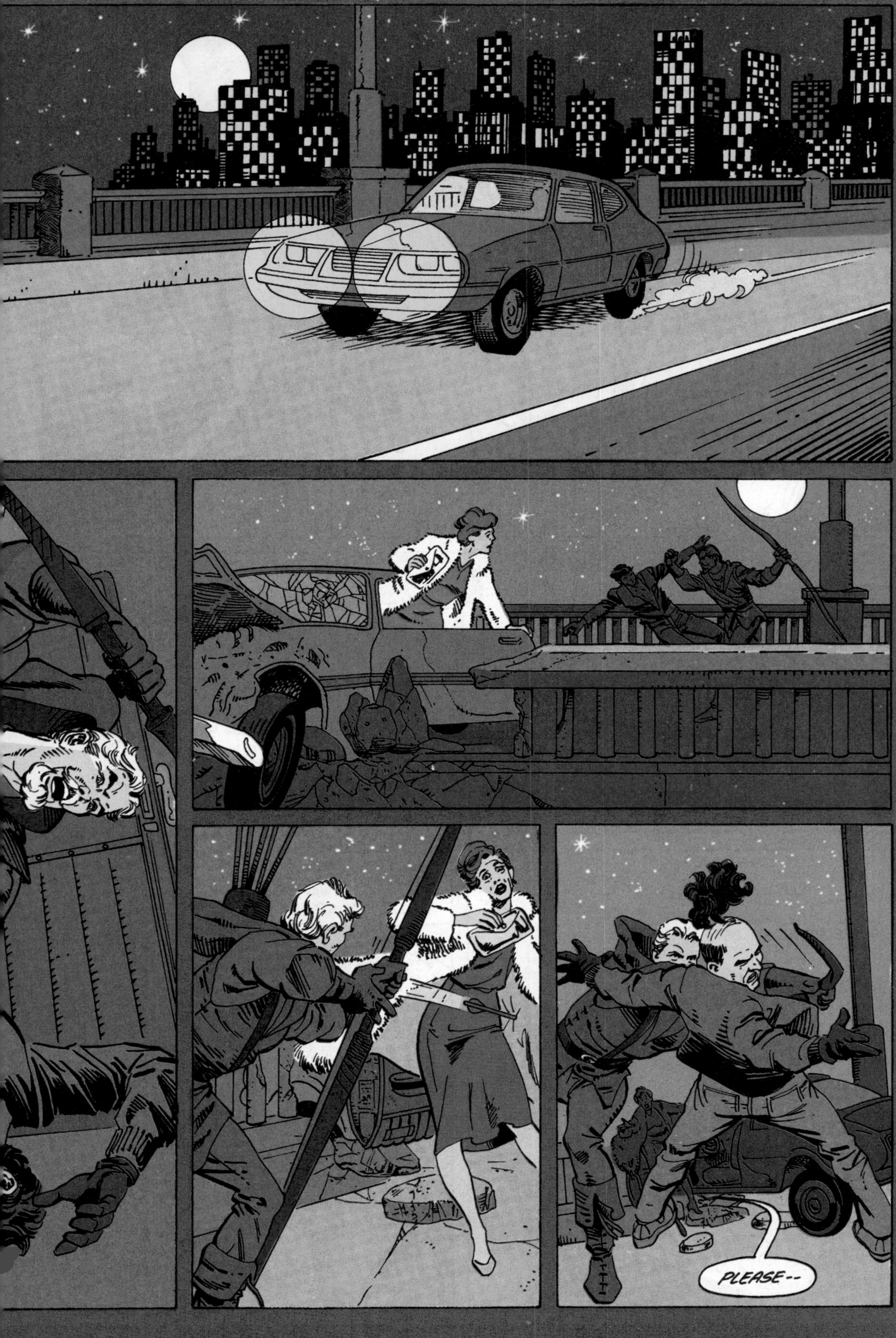
PLEASE--

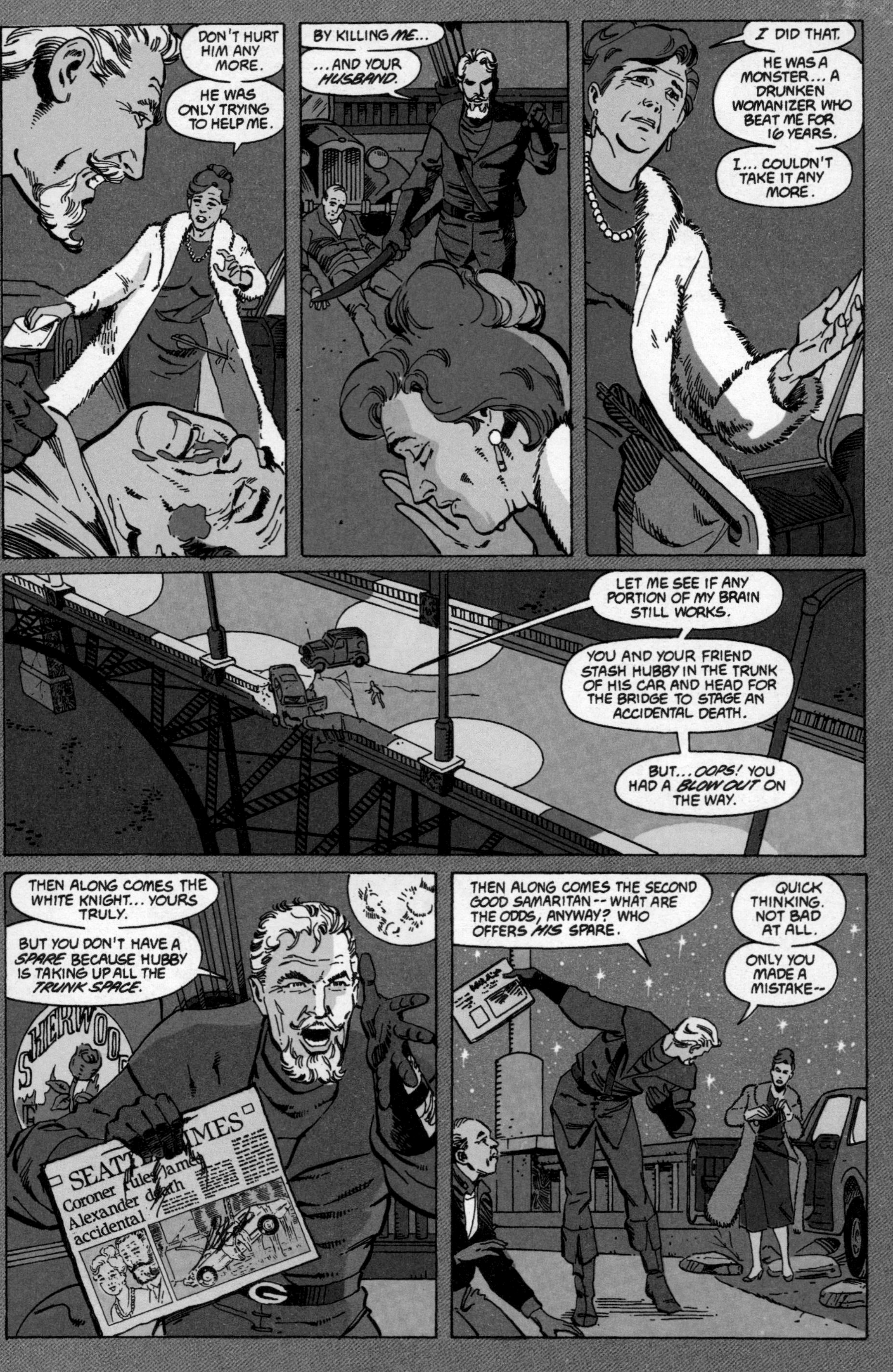
DON'T HURT HIM ANY MORE.
HE WAS ONLY TRYING TO HELP ME.
BY KILLING *ME*...
...AND YOUR *HUSBAND*.
I DID THAT.
HE WAS A MONSTER... A DRUNKEN WOMANIZER WHO BEAT ME FOR 16 YEARS.
I... COULDN'T TAKE IT ANY MORE.
LET ME SEE IF ANY PORTION OF MY BRAIN STILL WORKS.
YOU AND YOUR FRIEND STASH HUBBY IN THE TRUNK OF HIS CAR AND HEAD FOR THE BRIDGE TO STAGE AN ACCIDENTAL DEATH.
BUT... *OOPS!* YOU HAD A *BLOW OUT* ON THE WAY.
THEN ALONG COMES THE WHITE KNIGHT... YOURS TRULY.
BUT YOU DON'T HAVE A *SPARE* BECAUSE HUBBY IS TAKING UP ALL THE *TRUNK SPACE*.
SEATTLE TIMES
Coroner rules James Alexander death accidental
THEN ALONG COMES THE SECOND GOOD SAMARITAN -- WHAT ARE THE ODDS, ANYWAY? WHO OFFERS *HIS* SPARE.
QUICK THINKING. NOT BAD AT ALL.
ONLY YOU MADE A MISTAKE--

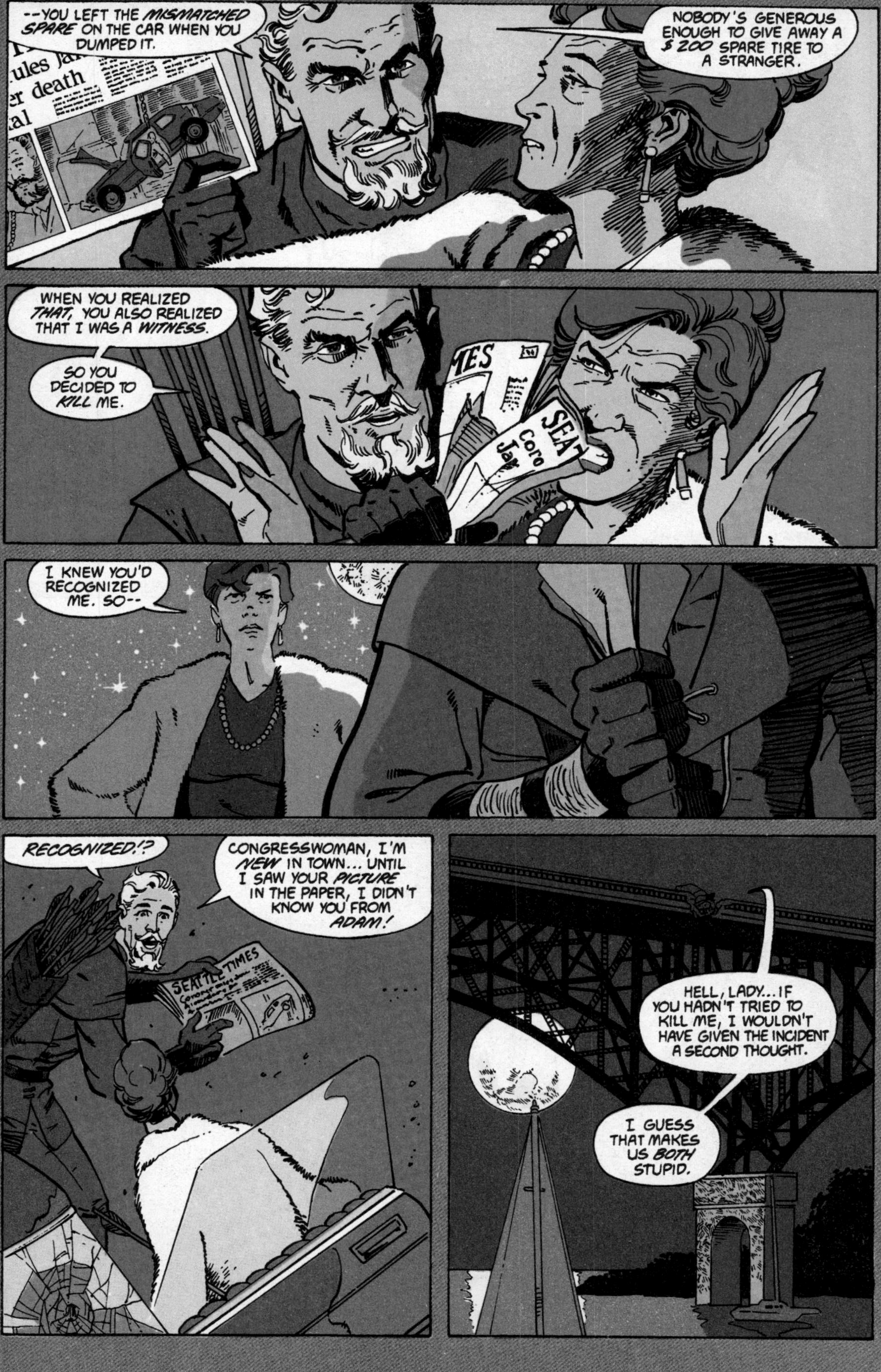
--YOU LEFT THE MISMATCHED SPARE ON THE CAR WHEN YOU DUMPED IT.
NOBODY'S GENEROUS ENOUGH TO GIVE AWAY A $200 SPARE TIRE TO A STRANGER.
WHEN YOU REALIZED THAT, YOU ALSO REALIZED THAT I WAS A WITNESS.
SO YOU DECIDED TO KILL ME.
I KNEW YOU'D RECOGNIZED ME. SO--
RECOGNIZED!?
CONGRESSWOMAN, I'M NEW IN TOWN... UNTIL I SAW YOUR PICTURE IN THE PAPER, I DIDN'T KNOW YOU FROM ADAM!
SEATTLE TIMES
HELL, LADY... IF YOU HADN'T TRIED TO KILL ME, I WOULDN'T HAVE GIVEN THE INCIDENT A SECOND THOUGHT.
I GUESS THAT MAKES US BOTH STUPID.

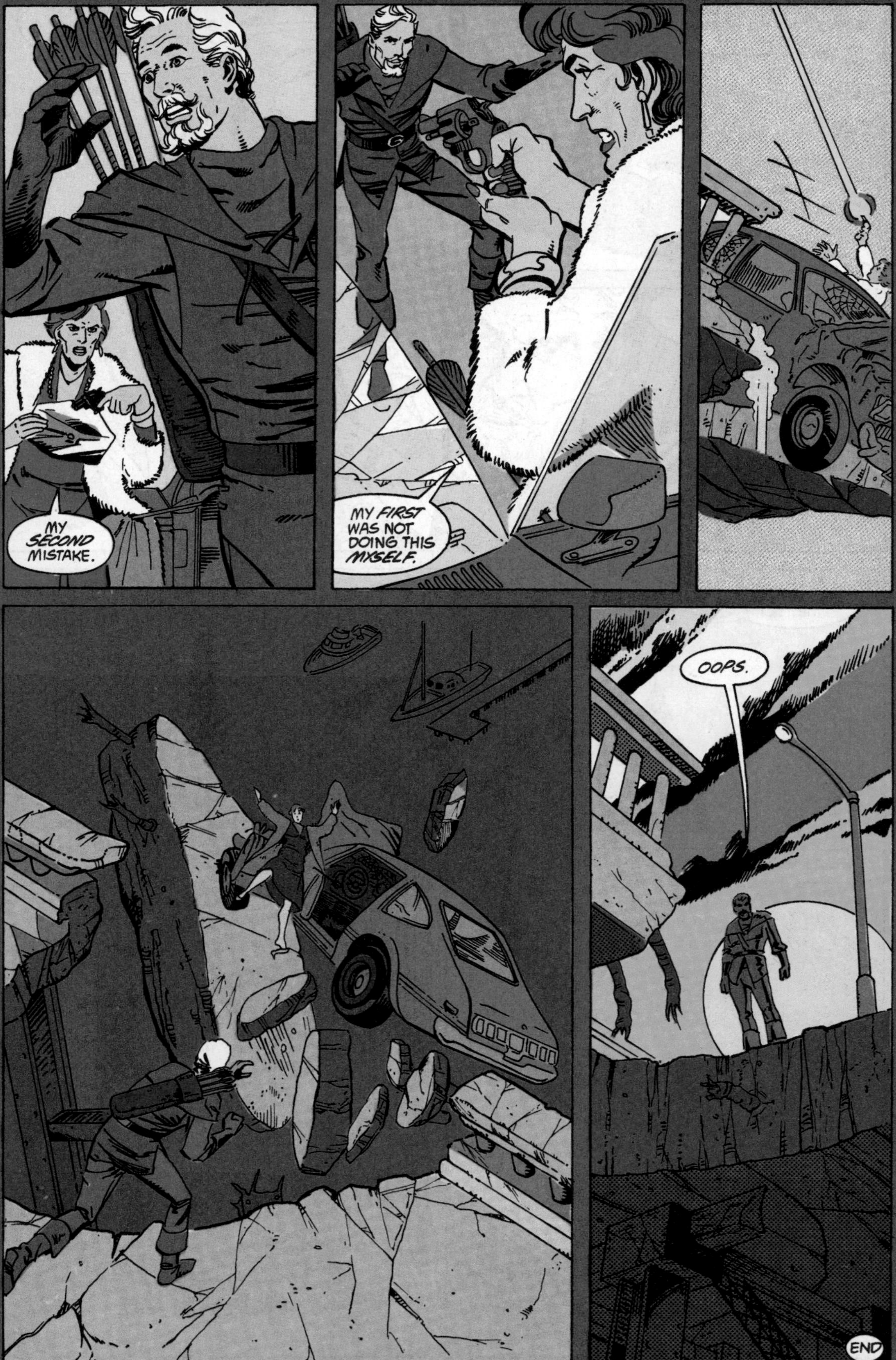
MY SECOND MISTAKE.
MY FIRST WAS NOT DOING THIS MYSELF.
OOPS.
END

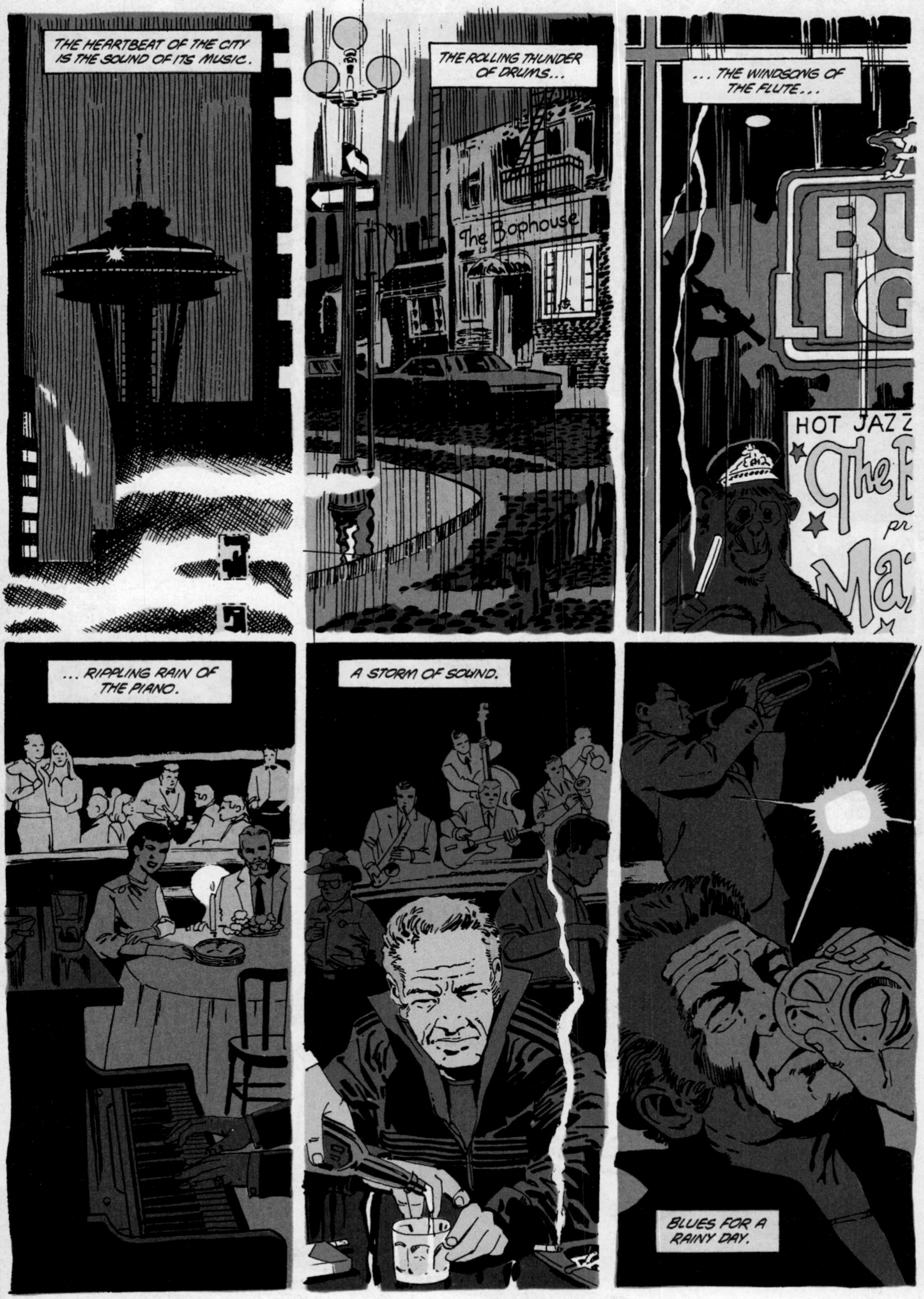
THE HEARTBEAT OF THE CITY IS THE SOUND OF ITS MUSIC.
THE ROLLING THUNDER OF DRUMS...
The Bophouse
... THE WINDSONG OF THE FLUTE...
HOT JAZZ
... RIPPLING RAIN OF THE PIANO.
A STORM OF SOUND.
BLUES FOR A RAINY DAY.

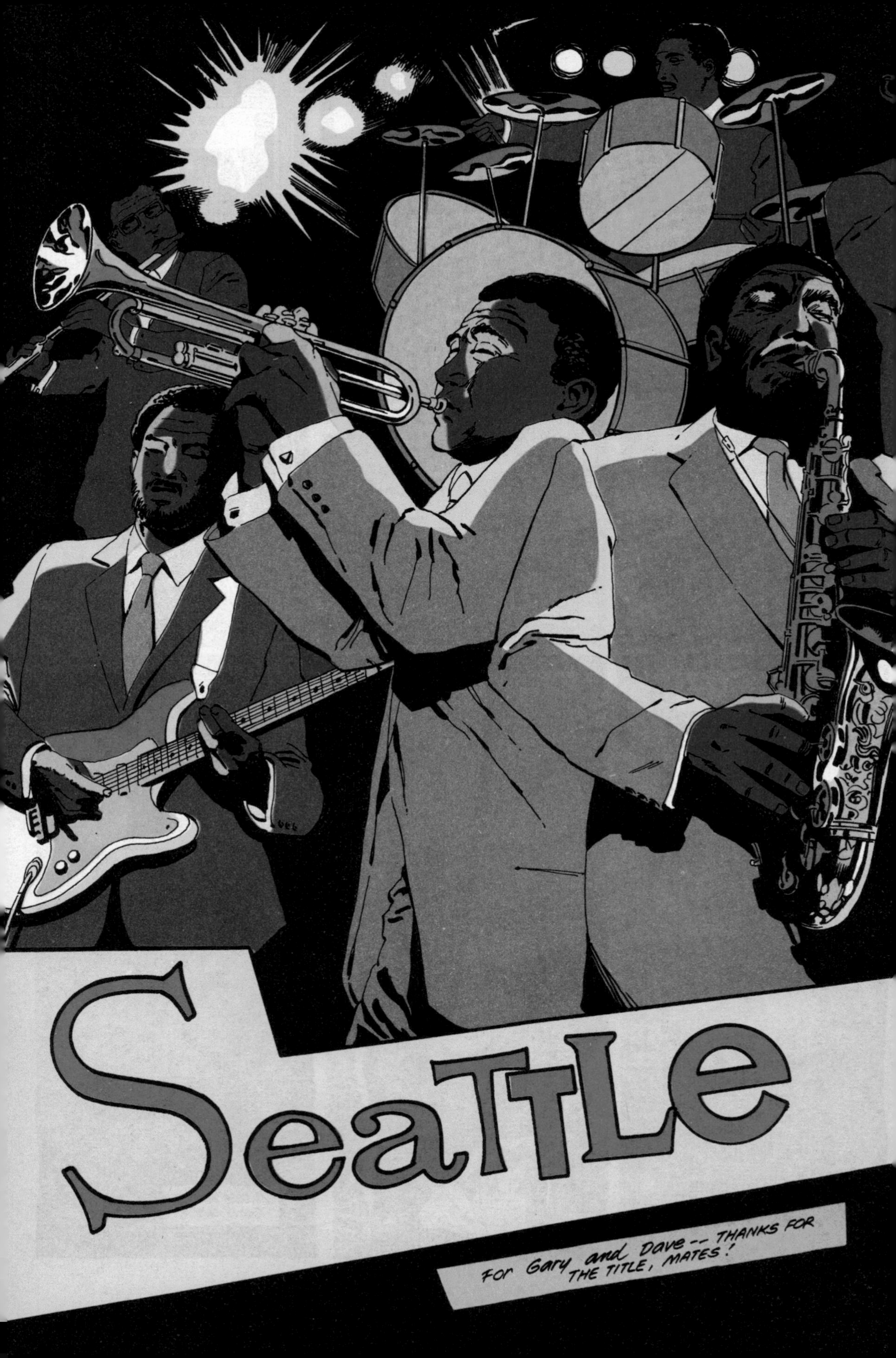
Seattle
For Gary and Dave -- THANKS FOR THE TITLE, MATES!

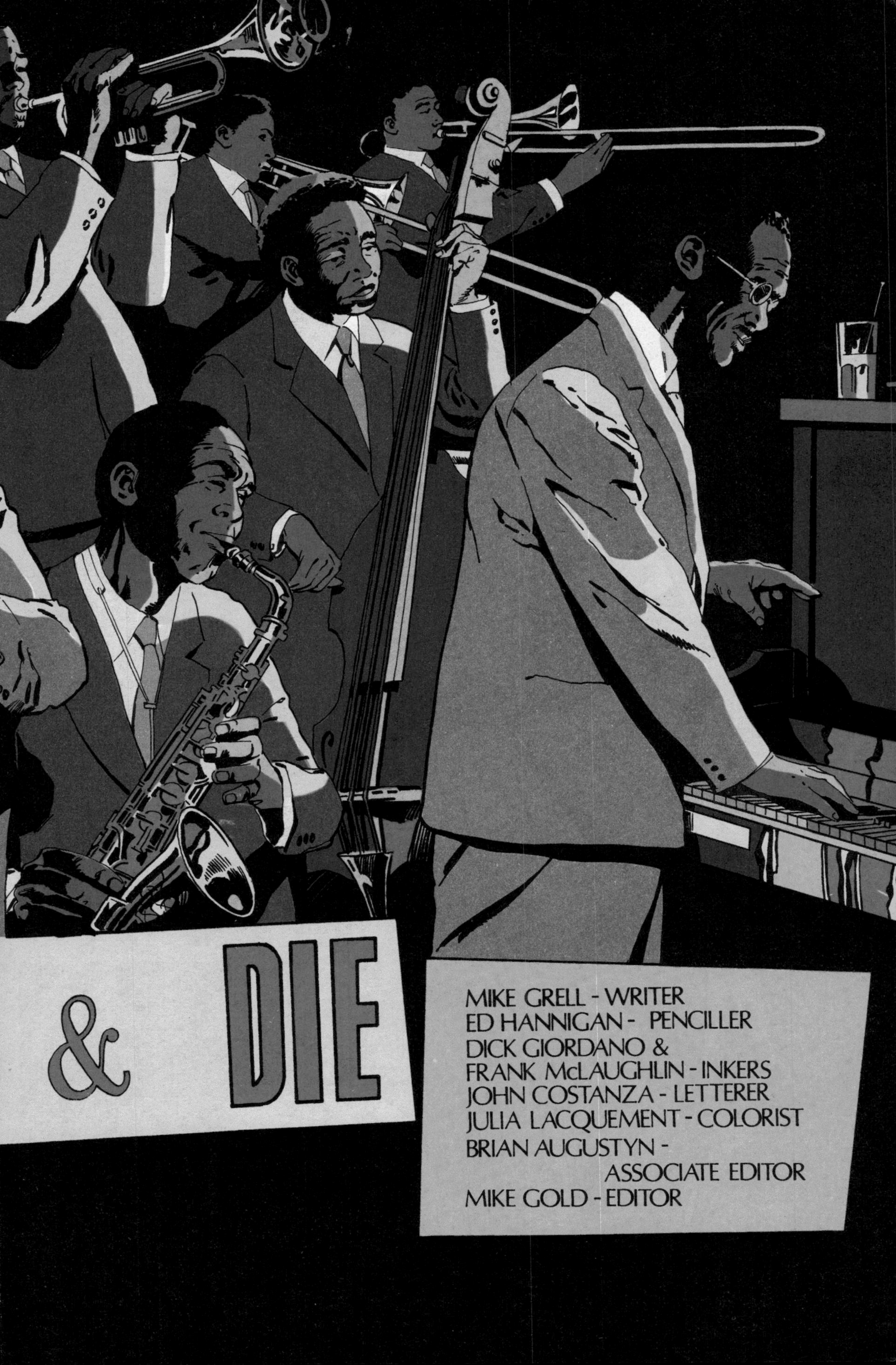

&
DIE
MIKE GRELL - WRITER
ED HANNIGAN - PENCILLER
DICK GIORDANO &
FRANK McLAUGHLIN - INKERS
JOHN COSTANZA - LETTERER
JULIA LACQUEMENT - COLORIST
BRIAN AUGUSTYN -
ASSOCIATE EDITOR
MIKE GOLD - EDITOR

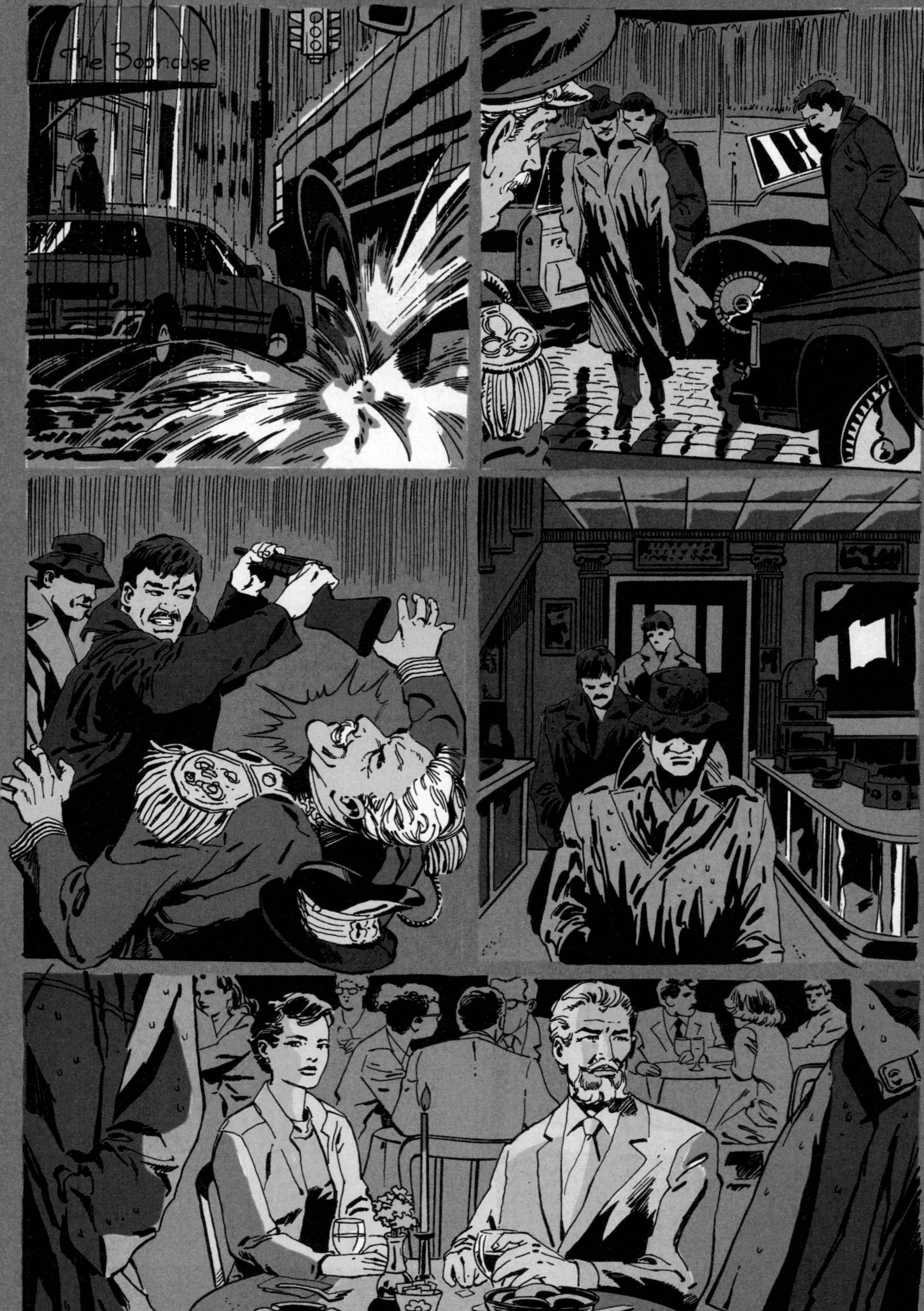
The Boohouse

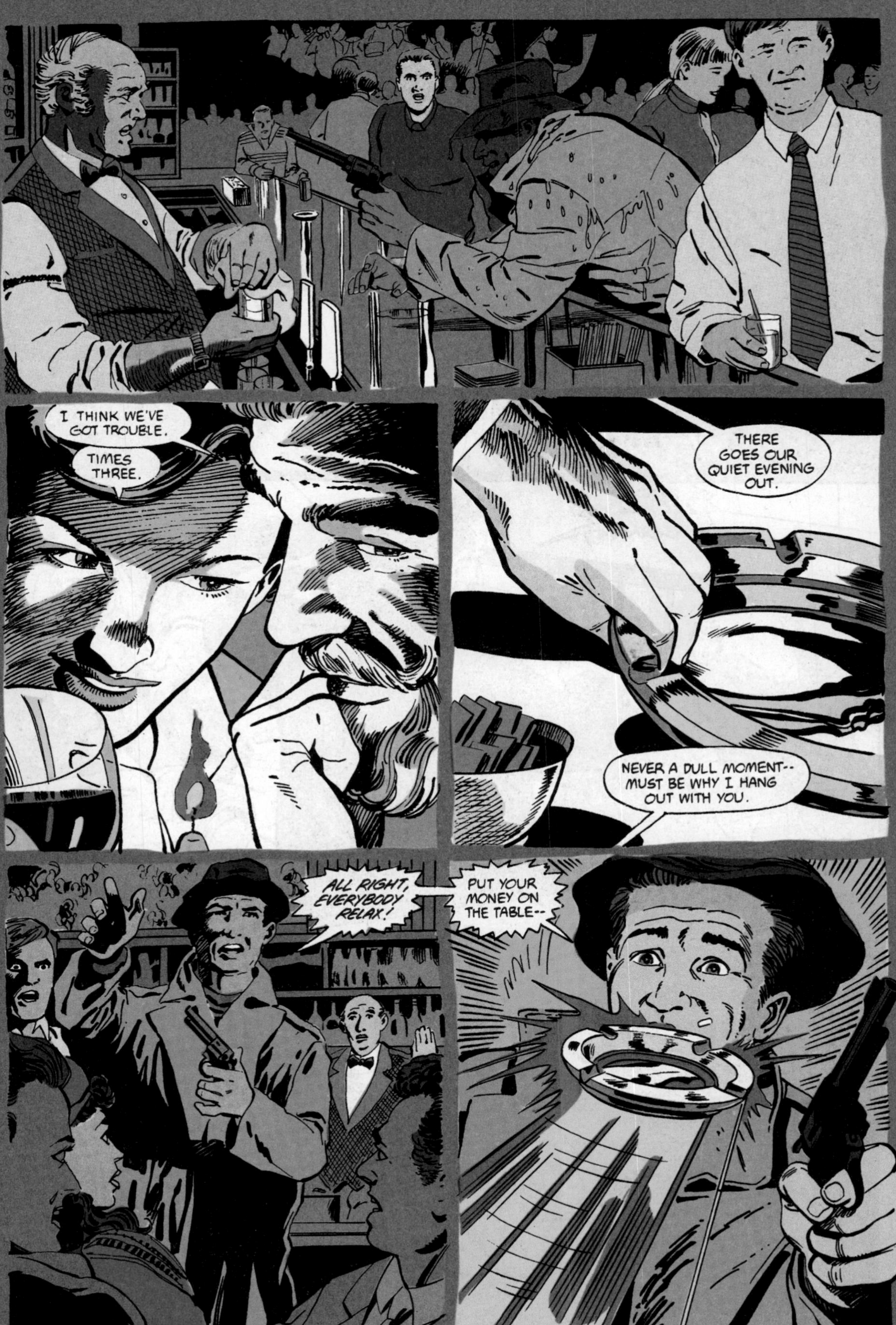

I THINK WE'VE GOT TROUBLE.
TIMES THREE.
THERE GOES OUR QUIET EVENING OUT.
NEVER A DULL MOMENT-- MUST BE WHY I HANG OUT WITH YOU.
ALL RIGHT, EVERYBODY RELAX!
PUT YOUR MONEY ON THE TABLE--

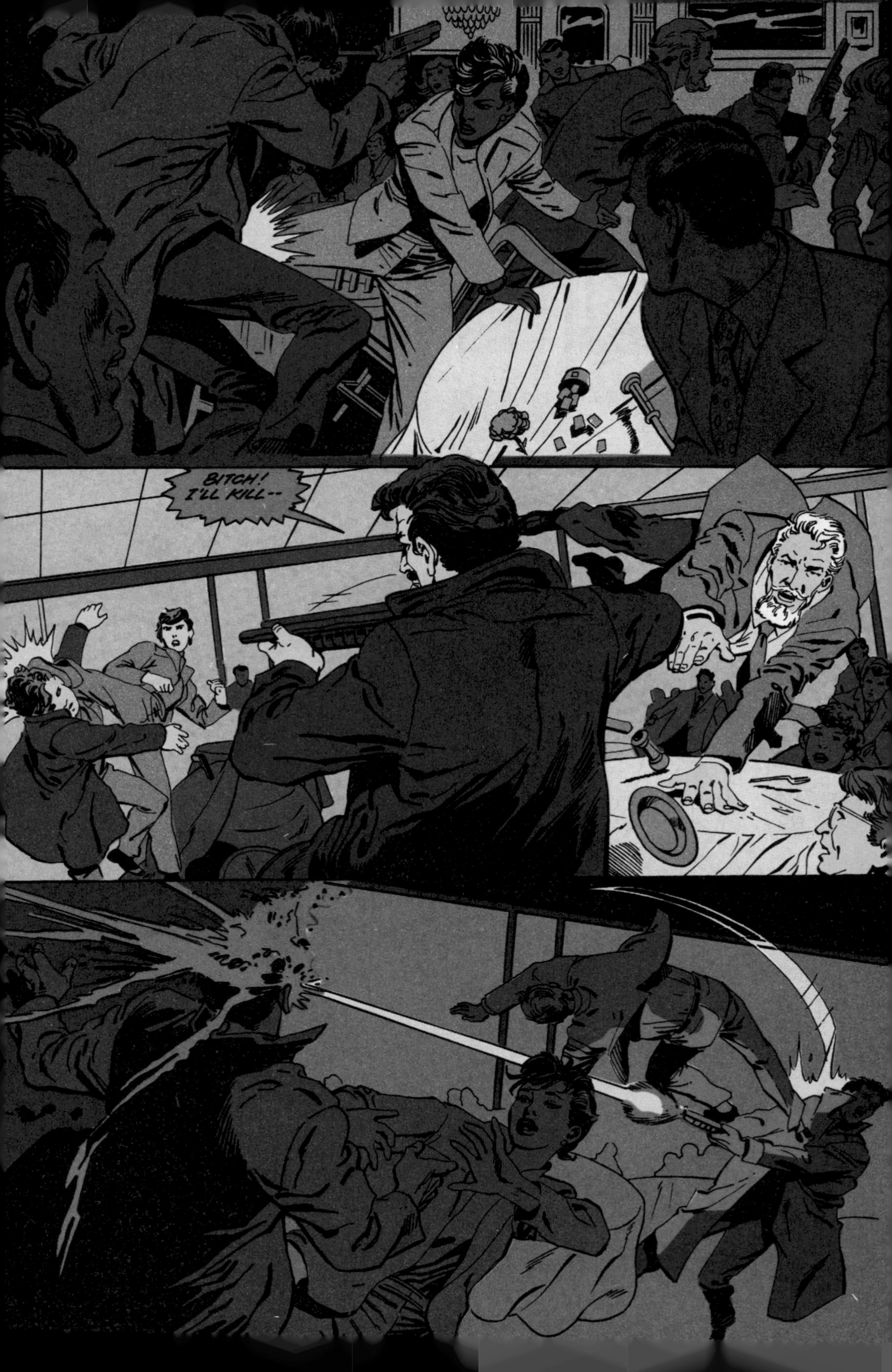
BITCH! I'LL KILL--

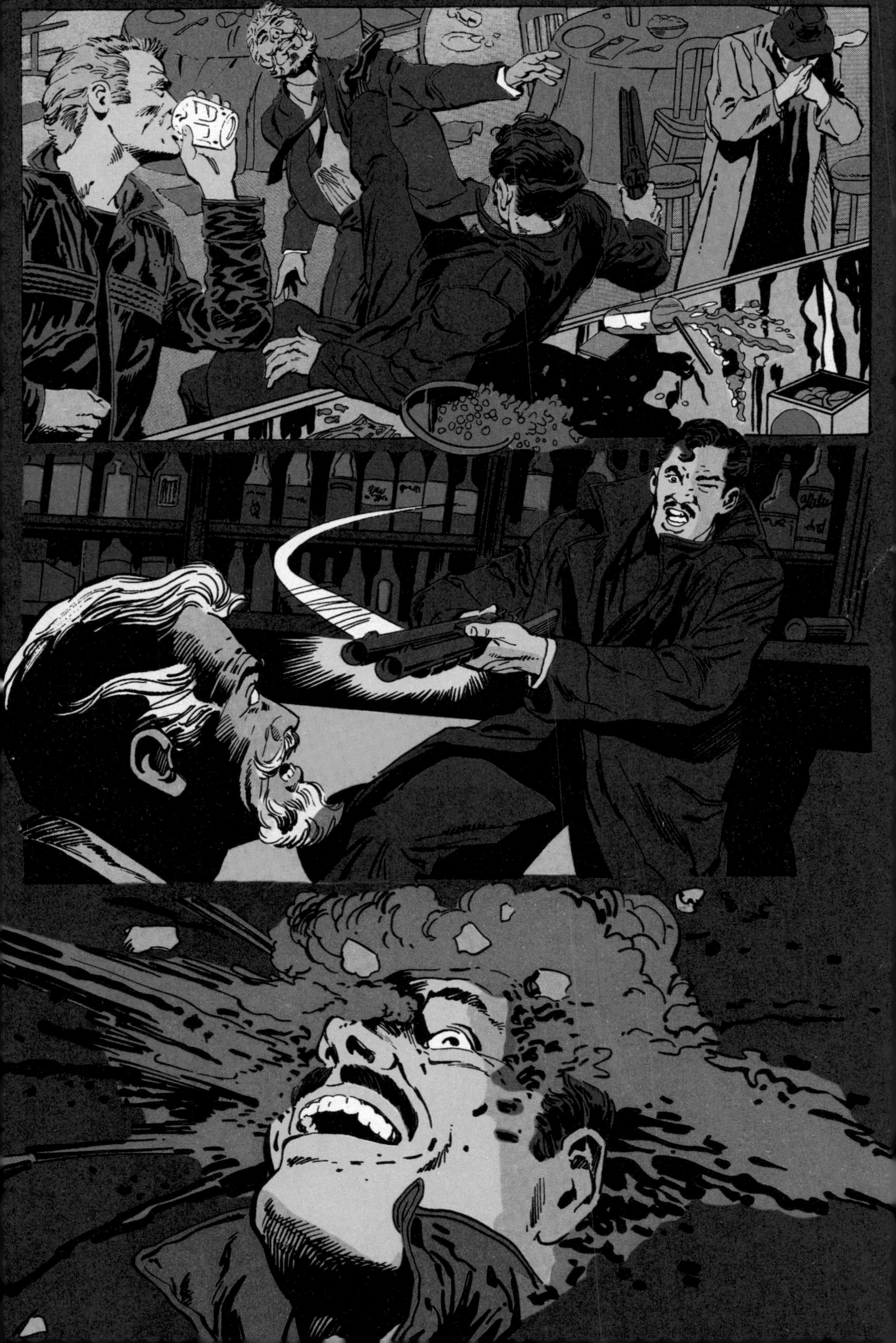

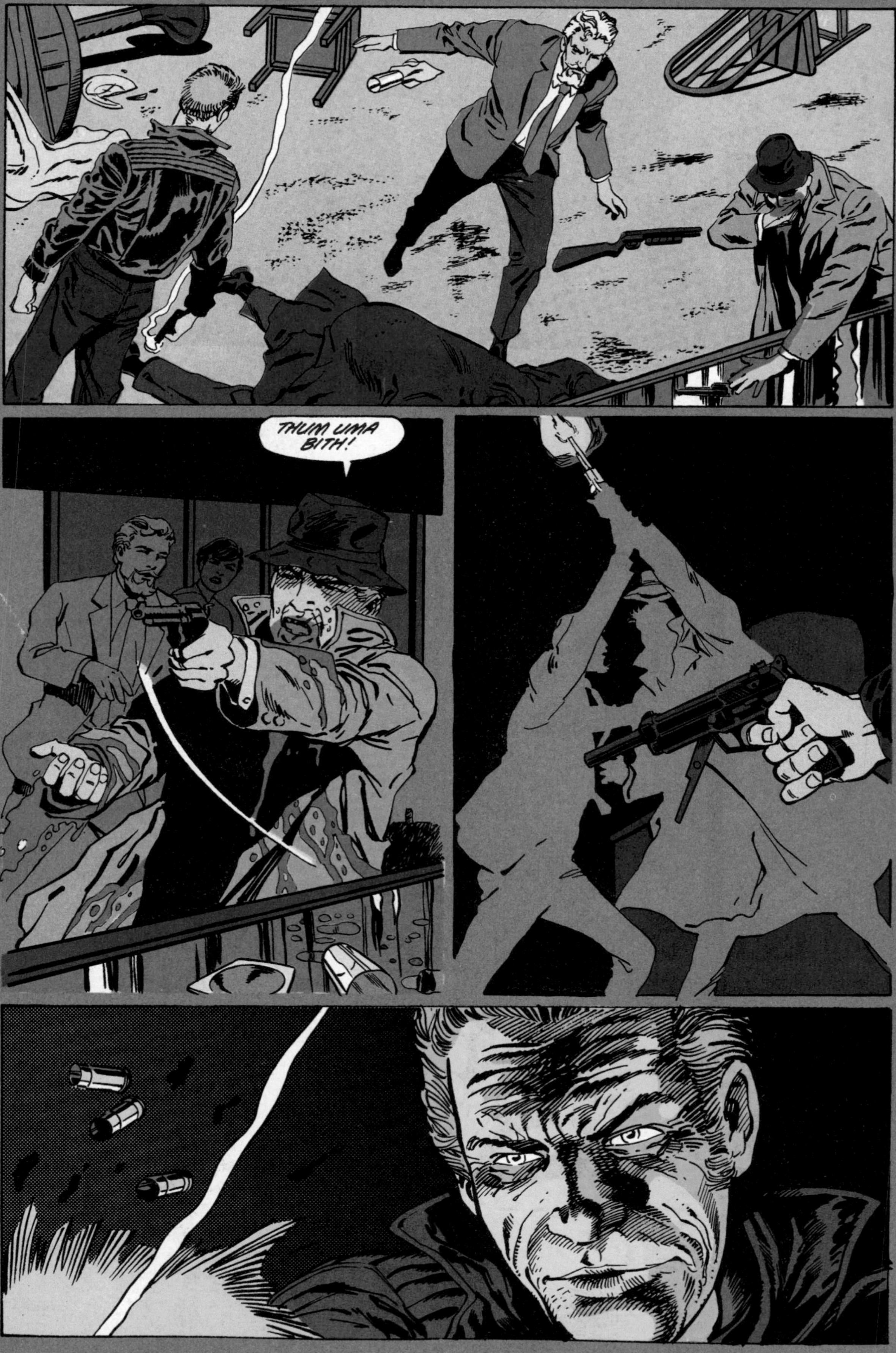
THUM UMA BITH!

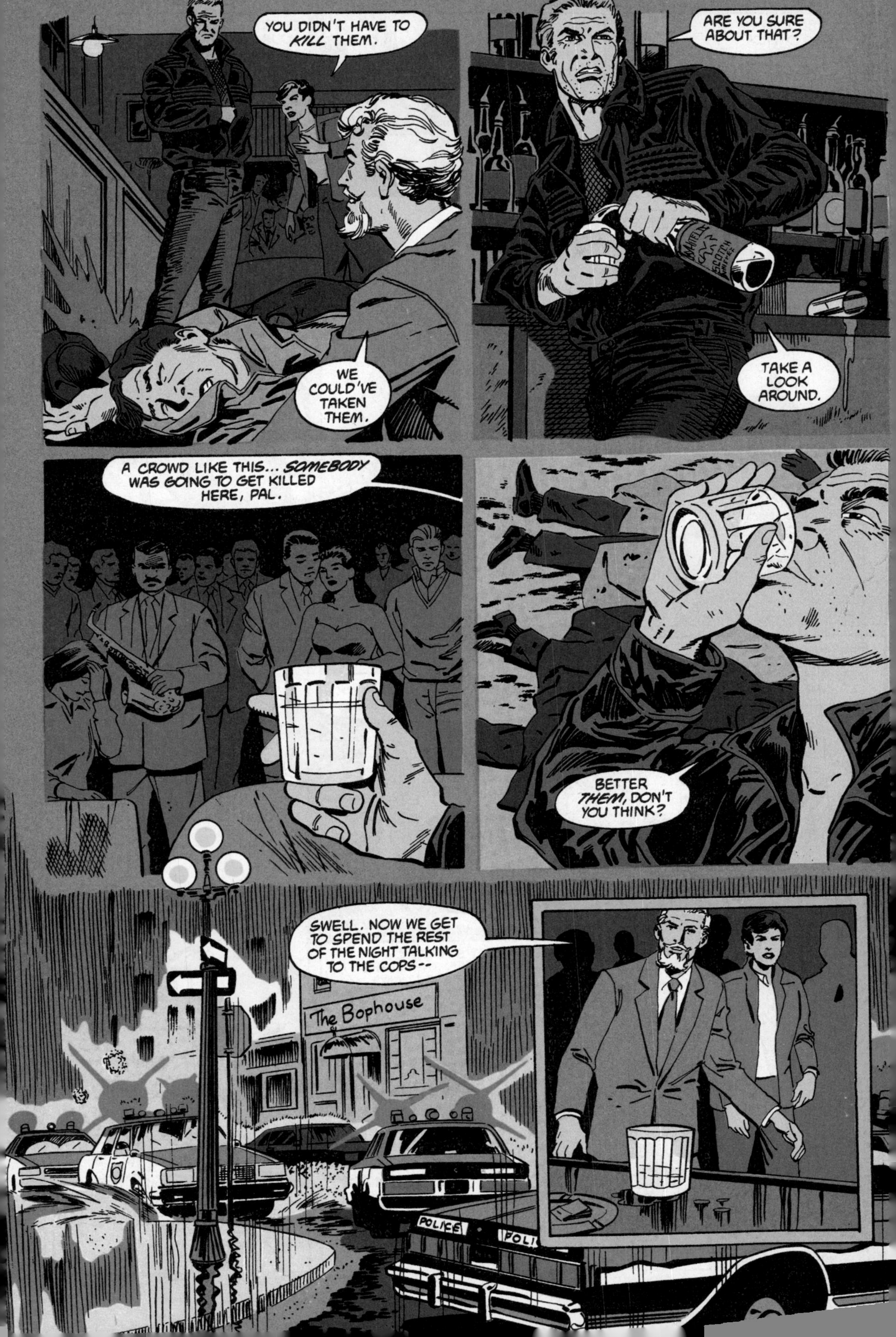
YOU DIDN'T HAVE TO KILL THEM.
WE COULD'VE TAKEN THEM.
ARE YOU SURE ABOUT THAT?
TAKE A LOOK AROUND.
A CROWD LIKE THIS... SOMEBODY WAS GOING TO GET KILLED HERE, PAL.
BETTER THEM, DON'T YOU THINK?
SWELL. NOW WE GET TO SPEND THE REST OF THE NIGHT TALKING TO THE COPS--
The Bophouse
POLICE

...THOUGHT HE WAS ONE OF *YOURS*.

HELL, NO! NOT WITH A *SELECTIVE FIRE* AUTOMATIC.

WELL *WHOEVER* HE WAS, HE SAVED MY LIFE AND MAYBE A LOT OF OTHERS HERE TONIGHT.

I DON'T CARE, QUEEN.

EVERY TIME GUYS LIKE YOU, OR YOUR LADY FRIEND, OR THIS JERK WITH A CANNON PULLS SOME STUNT, THE PRESS JUMPS ON IT AND THE *MAYOR* JUMPS ON *ME*.

SEEMS LIKE A TIME OR TWO WE'VE DONE YOU A *FAVOR*, LT. CAMERON.

I DON'T NEED *YOU* TO REMIND ME OF THAT.

YOU WANT TO BUST SOME PUNK'S HEAD ON THE STREET, FINE...

...BUT IT'S ANOTHER STORY WHEN THERE ARE DEAD BODIES LYING AROUND.

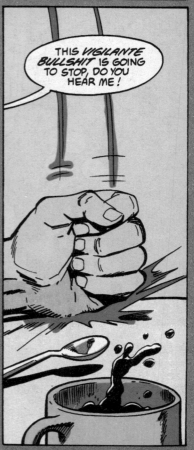

THIS *VIGILANTE BULLSHIT* IS GOING TO STOP, DO YOU HEAR ME!

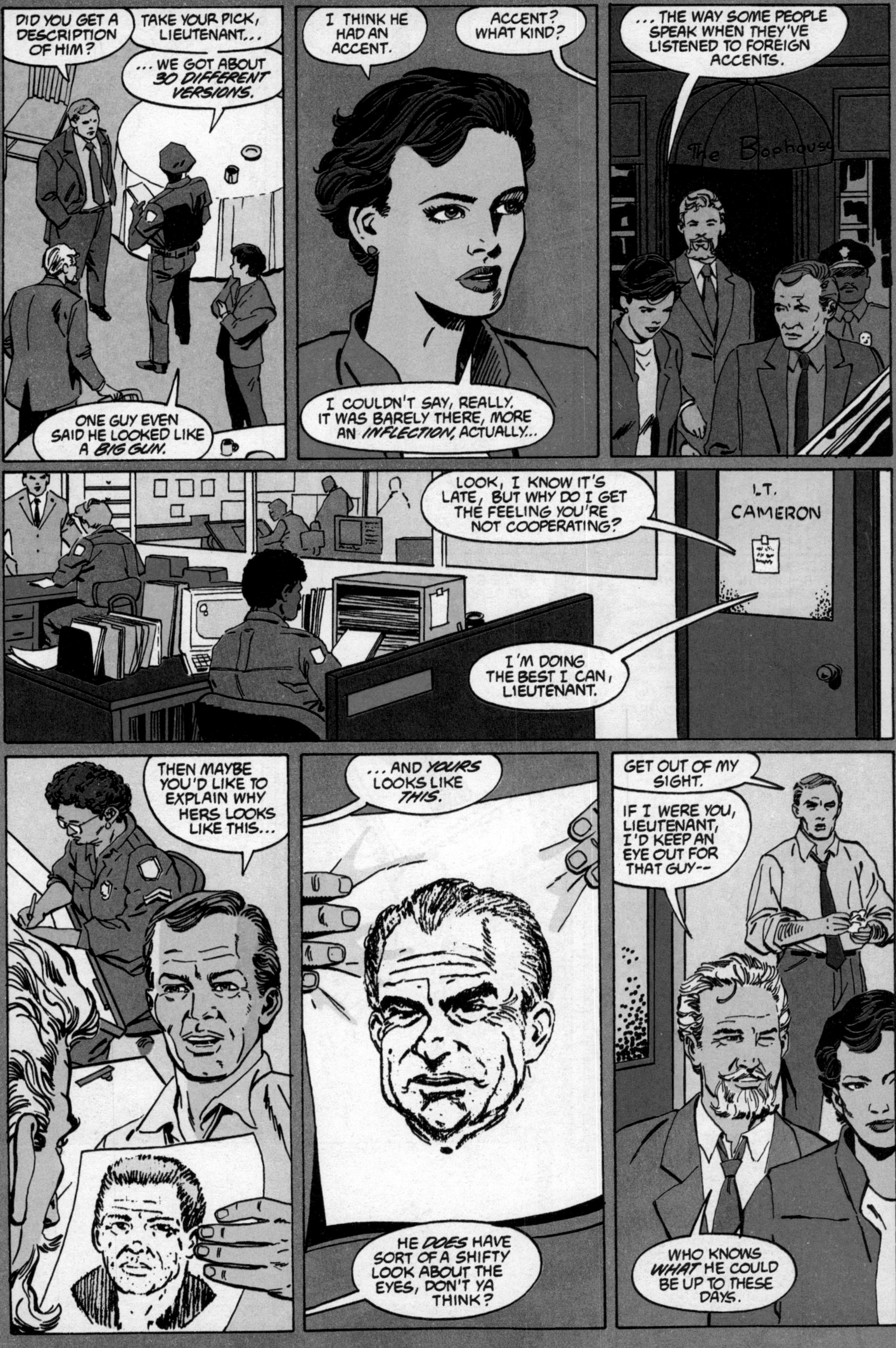
DID YOU GET A DESCRIPTION OF HIM?
TAKE YOUR PICK, LIEUTENANT...
...WE GOT ABOUT 30 DIFFERENT VERSIONS.
ONE GUY EVEN SAID HE LOOKED LIKE A BIG GUN.
I THINK HE HAD AN ACCENT.
ACCENT? WHAT KIND?
I COULDN'T SAY, REALLY. IT WAS BARELY THERE, MORE AN INFLECTION, ACTUALLY...
...THE WAY SOME PEOPLE SPEAK WHEN THEY'VE LISTENED TO FOREIGN ACCENTS.
The Bophouse
LOOK, I KNOW IT'S LATE, BUT WHY DO I GET THE FEELING YOU'RE NOT COOPERATING?
LT. CAMERON
I'M DOING THE BEST I CAN, LIEUTENANT.
THEN MAYBE YOU'D LIKE TO EXPLAIN WHY HERS LOOKS LIKE THIS...
...AND YOURS LOOKS LIKE THIS.
HE DOES HAVE SORT OF A SHIFTY LOOK ABOUT THE EYES, DON'T YA THINK?
GET OUT OF MY SIGHT.
IF I WERE YOU, LIEUTENANT, I'D KEEP AN EYE OUT FOR THAT GUY--
WHO KNOWS WHAT HE COULD BE UP TO THESE DAYS.

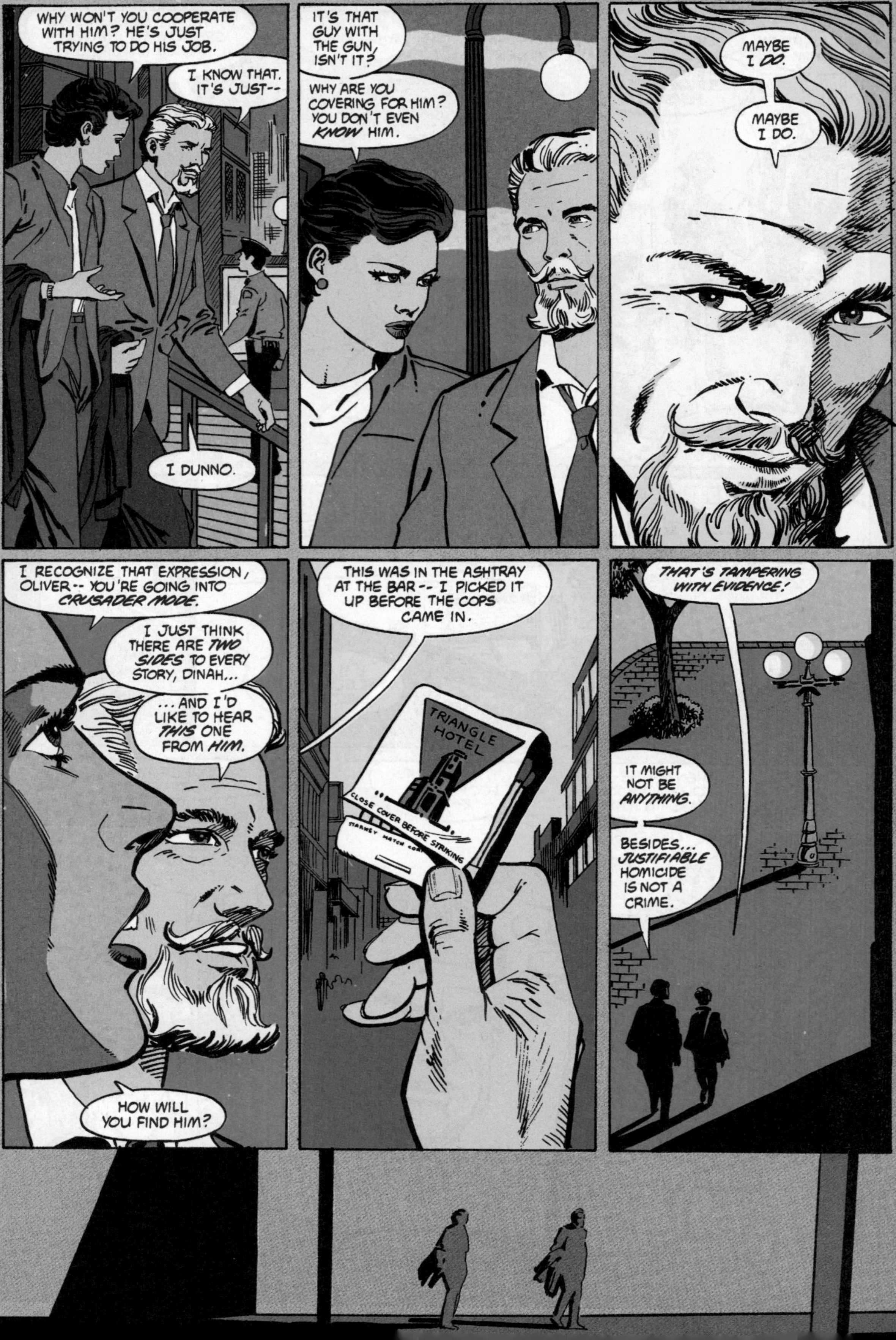

WHY WON'T YOU COOPERATE WITH HIM? HE'S JUST TRYING TO DO HIS JOB.
I KNOW THAT. IT'S JUST--
I DUNNO.
IT'S THAT GUY WITH THE GUN, ISN'T IT?
WHY ARE YOU COVERING FOR HIM? YOU DON'T EVEN KNOW HIM.
MAYBE I DO.
MAYBE I DO.
I RECOGNIZE THAT EXPRESSION, OLIVER-- YOU'RE GOING INTO CRUSADER MODE.
I JUST THINK THERE ARE TWO SIDES TO EVERY STORY, DINAH...
...AND I'D LIKE TO HEAR THIS ONE FROM HIM.
HOW WILL YOU FIND HIM?
THIS WAS IN THE ASHTRAY AT THE BAR-- I PICKED IT UP BEFORE THE COPS CAME IN.
TRIANGLE HOTEL
CLOSE COVER BEFORE STRIKING
THAT'S TAMPERING WITH EVIDENCE!
IT MIGHT NOT BE ANYTHING.
BESIDES... JUSTIFIABLE HOMICIDE IS NOT A CRIME.

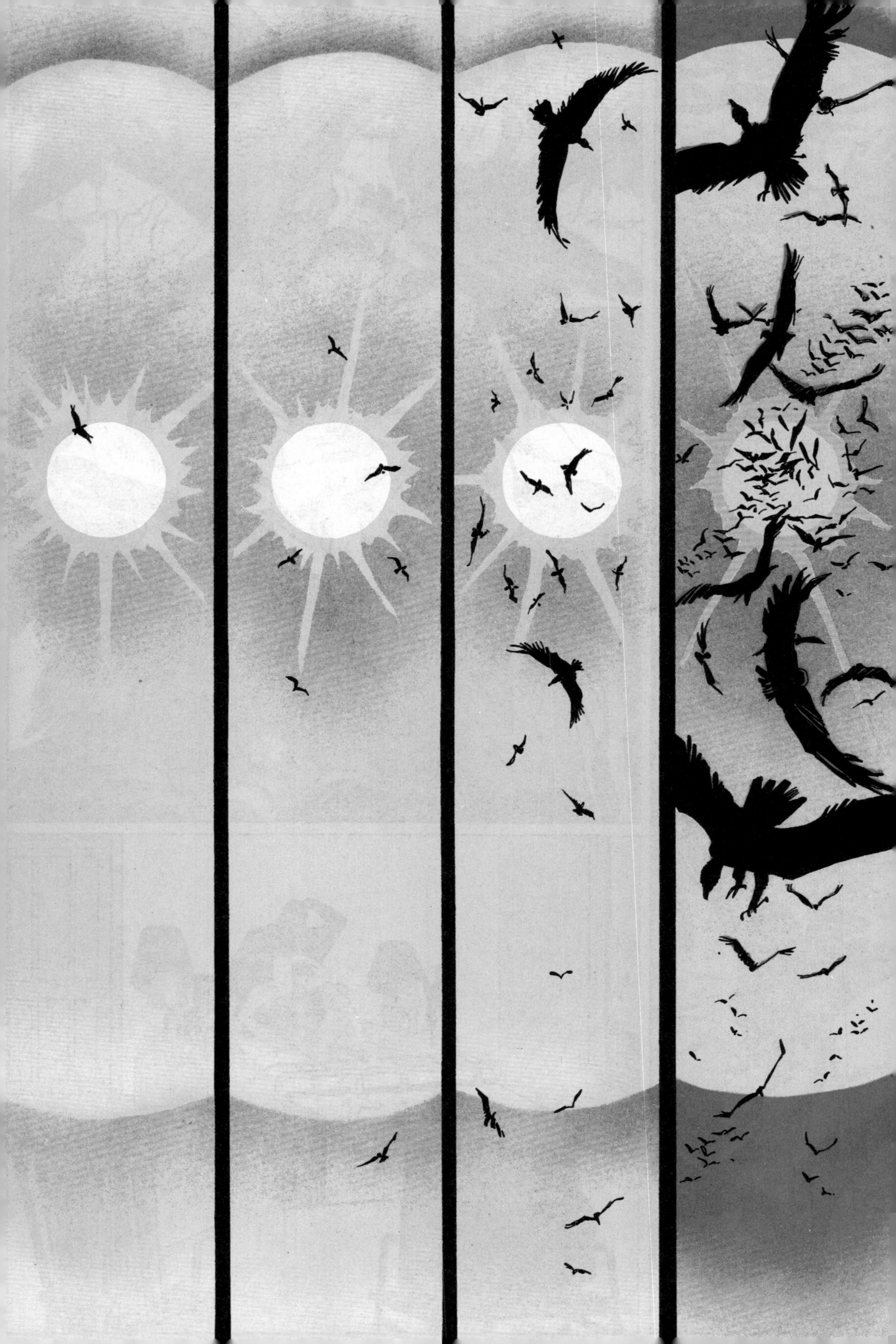

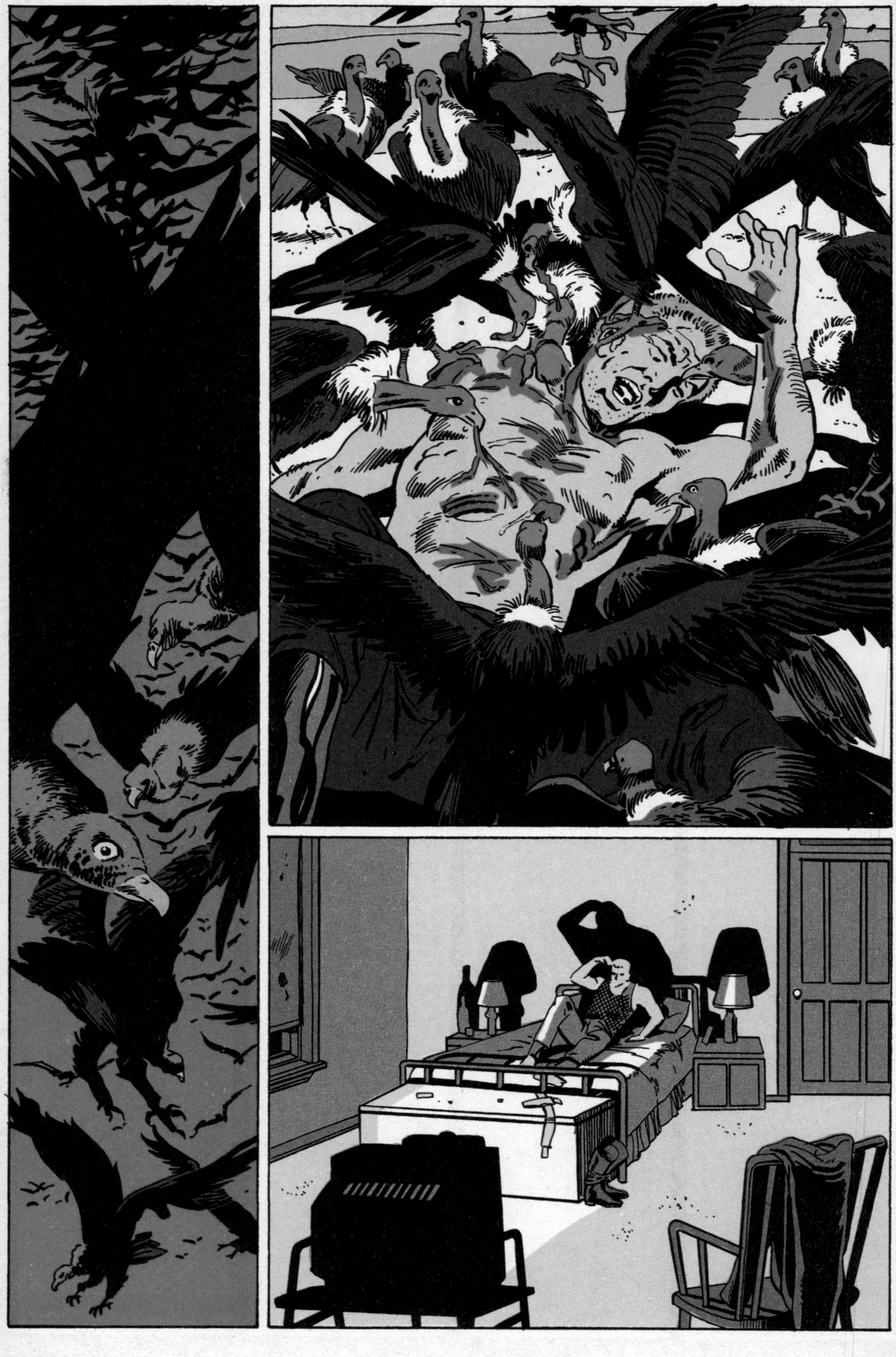

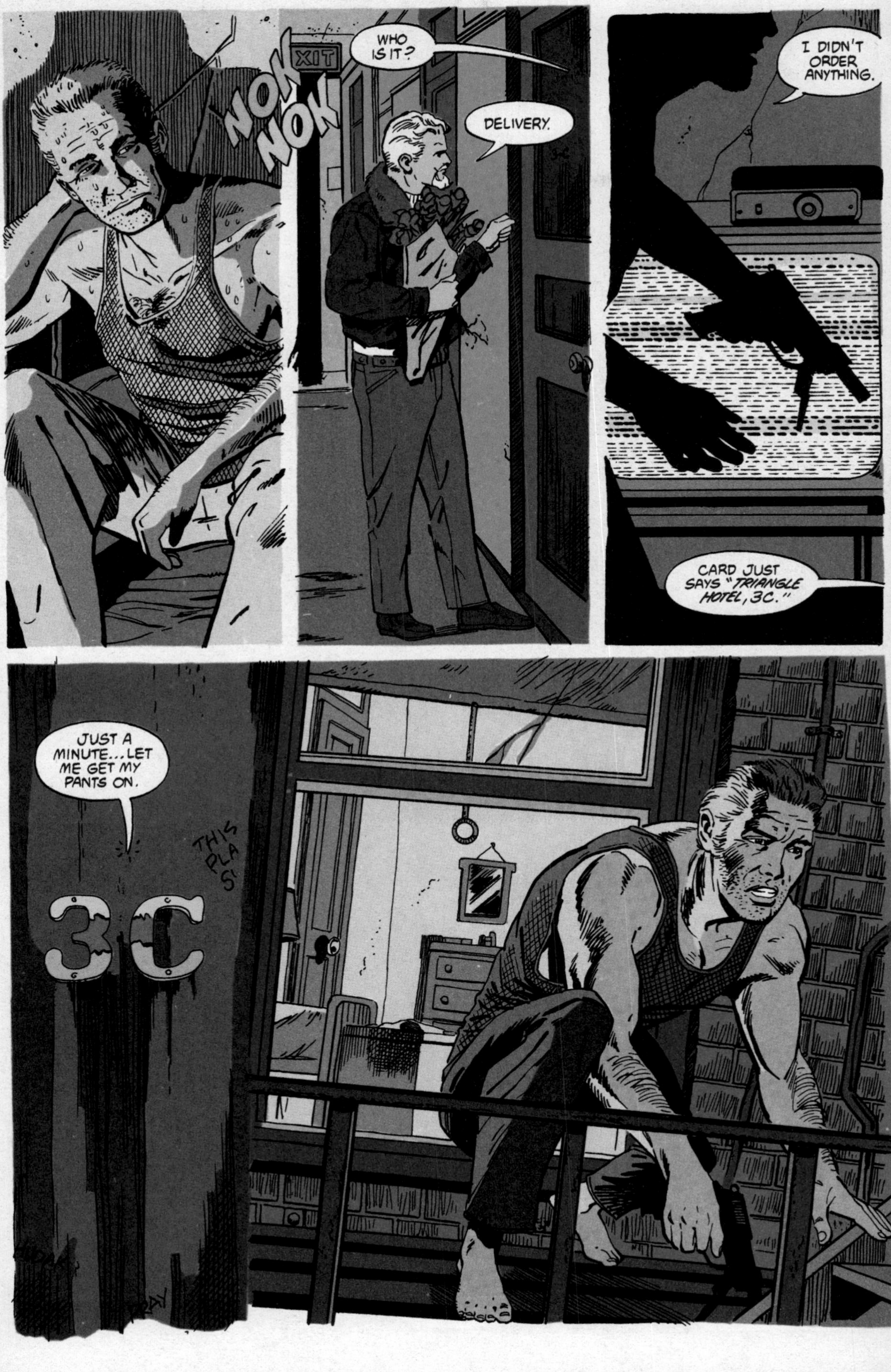
NOK NOK
XIT
WHO IS IT?
DELIVERY.
I DIDN'T ORDER ANYTHING.
CARD JUST SAYS "TRIANGLE HOTEL, 3C."
JUST A MINUTE... LET ME GET MY PANTS ON.
3C

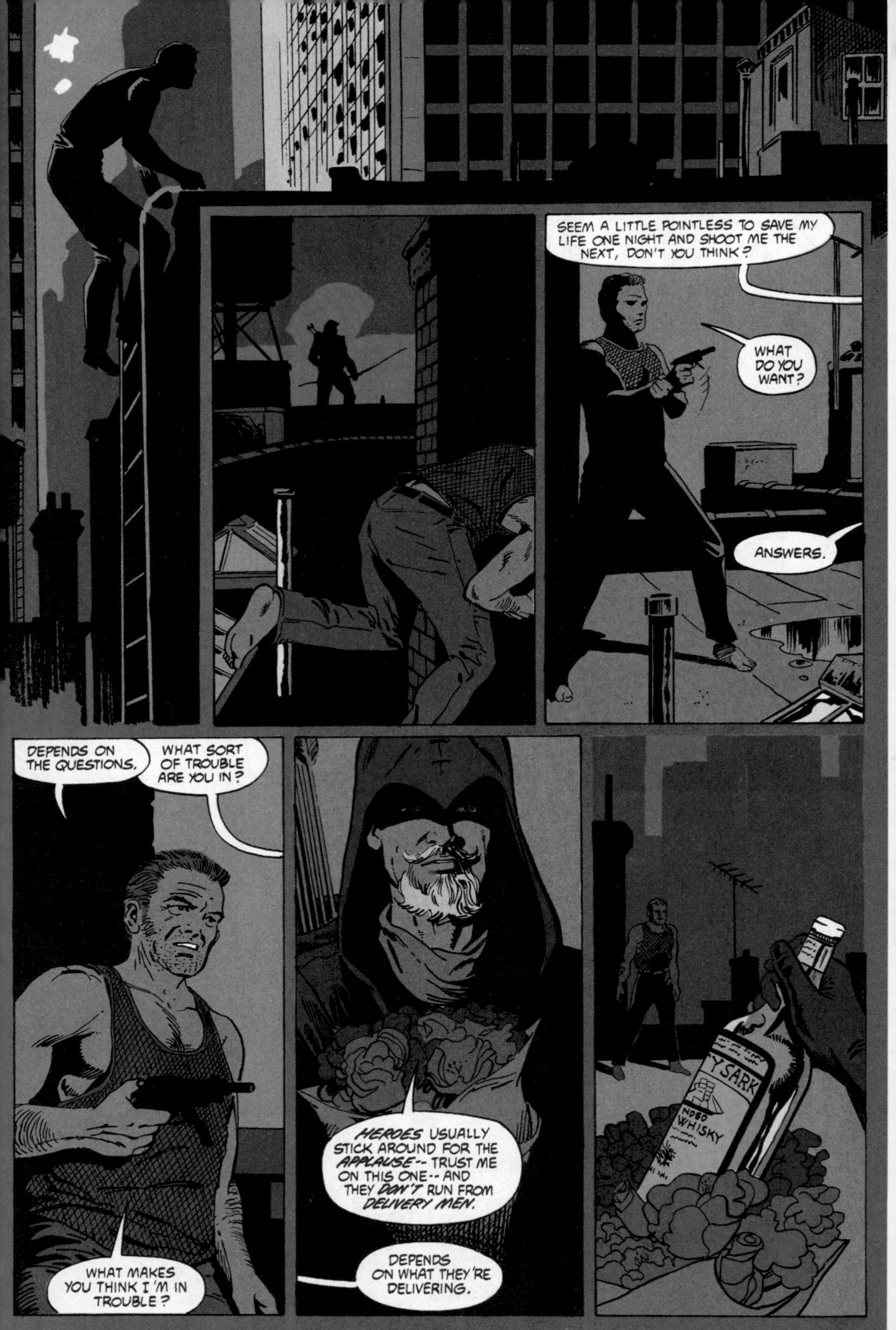
SEEM A LITTLE POINTLESS TO SAVE MY LIFE ONE NIGHT AND SHOOT ME THE NEXT, DON'T YOU THINK?
WHAT DO YOU WANT?
ANSWERS.
DEPENDS ON THE QUESTIONS.
WHAT SORT OF TROUBLE ARE YOU IN?
WHAT MAKES YOU THINK I'M IN TROUBLE?
HEROES USUALLY STICK AROUND FOR THE APPLAUSE-- TRUST ME ON THIS ONE-- AND THEY DON'T RUN FROM DELIVERY MEN.
DEPENDS ON WHAT THEY'RE DELIVERING.
WHISKY

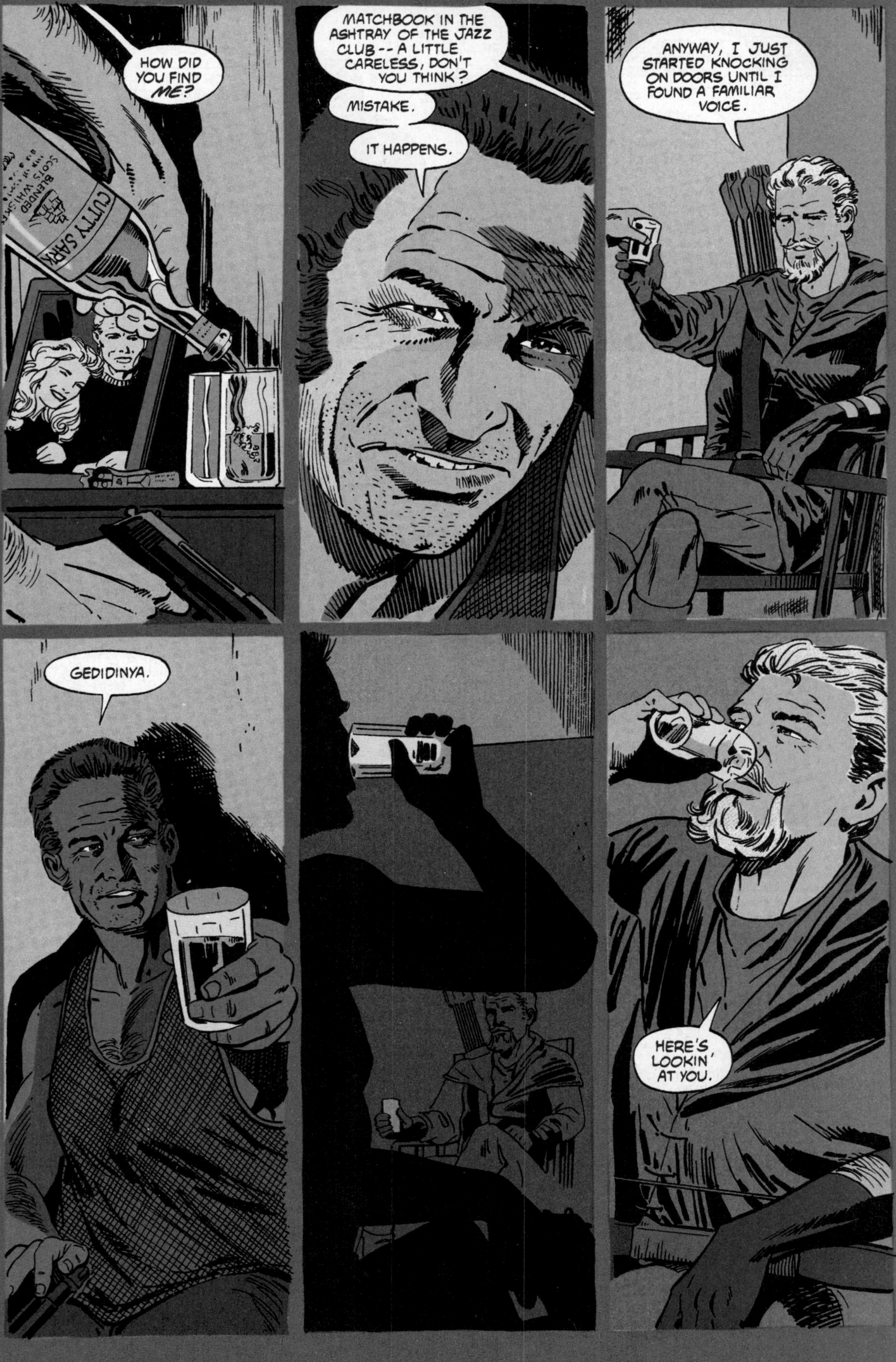
HOW DID YOU FIND ME?
CUTTY SARK
BLENDED SCOTS WHISKY
MATCHBOOK IN THE ASHTRAY OF THE JAZZ CLUB -- A LITTLE CARELESS, DON'T YOU THINK?
MISTAKE.
IT HAPPENS.
ANYWAY, I JUST STARTED KNOCKING ON DOORS UNTIL I FOUND A FAMILIAR VOICE.
GEDIDINYA.
HERE'S LOOKIN' AT YOU.

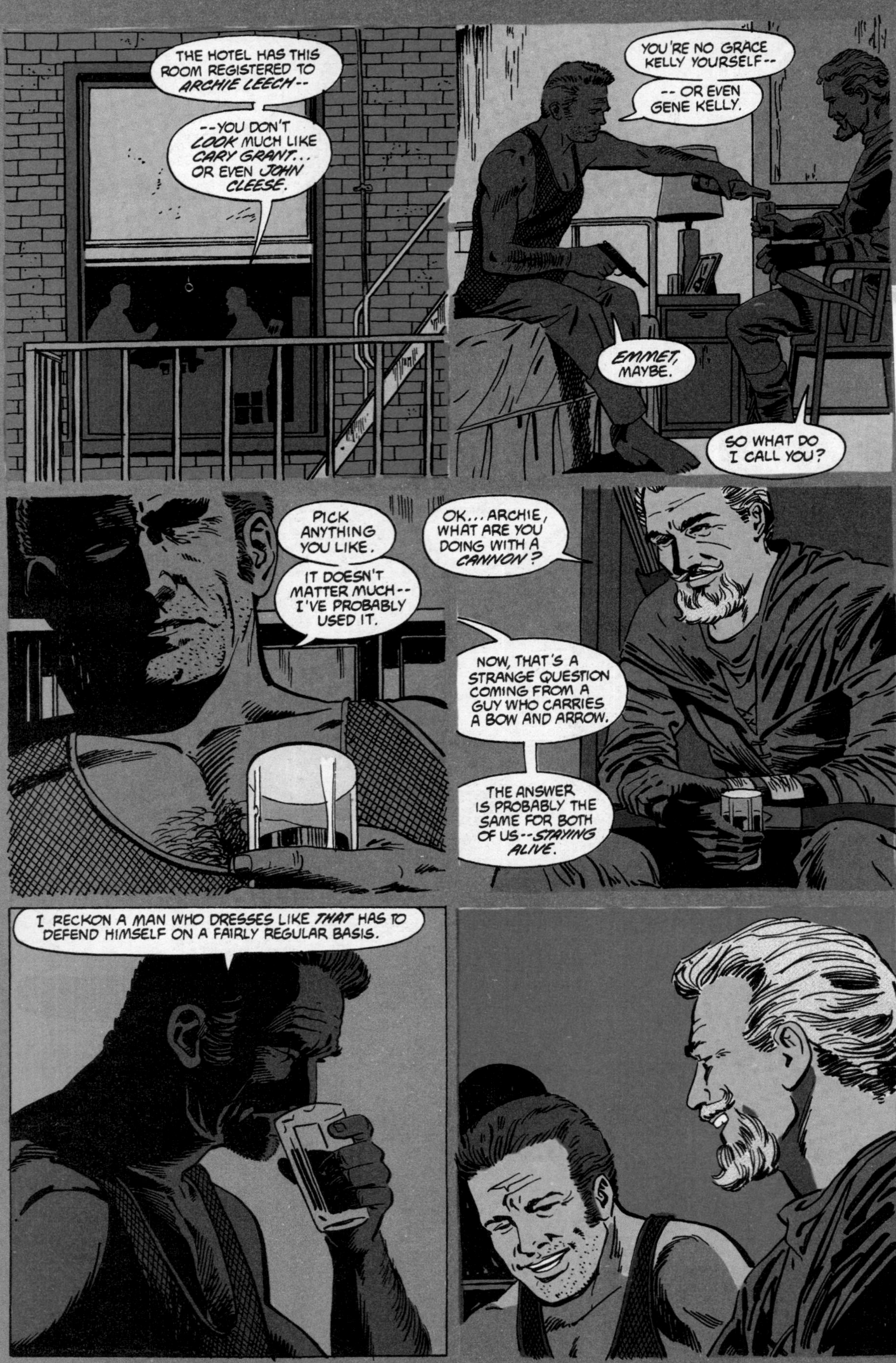
THE HOTEL HAS THIS ROOM REGISTERED TO ARCHIE LEECH--
--YOU DON'T LOOK MUCH LIKE CARY GRANT... OR EVEN JOHN CLEESE.
YOU'RE NO GRACE KELLY YOURSELF--
--OR EVEN GENE KELLY.
EMMET, MAYBE.
SO WHAT DO I CALL YOU?
PICK ANYTHING YOU LIKE.
IT DOESN'T MATTER MUCH--I'VE PROBABLY USED IT.
OK... ARCHIE, WHAT ARE YOU DOING WITH A CANNON?
NOW, THAT'S A STRANGE QUESTION COMING FROM A GUY WHO CARRIES A BOW AND ARROW.
THE ANSWER IS PROBABLY THE SAME FOR BOTH OF US--STAYING ALIVE.
I RECKON A MAN WHO DRESSES LIKE THAT HAS TO DEFEND HIMSELF ON A FAIRLY REGULAR BASIS.

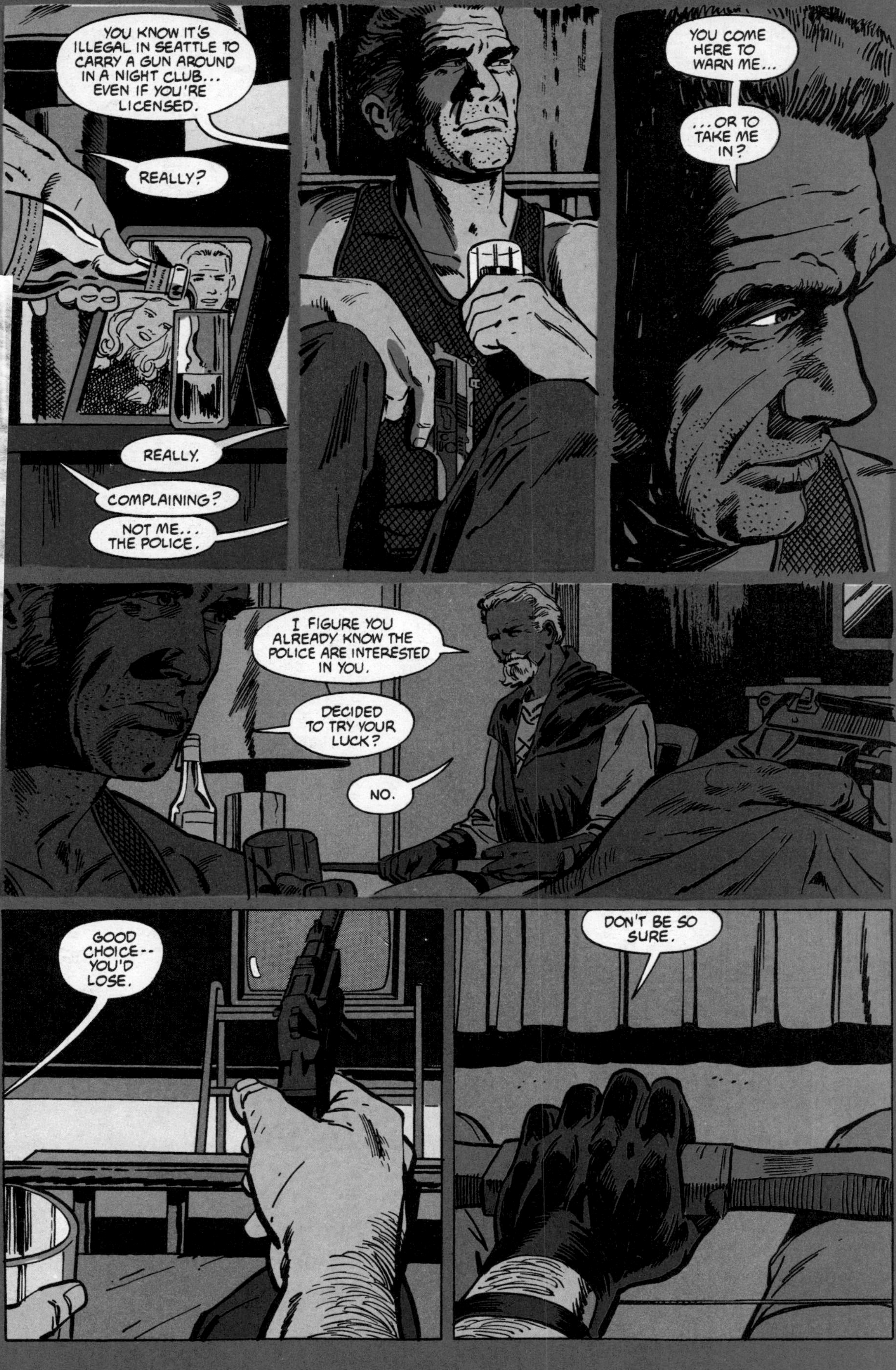
YOU KNOW IT'S ILLEGAL IN SEATTLE TO CARRY A GUN AROUND IN A NIGHT CLUB... EVEN IF YOU'RE LICENSED.
REALLY?
REALLY.
COMPLAINING?
NOT ME... THE POLICE.
YOU COME HERE TO WARN ME...
...OR TO TAKE ME IN?
I FIGURE YOU ALREADY KNOW THE POLICE ARE INTERESTED IN YOU.
DECIDED TO TRY YOUR LUCK?
NO.
GOOD CHOICE-- YOU'D LOSE.
DON'T BE SO SURE.

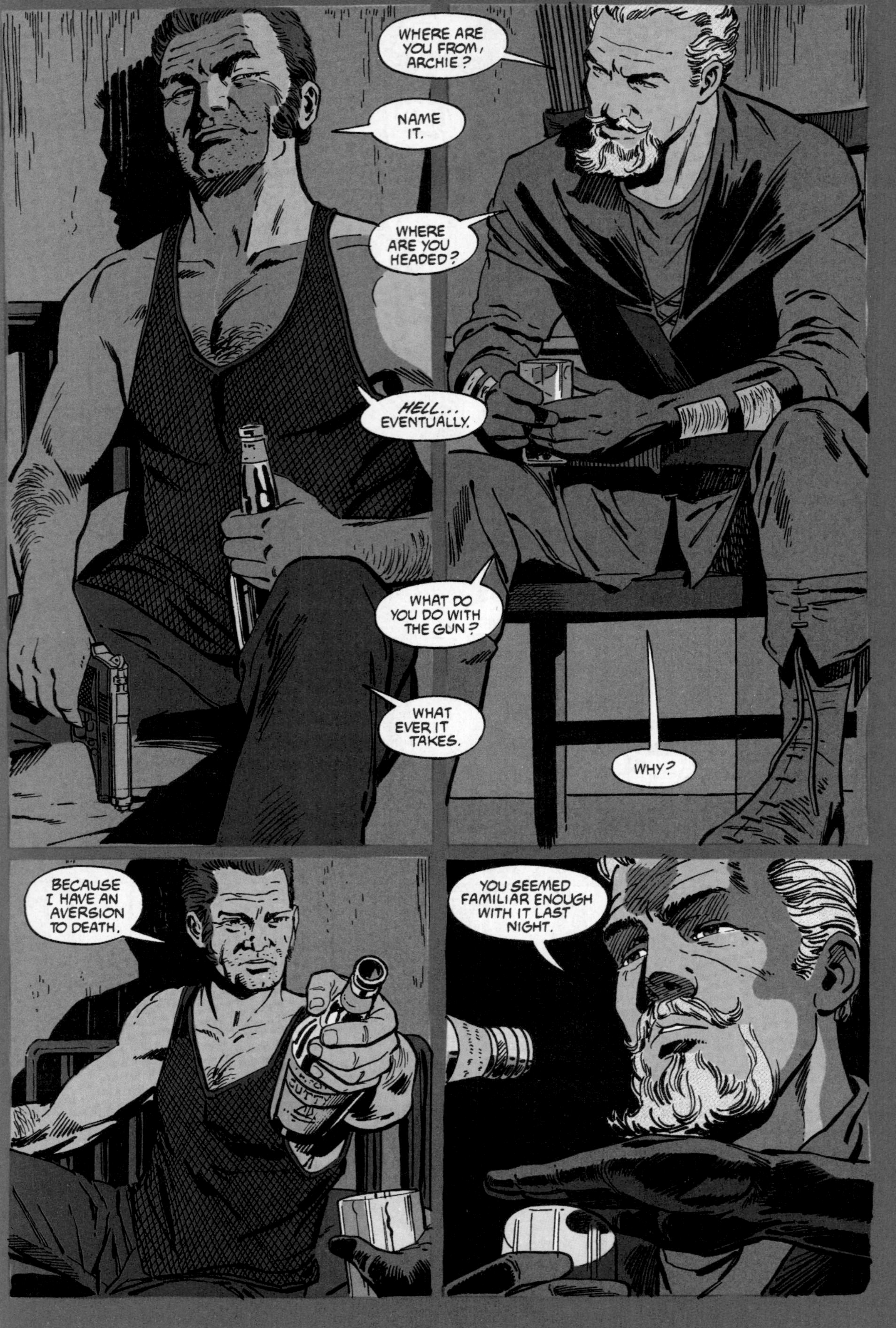
WHERE ARE YOU FROM, ARCHIE?
NAME IT.
WHERE ARE YOU HEADED?
HELL... EVENTUALLY.
WHAT DO YOU DO WITH THE GUN?
WHAT EVER IT TAKES.
WHY?
BECAUSE I HAVE AN AVERSION TO DEATH.
YOU SEEMED FAMILIAR ENOUGH WITH IT LAST NIGHT.

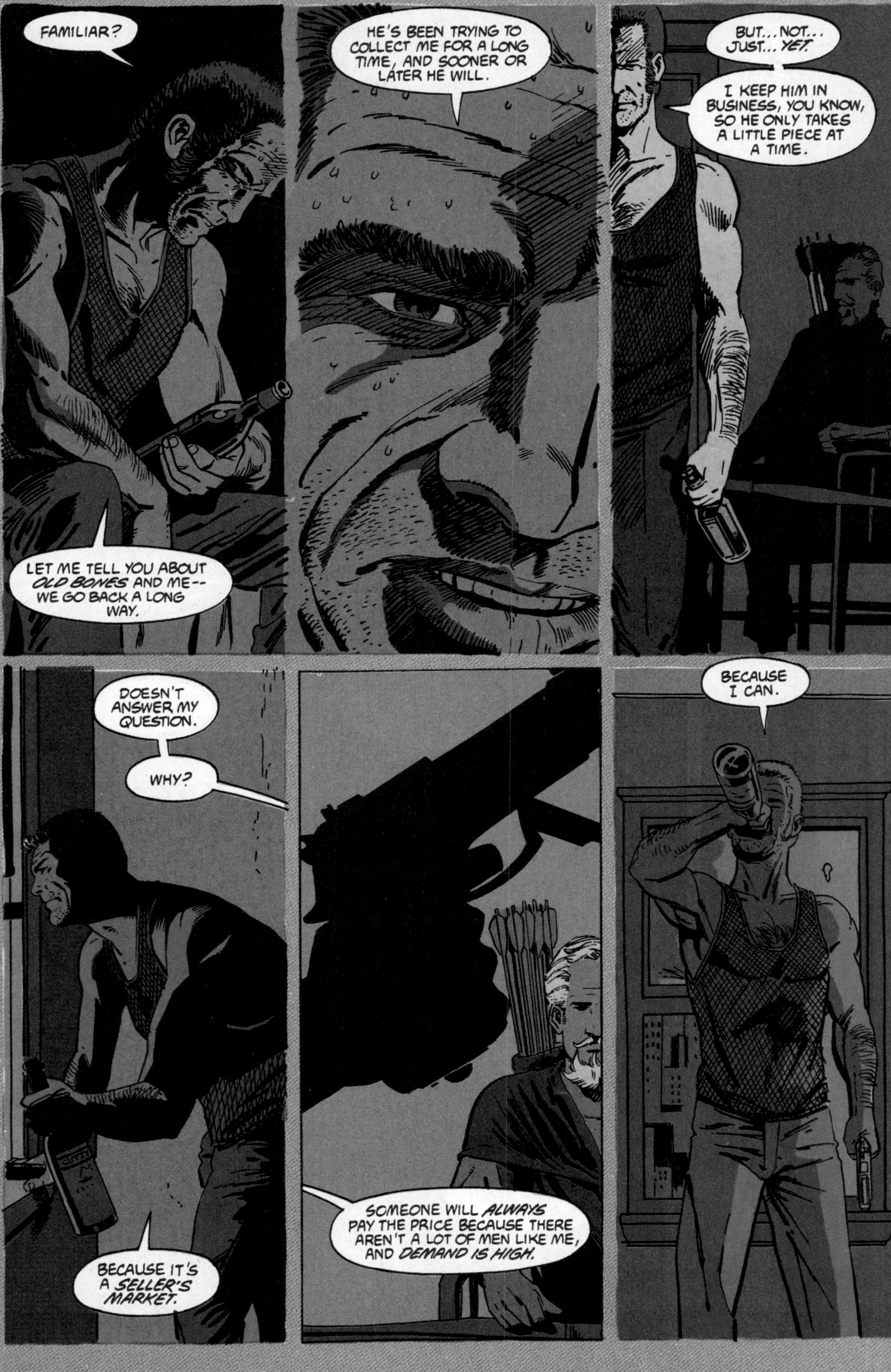
FAMILIAR?
LET ME TELL YOU ABOUT *OLD BONES* AND ME-- WE GO BACK A LONG WAY.
HE'S BEEN TRYING TO COLLECT ME FOR A LONG TIME, AND SOONER OR LATER HE WILL.
BUT... NOT... JUST... *YET.*
I KEEP HIM IN BUSINESS, YOU KNOW, SO HE ONLY TAKES A LITTLE PIECE AT A TIME.
DOESN'T ANSWER MY QUESTION.
WHY?
BECAUSE IT'S A *SELLER'S MARKET.*
SOMEONE WILL *ALWAYS* PAY THE PRICE BECAUSE THERE AREN'T A LOT OF MEN LIKE ME, AND *DEMAND IS HIGH.*
BECAUSE I CAN.

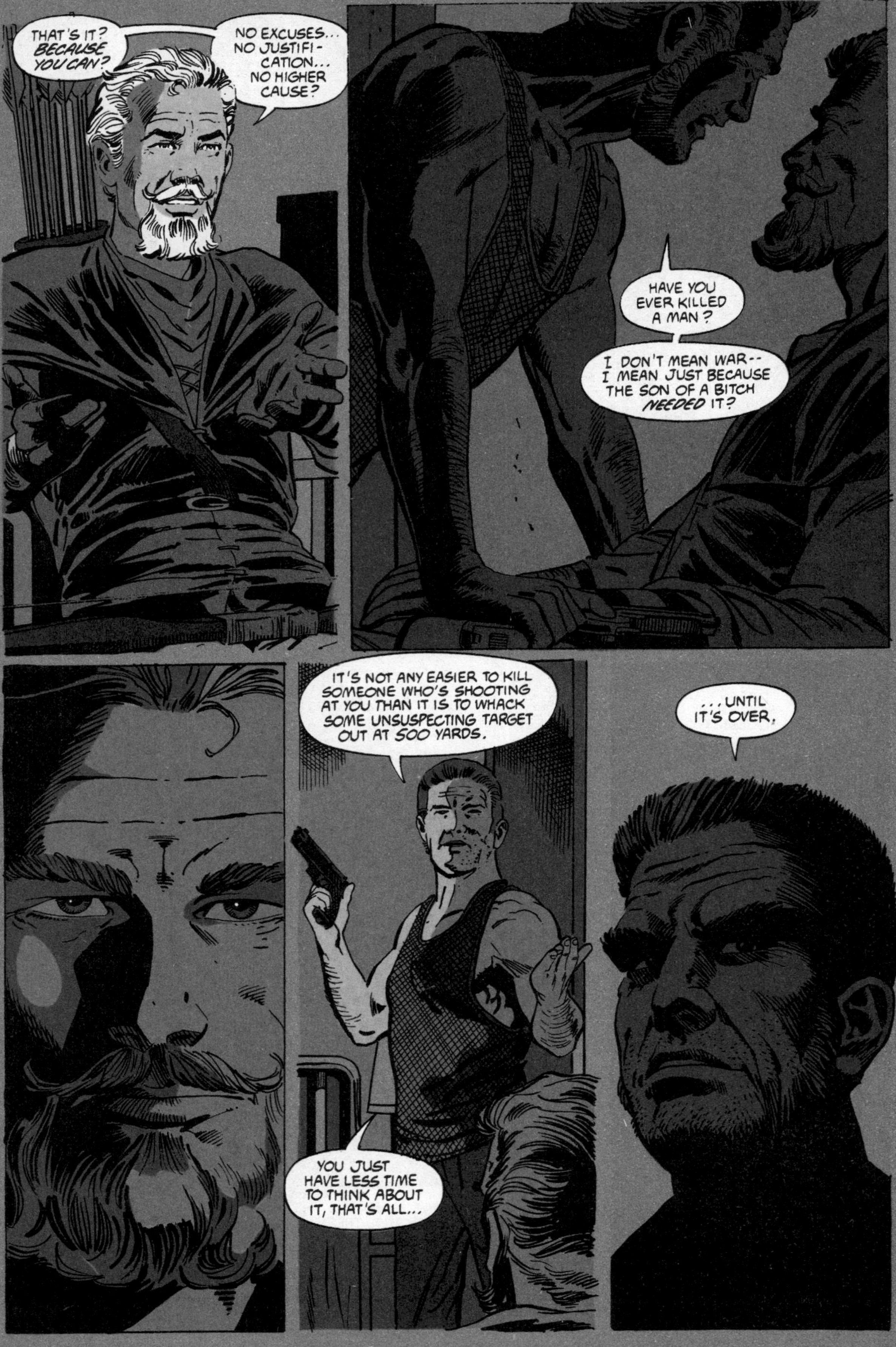
THAT'S IT? BECAUSE YOU CAN?
NO EXCUSES... NO JUSTIFI-CATION... NO HIGHER CAUSE?
HAVE YOU EVER KILLED A MAN?
I DON'T MEAN WAR-- I MEAN JUST BECAUSE THE SON OF A BITCH NEEDED IT?
IT'S NOT ANY EASIER TO KILL SOMEONE WHO'S SHOOTING AT YOU THAN IT IS TO WHACK SOME UNSUSPECTING TARGET OUT AT 500 YARDS.
YOU JUST HAVE LESS TIME TO THINK ABOUT IT, THAT'S ALL...
...UNTIL IT'S OVER.

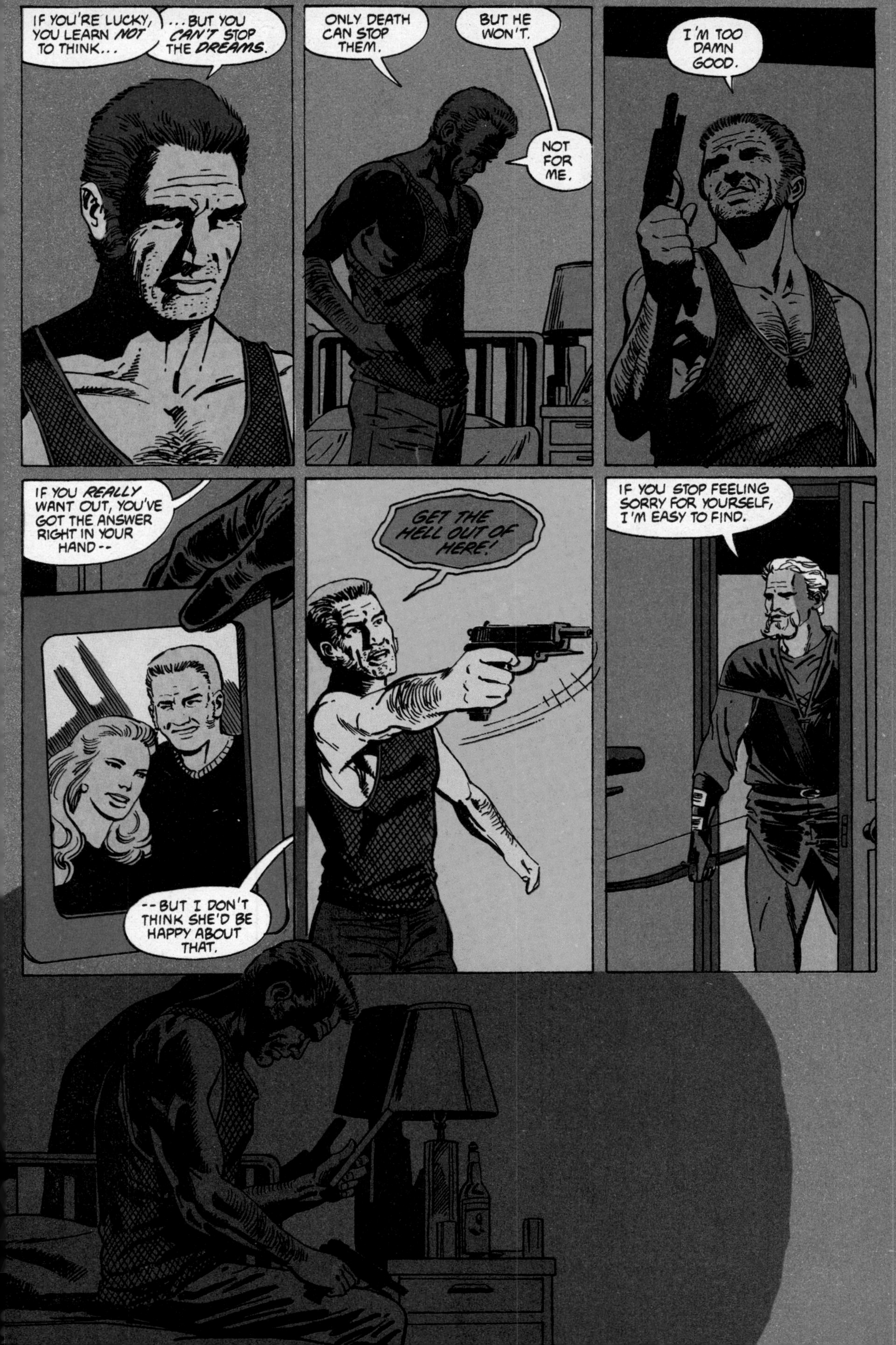
IF YOU'RE LUCKY, YOU LEARN NOT TO THINK...
...BUT YOU CAN'T STOP THE DREAMS.
ONLY DEATH CAN STOP THEM.
BUT HE WON'T.
NOT FOR ME.
I'M TOO DAMN GOOD.
IF YOU REALLY WANT OUT, YOU'VE GOT THE ANSWER RIGHT IN YOUR HAND--
--BUT I DON'T THINK SHE'D BE HAPPY ABOUT THAT.
GET THE HELL OUT OF HERE!
IF YOU STOP FEELING SORRY FOR YOURSELF, I'M EASY TO FIND.

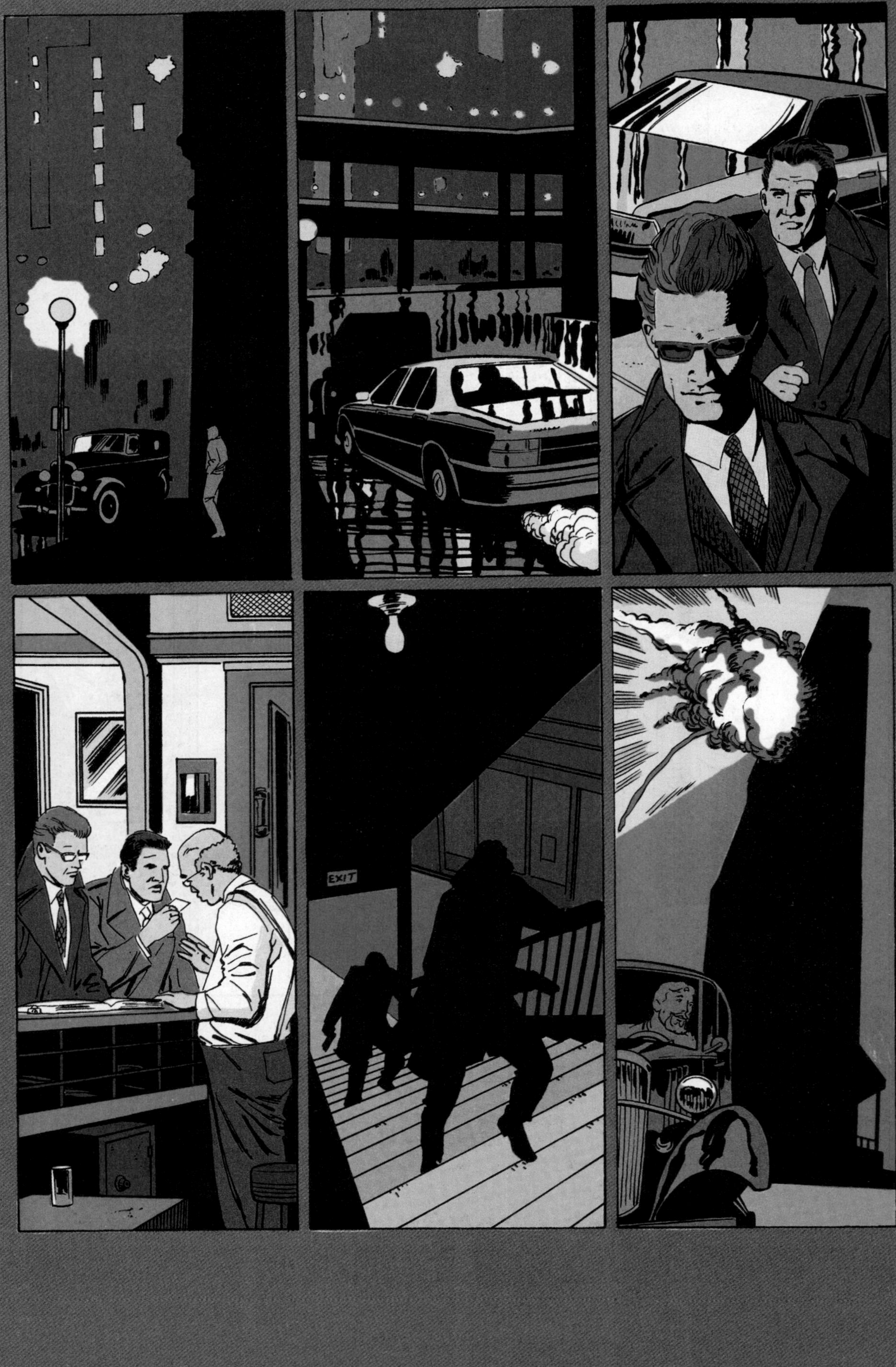
EXIT

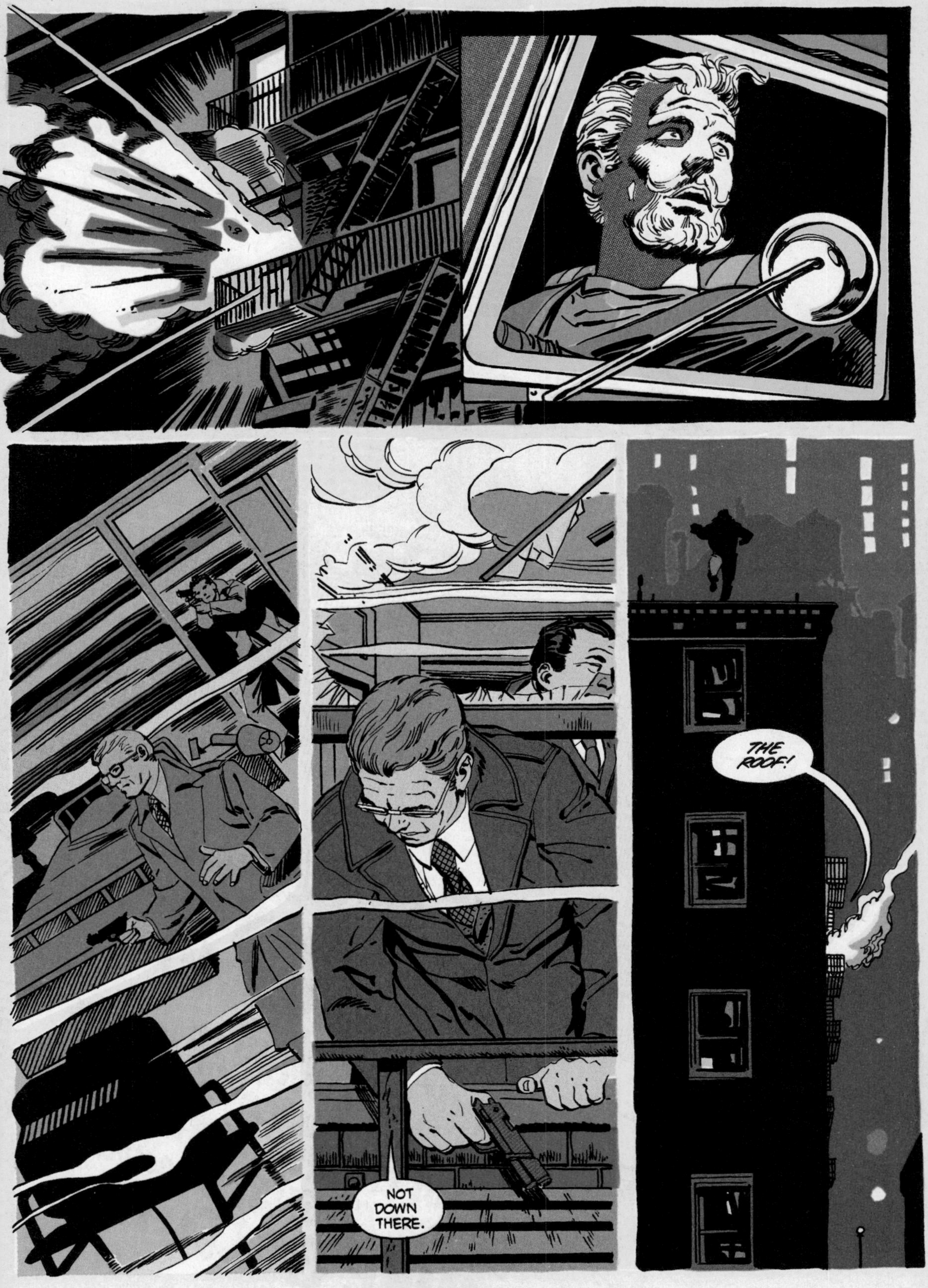
NOT DOWN THERE.
THE ROOF!

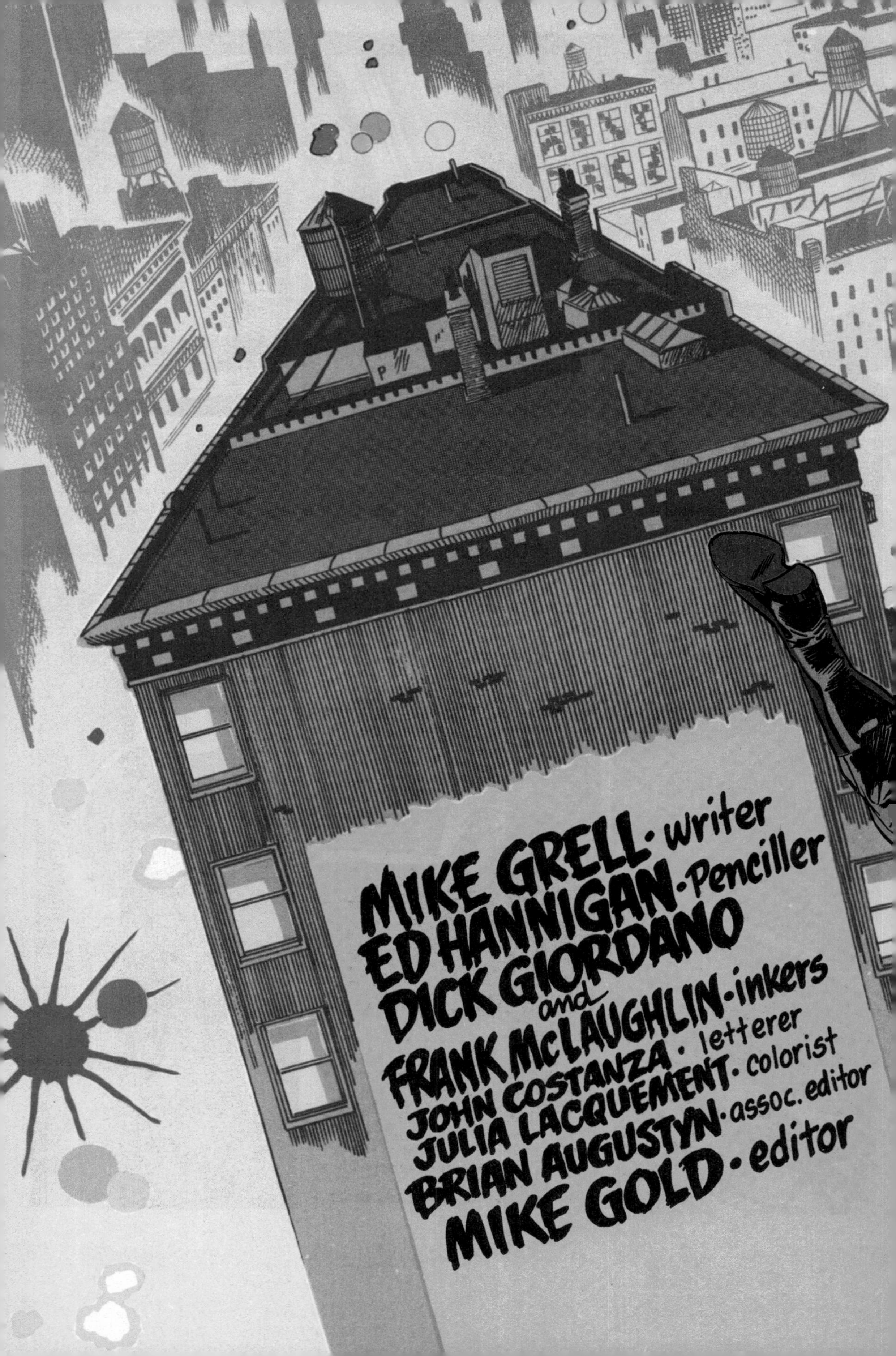
MIKE GRELL · writer
ED HANNIGAN · Penciller
DICK GIORDANO
and
FRANK McLAUGHLIN · inkers
JOHN COSTANZA · letterer
JULIA LACQUEMENT · colorist
BRIAN AUGUSTYN · assoc. editor
MIKE GOLD · editor

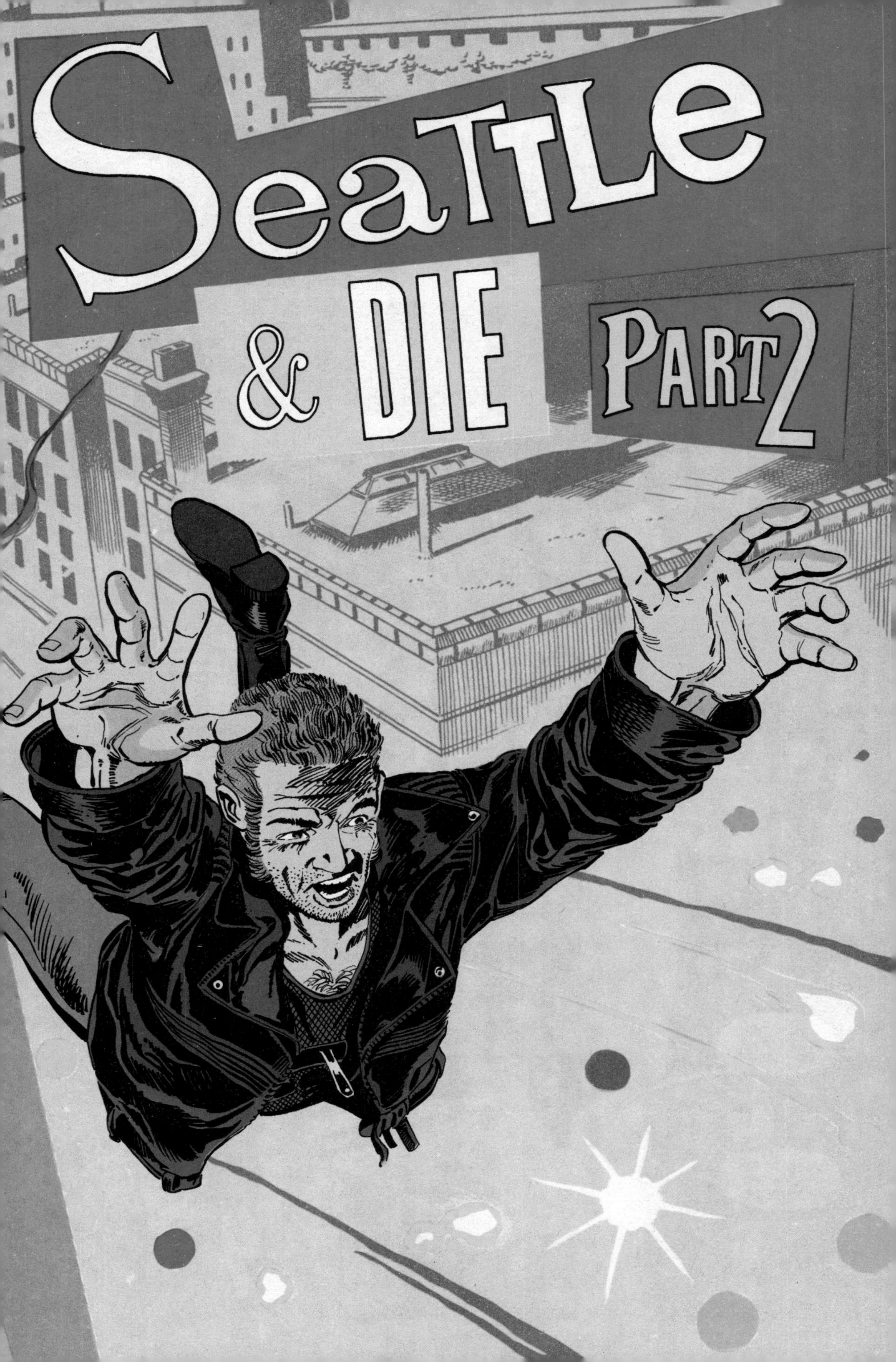
Seattle
& DIE
PART 2

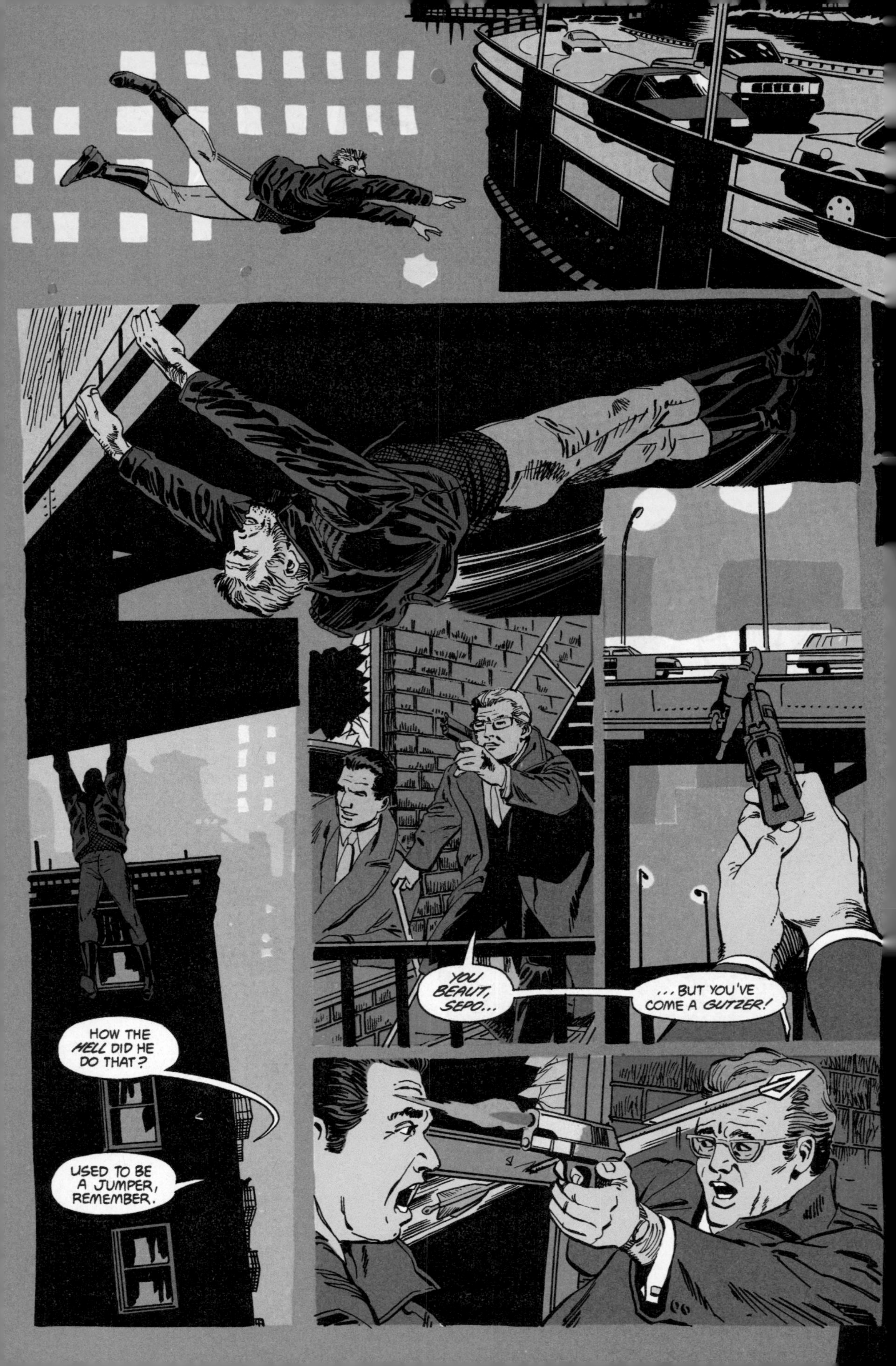
YOU BEAUT, SEPO...
...BUT YOU'VE COME A GUTZER!
HOW THE HELL DID HE DO THAT?
USED TO BE A JUMPER, REMEMBER.

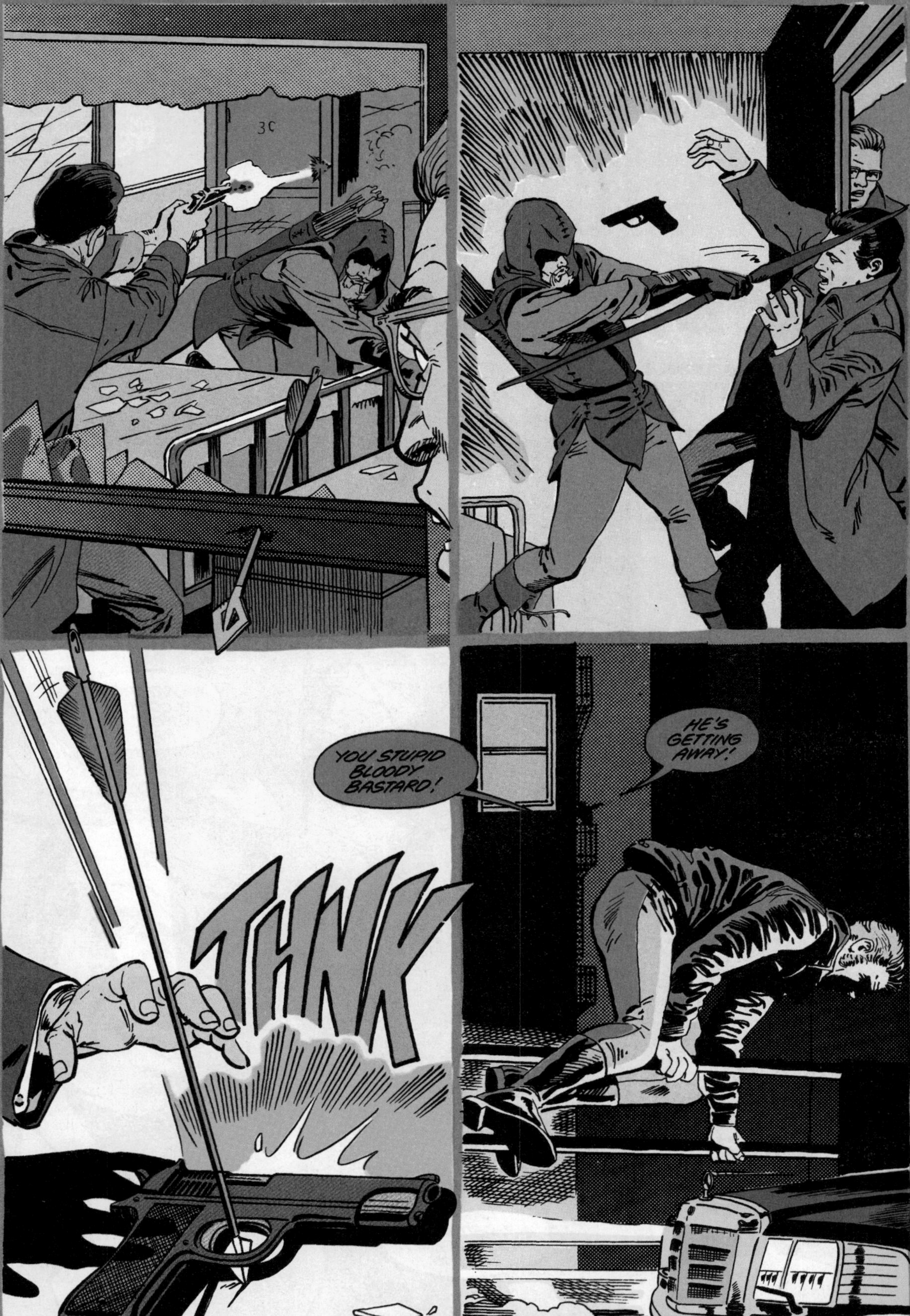
3C
THNK
YOU STUPID BLOODY BASTARD!
HE'S GETTING AWAY!

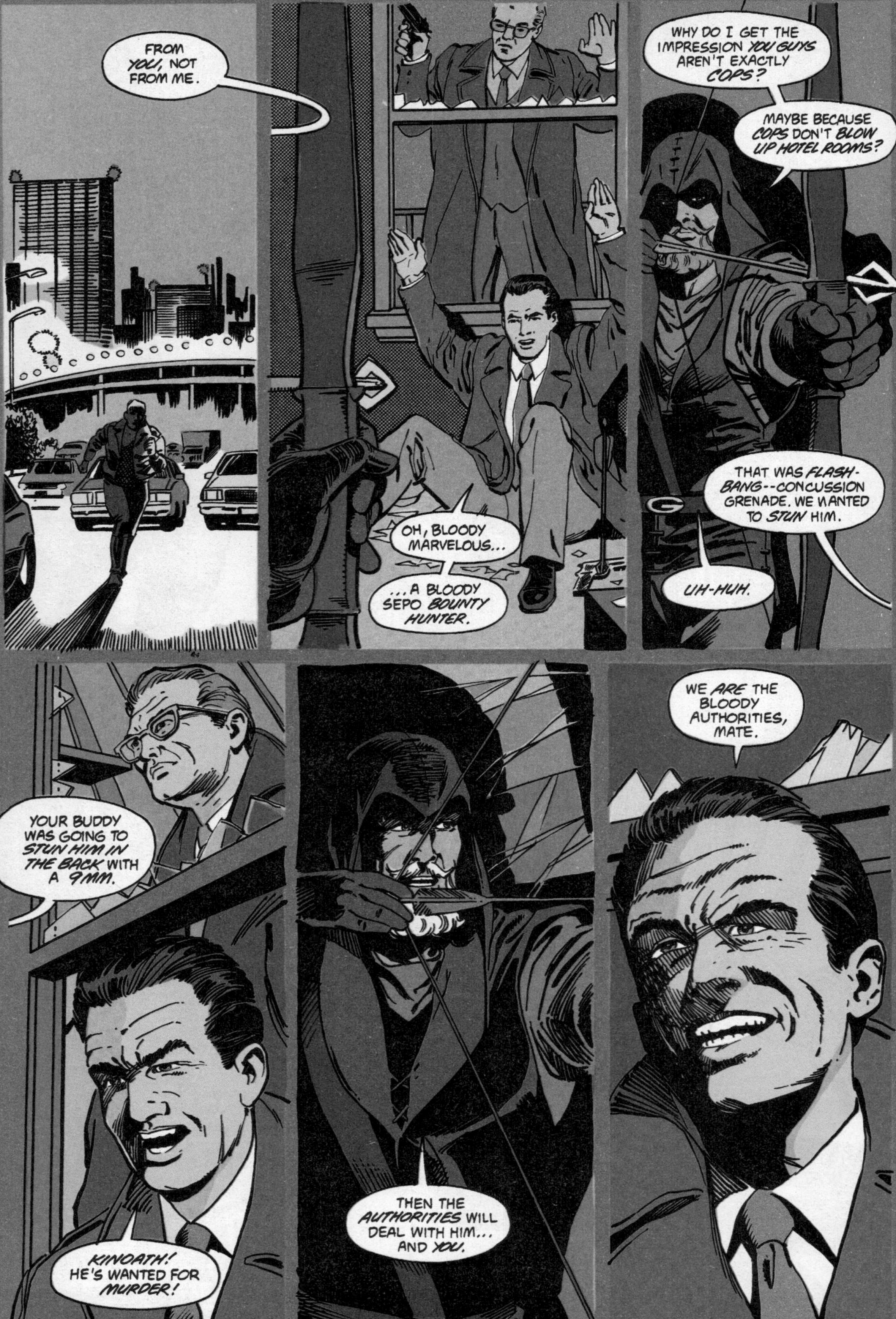
FROM YOU, NOT FROM ME.
OH, BLOODY MARVELOUS...
...A BLOODY SEPO BOUNTY HUNTER.
WHY DO I GET THE IMPRESSION YOU GUYS AREN'T EXACTLY COPS?
MAYBE BECAUSE COPS DON'T BLOW UP HOTEL ROOMS?
THAT WAS FLASH-BANG--CONCUSSION GRENADE. WE WANTED TO STUN HIM.
UH-HUH.
YOUR BUDDY WAS GOING TO STUN HIM IN THE BACK WITH A 9MM.
KINOATH! HE'S WANTED FOR MURDER!
THEN THE AUTHORITIES WILL DEAL WITH HIM... AND YOU.
WE ARE THE BLOODY AUTHORITIES, MATE.

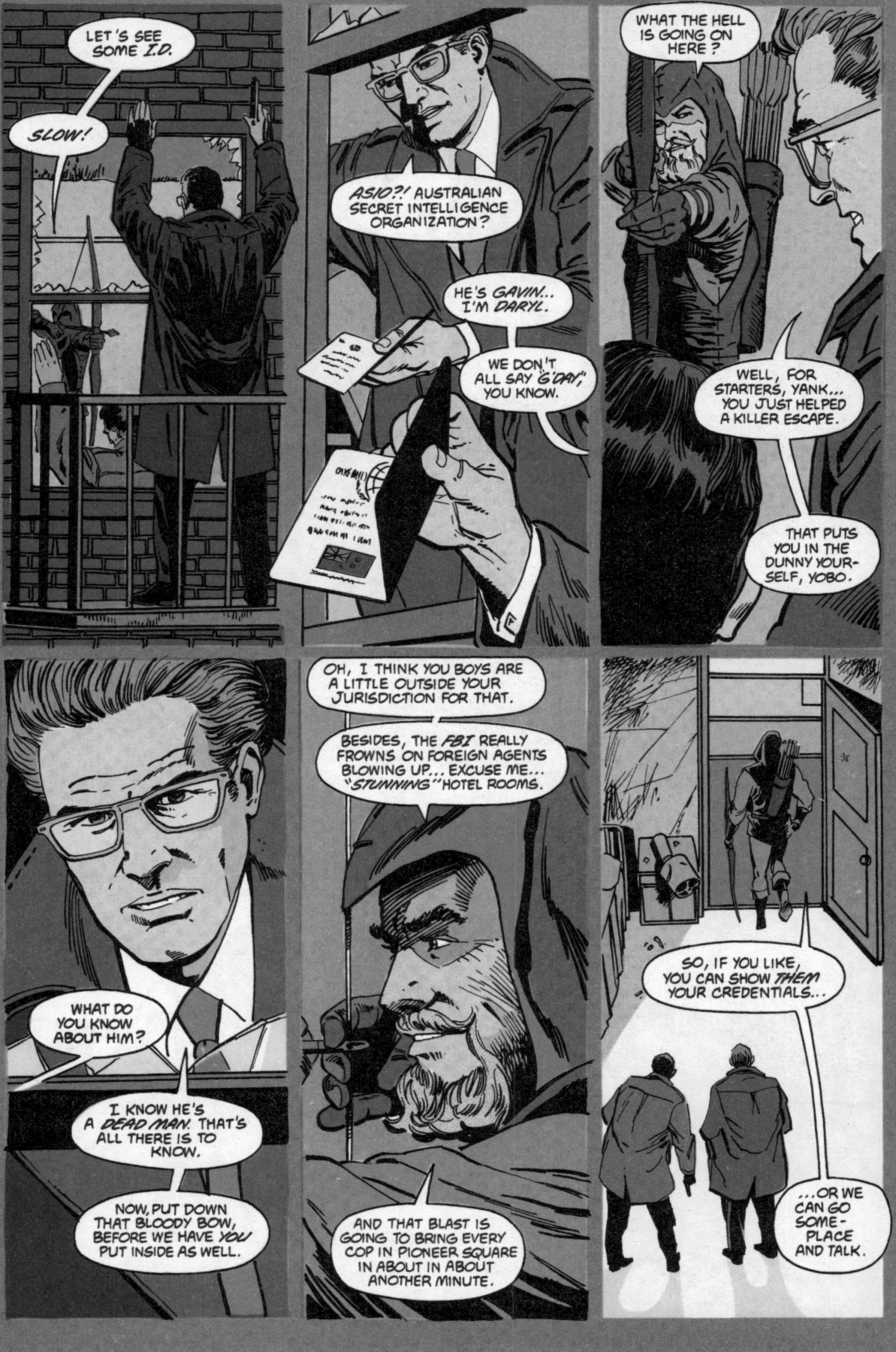

LET'S SEE SOME I.D.
SLOW!
ASIO?! AUSTRALIAN SECRET INTELLIGENCE ORGANIZATION?
HE'S GAVIN... I'M DARYL.
WE DON'T ALL SAY "G'DAY," YOU KNOW.
WHAT THE HELL IS GOING ON HERE?
WELL, FOR STARTERS, YANK... YOU JUST HELPED A KILLER ESCAPE.
THAT PUTS YOU IN THE DUNNY YOURSELF, YOBO.
WHAT DO YOU KNOW ABOUT HIM?
I KNOW HE'S A DEAD MAN. THAT'S ALL THERE IS TO KNOW.
NOW, PUT DOWN THAT BLOODY BOW, BEFORE WE HAVE YOU PUT INSIDE AS WELL.
OH, I THINK YOU BOYS ARE A LITTLE OUTSIDE YOUR JURISDICTION FOR THAT.
BESIDES, THE FBI REALLY FROWNS ON FOREIGN AGENTS BLOWING UP... EXCUSE ME... "STUNNING" HOTEL ROOMS.
AND THAT BLAST IS GOING TO BRING EVERY COP IN PIONEER SQUARE IN ABOUT IN ABOUT ANOTHER MINUTE.
SO, IF YOU LIKE, YOU CAN SHOW THEM YOUR CREDENTIALS...
...OR WE CAN GO SOME-PLACE AND TALK.

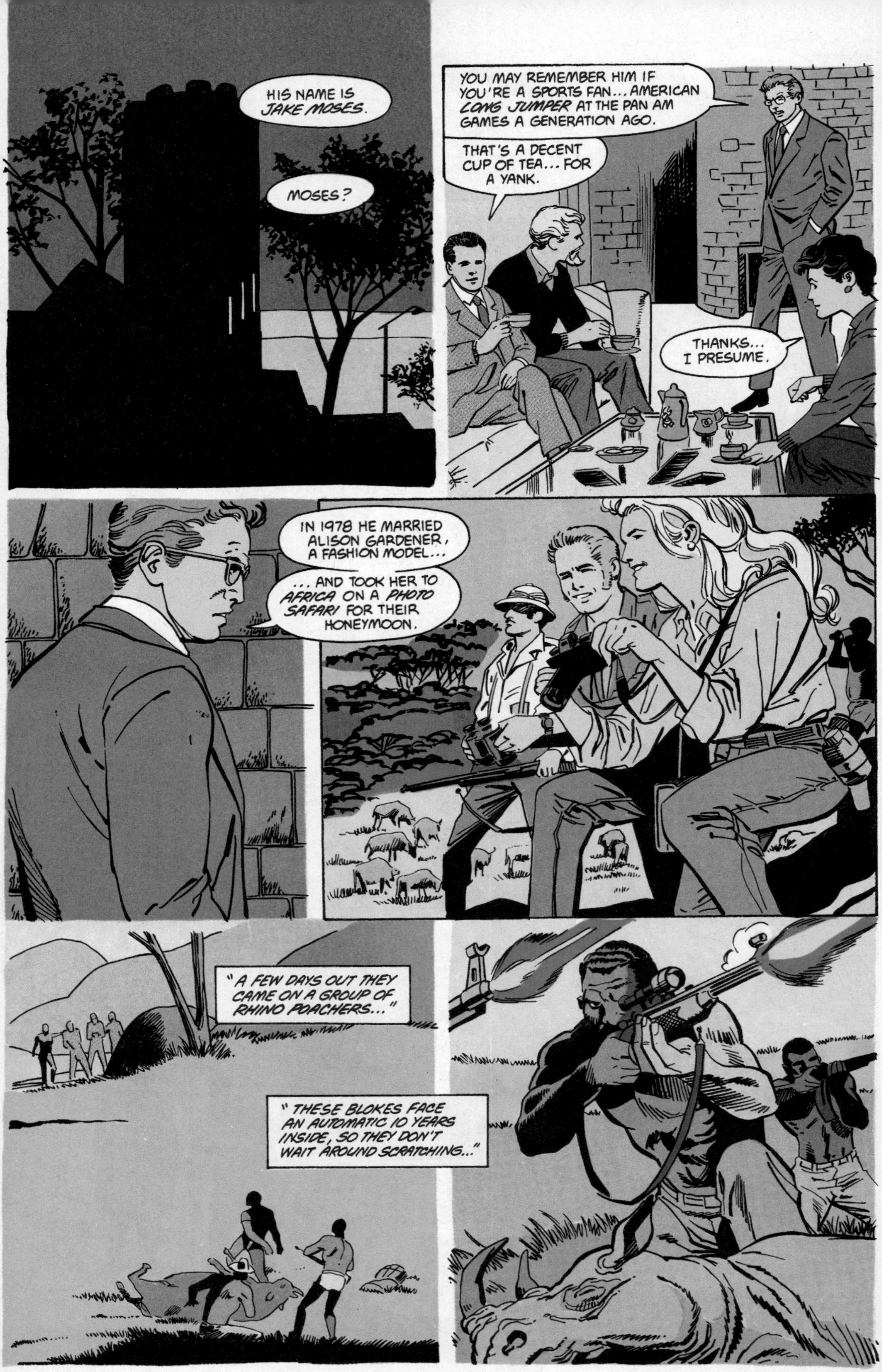
HIS NAME IS JAKE MOSES.
MOSES?
YOU MAY REMEMBER HIM IF YOU'RE A SPORTS FAN... AMERICAN LONG JUMPER AT THE PAN AM GAMES A GENERATION AGO.
THAT'S A DECENT CUP OF TEA... FOR A YANK.
THANKS... I PRESUME.
IN 1978 HE MARRIED ALISON GARDENER, A FASHION MODEL...
...AND TOOK HER TO AFRICA ON A PHOTO SAFARI FOR THEIR HONEYMOON.
"A FEW DAYS OUT THEY CAME ON A GROUP OF RHINO POACHERS..."
"THESE BLOKES FACE AN AUTOMATIC 10 YEARS INSIDE, SO THEY DON'T WAIT AROUND SCRATCHING..."

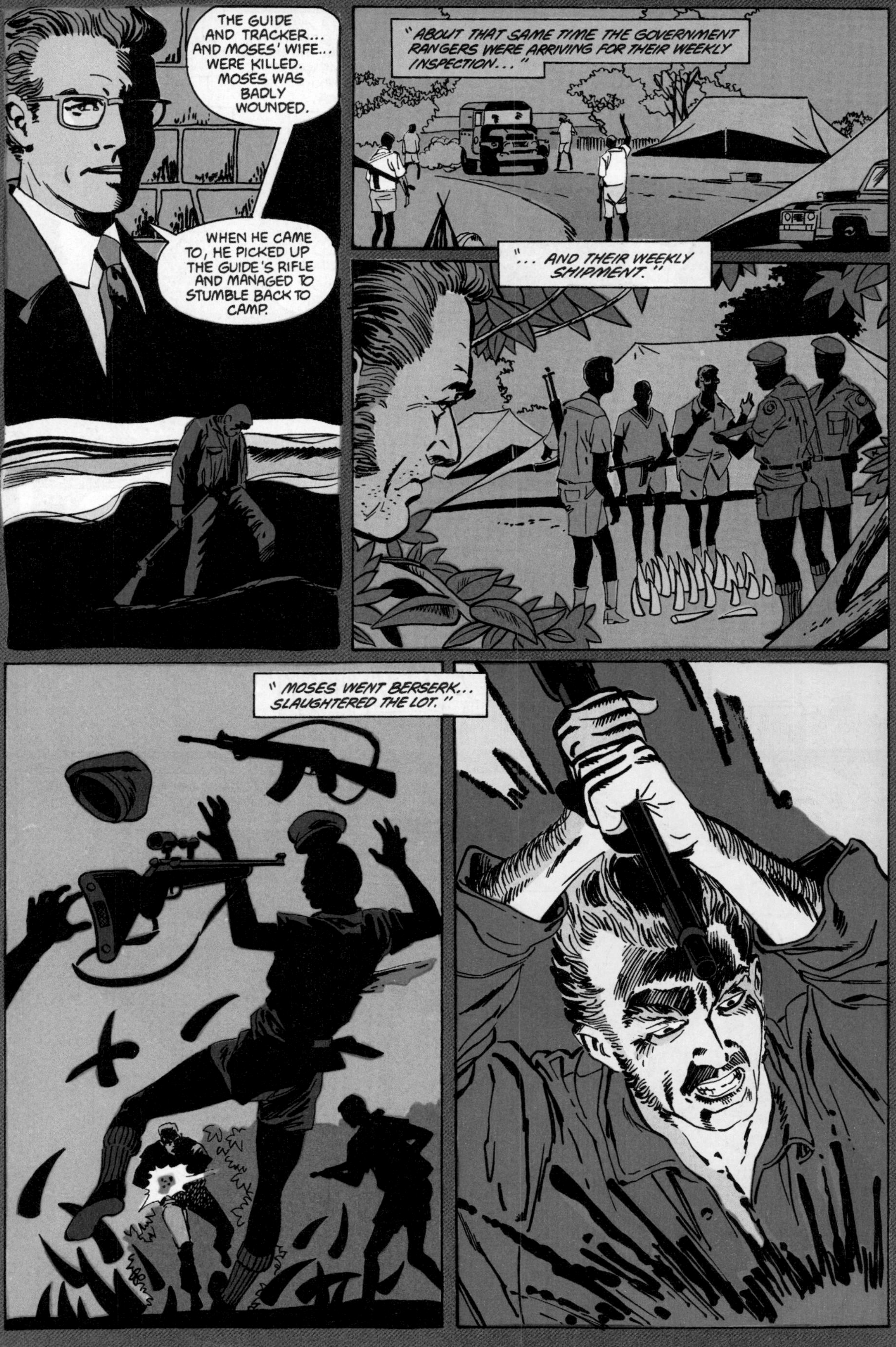
THE GUIDE AND TRACKER... AND MOSES' WIFE... WERE KILLED. MOSES WAS BADLY WOUNDED.
WHEN HE CAME TO, HE PICKED UP THE GUIDE'S RIFLE AND MANAGED TO STUMBLE BACK TO CAMP.
"ABOUT THAT SAME TIME THE GOVERNMENT RANGERS WERE ARRIVING FOR THEIR WEEKLY INSPECTION..."
"... AND THEIR WEEKLY SHIPMENT."
"MOSES WENT BERSERK... SLAUGHTERED THE LOT."

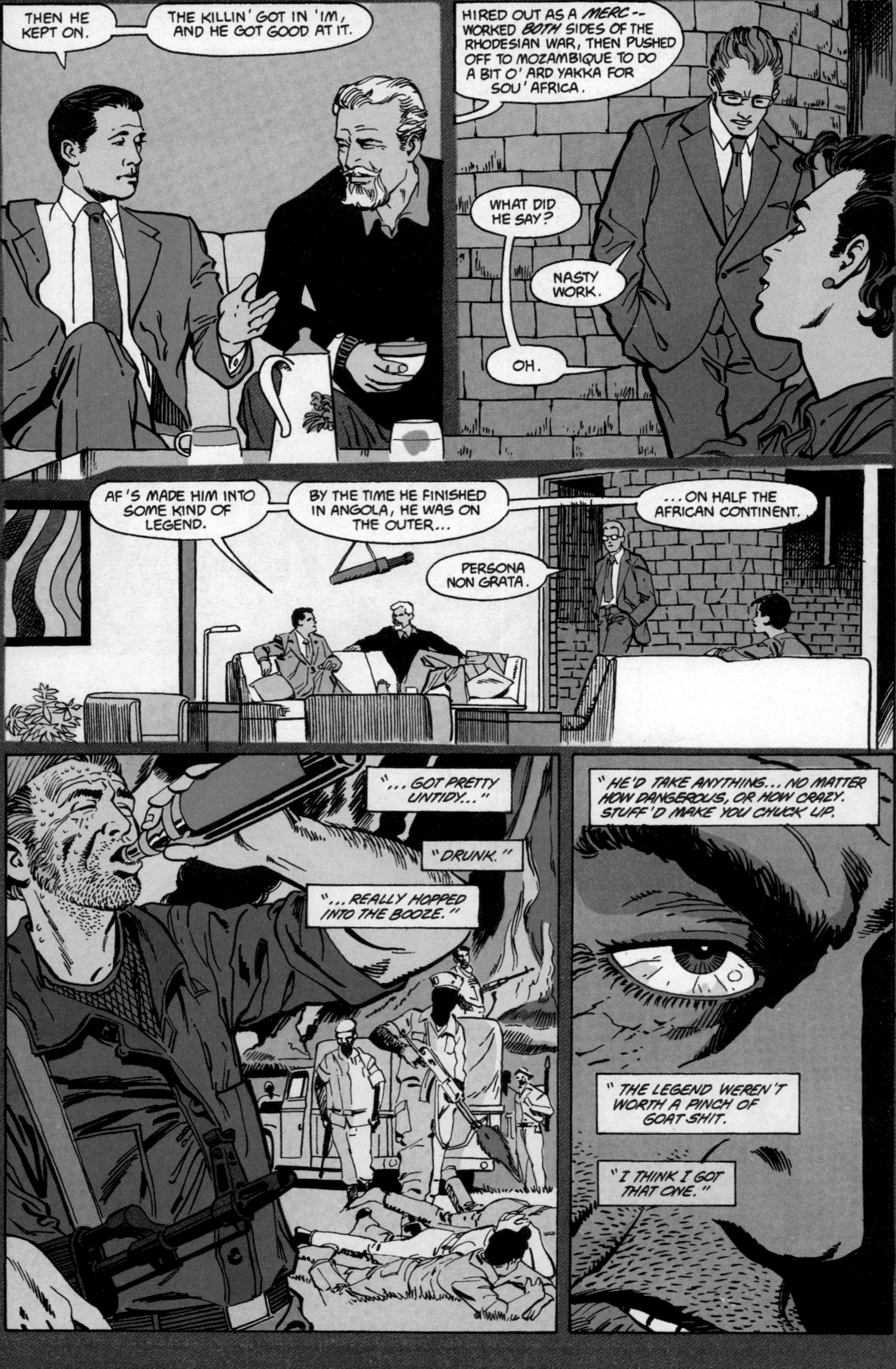
THEN HE KEPT ON.
THE KILLIN' GOT IN 'IM, AND HE GOT GOOD AT IT.
HIRED OUT AS A MERC -- WORKED BOTH SIDES OF THE RHODESIAN WAR, THEN PUSHED OFF TO MOZAMBIQUE TO DO A BIT O' ARD YAKKA FOR SOU' AFRICA.
WHAT DID HE SAY?
NASTY WORK.
OH.
AF'S MADE HIM INTO SOME KIND OF LEGEND.
BY THE TIME HE FINISHED IN ANGOLA, HE WAS ON THE OUTER...
...ON HALF THE AFRICAN CONTINENT.
PERSONA NON GRATA.
"...GOT PRETTY UNTIDY..."
"DRUNK."
"...REALLY HOPPED INTO THE BOOZE."
"HE'D TAKE ANYTHING... NO MATTER HOW DANGEROUS, OR HOW CRAZY. STUFF'D MAKE YOU CHUCK UP.
"THE LEGEND WEREN'T WORTH A PINCH OF GOAT SHIT.
"I THINK I GOT THAT ONE."

WHAT I WANT TO KNOW IS WHAT THE *ASIO* WANT HIM FOR.

GOT THE *TASSIE MAP*, GAZZA?

YAIR. HERE Y'GO.

SOUTHERN AUSTRAL

ON THE EAST COAST OF TASMANIA, NEAR HOBART, THERE'S A NAVAL BASE-- SERVICES MORE THAN JUST AUSTRALIAN SHIPS.

S O U

CTORIA

MELBOURNE

140

BASS STRAIT

40

TASMA.

Hobart

TASMANIA

DIAN OS

CANBERRA

IN OCTOBER OF '87 THERE WAS AN *IRANIAN* SHIP DOCKED THERE TO PICK UP A LOAD OF *AMERICAN MUNITIONS.*

MOSES AND HIS CREW OF MERCS *BLEW IT UP.*

SEEMS LIKE SOMETHING TO *CONGRATULATE* HIM FOR.

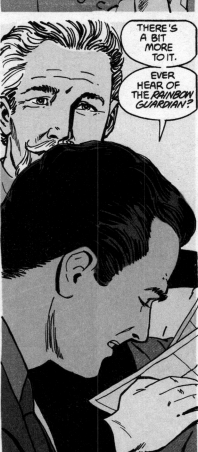

THERE'S A BIT MORE TO IT. EVER HEAR OF THE *RAINBOW GUARDIAN?*

JESUS.

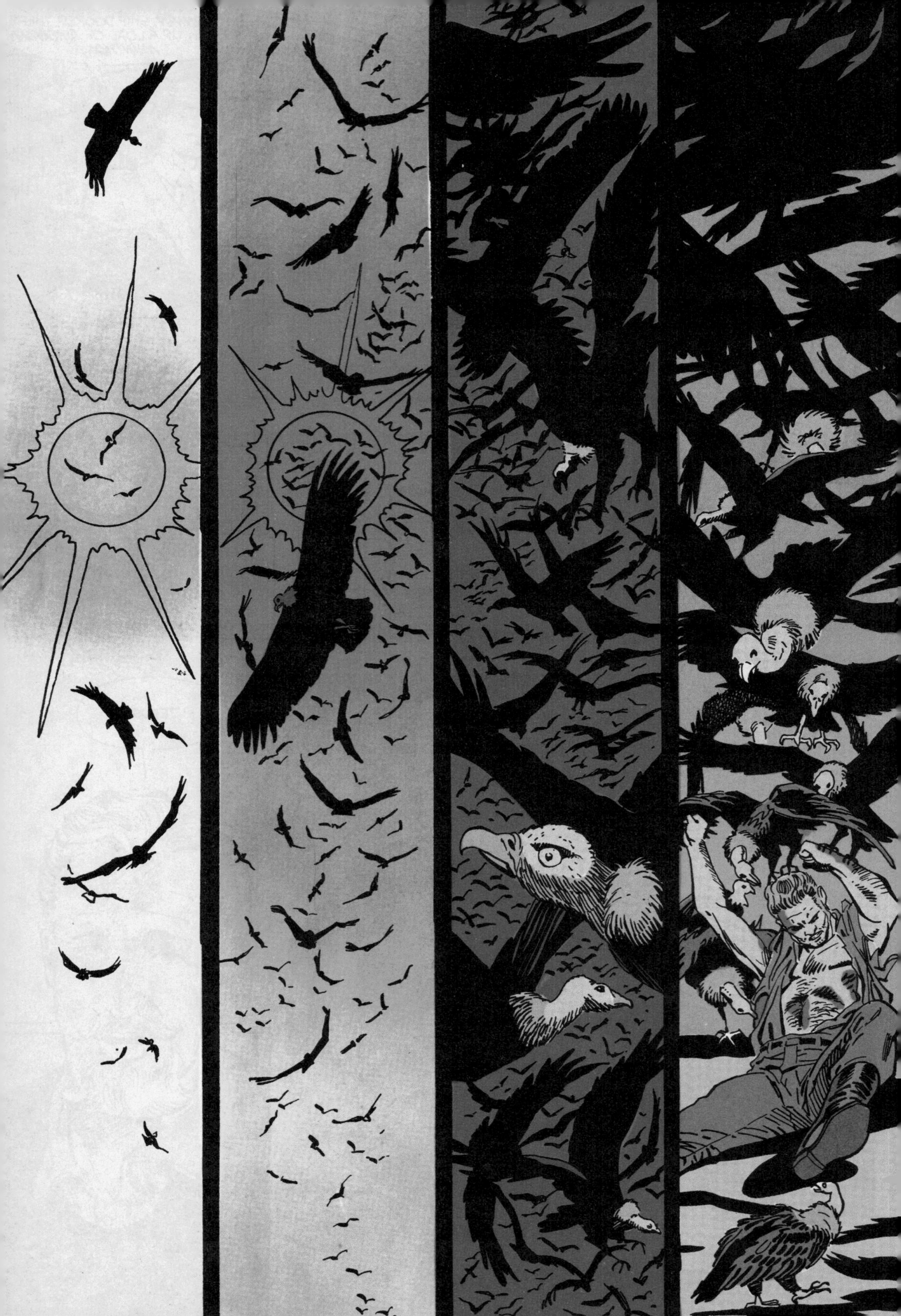

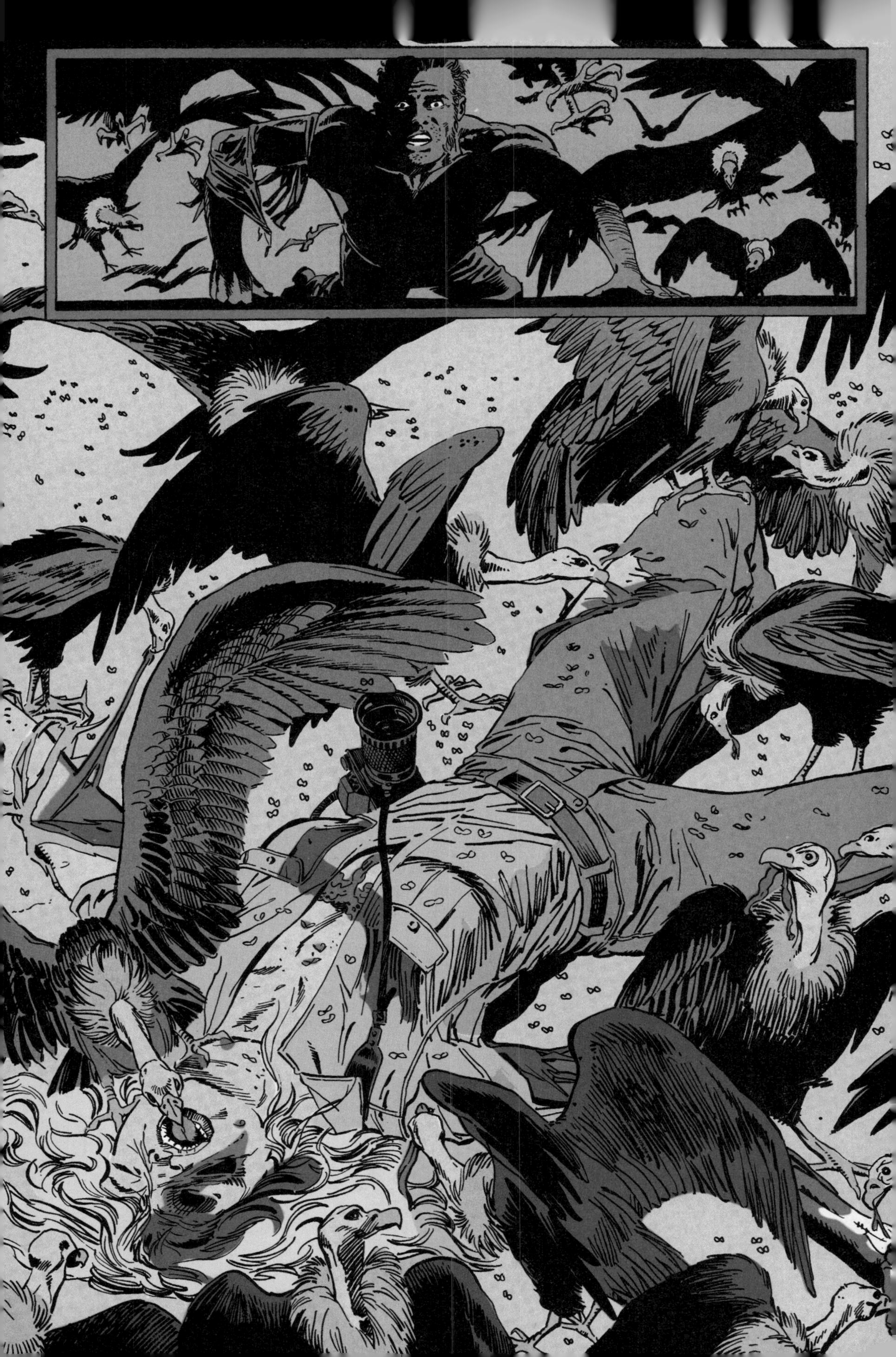

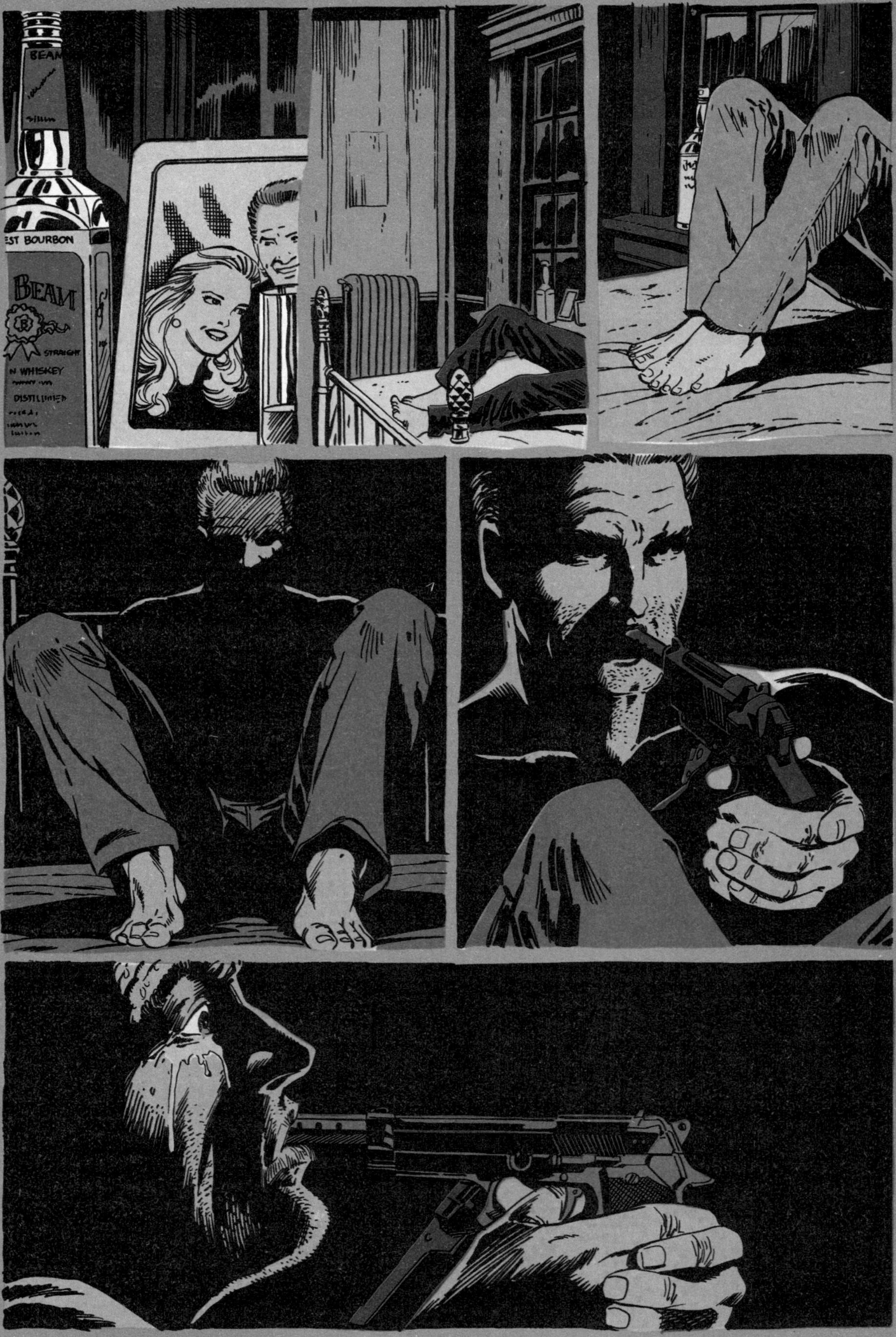
BEAM
EST BOURBON
BEAM
STRAIGHT
N WHISKEY

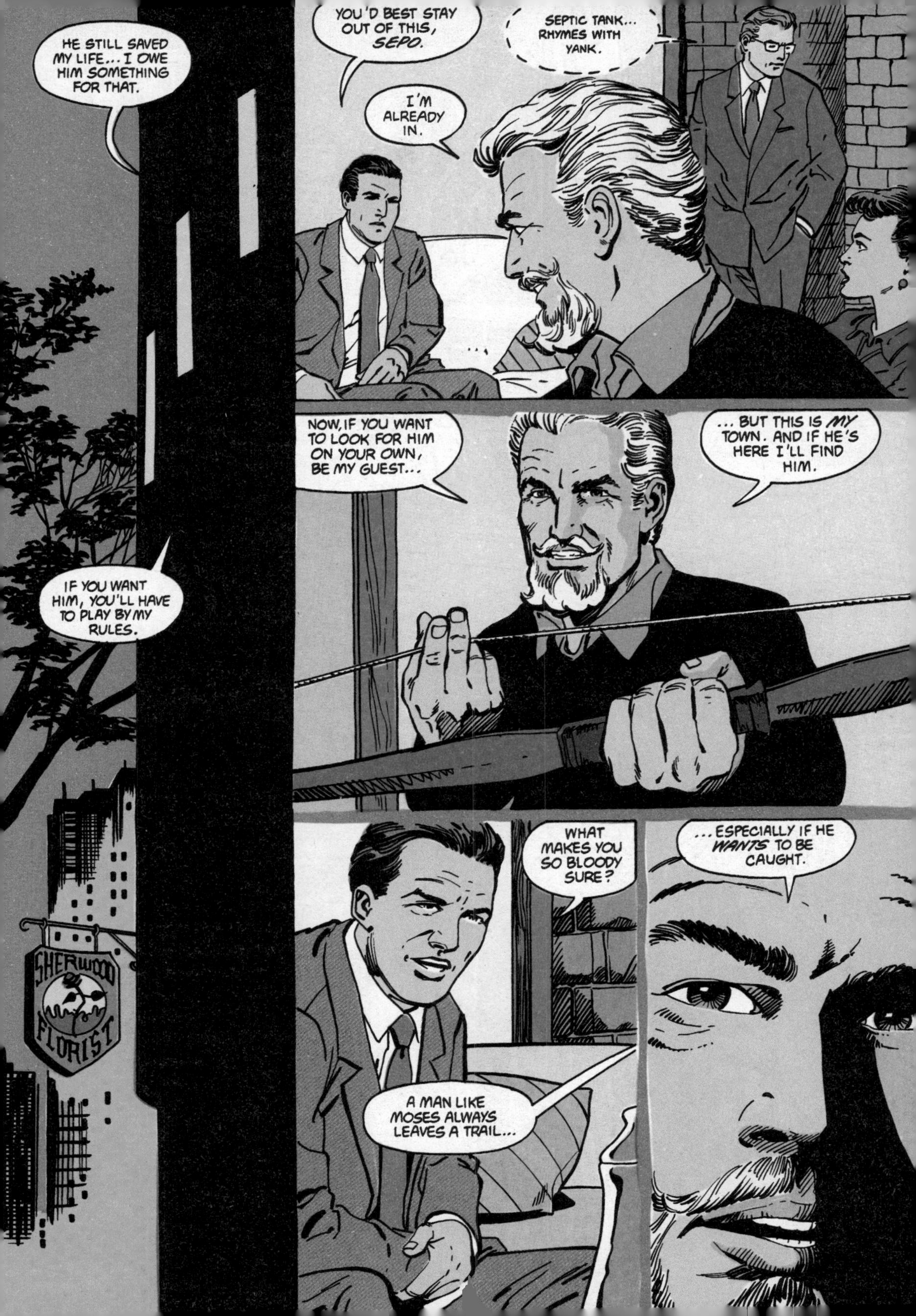
HE STILL SAVED MY LIFE... I OWE HIM SOMETHING FOR THAT.
YOU'D BEST STAY OUT OF THIS, SEPO.
SEPTIC TANK... RHYMES WITH YANK.
I'M ALREADY IN.
...
IF YOU WANT HIM, YOU'LL HAVE TO PLAY BY MY RULES.
NOW, IF YOU WANT TO LOOK FOR HIM ON YOUR OWN, BE MY GUEST...
... BUT THIS IS MY TOWN. AND IF HE'S HERE I'LL FIND HIM.
WHAT MAKES YOU SO BLOODY SURE?
A MAN LIKE MOSES ALWAYS LEAVES A TRAIL...
... ESPECIALLY IF HE WANTS TO BE CAUGHT.
SHERWOOD FLORIST

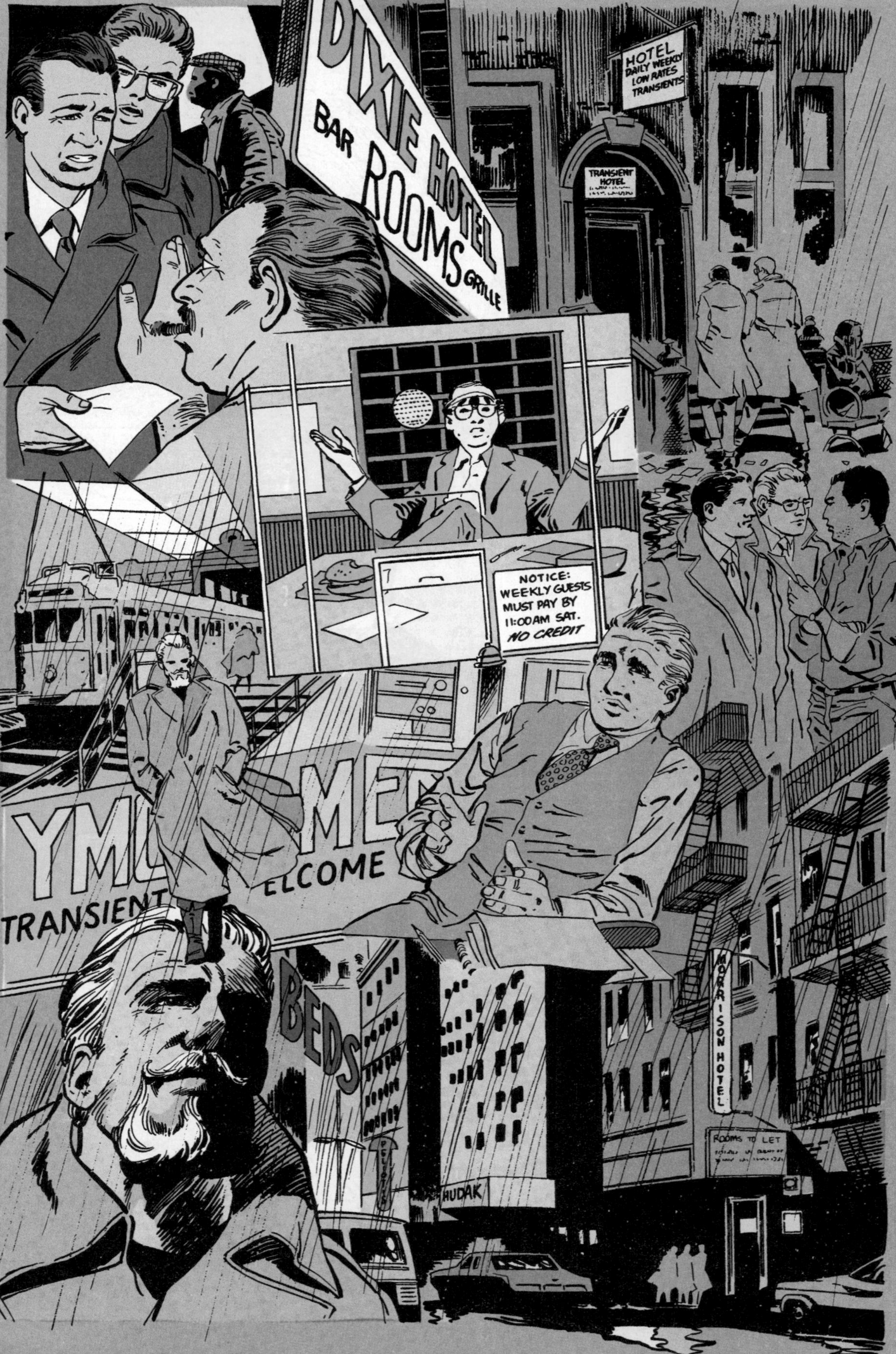
DIXIE HOTEL
BAR
ROOMS
GRILLE
HOTEL
DAILY WEEKLY
LOW RATES
TRANSIENTS
TRANSIENT
HOTEL
NOTICE:
WEEKLY GUESTS
MUST PAY BY
11:00AM SAT.
NO CREDIT
YM
ME
ELCOME
TRANSIENT
BEDS
MORRISON HOTEL
ROOMS TO LET
HUDAK

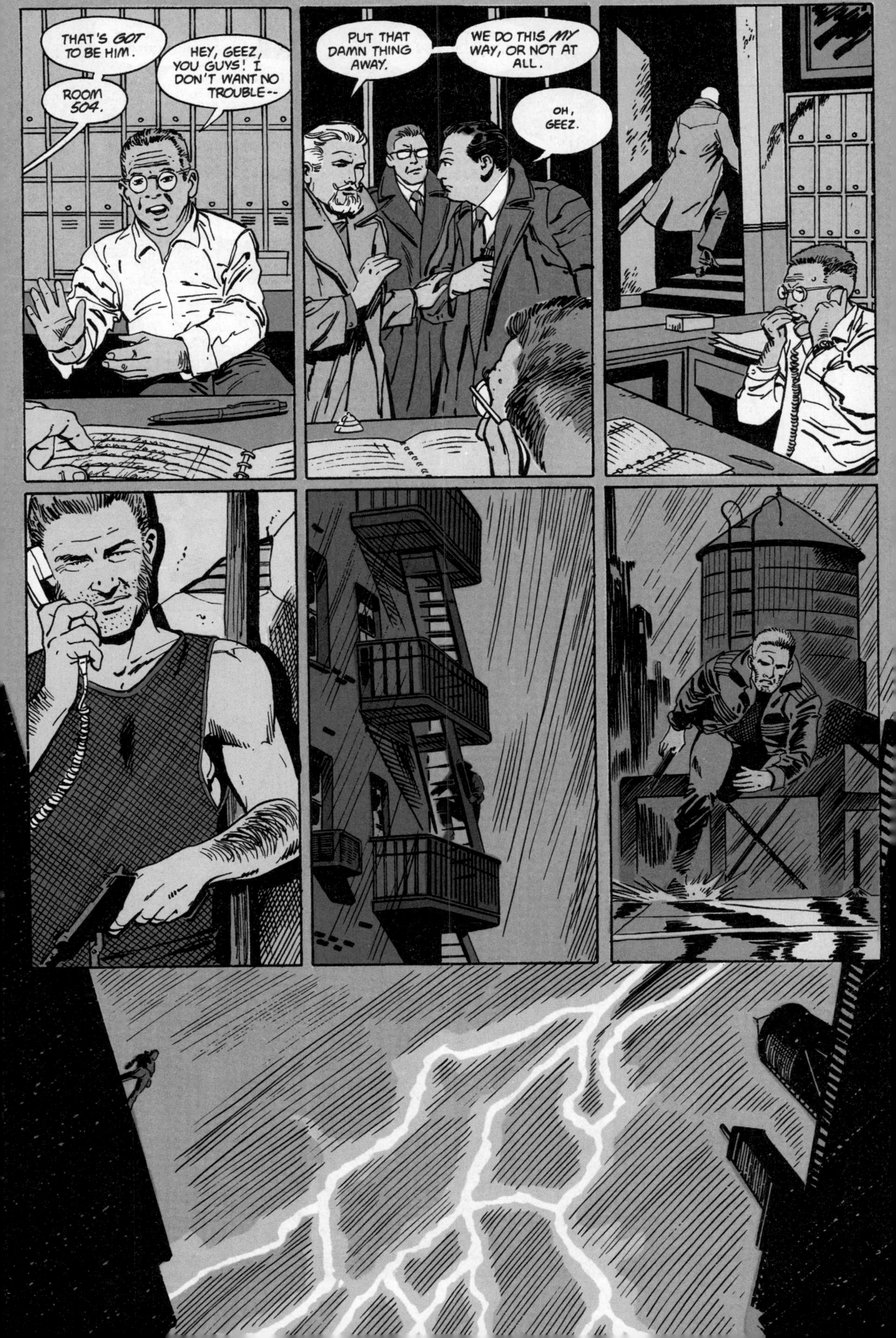

THAT'S GOT TO BE HIM.
ROOM 504.
HEY, GEEZ, YOU GUYS! I DON'T WANT NO TROUBLE--
PUT THAT DAMN THING AWAY.
WE DO THIS MY WAY, OR NOT AT ALL.
OH, GEEZ.

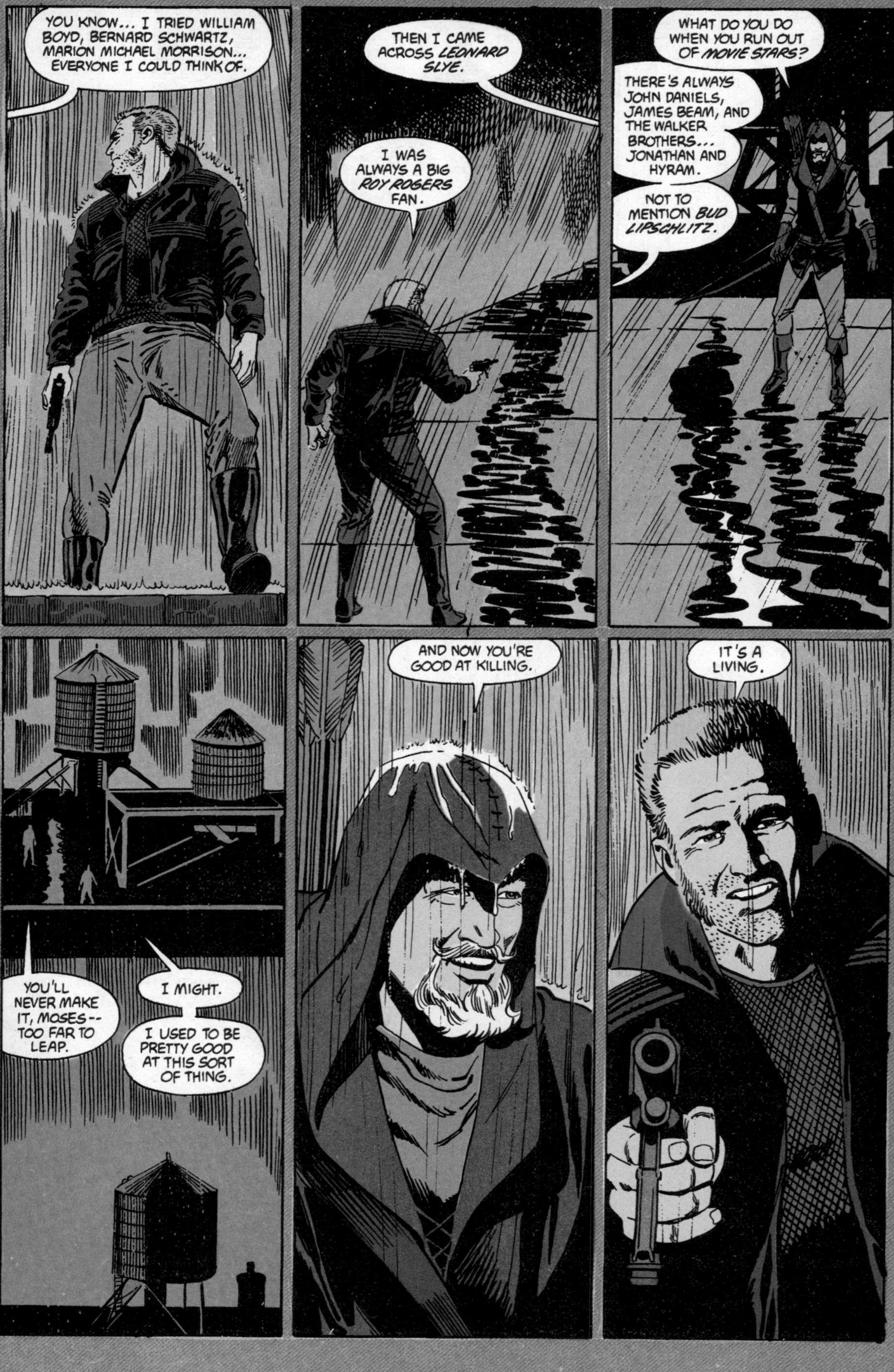
YOU KNOW... I TRIED WILLIAM BOYD, BERNARD SCHWARTZ, MARION MICHAEL MORRISON... EVERYONE I COULD THINK OF.
THEN I CAME ACROSS *LEONARD SLYE*.
I WAS ALWAYS A BIG *ROY ROGERS* FAN.
WHAT DO YOU DO WHEN YOU RUN OUT OF *MOVIE STARS?*
THERE'S ALWAYS JOHN DANIELS, JAMES BEAM, AND THE WALKER BROTHERS... JONATHAN AND HYRAM.
NOT TO MENTION *BUD LIPSCHLITZ*.
YOU'LL NEVER MAKE IT, MOSES-- TOO FAR TO LEAP.
I MIGHT.
I USED TO BE PRETTY GOOD AT THIS SORT OF THING.
AND NOW YOU'RE GOOD AT KILLING.
IT'S A LIVING.

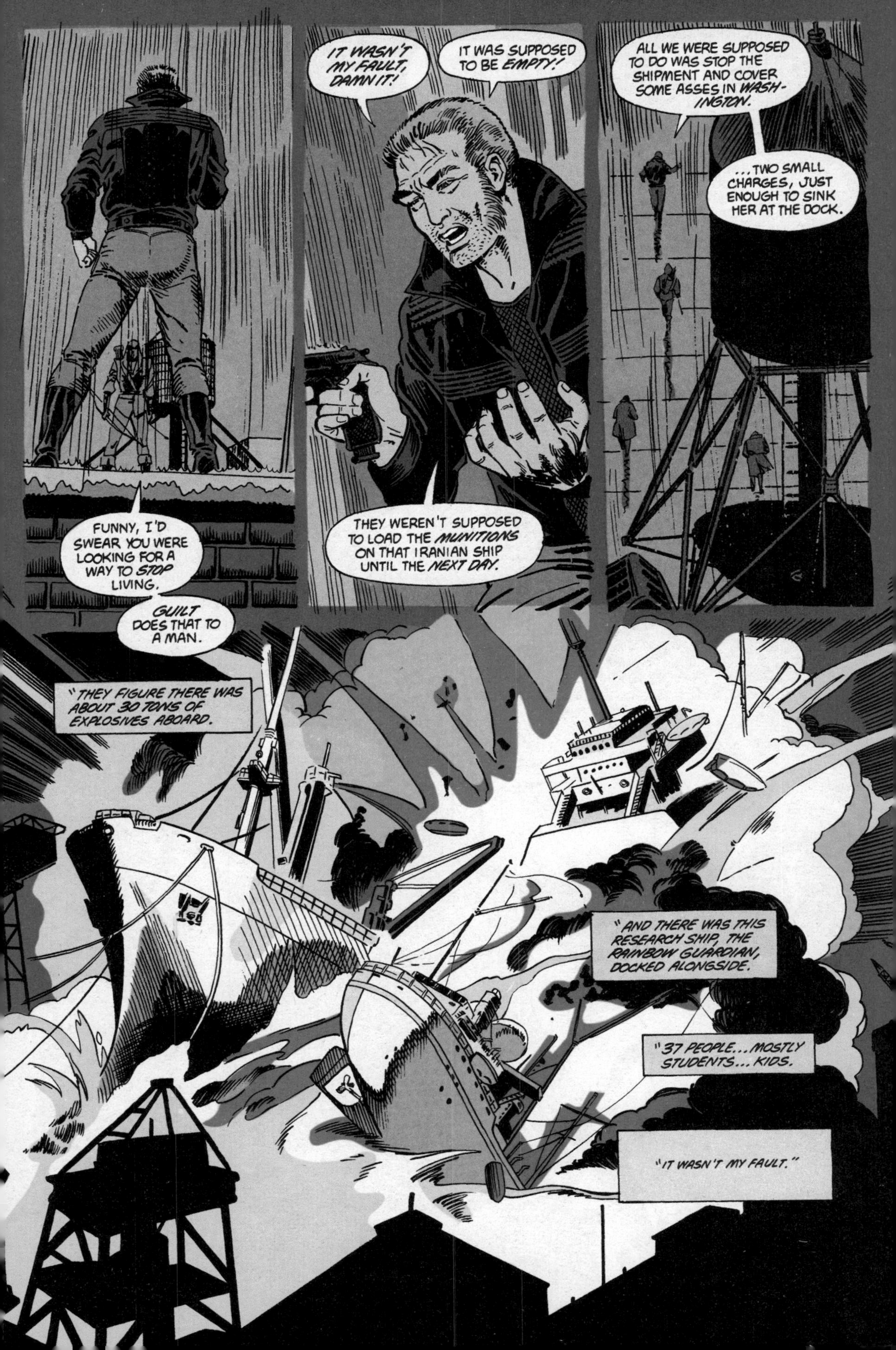
IT WASN'T MY FAULT, DAMN IT!
IT WAS SUPPOSED TO BE EMPTY!
ALL WE WERE SUPPOSED TO DO WAS STOP THE SHIPMENT AND COVER SOME ASSES IN WASH-INGTON.
...TWO SMALL CHARGES, JUST ENOUGH TO SINK HER AT THE DOCK.
FUNNY, I'D SWEAR YOU WERE LOOKING FOR A WAY TO STOP LIVING.
GUILT DOES THAT TO A MAN.
THEY WEREN'T SUPPOSED TO LOAD THE MUNITIONS ON THAT IRANIAN SHIP UNTIL THE NEXT DAY.
"THEY FIGURE THERE WAS ABOUT 30 TONS OF EXPLOSIVES ABOARD.
"AND THERE WAS THIS RESEARCH SHIP, THE RAINBOW GUARDIAN, DOCKED ALONGSIDE.
"37 PEOPLE... MOSTLY STUDENTS... KIDS.
"IT WASN'T MY FAULT."

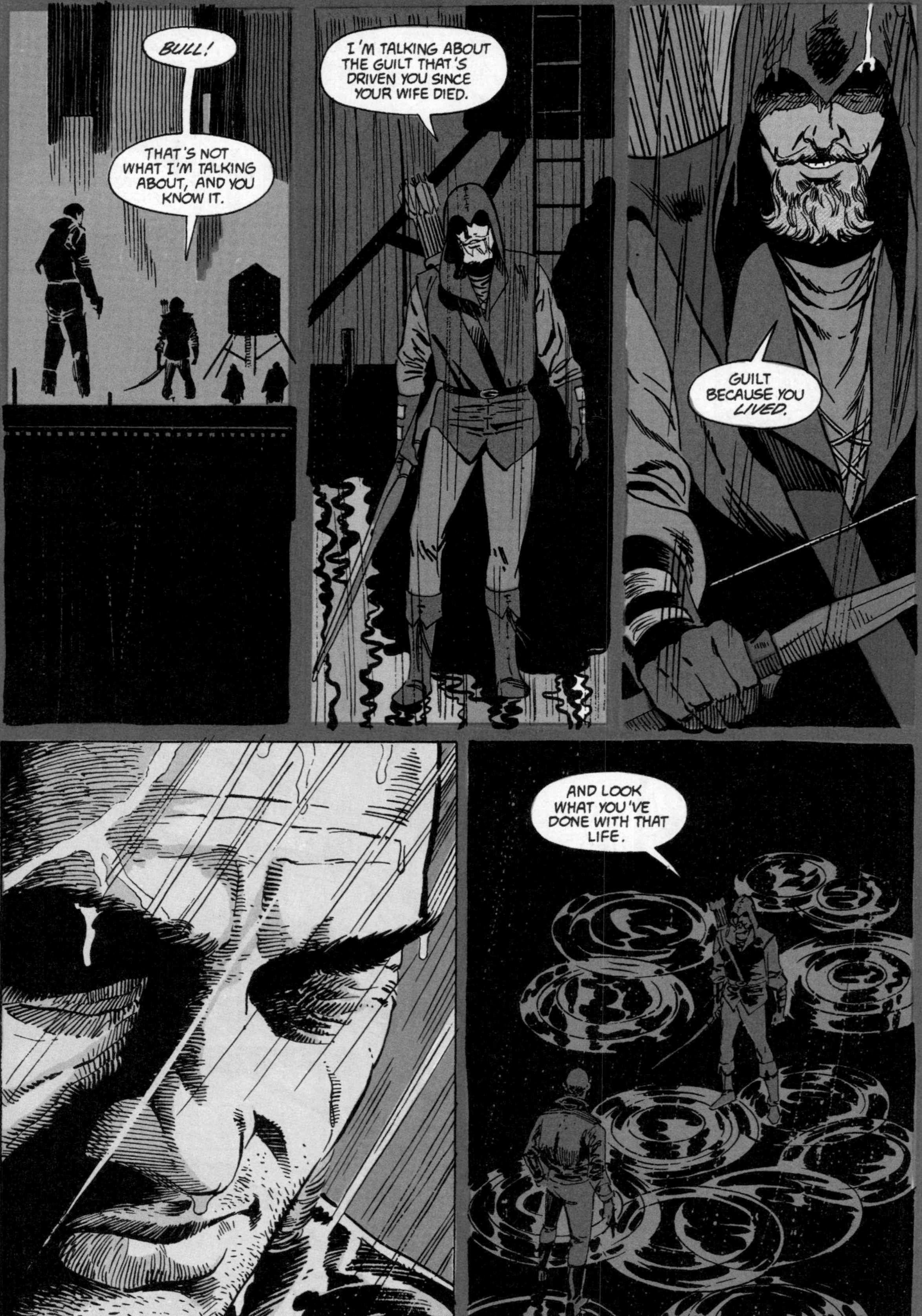
BULL!
THAT'S NOT WHAT I'M TALKING ABOUT, AND YOU KNOW IT.
I'M TALKING ABOUT THE GUILT THAT'S DRIVEN YOU SINCE YOUR WIFE DIED.
GUILT BECAUSE YOU *LIVED.*
AND LOOK WHAT YOU'VE DONE WITH THAT LIFE.

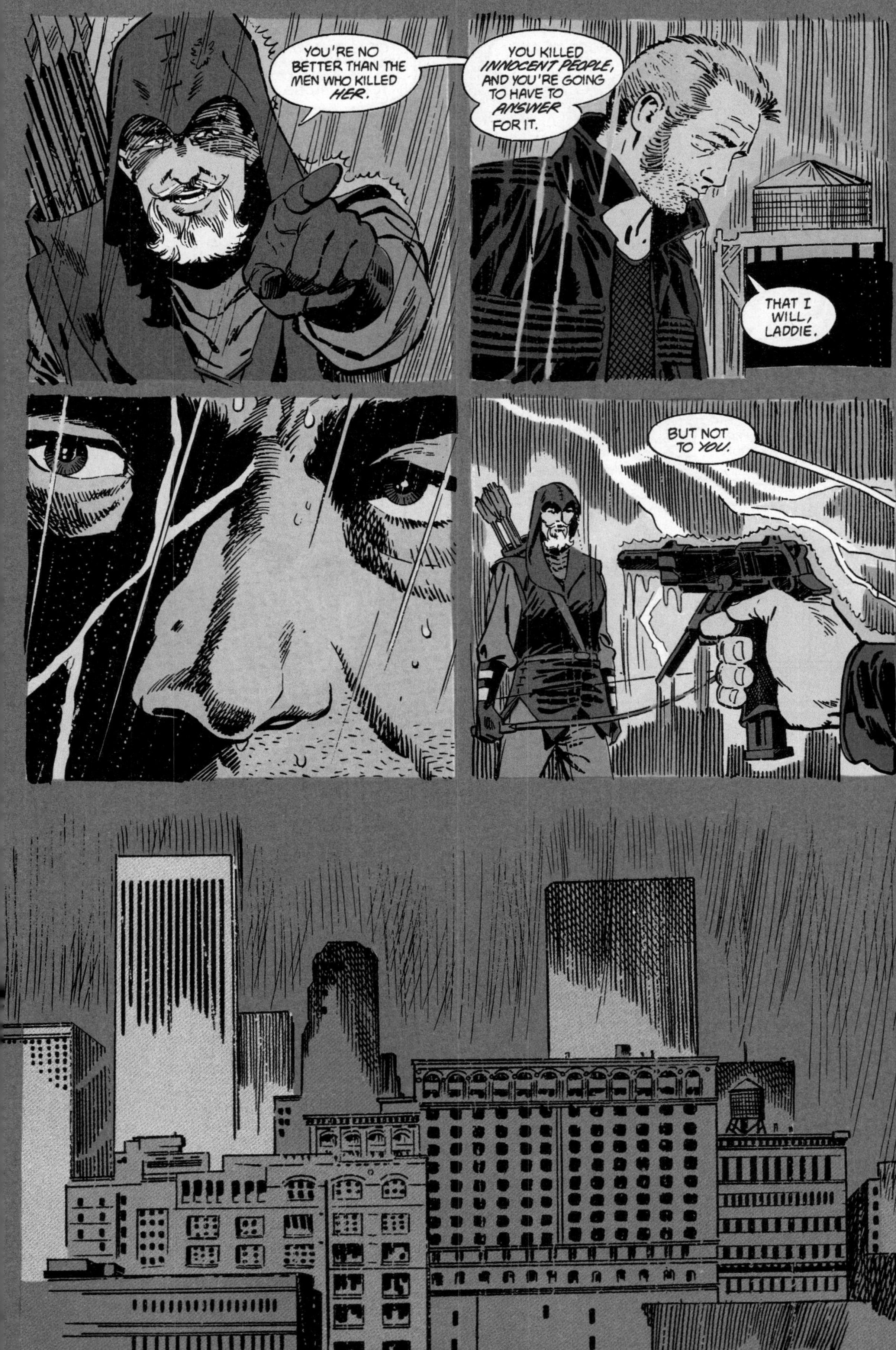
YOU'RE NO BETTER THAN THE MEN WHO KILLED HER.
YOU KILLED INNOCENT PEOPLE, AND YOU'RE GOING TO HAVE TO ANSWER FOR IT.
THAT I WILL, LADDIE.
BUT NOT TO YOU.

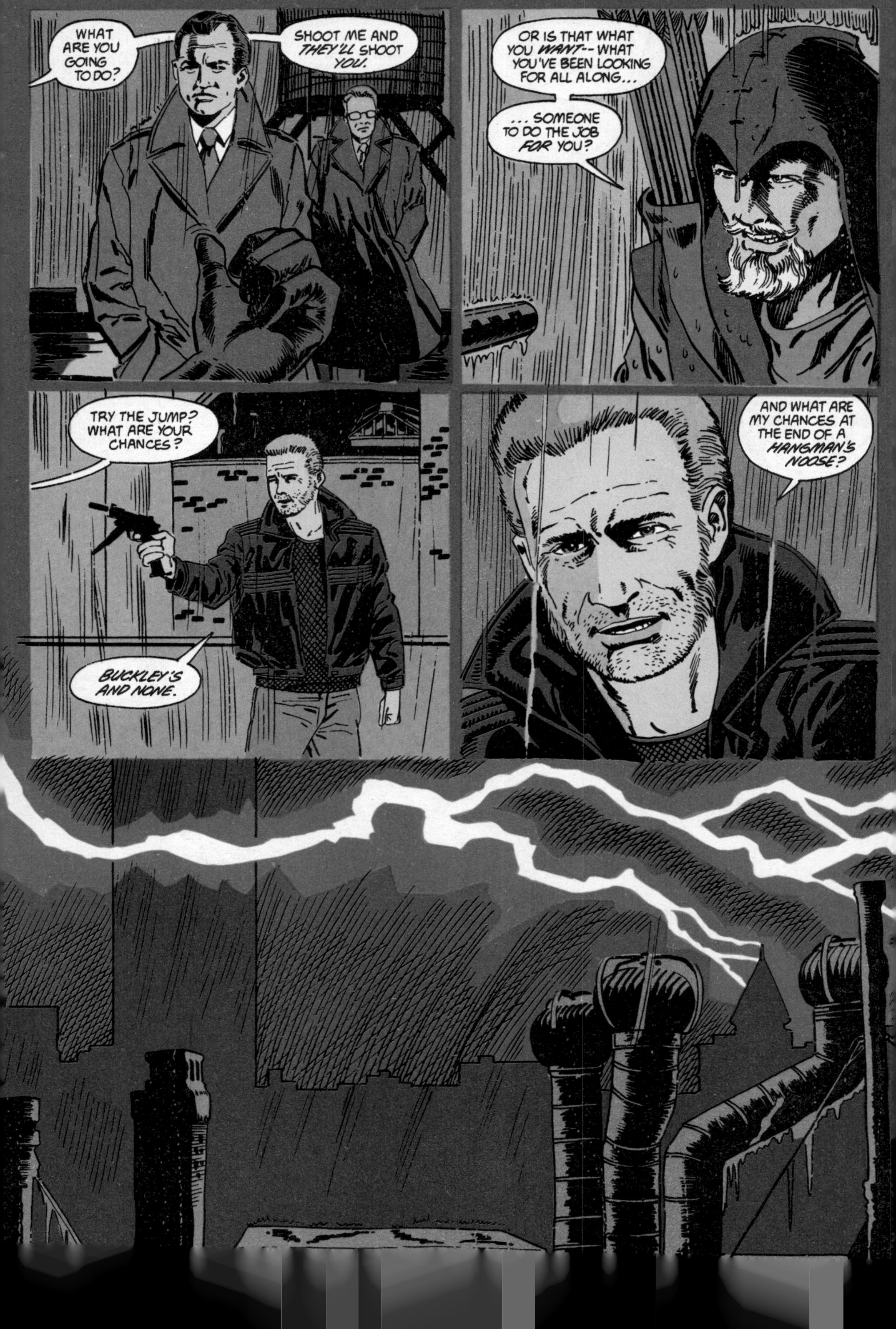
WHAT ARE YOU GOING TO DO?
SHOOT ME AND THEY'LL SHOOT YOU.
OR IS THAT WHAT YOU WANT-- WHAT YOU'VE BEEN LOOKING FOR ALL ALONG...
... SOMEONE TO DO THE JOB FOR YOU?
TRY THE JUMP? WHAT ARE YOUR CHANCES?
BUCKLEY'S AND NONE.
AND WHAT ARE MY CHANCES AT THE END OF A HANGMAN'S NOOSE?

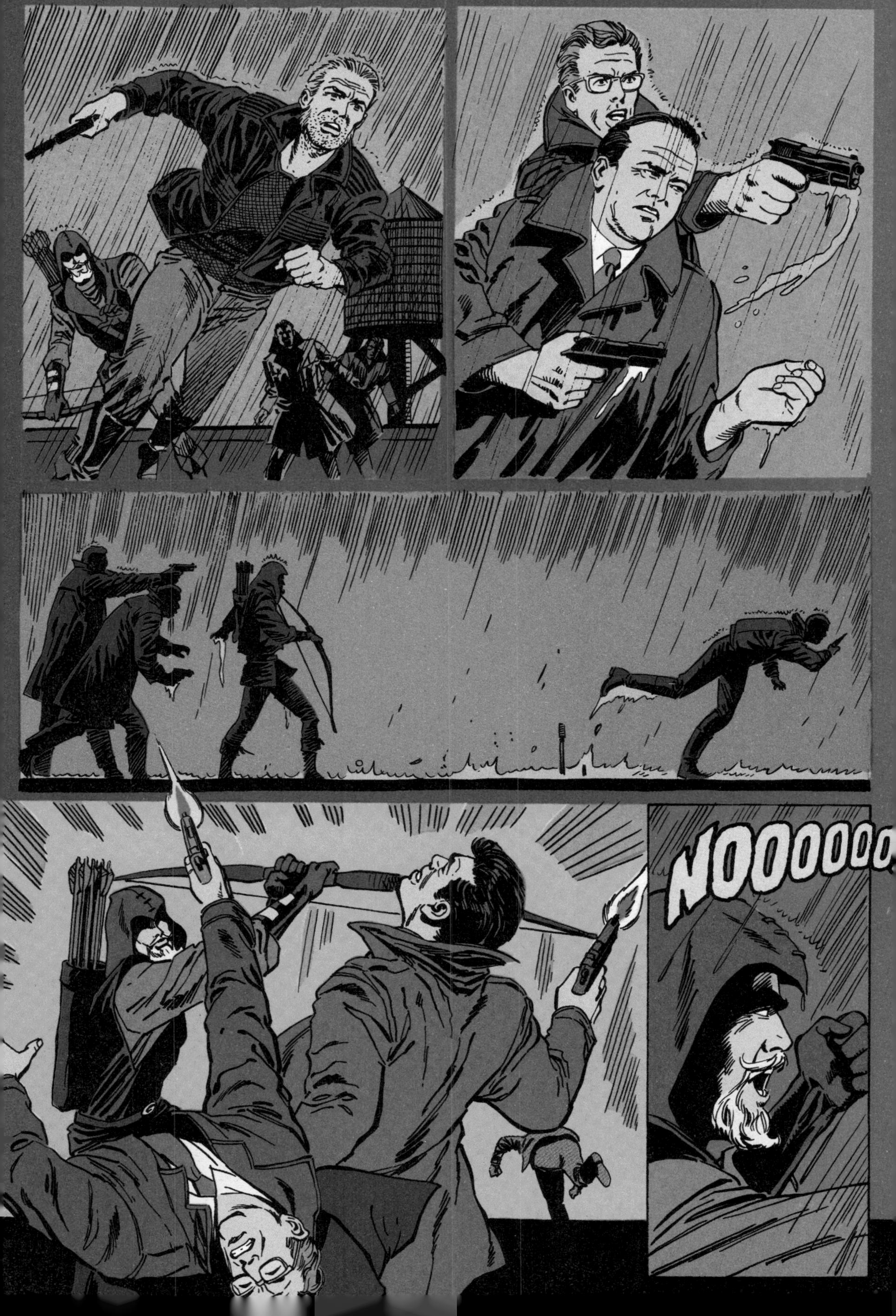
NOOOOOO!

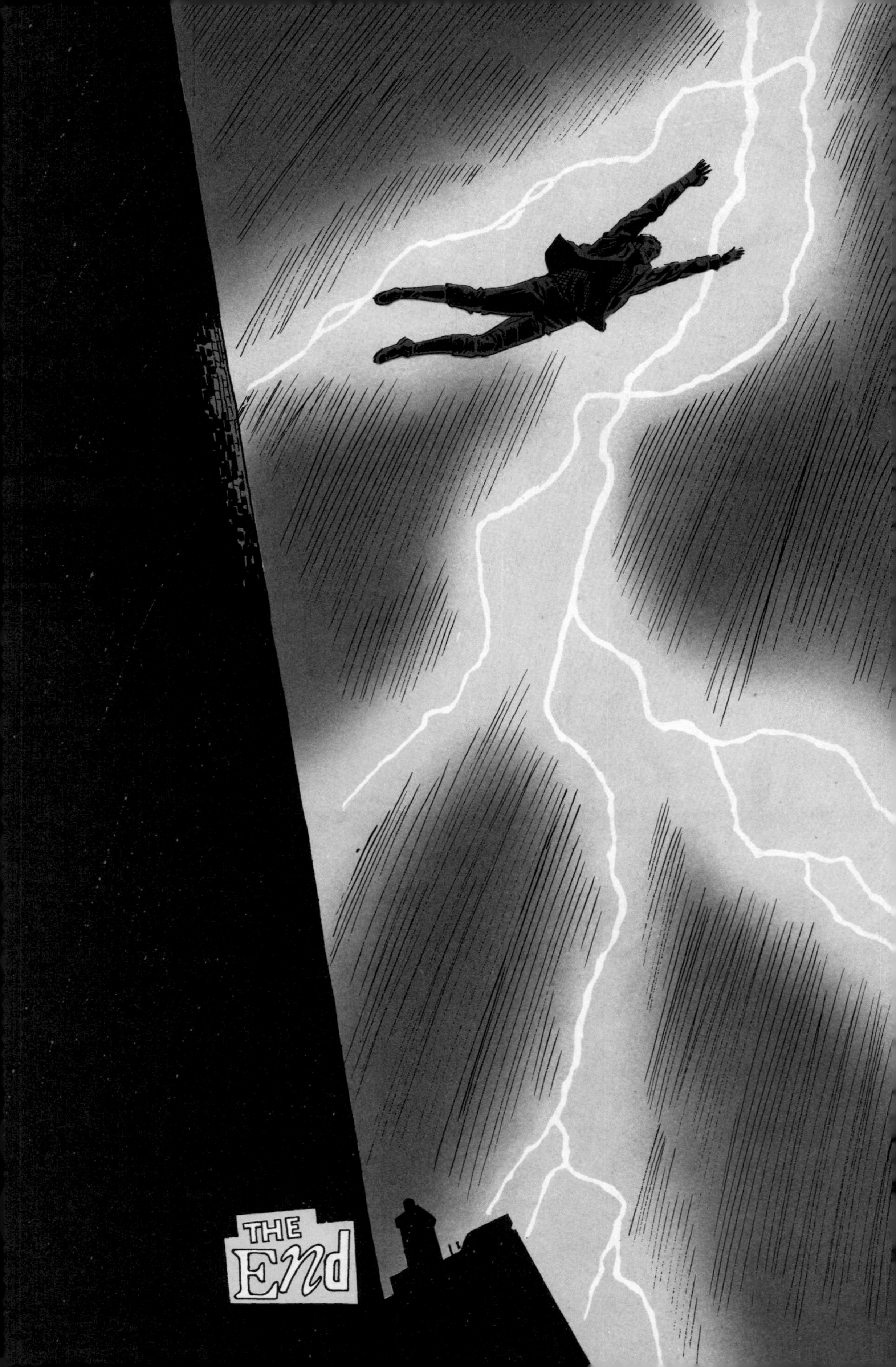
THE End

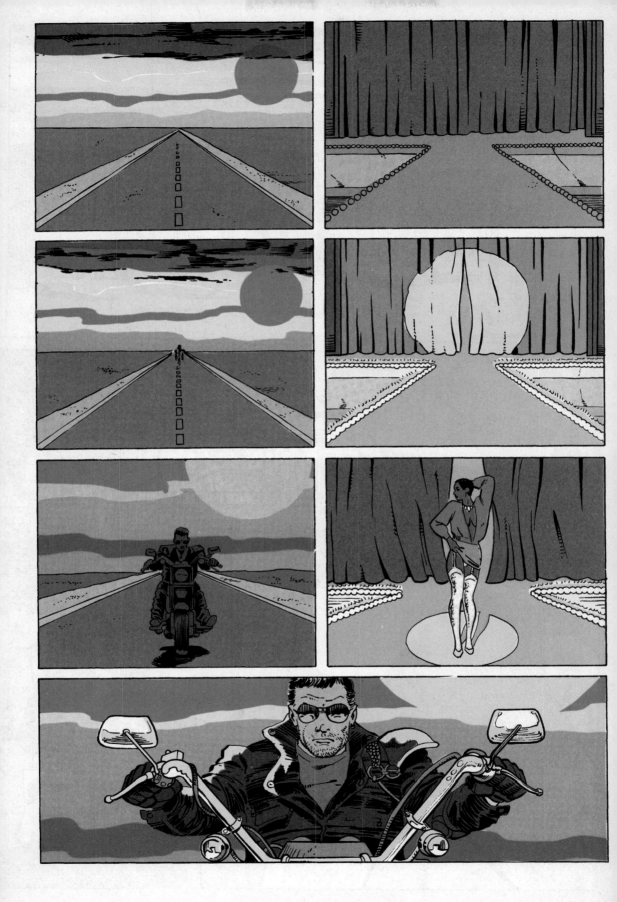

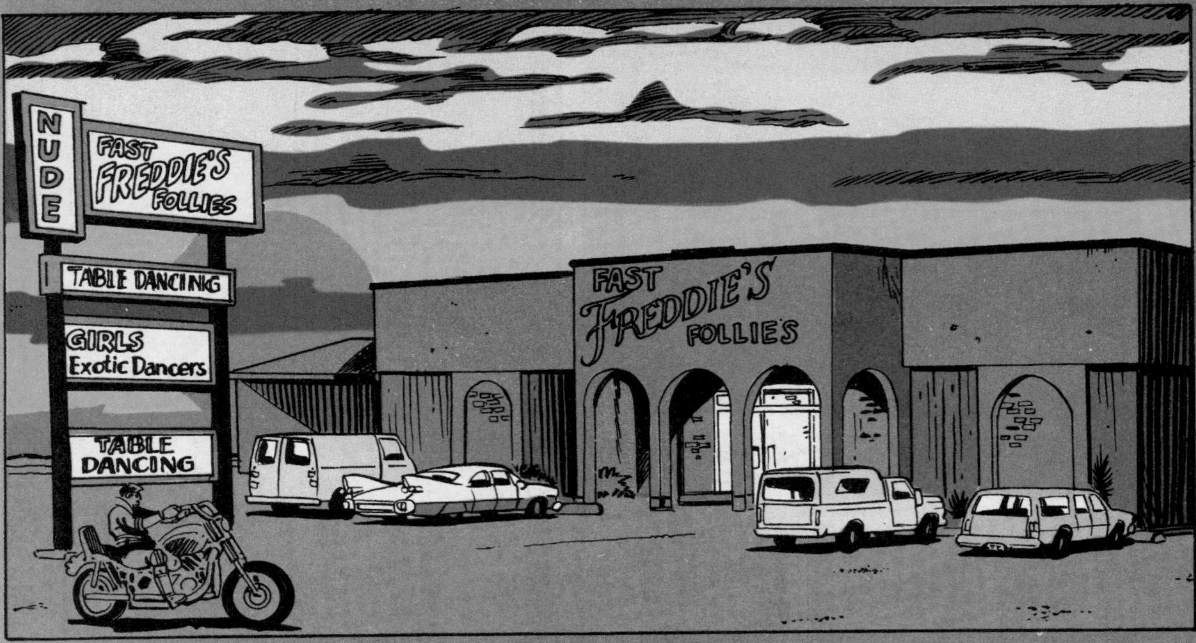
NUDE
FAST FREDDIE'S FOLLIES
TABLE DANCING
GIRLS
Exotic Dancers
TABLE DANCING
FAST FREDDIE'S FOLLIES

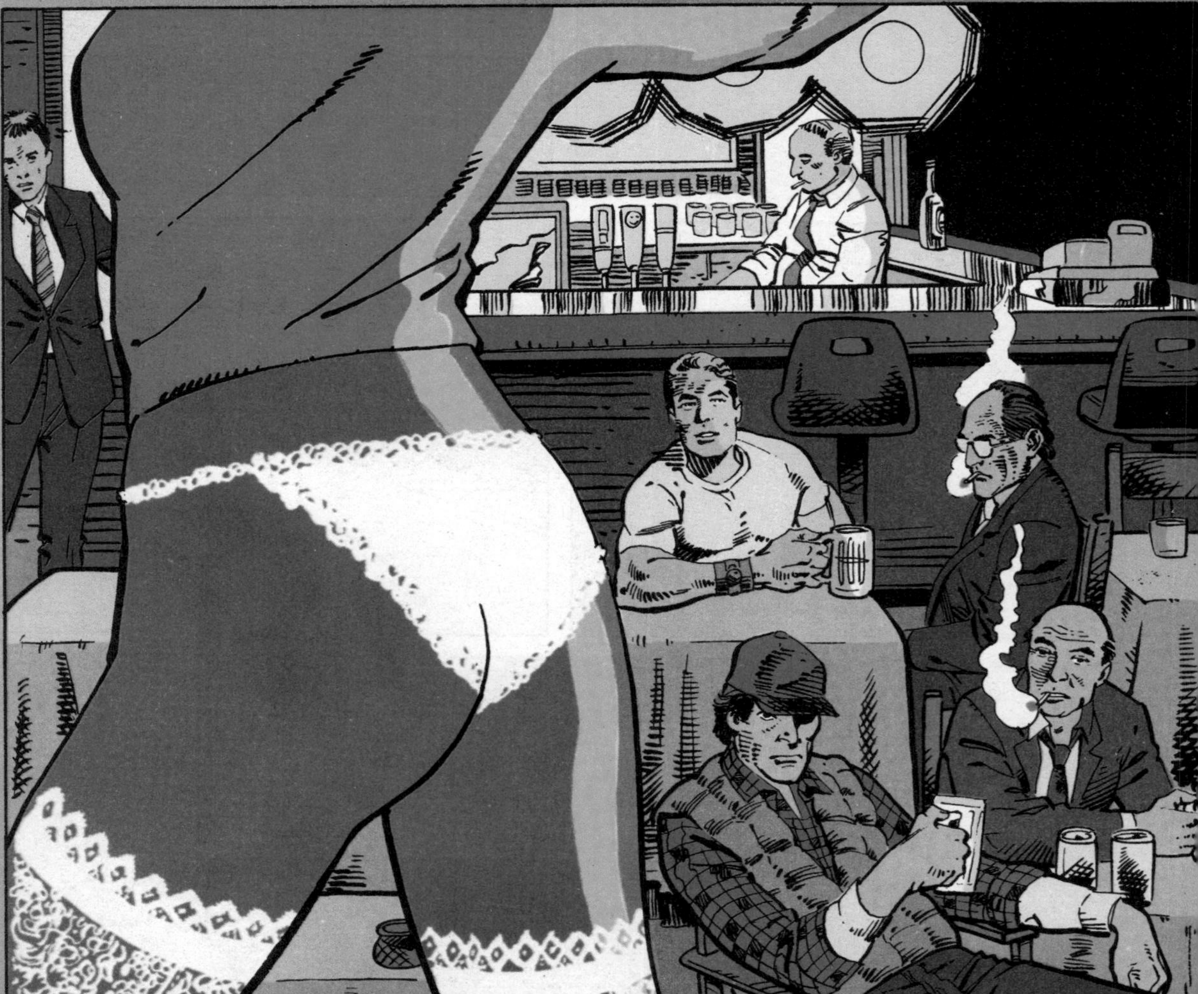

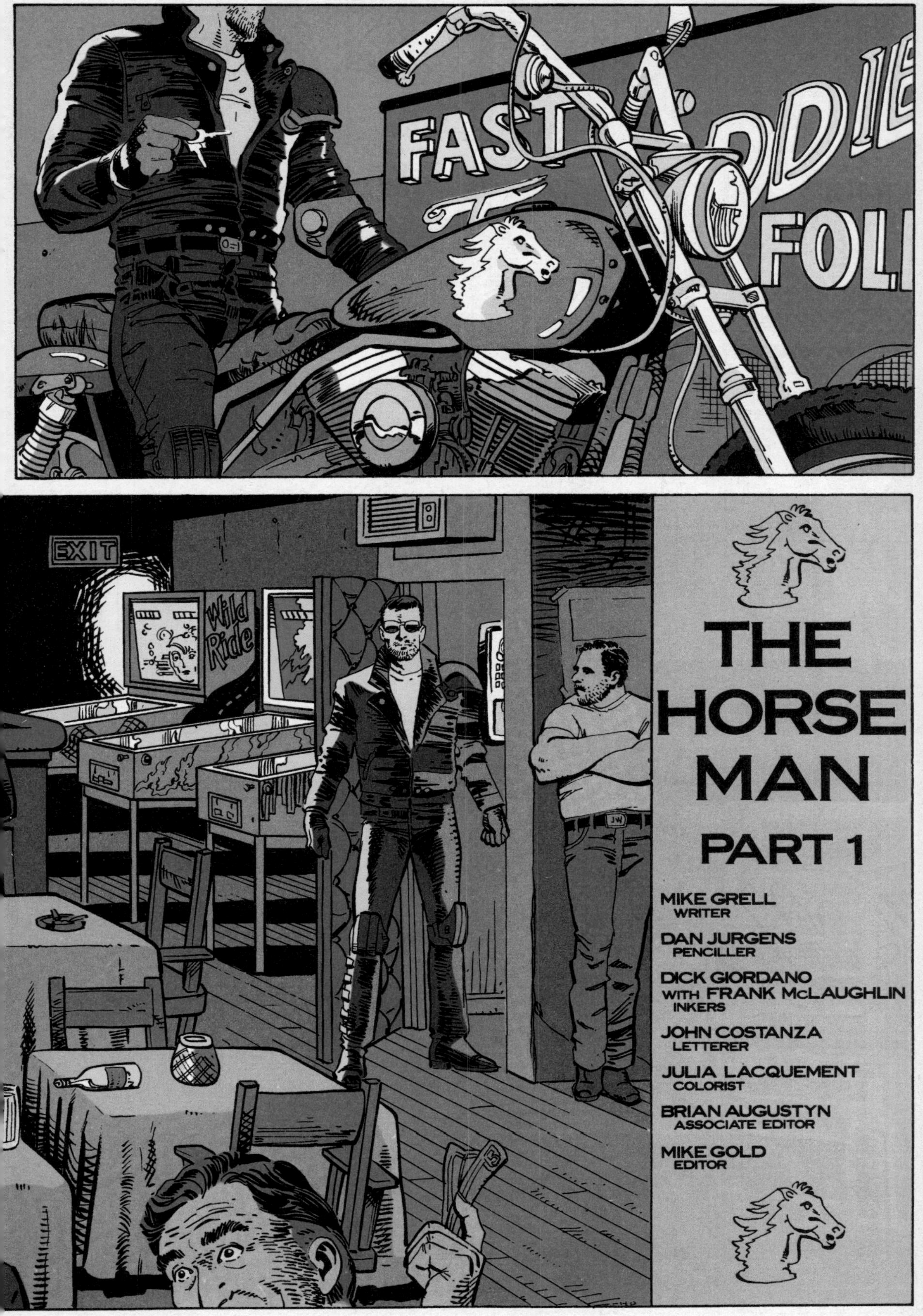
FAST
ODIE
FOLI
EXIT
Wild Ride
THE HORSE MAN
PART 1
MIKE GRELL
WRITER
DAN JURGENS
PENCILLER
DICK GIORDANO
WITH FRANK McLAUGHLIN
INKERS
JOHN COSTANZA
LETTERER
JULIA LACQUEMENT
COLORIST
BRIAN AUGUSTYN
ASSOCIATE EDITOR
MIKE GOLD
EDITOR

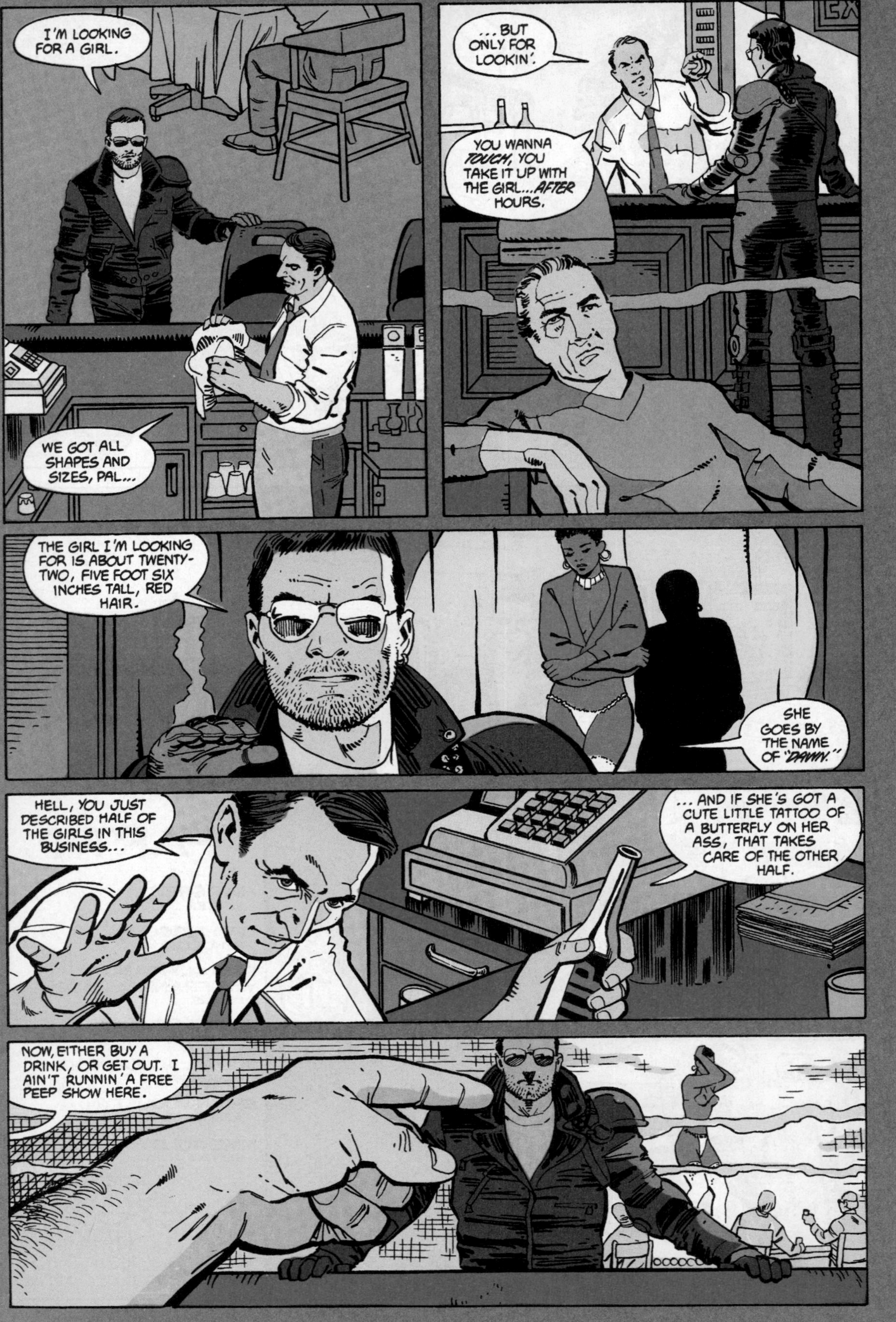
I'M LOOKING FOR A GIRL.
WE GOT ALL SHAPES AND SIZES, PAL...
...BUT ONLY FOR LOOKIN'.
YOU WANNA TOUCH, YOU TAKE IT UP WITH THE GIRL... AFTER HOURS.
THE GIRL I'M LOOKING FOR IS ABOUT TWENTY-TWO, FIVE FOOT SIX INCHES TALL, RED HAIR.
SHE GOES BY THE NAME OF "DAWN."
HELL, YOU JUST DESCRIBED HALF OF THE GIRLS IN THIS BUSINESS...
...AND IF SHE'S GOT A CUTE LITTLE TATTOO OF A BUTTERFLY ON HER ASS, THAT TAKES CARE OF THE OTHER HALF.
NOW, EITHER BUY A DRINK, OR GET OUT. I AIN'T RUNNIN' A FREE PEEP SHOW HERE.

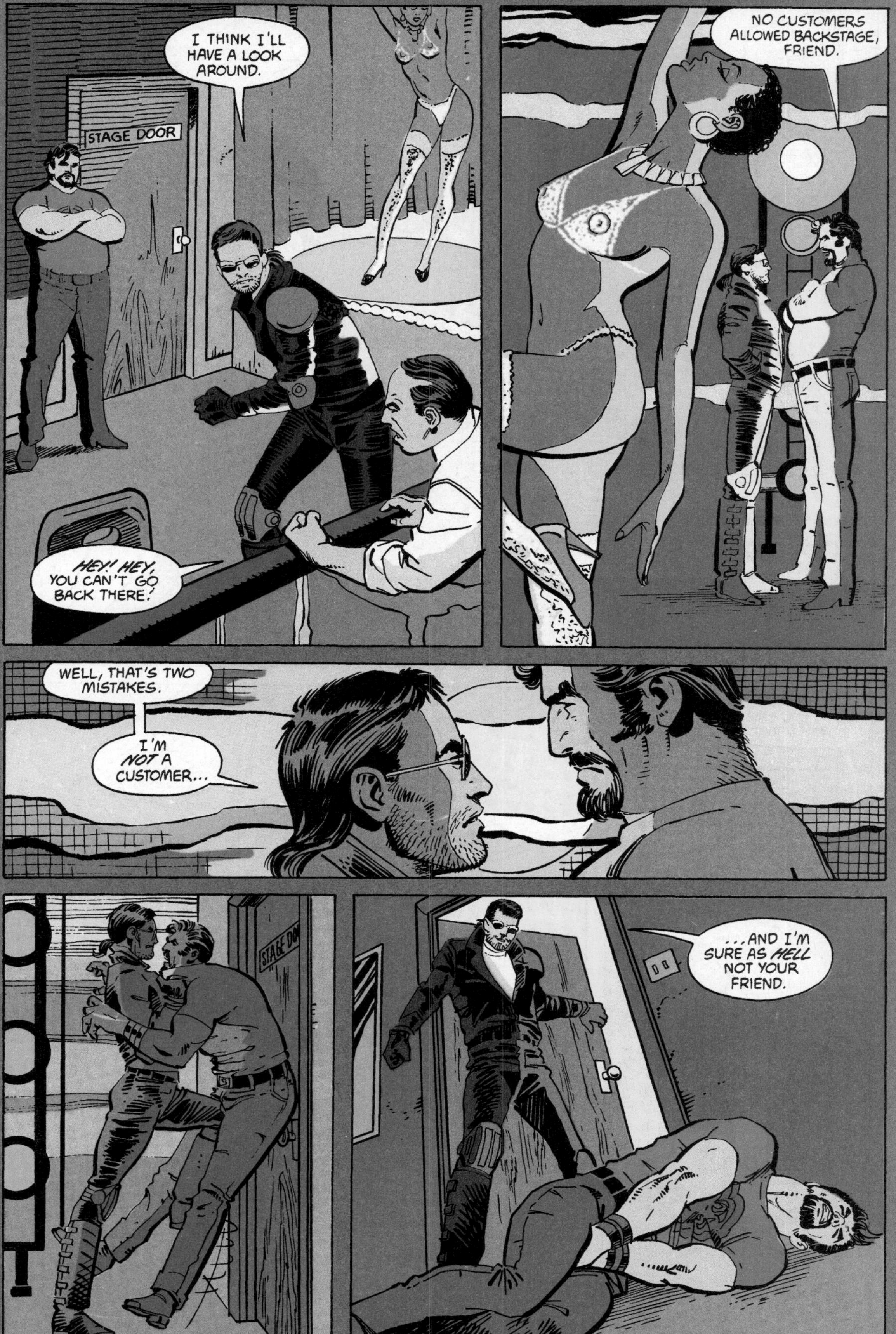
I THINK I'LL HAVE A LOOK AROUND.
STAGE DOOR
HEY! HEY, YOU CAN'T GO BACK THERE!
NO CUSTOMERS ALLOWED BACKSTAGE, FRIEND.
WELL, THAT'S TWO MISTAKES.
I'M NOT A CUSTOMER...
...AND I'M SURE AS HELL NOT YOUR FRIEND.

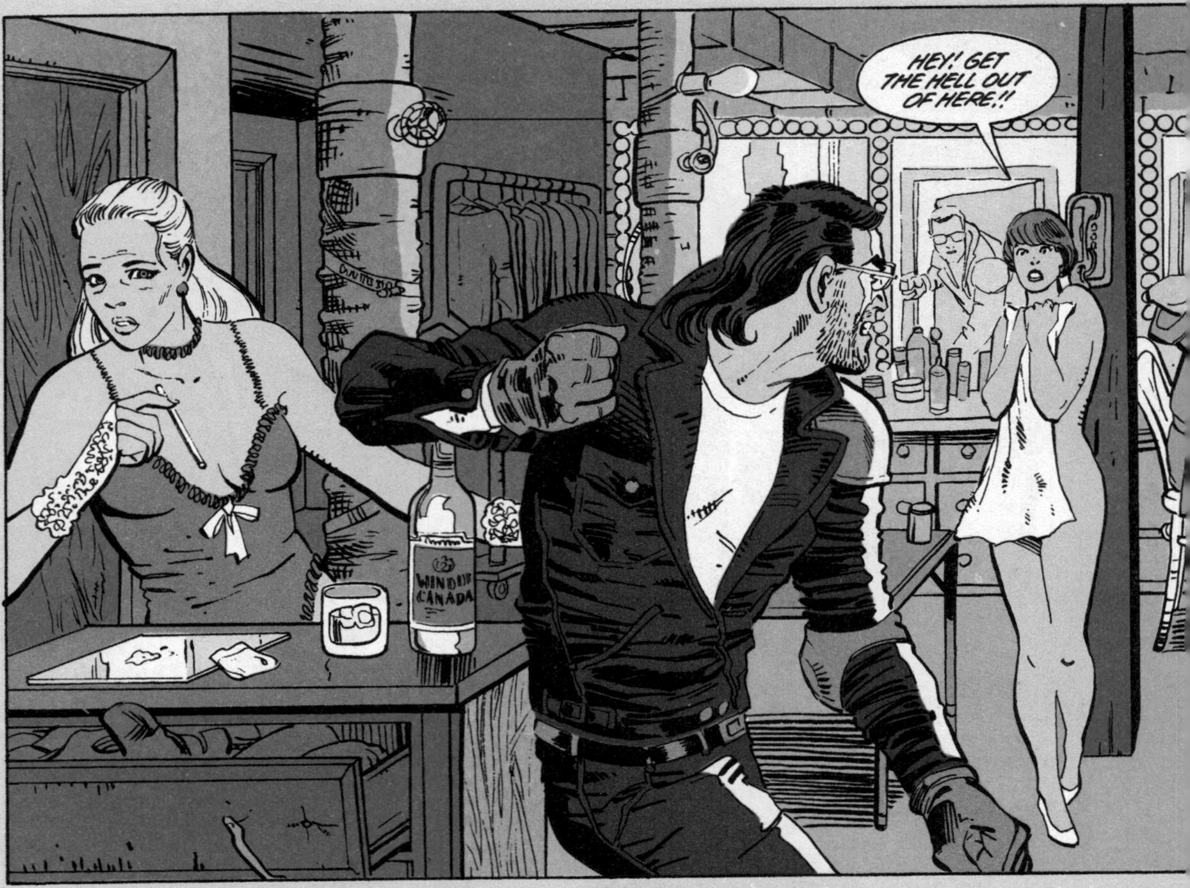
HEY! GET THE HELL OUT OF HERE!!
WINDSOR CANADA

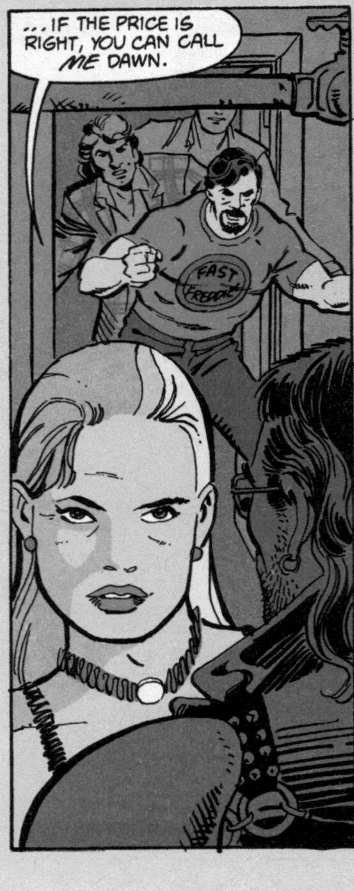
...IF THE PRICE IS RIGHT, YOU CAN CALL ME DAWN.
FAST FREDDIE'S

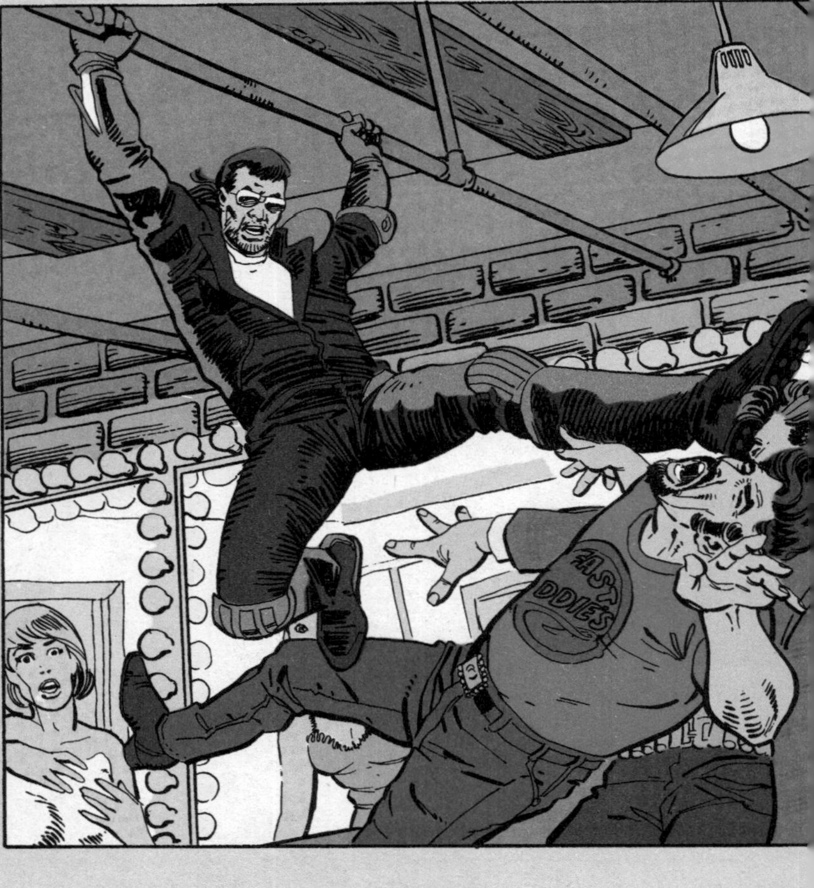
FAST DDIES

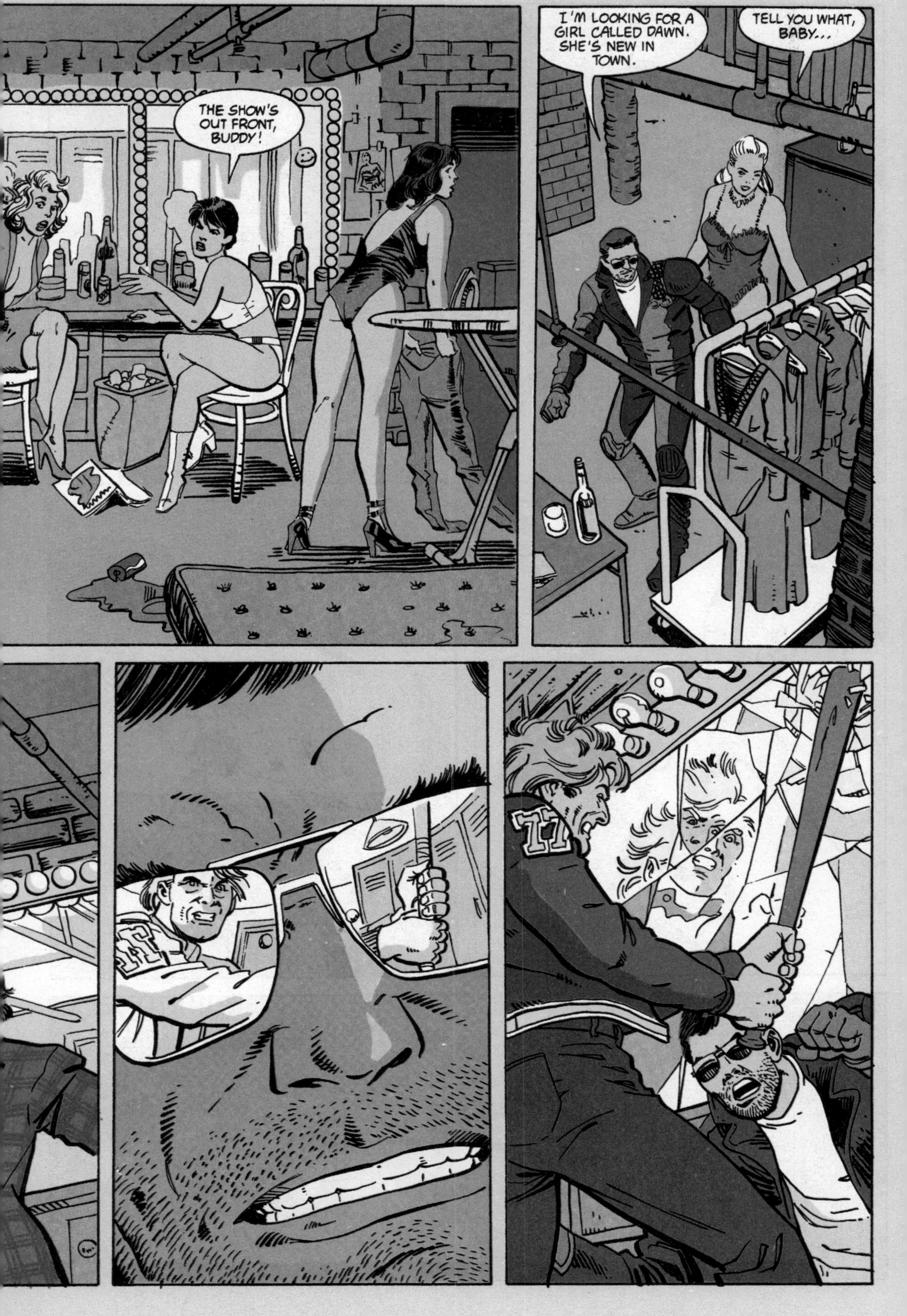
THE SHOW'S OUT FRONT, BUDDY!
I'M LOOKING FOR A GIRL CALLED DAWN. SHE'S NEW IN TOWN.
TELL YOU WHAT, BABY...

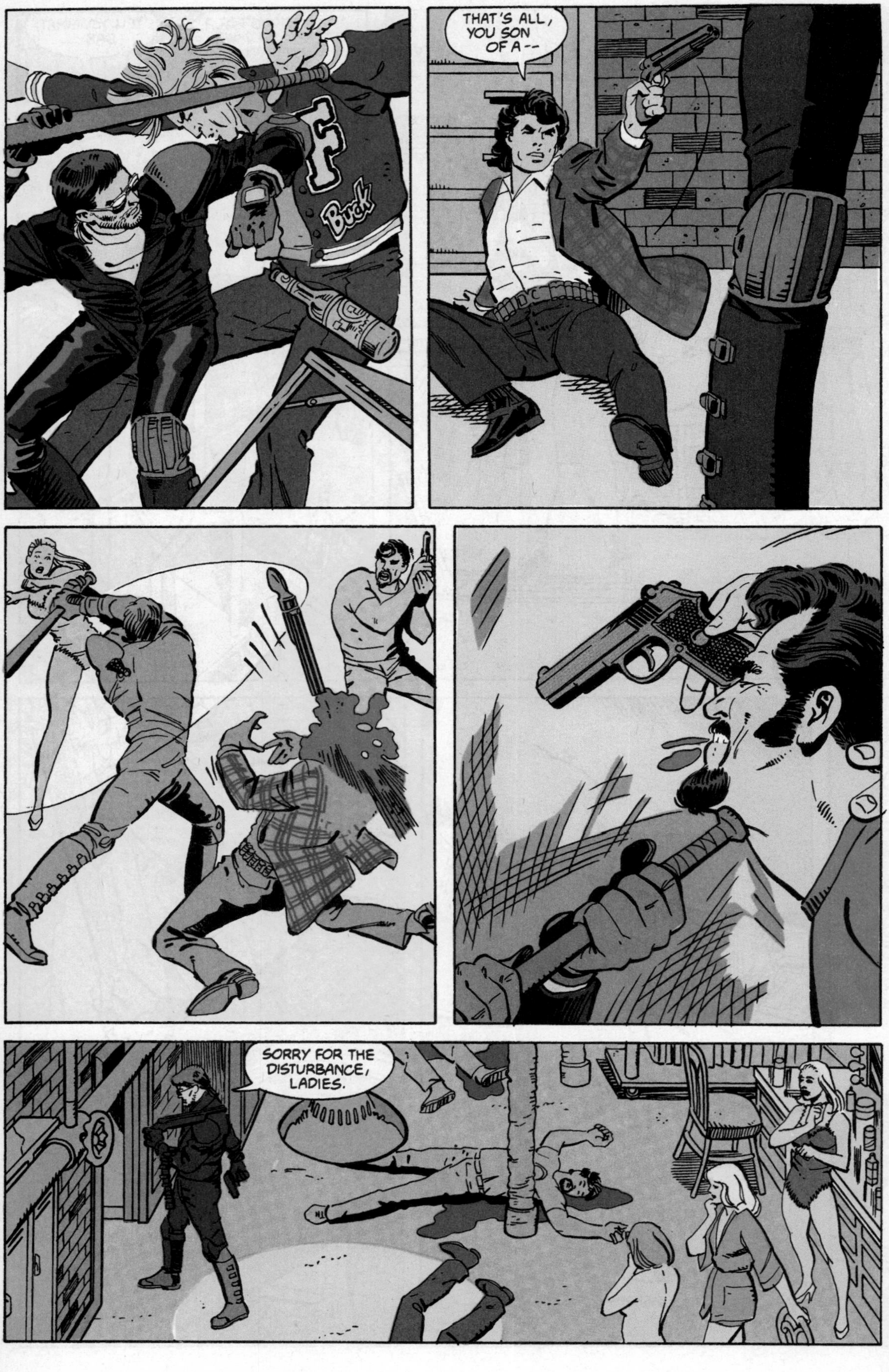
THAT'S ALL, YOU SON OF A--
SORRY FOR THE DISTURBANCE, LADIES.

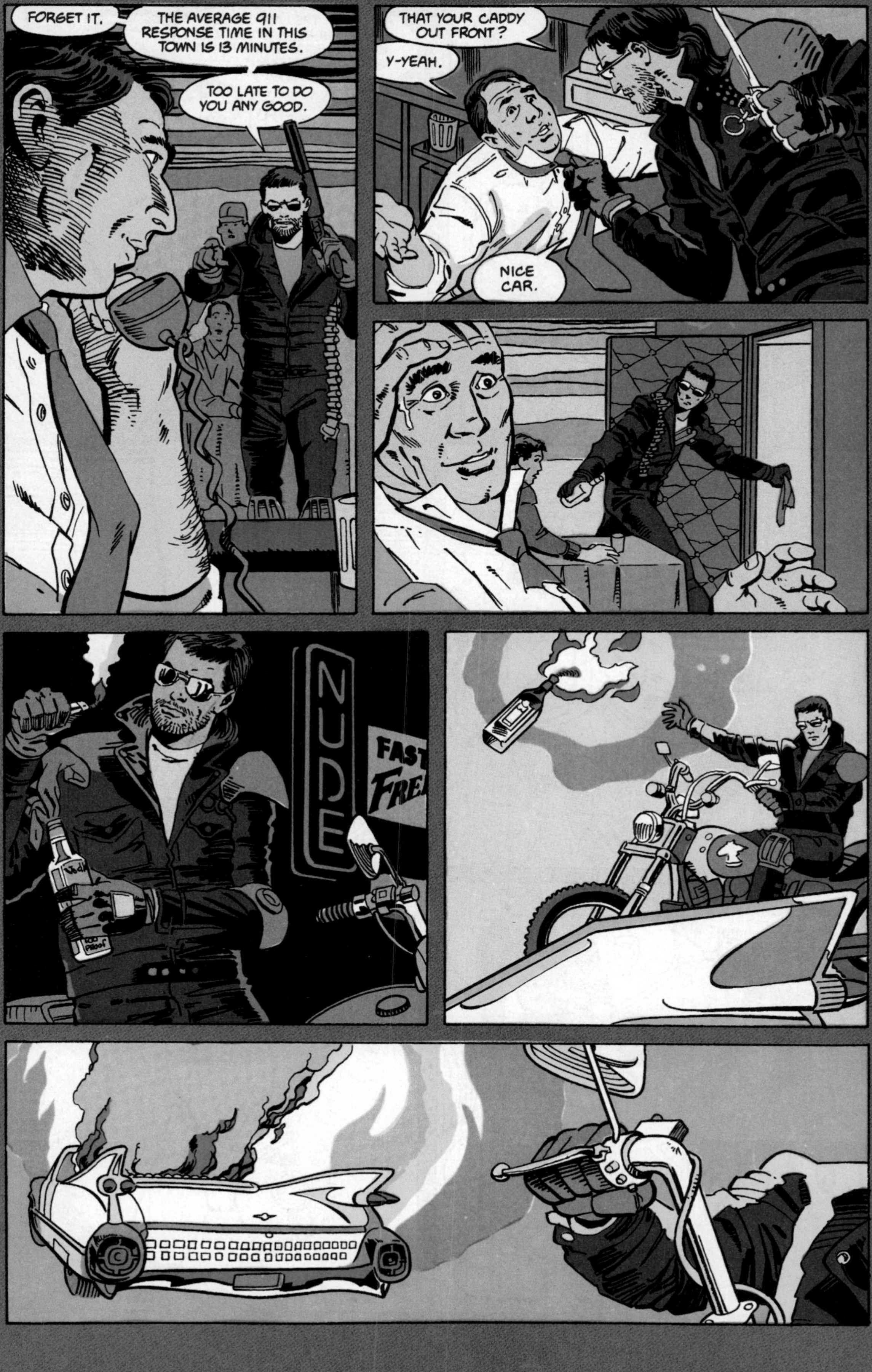
FORGET IT.
THE AVERAGE 911 RESPONSE TIME IN THIS TOWN IS 13 MINUTES.
TOO LATE TO DO YOU ANY GOOD.
THAT YOUR CADDY OUT FRONT?
Y-YEAH.
NICE CAR.
NUDE
FAST
FREE

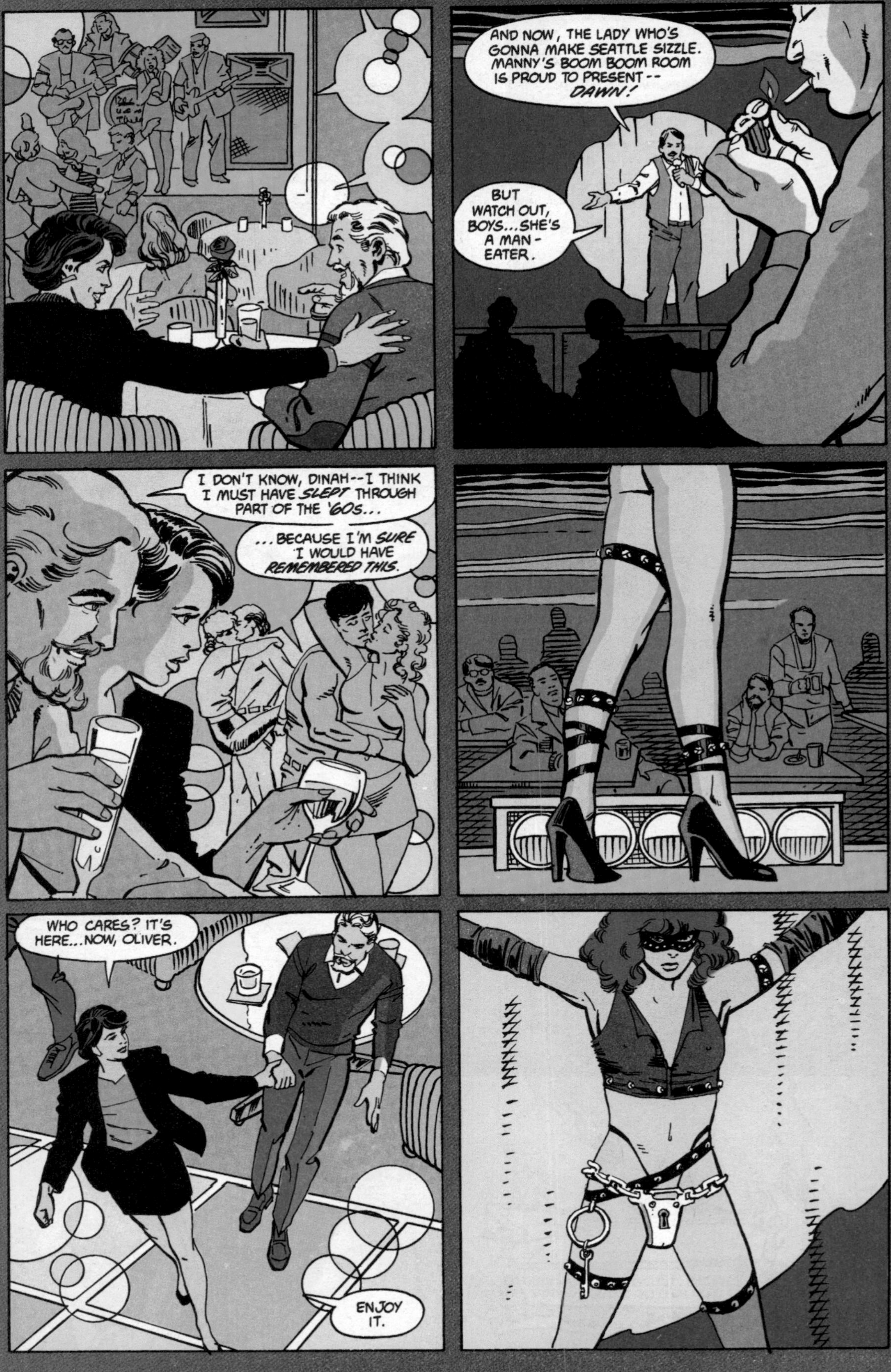
AND NOW, THE LADY WHO'S GONNA MAKE SEATTLE SIZZLE. MANNY'S BOOM BOOM ROOM IS PROUD TO PRESENT -- DAWN!
BUT WATCH OUT, BOYS... SHE'S A MAN-EATER.
I DON'T KNOW, DINAH-- I THINK I MUST HAVE SLEPT THROUGH PART OF THE '60s...
...BECAUSE I'M SURE I WOULD HAVE REMEMBERED THIS.
WHO CARES? IT'S HERE... NOW, OLIVER.
ENJOY IT.

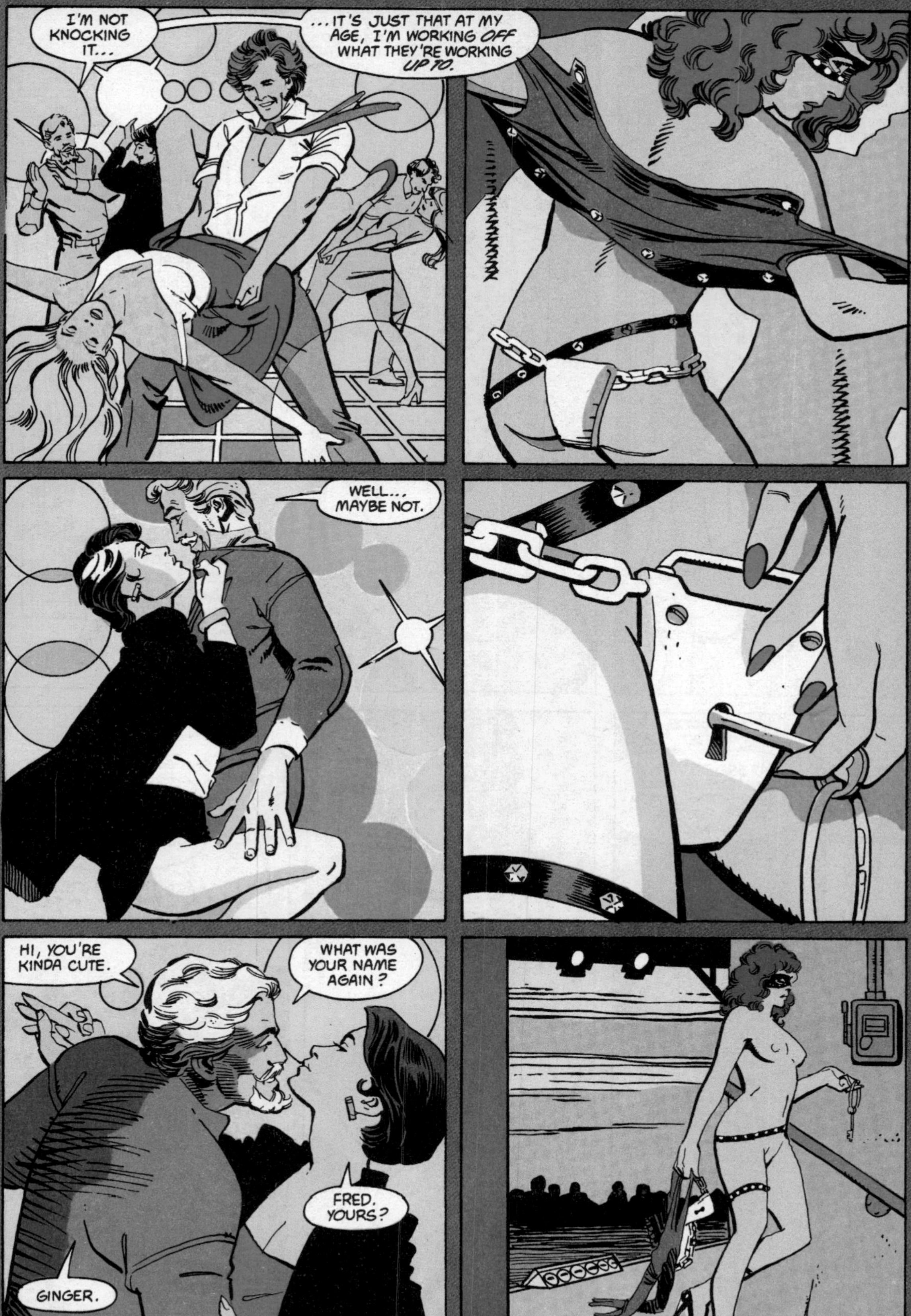
I'M NOT KNOCKING IT...
...IT'S JUST THAT AT MY AGE, I'M WORKING *OFF* WHAT THEY'RE WORKING *UP TO*.
WELL... MAYBE NOT.
HI, YOU'RE KINDA CUTE.
WHAT WAS YOUR NAME AGAIN?
FRED. YOURS?
GINGER.

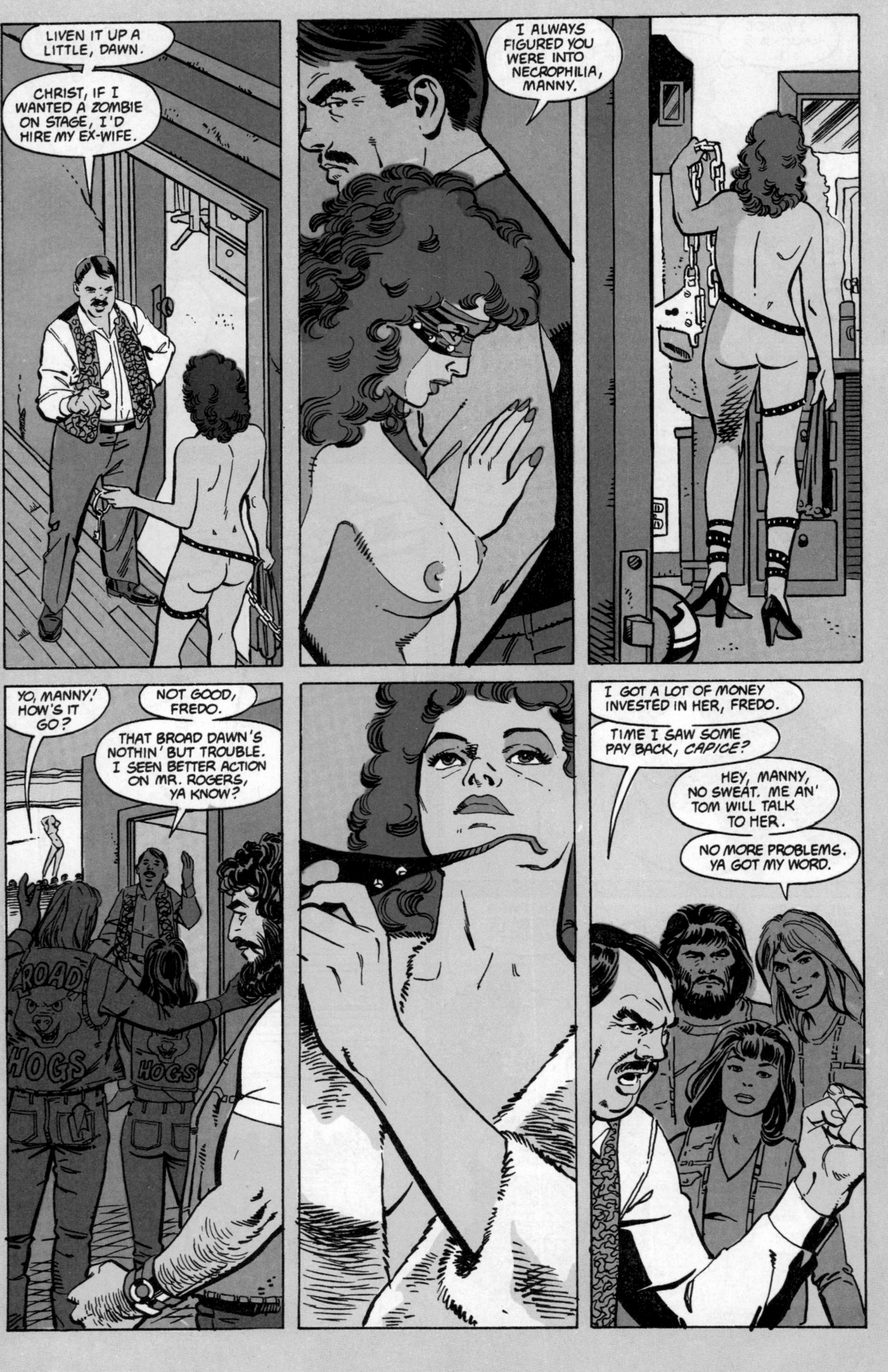

LIVEN IT UP A LITTLE, DAWN.
CHRIST, IF I WANTED A ZOMBIE ON STAGE, I'D HIRE MY EX-WIFE.
I ALWAYS FIGURED YOU WERE INTO NECROPHILIA, MANNY.
YO, MANNY! HOW'S IT GO?
NOT GOOD, FREDO.
THAT BROAD DAWN'S NOTHIN' BUT TROUBLE. I SEEN BETTER ACTION ON MR. ROGERS, YA KNOW?
ROAD HOGS
HOGS
I GOT A LOT OF MONEY INVESTED IN HER, FREDO.
TIME I SAW SOME PAY BACK, *CAPICE?*
HEY, MANNY, NO SWEAT. ME AN' TOM WILL TALK TO HER.
NO MORE PROBLEMS. YA GOT MY WORD.

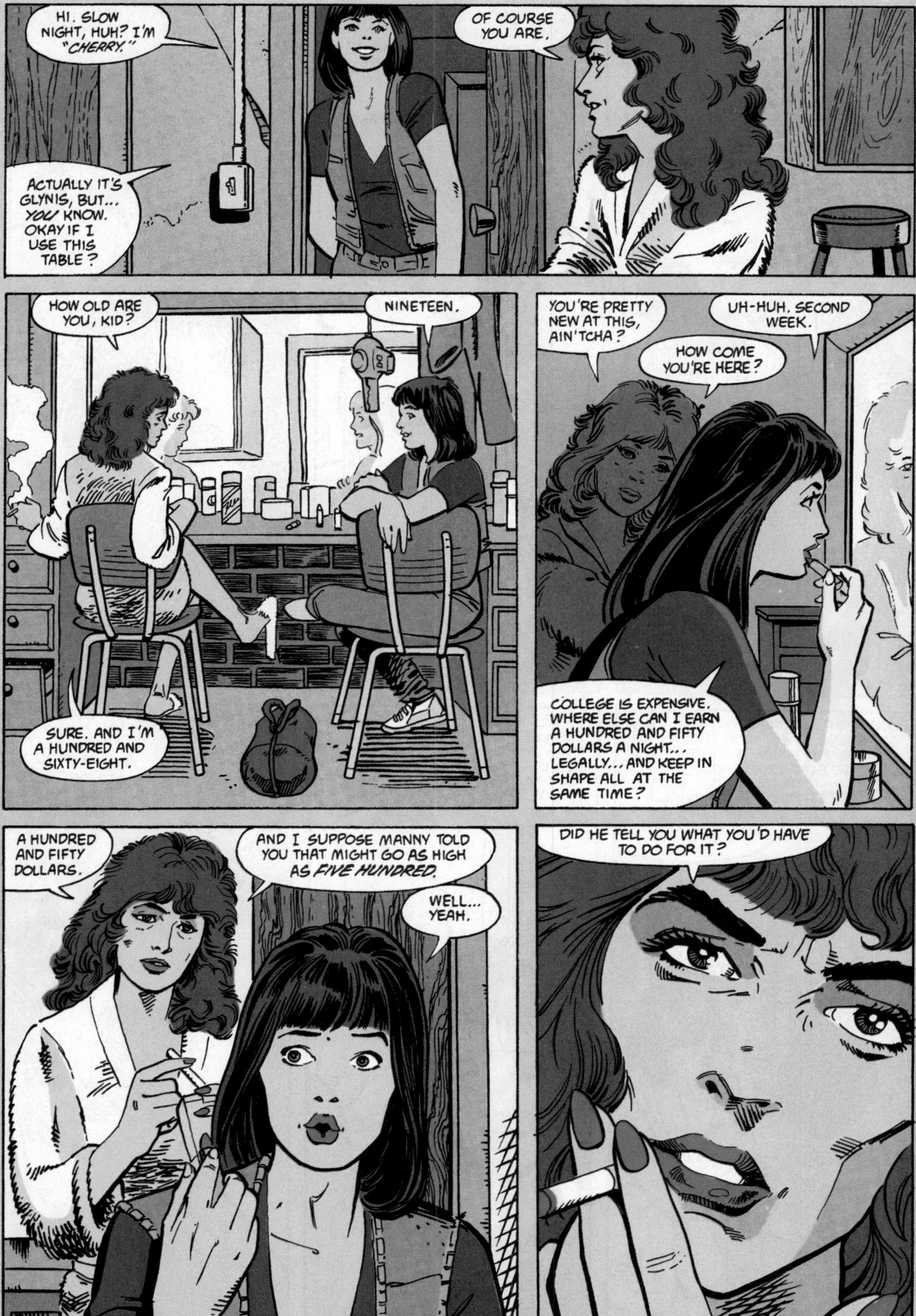
HI. SLOW NIGHT, HUH? I'M "CHERRY."
OF COURSE YOU ARE.
ACTUALLY IT'S GLYNIS, BUT... YOU KNOW. OKAY IF I USE THIS TABLE?
HOW OLD ARE YOU, KID?
NINETEEN.
SURE. AND I'M A HUNDRED AND SIXTY-EIGHT.
YOU'RE PRETTY NEW AT THIS, AIN'TCHA?
UH-HUH. SECOND WEEK.
HOW COME YOU'RE HERE?
COLLEGE IS EXPENSIVE. WHERE ELSE CAN I EARN A HUNDRED AND FIFTY DOLLARS A NIGHT... LEGALLY... AND KEEP IN SHAPE ALL AT THE SAME TIME?
A HUNDRED AND FIFTY DOLLARS.
AND I SUPPOSE MANNY TOLD YOU THAT MIGHT GO AS HIGH AS FIVE HUNDRED.
WELL... YEAH.
DID HE TELL YOU WHAT YOU'D HAVE TO DO FOR IT?

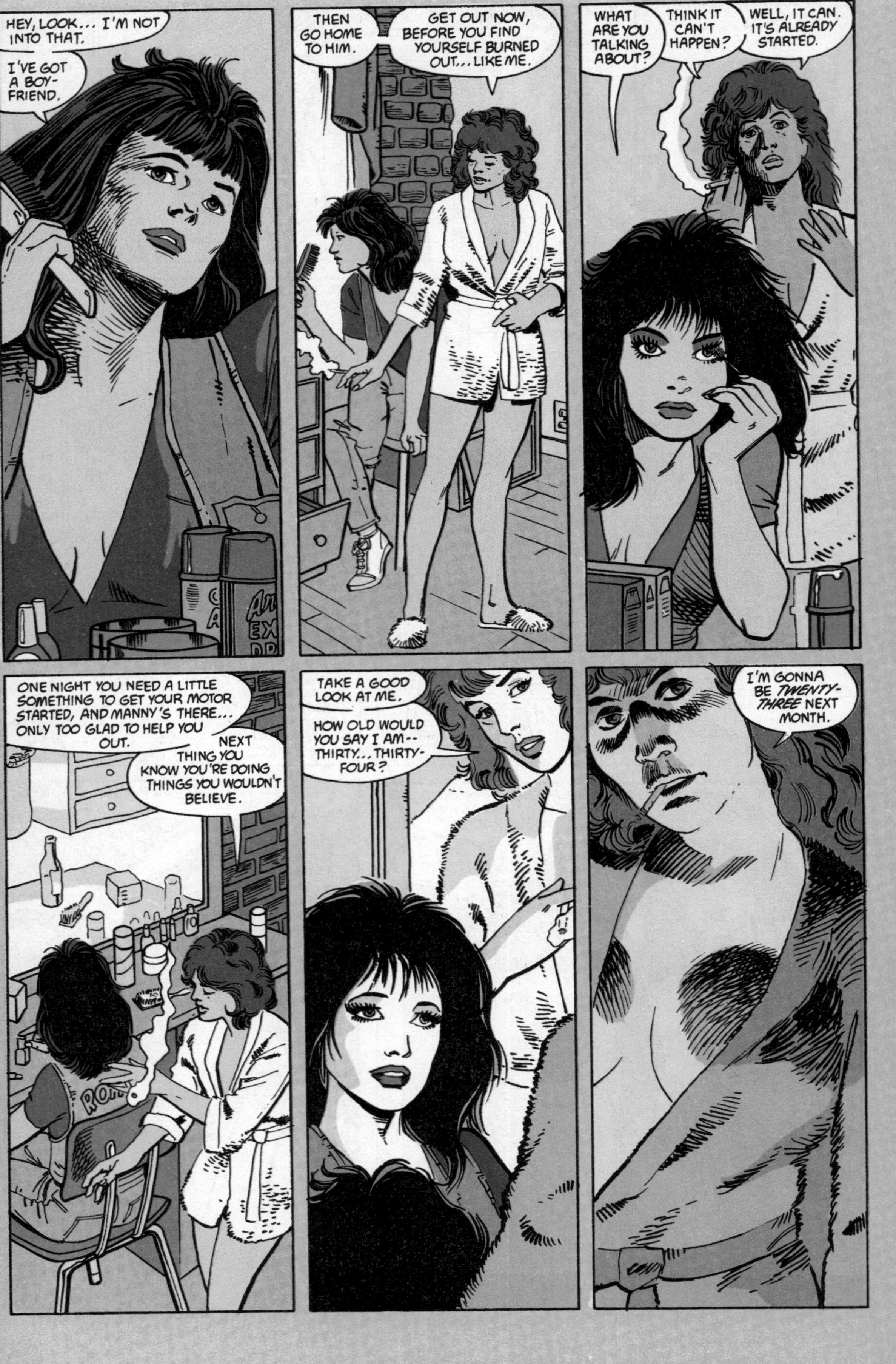
HEY, LOOK... I'M NOT INTO THAT.
I'VE GOT A BOY-FRIEND.
THEN GO HOME TO HIM.
GET OUT NOW, BEFORE YOU FIND YOURSELF BURNED OUT... LIKE ME.
WHAT ARE YOU TALKING ABOUT?
THINK IT CAN'T HAPPEN?
WELL, IT CAN. IT'S ALREADY STARTED.
ONE NIGHT YOU NEED A LITTLE SOMETHING TO GET YOUR MOTOR STARTED, AND MANNY'S THERE... ONLY TOO GLAD TO HELP YOU OUT.
NEXT THING YOU KNOW YOU'RE DOING THINGS YOU WOULDN'T BELIEVE.
TAKE A GOOD LOOK AT ME.
HOW OLD WOULD YOU SAY I AM-- THIRTY... THIRTY-FOUR?
I'M GONNA BE TWENTY-THREE NEXT MONTH.

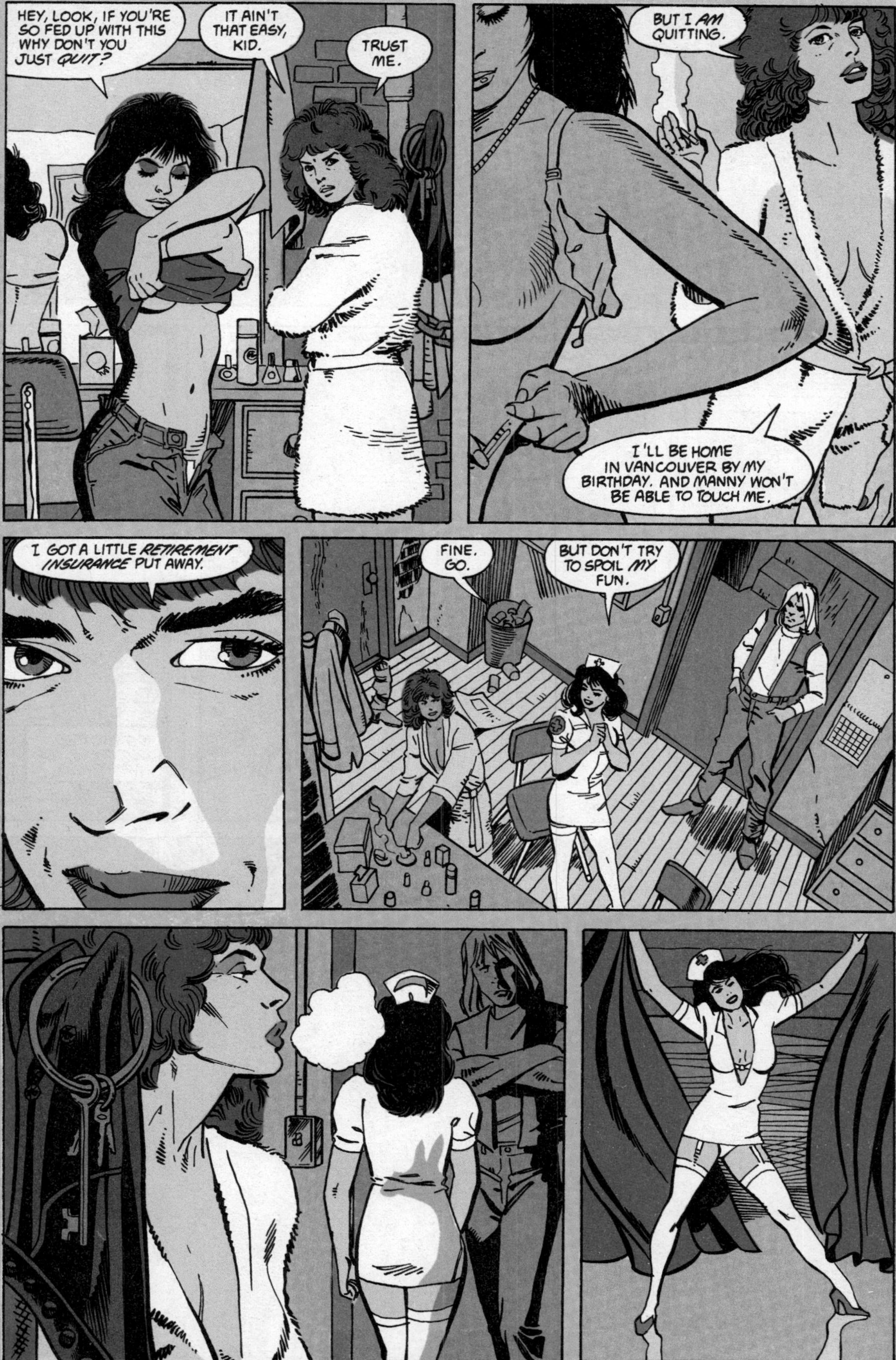
HEY, LOOK, IF YOU'RE SO FED UP WITH THIS WHY DON'T YOU JUST QUIT?
IT AIN'T THAT EASY, KID.
TRUST ME.
BUT I AM QUITTING.
I'LL BE HOME IN VANCOUVER BY MY BIRTHDAY. AND MANNY WON'T BE ABLE TO TOUCH ME.
I GOT A LITTLE RETIREMENT INSURANCE PUT AWAY.
FINE. GO.
BUT DON'T TRY TO SPOIL MY FUN.

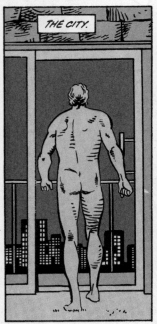

THE CITY.

SOMETHING IN THE RHYTHM THAT FLOWS WITH YOUR BLOOD.

NIGHTS LIKE THIS, IT CALLS.

WOULDN'T DO ANY GOOD TO TRY TO SLEEP ANYWAY.

SOMEWHERE OUT THERE, IT'S HAPPENING.

IT'S JUST A QUESTION OF FINDING IT.

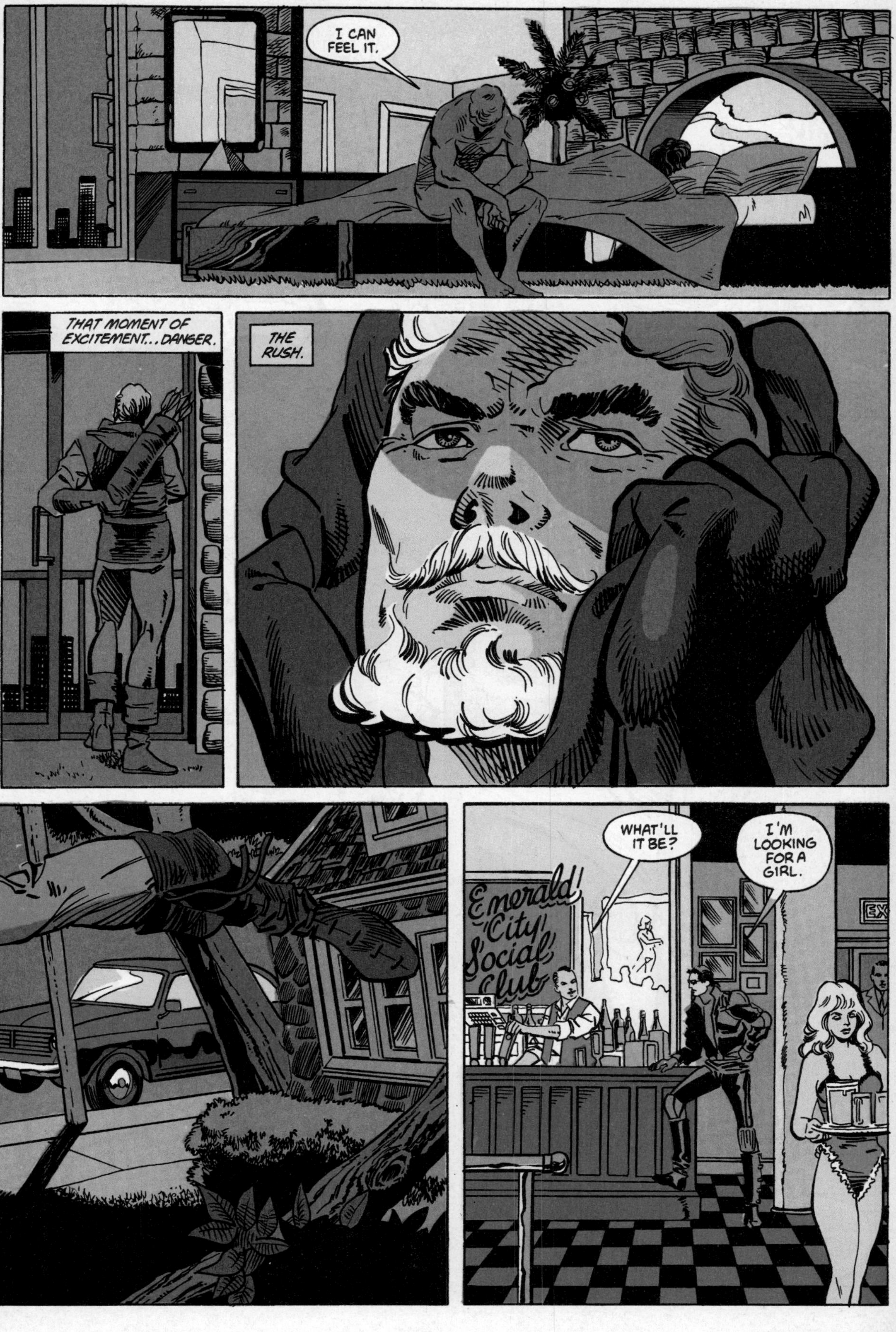
I CAN FEEL IT.
THAT MOMENT OF EXCITEMENT... DANGER.
THE RUSH.
WHAT'LL IT BE?
I'M LOOKING FOR A GIRL.
Emerald City Social Club

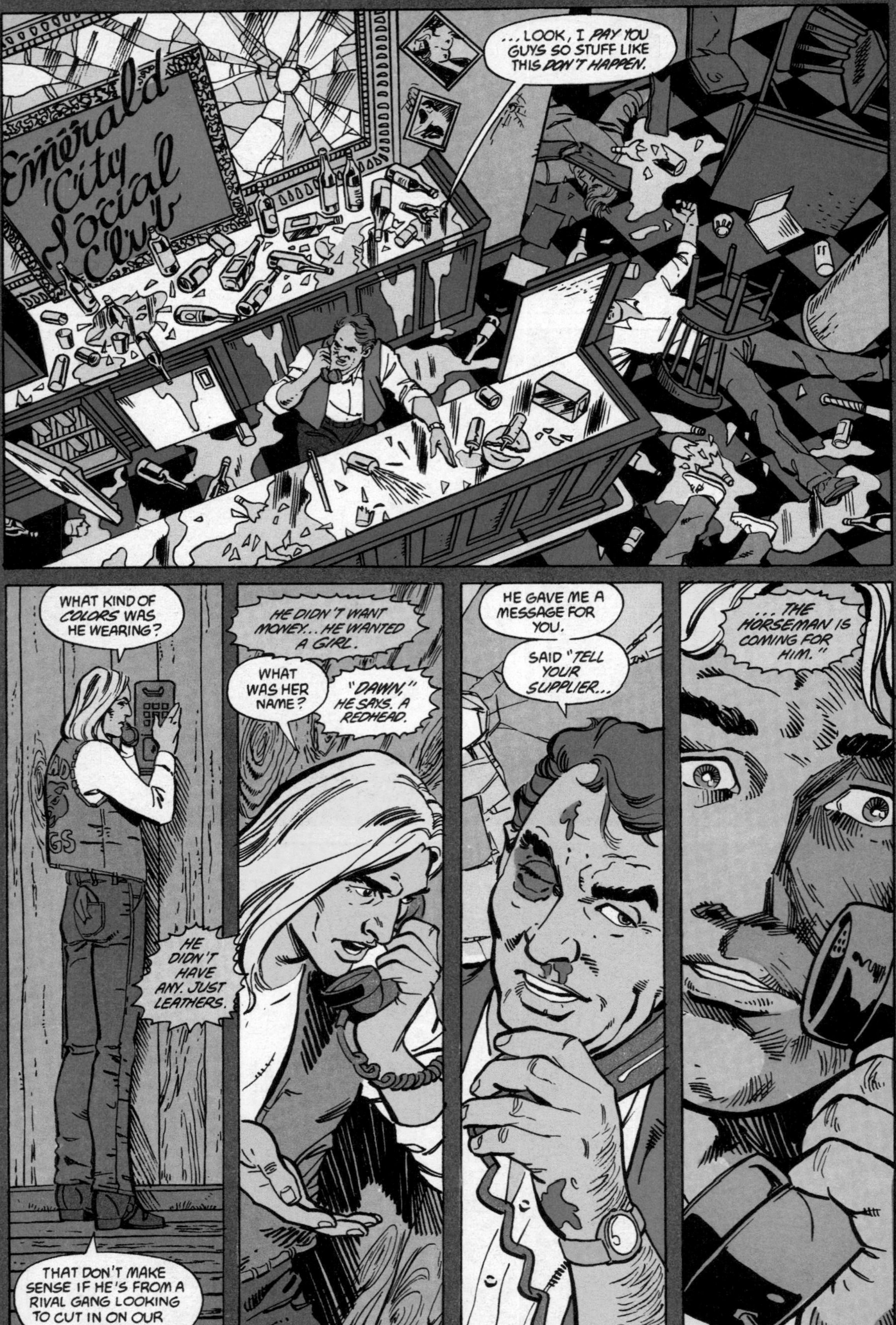

Emerald City Social Club
...LOOK, I PAY YOU GUYS SO STUFF LIKE THIS DON'T HAPPEN.
WHAT KIND OF COLORS WAS HE WEARING?
HE DIDN'T HAVE ANY. JUST LEATHERS.
THAT DON'T MAKE SENSE IF HE'S FROM A RIVAL GANG LOOKING TO CUT IN ON OUR TERRITORY...
HE DIDN'T WANT MONEY... HE WANTED A GIRL.
WHAT WAS HER NAME?
"DAWN," HE SAYS. A REDHEAD.
HE GAVE ME A MESSAGE FOR YOU.
SAID "TELL YOUR SUPPLIER...
...THE HORSEMAN IS COMING FOR HIM."

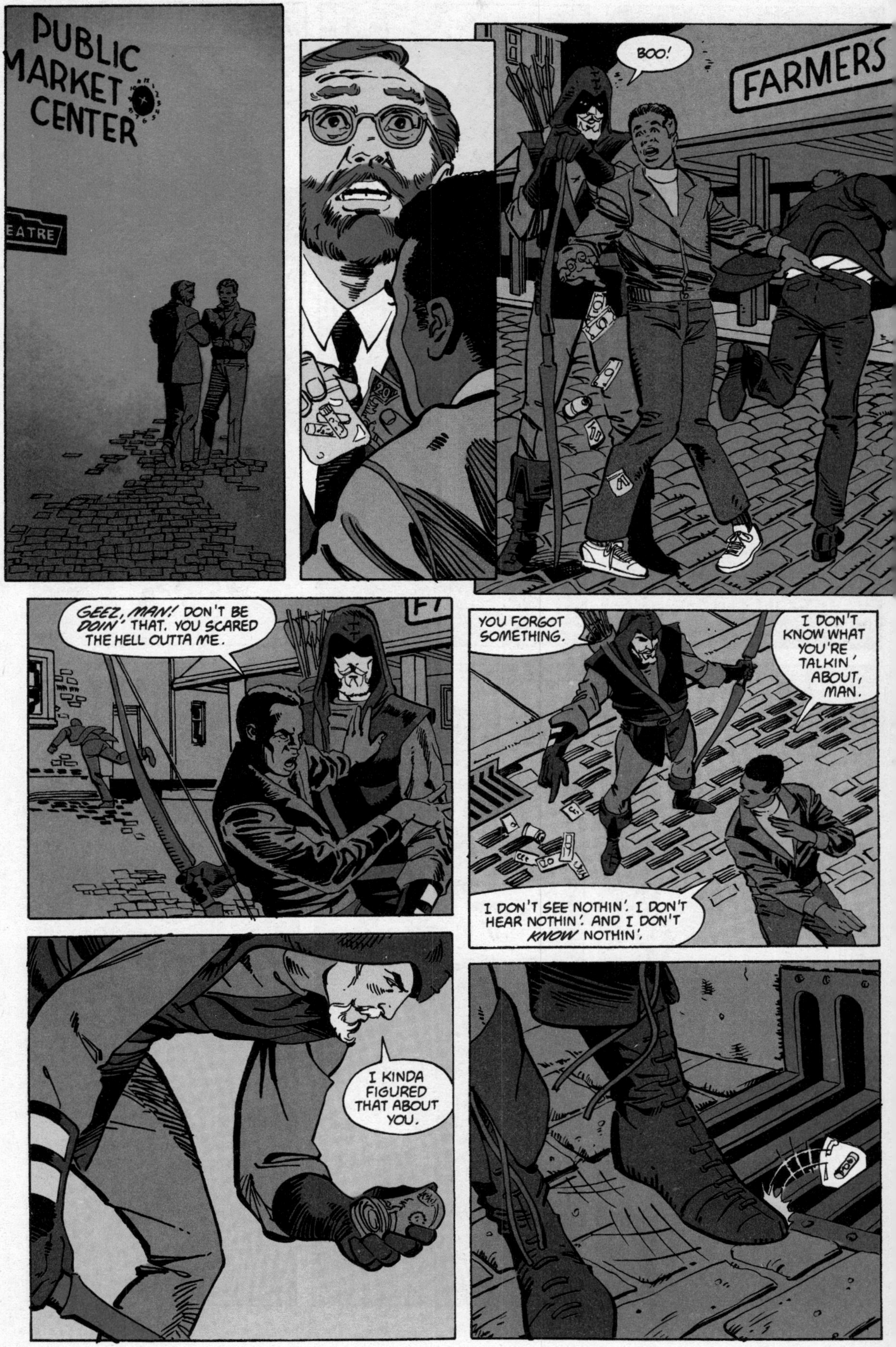
PUBLIC MARKET CENTER
EATRE
BOO!
FARMERS
GEEZ, MAN! DON'T BE DOIN' THAT. YOU SCARED THE HELL OUTTA ME.
YOU FORGOT SOMETHING.
I DON'T KNOW WHAT YOU'RE TALKIN' ABOUT, MAN.
I DON'T SEE NOTHIN'. I DON'T HEAR NOTHIN'. AND I DON'T KNOW NOTHIN'.
I KINDA FIGURED THAT ABOUT YOU.

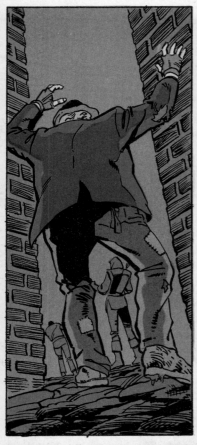

WHAT'S GOING ON, OLD TIMER?

THEY'RE GETTIN' WORSE, YA KNOW.

I SEEN SOME WEIRD SHIT, AND SOME SCARY SHIT...

BUT *NOTHING* LIKE THIS.

EVEN THE SPIDERS... NOTHING LIKE THIS.

NEVER SHOULD HAVE TRIED THAT STUFF.

HERE, POP. GET YOURSELF A ROOM...

AND PUT SOMETHING IN YOUR STOMACH BESIDES STERNO.

THEY WAS BIG HAIRY BASTARDS...TARANTULAS.

BUT NOTHING LIKE THIS.

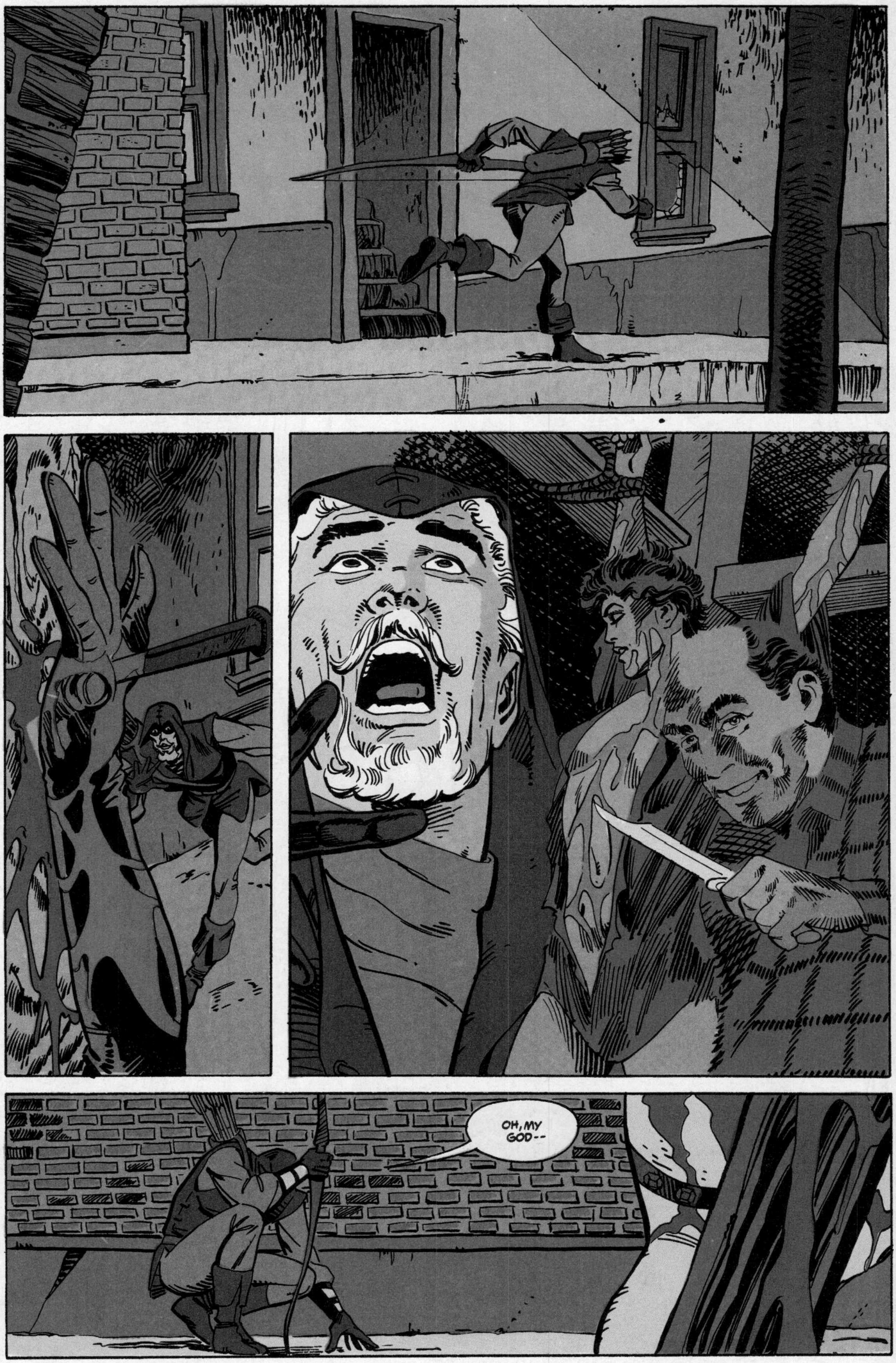
OH, MY GOD--

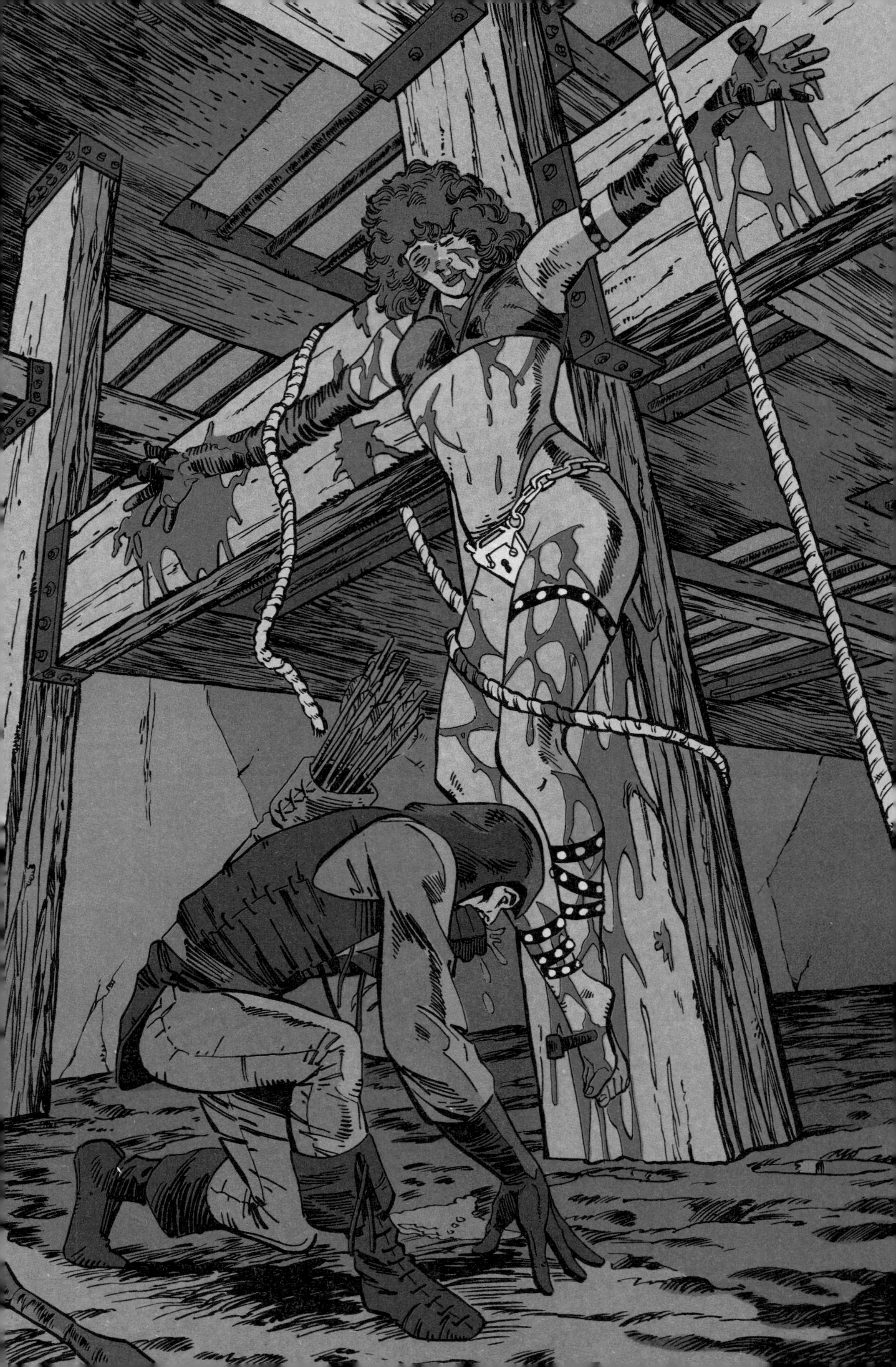

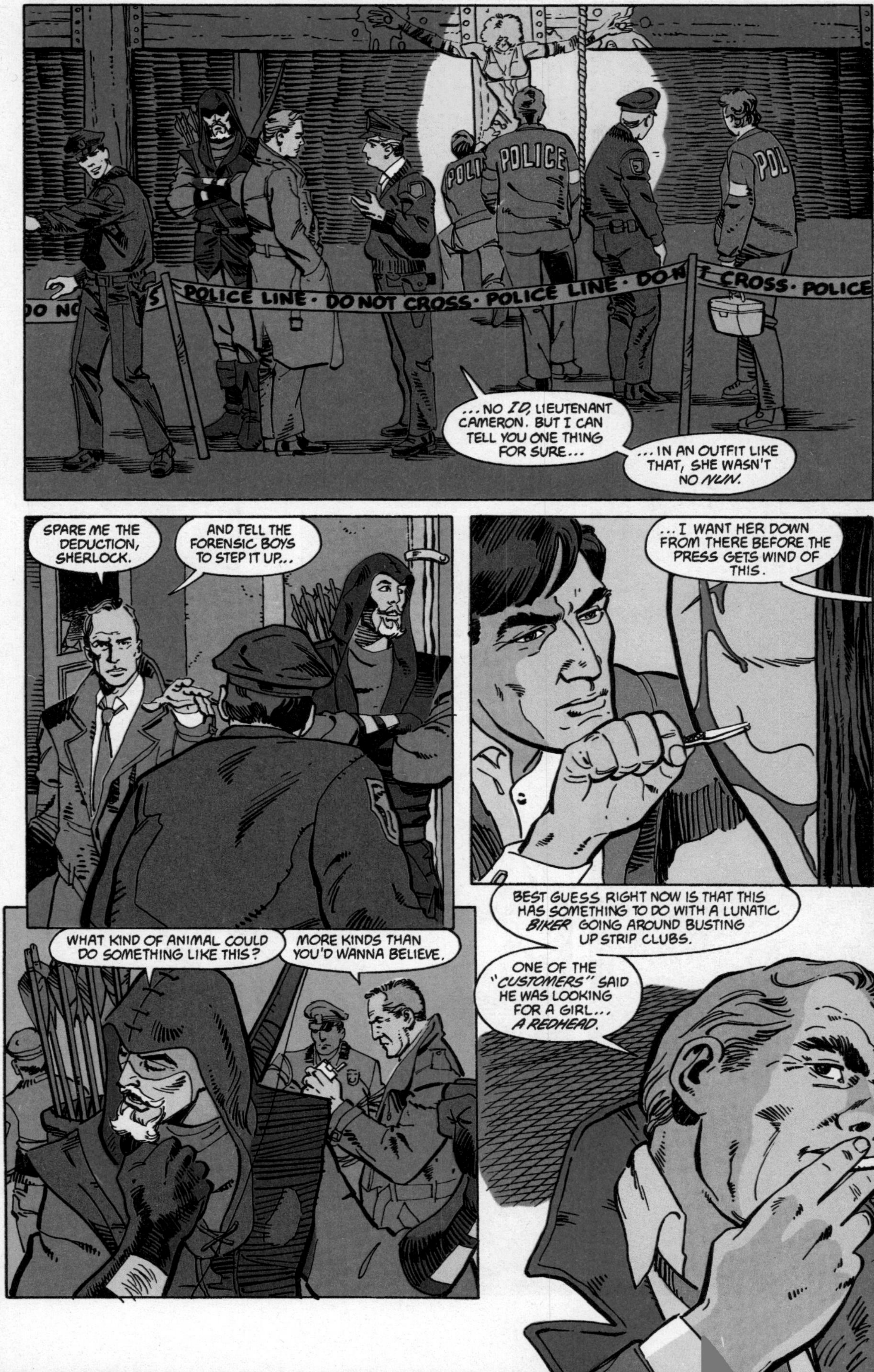
DO NOT CROSS · POLICE LINE · DO NOT CROSS · POLICE LINE · DO NOT CROSS · POLICE
...NO ID, LIEUTENANT CAMERON. BUT I CAN TELL YOU ONE THING FOR SURE...
...IN AN OUTFIT LIKE THAT, SHE WASN'T NO NUN.
SPARE ME THE DEDUCTION, SHERLOCK.
AND TELL THE FORENSIC BOYS TO STEP IT UP...
...I WANT HER DOWN FROM THERE BEFORE THE PRESS GETS WIND OF THIS.
BEST GUESS RIGHT NOW IS THAT THIS HAS SOMETHING TO DO WITH A LUNATIC BIKER GOING AROUND BUSTING UP STRIP CLUBS.
WHAT KIND OF ANIMAL COULD DO SOMETHING LIKE THIS?
MORE KINDS THAN YOU'D WANNA BELIEVE.
ONE OF THE "CUSTOMERS" SAID HE WAS LOOKING FOR A GIRL... A REDHEAD.

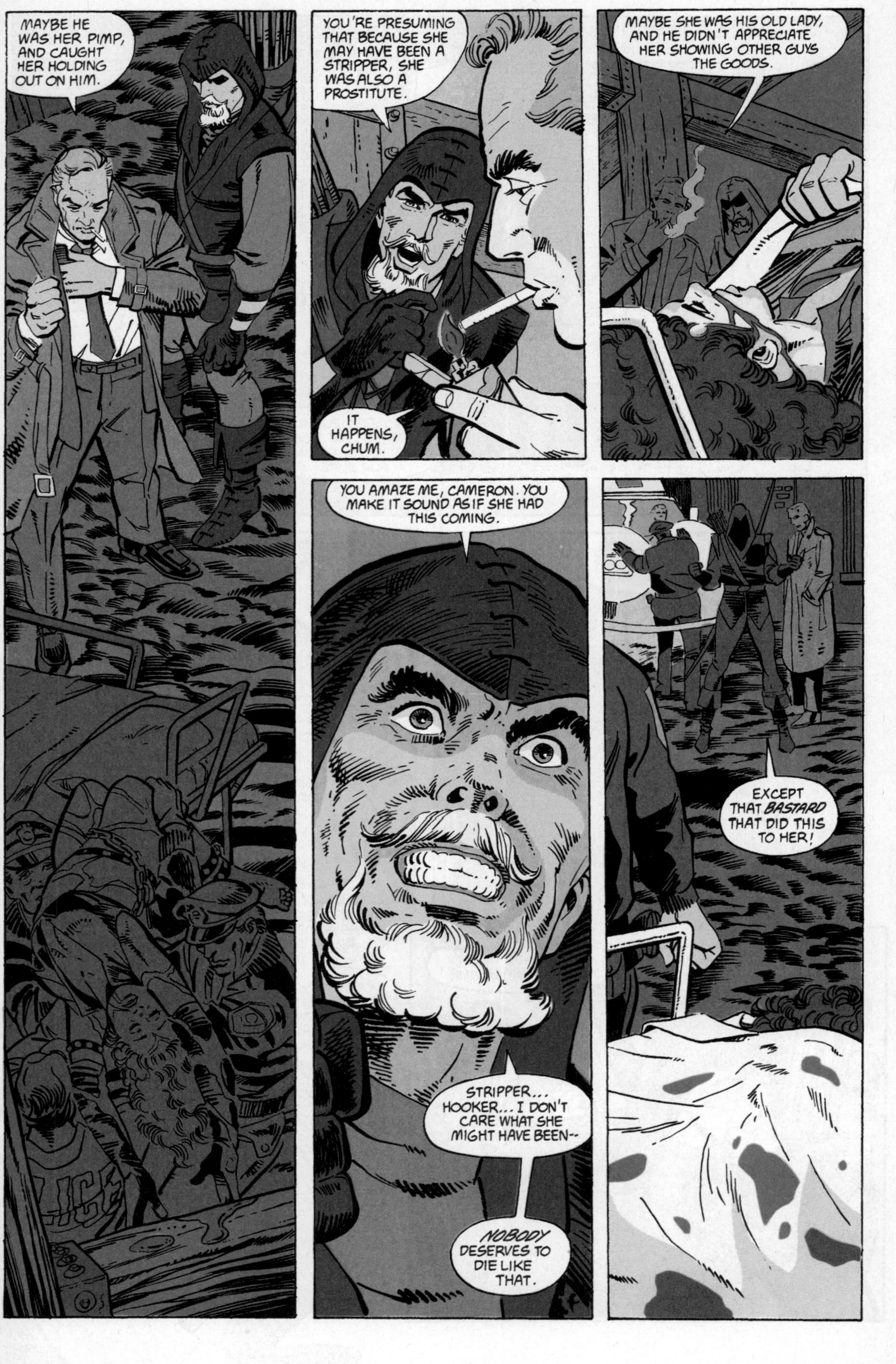
MAYBE HE WAS HER PIMP, AND CAUGHT HER HOLDING OUT ON HIM.
YOU'RE PRESUMING THAT BECAUSE SHE MAY HAVE BEEN A STRIPPER, SHE WAS ALSO A PROSTITUTE.
IT HAPPENS, CHUM.
MAYBE SHE WAS HIS OLD LADY, AND HE DIDN'T APPRECIATE HER SHOWING OTHER GUYS THE GOODS.
YOU AMAZE ME, CAMERON. YOU MAKE IT SOUND AS IF SHE HAD THIS COMING.
STRIPPER... HOOKER... I DON'T CARE WHAT SHE MIGHT HAVE BEEN--
NOBODY DESERVES TO DIE LIKE THAT.
EXCEPT THAT *BASTARD* THAT DID THIS TO HER!

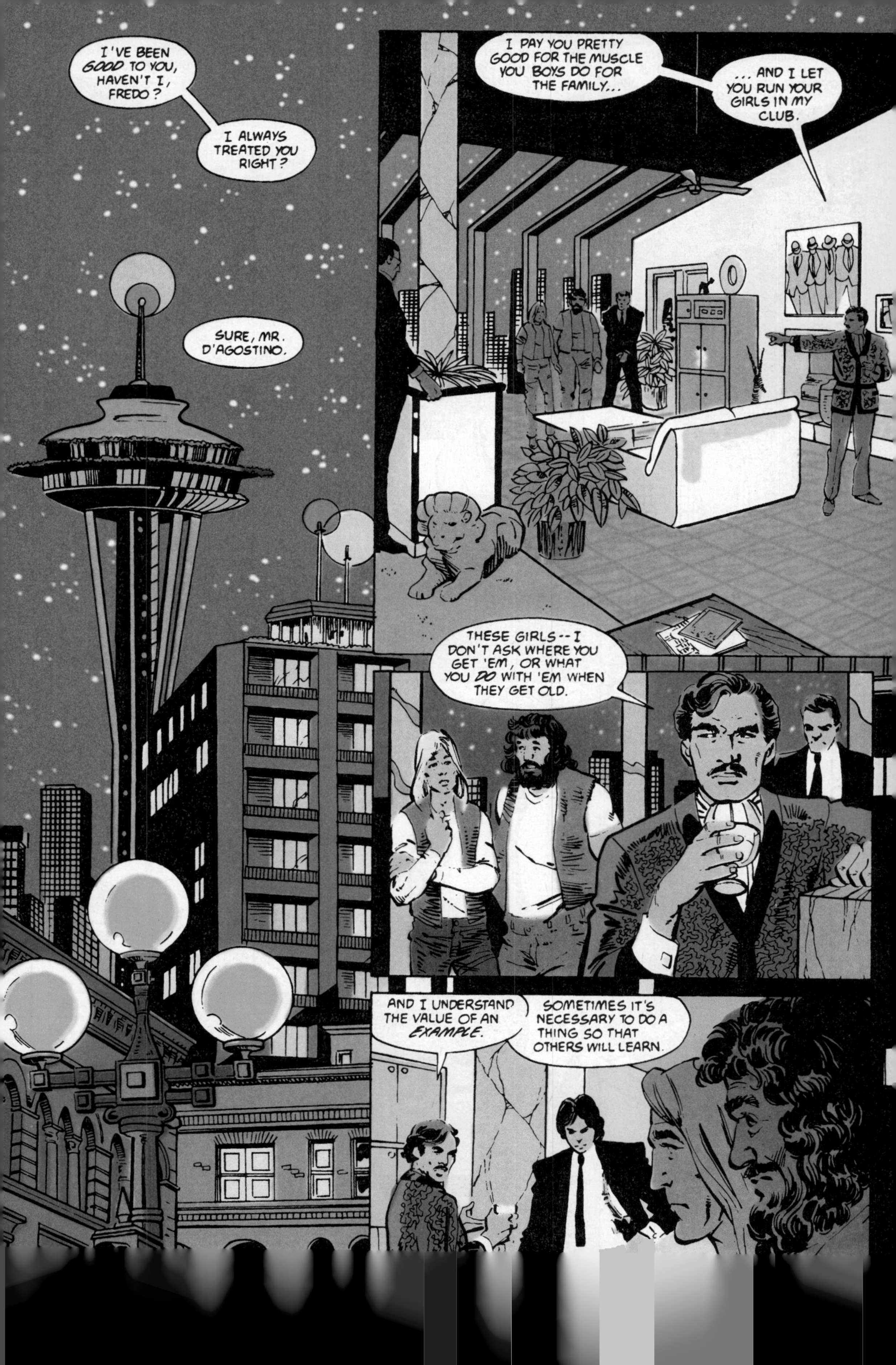
I'VE BEEN GOOD TO YOU, HAVEN'T I, FREDO?
I ALWAYS TREATED YOU RIGHT?
SURE, MR. D'AGOSTINO.
I PAY YOU PRETTY GOOD FOR THE MUSCLE YOU BOYS DO FOR THE FAMILY...
...AND I LET YOU RUN YOUR GIRLS IN MY CLUB.
THESE GIRLS -- I DON'T ASK WHERE YOU GET 'EM, OR WHAT YOU DO WITH 'EM WHEN THEY GET OLD.
AND I UNDERSTAND THE VALUE OF AN EXAMPLE.
SOMETIMES IT'S NECESSARY TO DO A THING SO THAT OTHERS WILL LEARN.

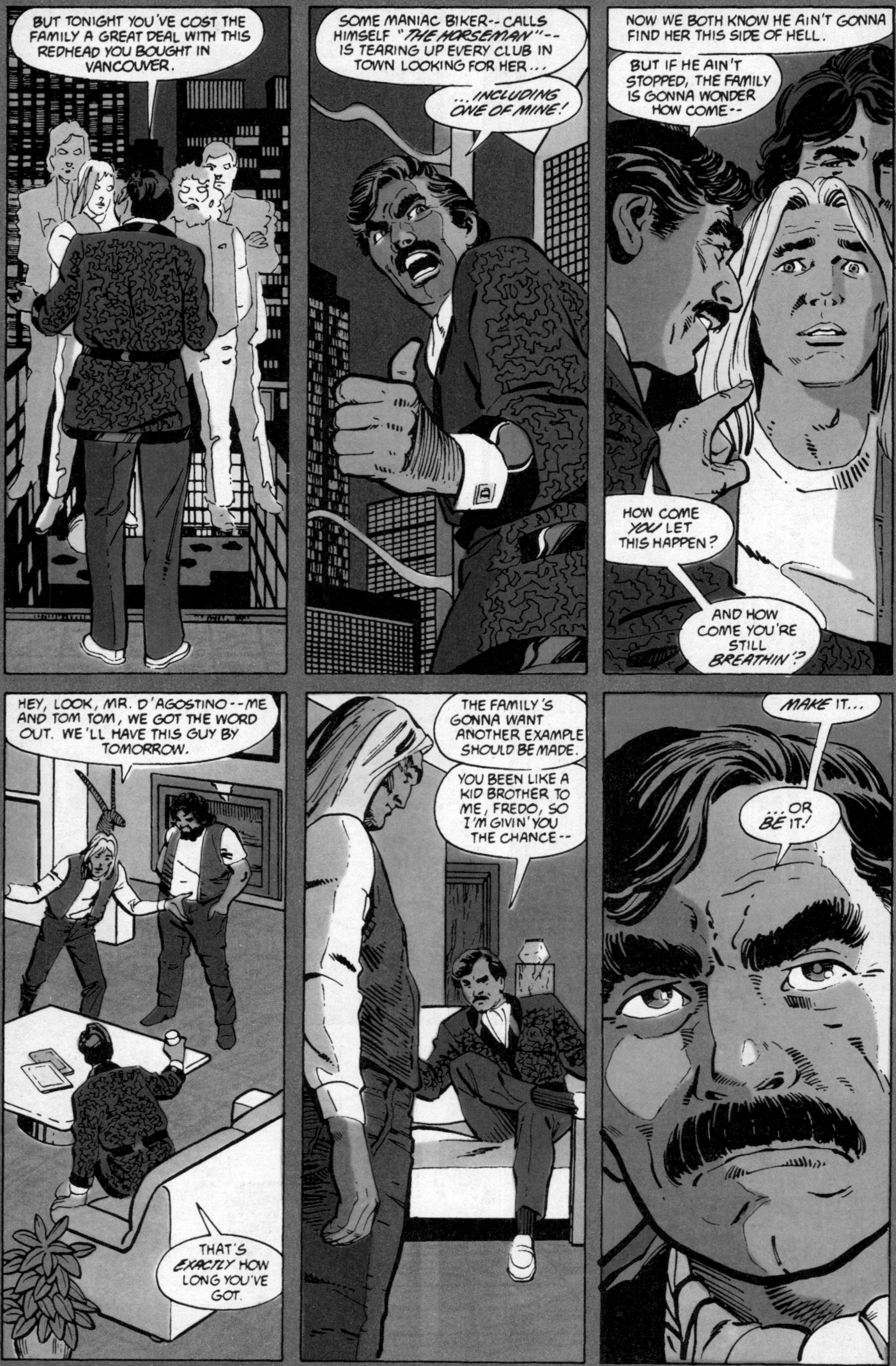
BUT TONIGHT YOU'VE COST THE FAMILY A GREAT DEAL WITH THIS REDHEAD YOU BOUGHT IN VANCOUVER.
SOME MANIAC BIKER-- CALLS HIMSELF "THE HORSEMAN"-- IS TEARING UP EVERY CLUB IN TOWN LOOKING FOR HER...
...INCLUDING ONE OF MINE!
NOW WE BOTH KNOW HE AIN'T GONNA FIND HER THIS SIDE OF HELL.
BUT IF HE AIN'T STOPPED, THE FAMILY IS GONNA WONDER HOW COME--
HOW COME YOU LET THIS HAPPEN?
AND HOW COME YOU'RE STILL BREATHIN'?
HEY, LOOK, MR. D'AGOSTINO--ME AND TOM TOM, WE GOT THE WORD OUT. WE'LL HAVE THIS GUY BY TOMORROW.
THAT'S EXACTLY HOW LONG YOU'VE GOT.
THE FAMILY'S GONNA WANT ANOTHER EXAMPLE SHOULD BE MADE.
YOU BEEN LIKE A KID BROTHER TO ME, FREDO, SO I'M GIVIN' YOU THE CHANCE--
MAKE IT...
...OR BE IT!

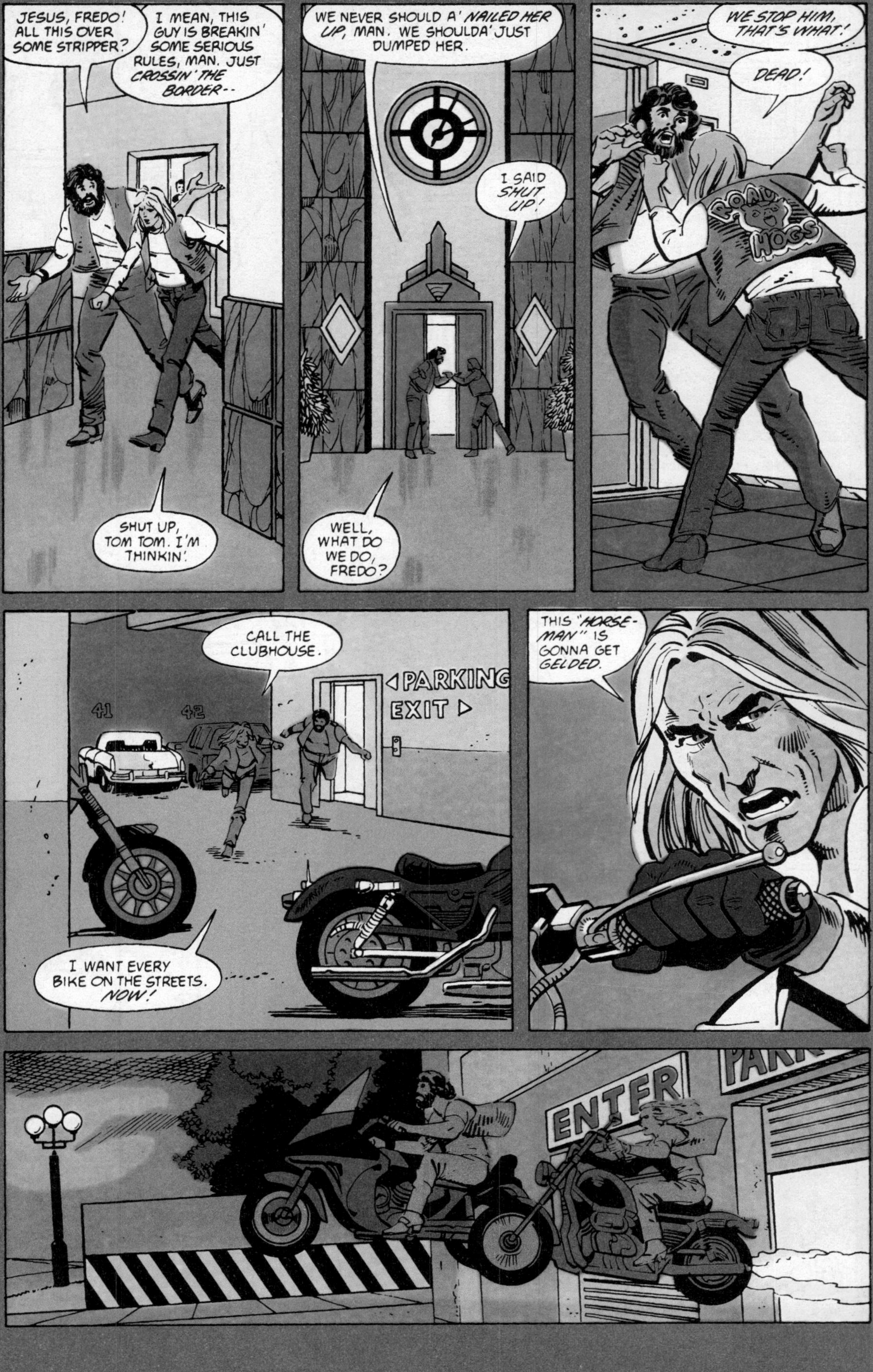
JESUS, FREDO! ALL THIS OVER SOME STRIPPER?
I MEAN, THIS GUY IS BREAKIN' SOME SERIOUS RULES, MAN. JUST CROSSIN' THE BORDER--
SHUT UP, TOM TOM. I'M THINKIN'.
WE NEVER SHOULD A' NAILED HER UP, MAN. WE SHOULDA' JUST DUMPED HER.
I SAID SHUT UP!
WELL, WHAT DO WE DO, FREDO?
WE STOP HIM, THAT'S WHAT!
DEAD!
ROAD HOGS
CALL THE CLUBHOUSE.
PARKING
EXIT
41
42
I WANT EVERY BIKE ON THE STREETS. NOW!
THIS "HORSE-MAN" IS GONNA GET GELDED.
ENTER

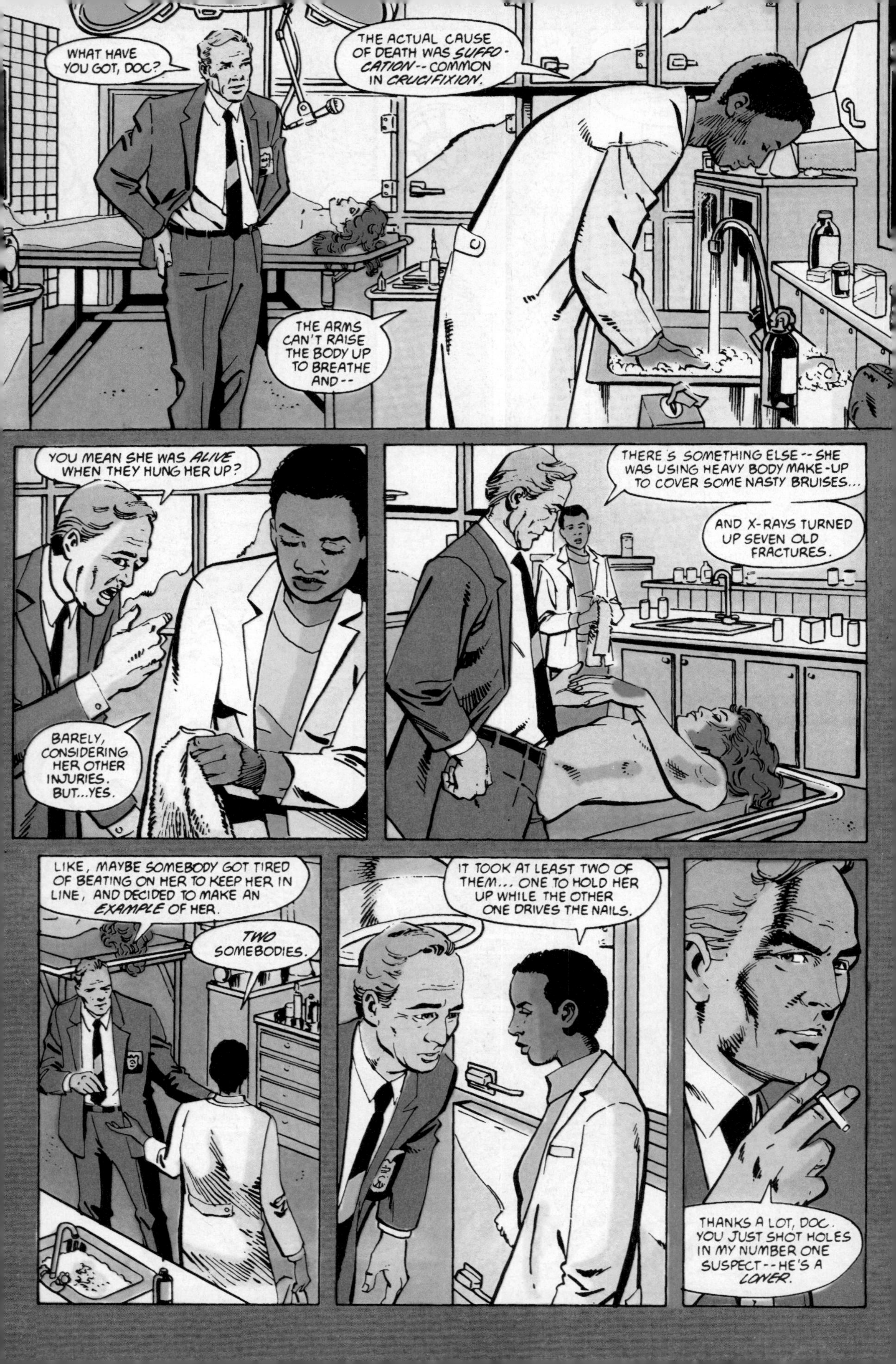
WHAT HAVE YOU GOT, DOC?
THE ACTUAL CAUSE OF DEATH WAS SUFFOCATION -- COMMON IN CRUCIFIXION.
THE ARMS CAN'T RAISE THE BODY UP TO BREATHE AND --
YOU MEAN SHE WAS ALIVE WHEN THEY HUNG HER UP?
BARELY, CONSIDERING HER OTHER INJURIES. BUT...YES.
THERE'S SOMETHING ELSE -- SHE WAS USING HEAVY BODY MAKE-UP TO COVER SOME NASTY BRUISES...
AND X-RAYS TURNED UP SEVEN OLD FRACTURES.
LIKE, MAYBE SOMEBODY GOT TIRED OF BEATING ON HER TO KEEP HER IN LINE, AND DECIDED TO MAKE AN EXAMPLE OF HER.
TWO SOMEBODIES.
IT TOOK AT LEAST TWO OF THEM... ONE TO HOLD HER UP WHILE THE OTHER ONE DRIVES THE NAILS.
THANKS A LOT, DOC. YOU JUST SHOT HOLES IN MY NUMBER ONE SUSPECT -- HE'S A LONER.

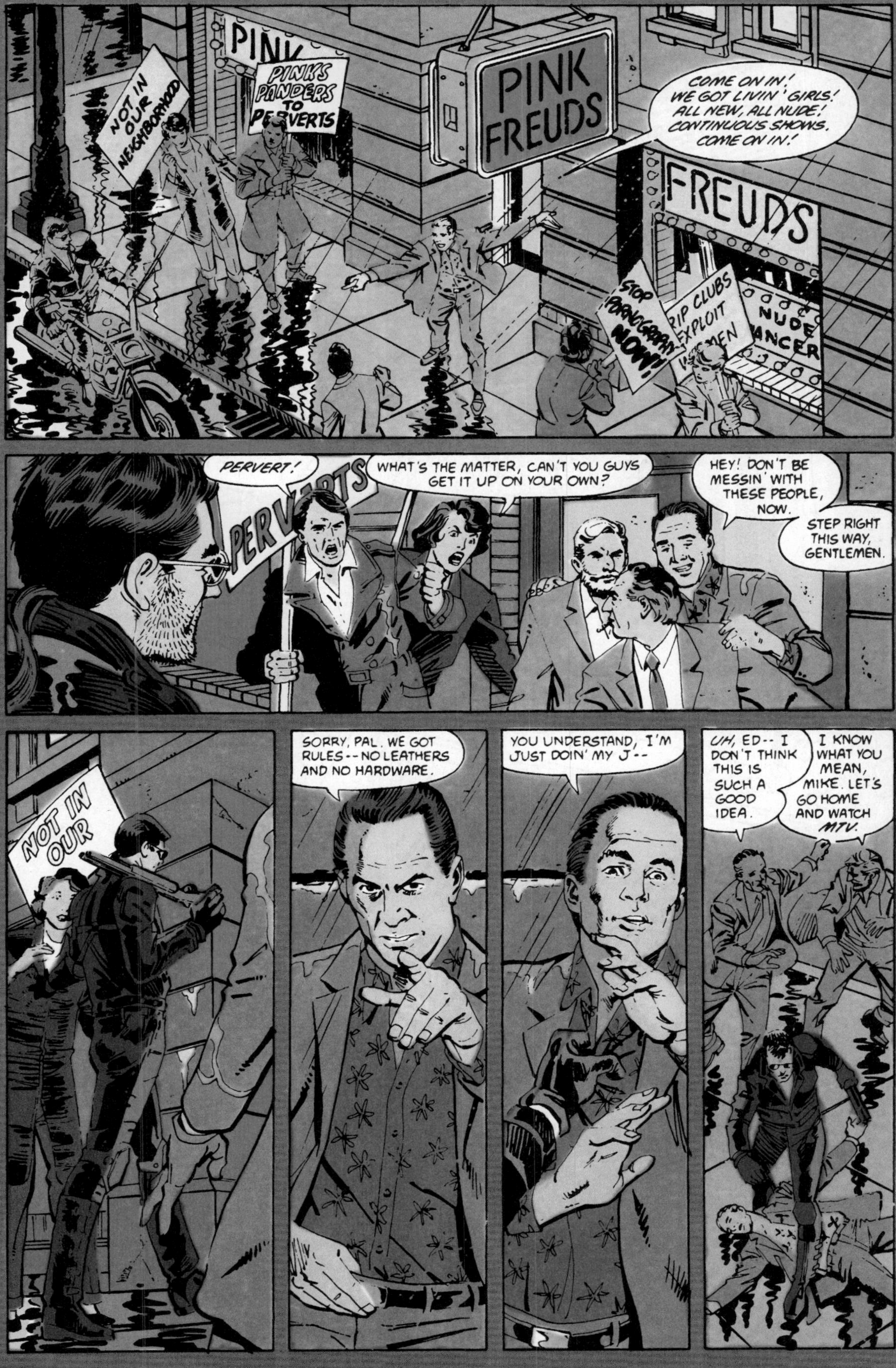
PINK
PINKS PANDERS TO PERVERTS
NOT IN OUR NEIGHBORHOOD
PINK FREUDS
COME ON IN! WE GOT LIVIN' GIRLS! ALL NEW, ALL NUDE! CONTINUOUS SHOWS. COME ON IN!
FREUDS
STOP PORNOGRAPHY NOW!
RIP CLUBS EXPLOIT
NUDE
ANCER
PERVERT!
WHAT'S THE MATTER, CAN'T YOU GUYS GET IT UP ON YOUR OWN?
HEY! DON'T BE MESSIN' WITH THESE PEOPLE, NOW.
STEP RIGHT THIS WAY, GENTLEMEN.
NOT IN OUR
SORRY, PAL. WE GOT RULES-- NO LEATHERS AND NO HARDWARE.
YOU UNDERSTAND, I'M JUST DOIN' MY J--
UH, ED-- I DON'T THINK THIS IS SUCH A GOOD IDEA.
I KNOW WHAT YOU MEAN, MIKE. LET'S GO HOME AND WATCH MTV.

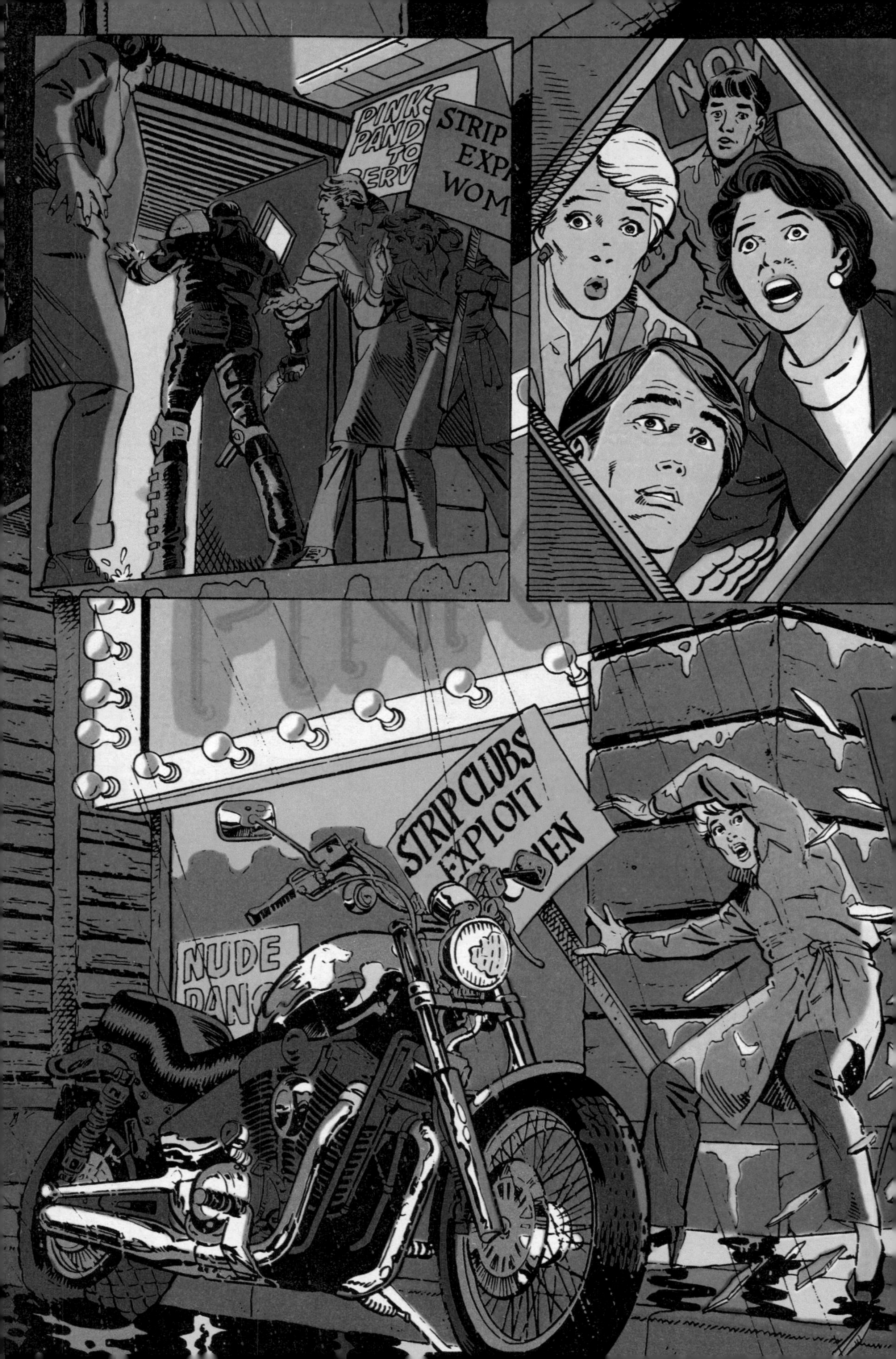
PINKS PAND TO ERV
STRIP EXP WOM
NOW
STRIP CLUBS EXPLOIT
NUDE DANC

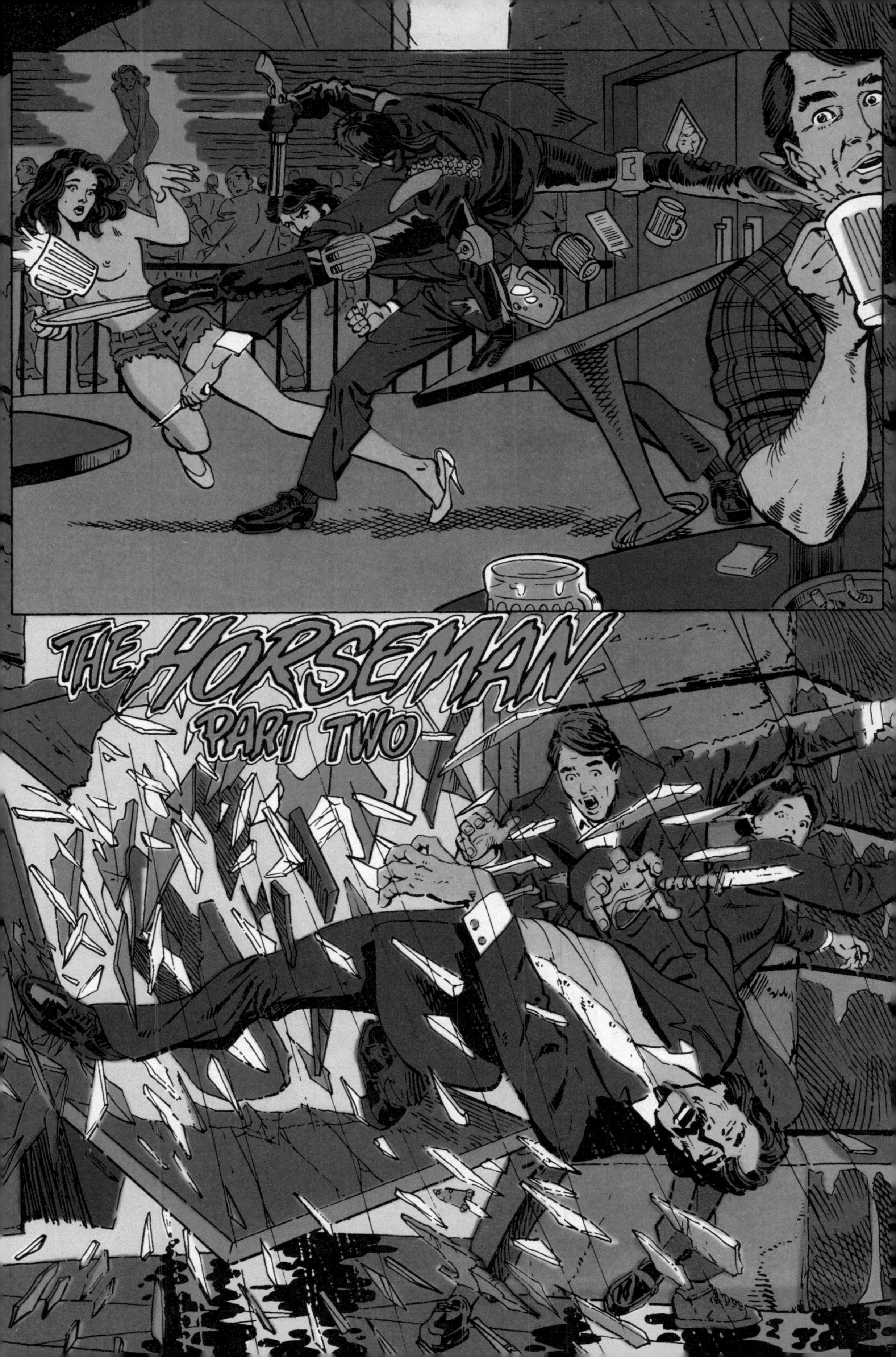
THE HORSEMAN
PART TWO

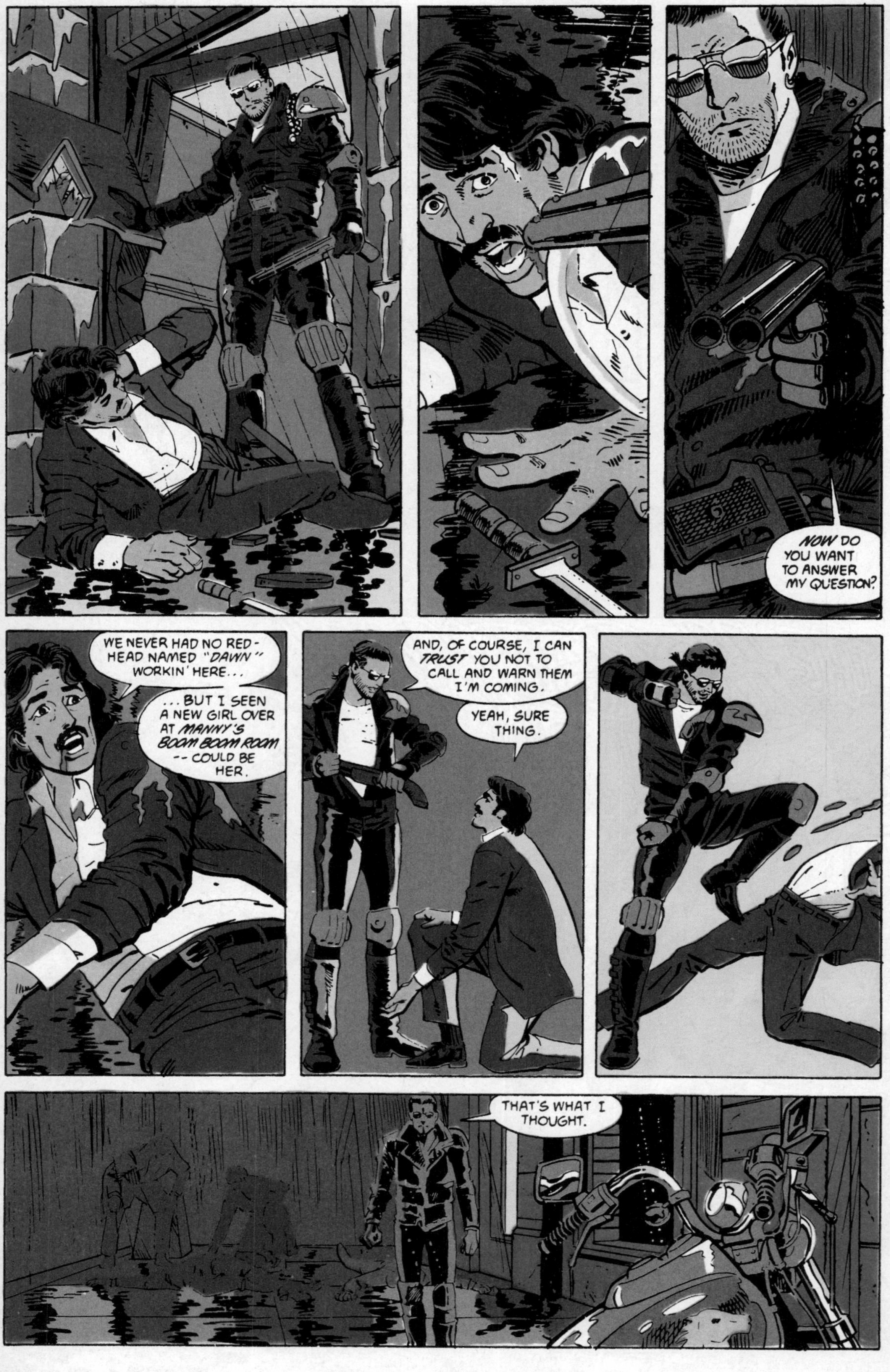

NOW DO YOU WANT TO ANSWER MY QUESTION?
WE NEVER HAD NO RED-HEAD NAMED "DAWN" WORKIN' HERE...
...BUT I SEEN A NEW GIRL OVER AT MANNY'S BOOM BOOM ROOM -- COULD BE HER.
AND, OF COURSE, I CAN TRUST YOU NOT TO CALL AND WARN THEM I'M COMING.
YEAH, SURE THING.
THAT'S WHAT I THOUGHT.

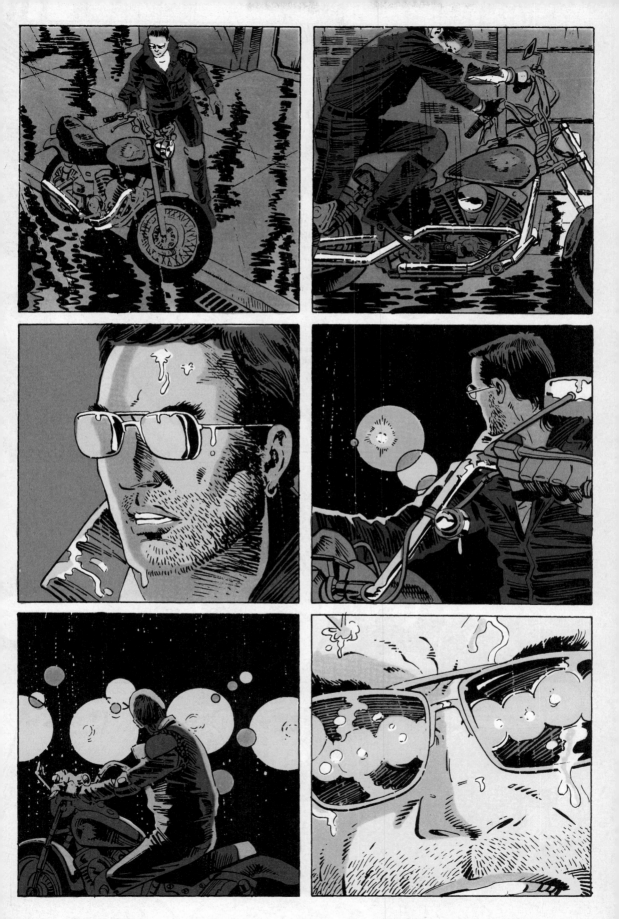

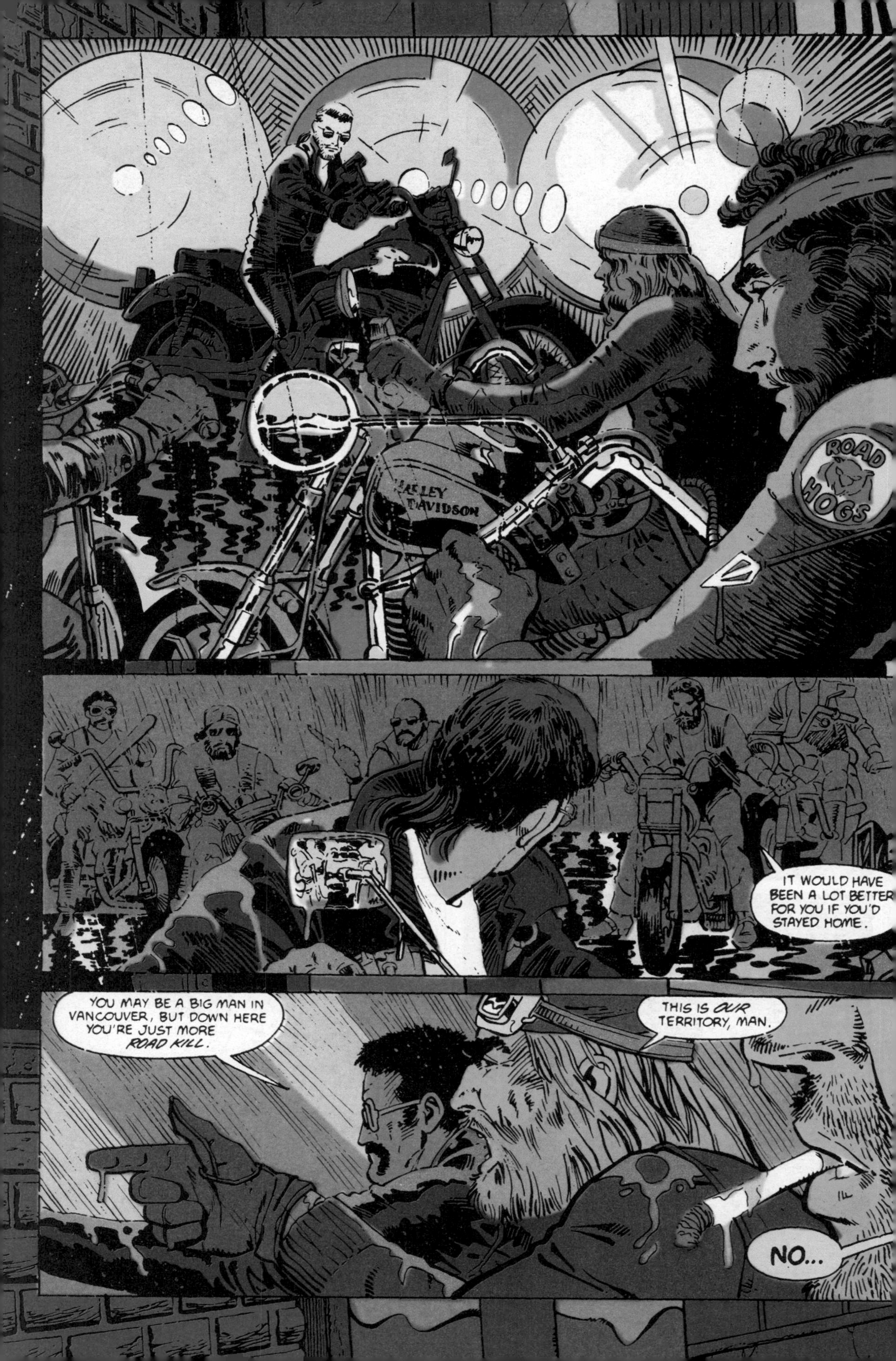

ROAD HOGS
HARLEY DAVIDSON
IT WOULD HAVE BEEN A LOT BETTER FOR YOU IF YOU'D STAYED HOME.
YOU MAY BE A BIG MAN IN VANCOUVER, BUT DOWN HERE YOU'RE JUST MORE *ROAD KILL*.
THIS IS *OUR* TERRITORY, MAN.
NO...

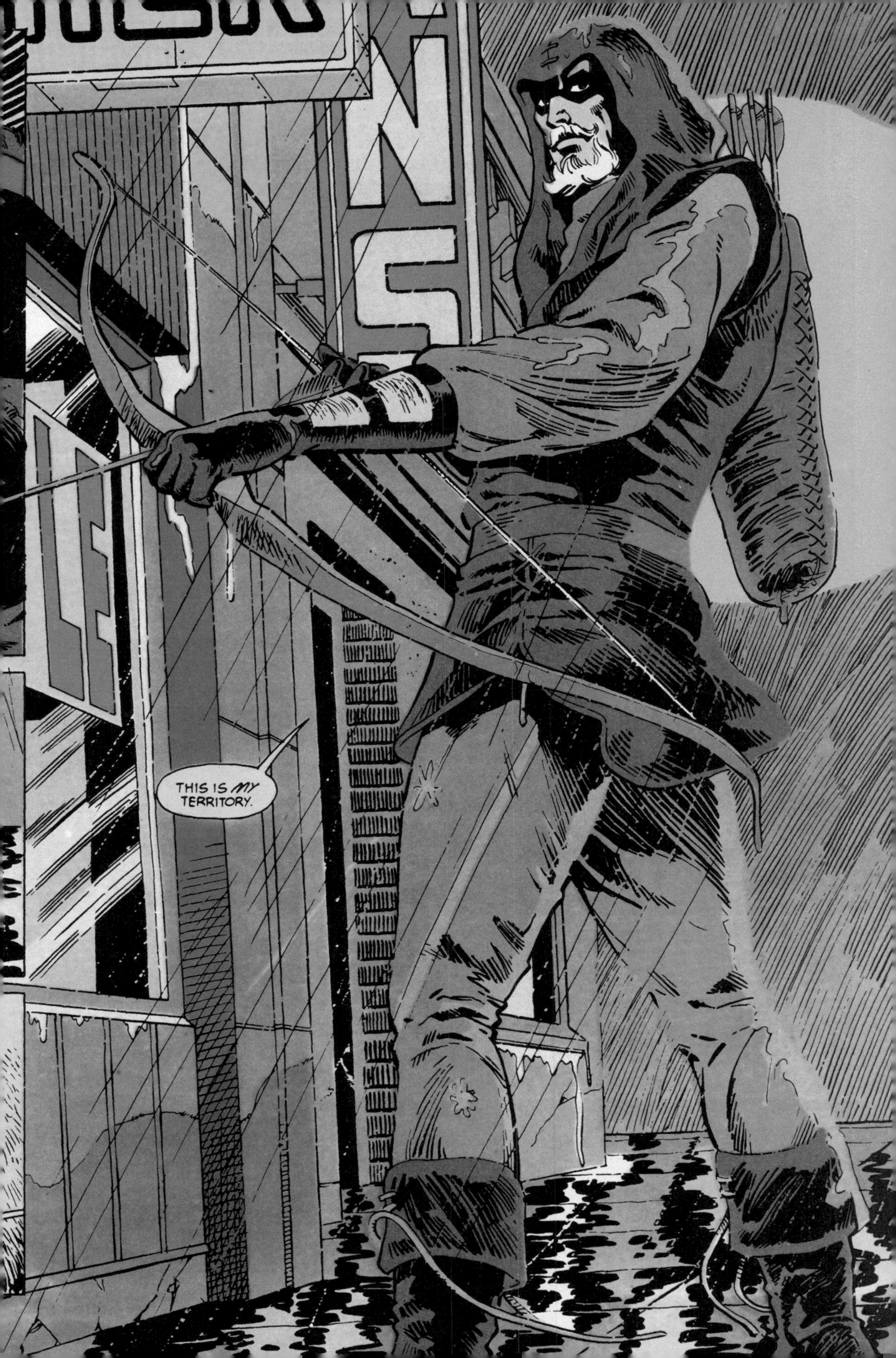
THIS IS *MY* TERRITORY.

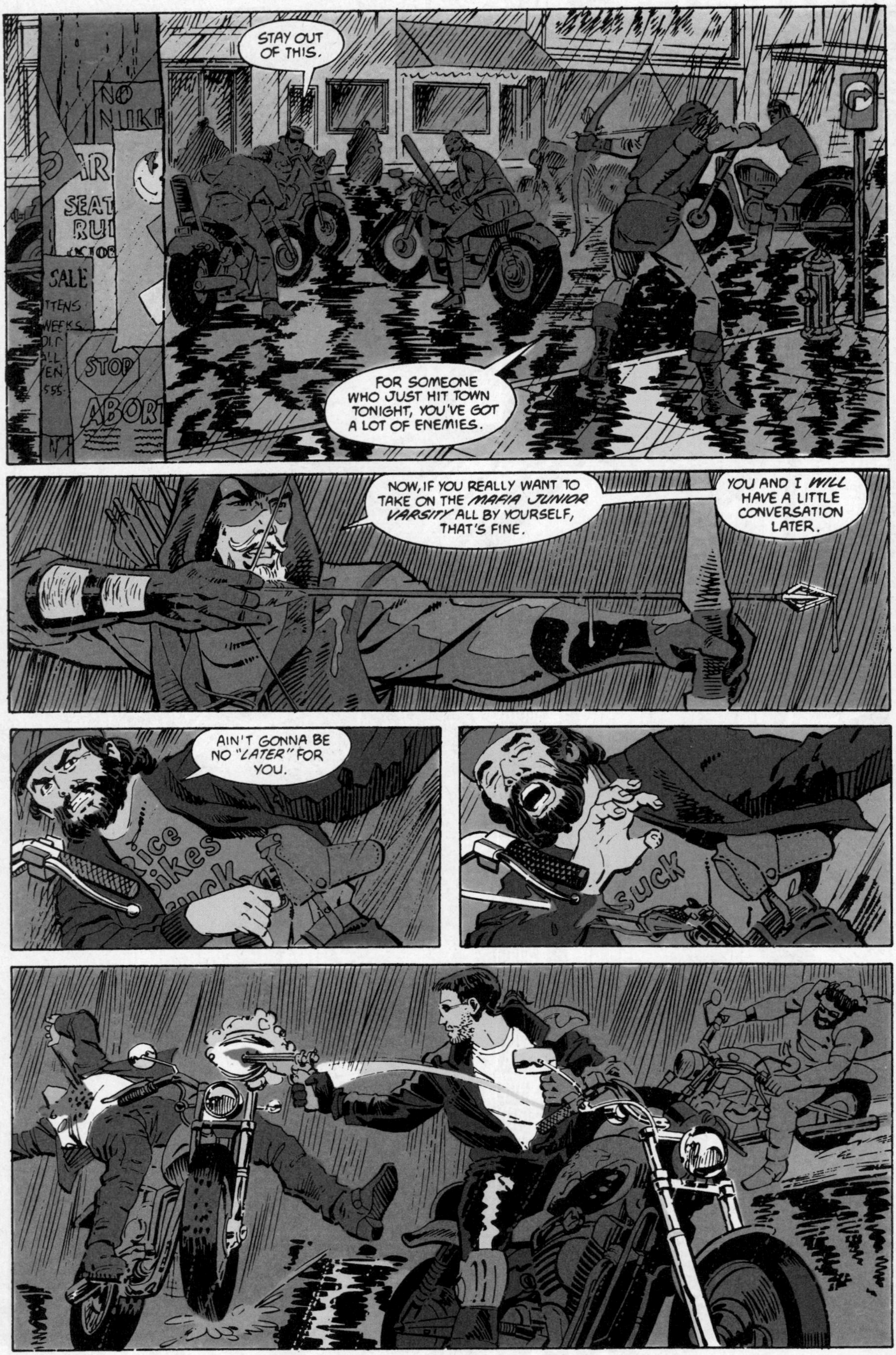
STAY OUT OF THIS.
SALE
STOP
FOR SOMEONE WHO JUST HIT TOWN TONIGHT, YOU'VE GOT A LOT OF ENEMIES.
NOW, IF YOU REALLY WANT TO TAKE ON THE *MAFIA JUNIOR VARSITY* ALL BY YOURSELF, THAT'S FINE.
YOU AND I ***WILL*** HAVE A LITTLE CONVERSATION LATER.
AIN'T GONNA BE NO "*LATER*" FOR YOU.
SUCK

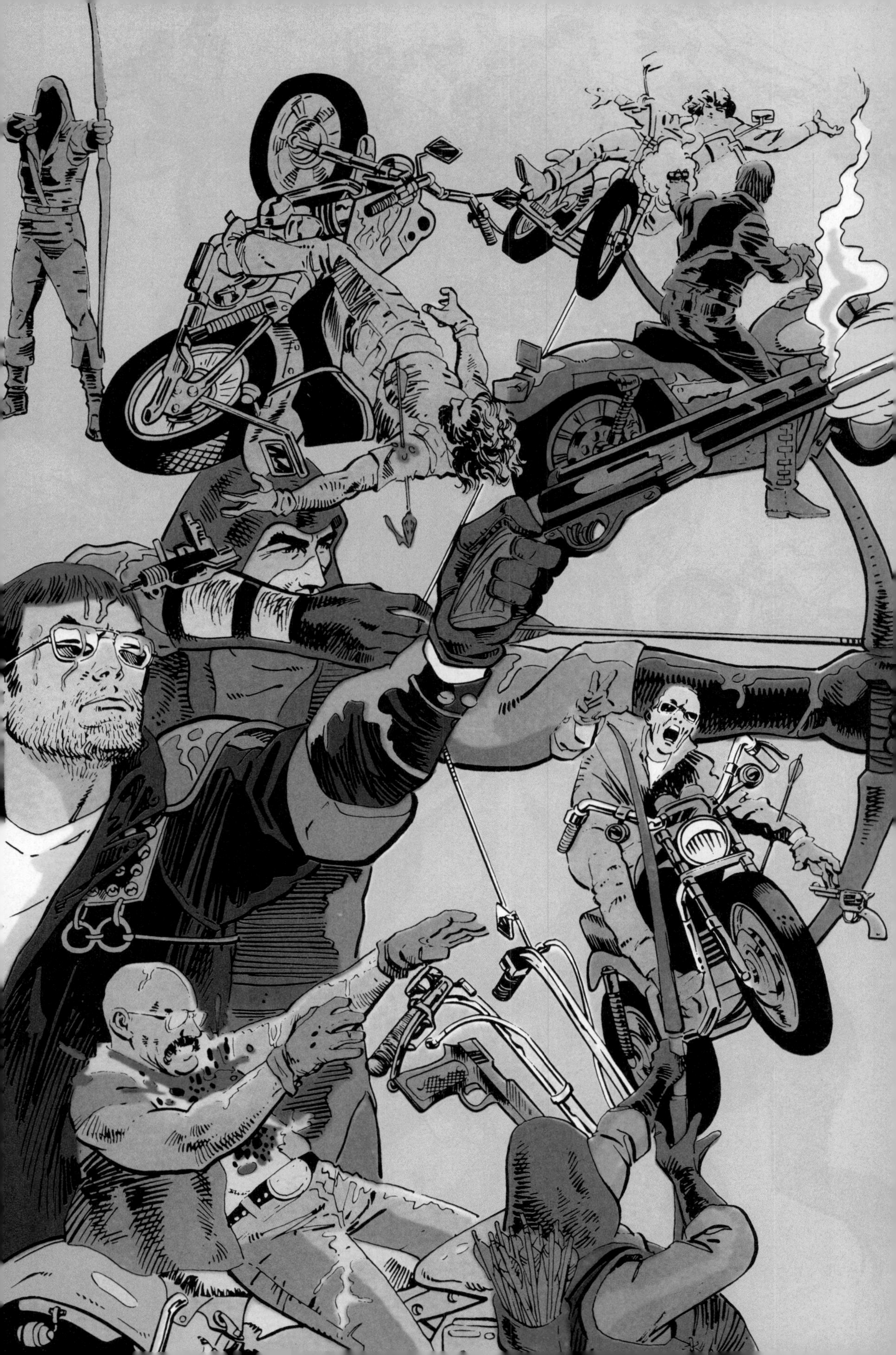

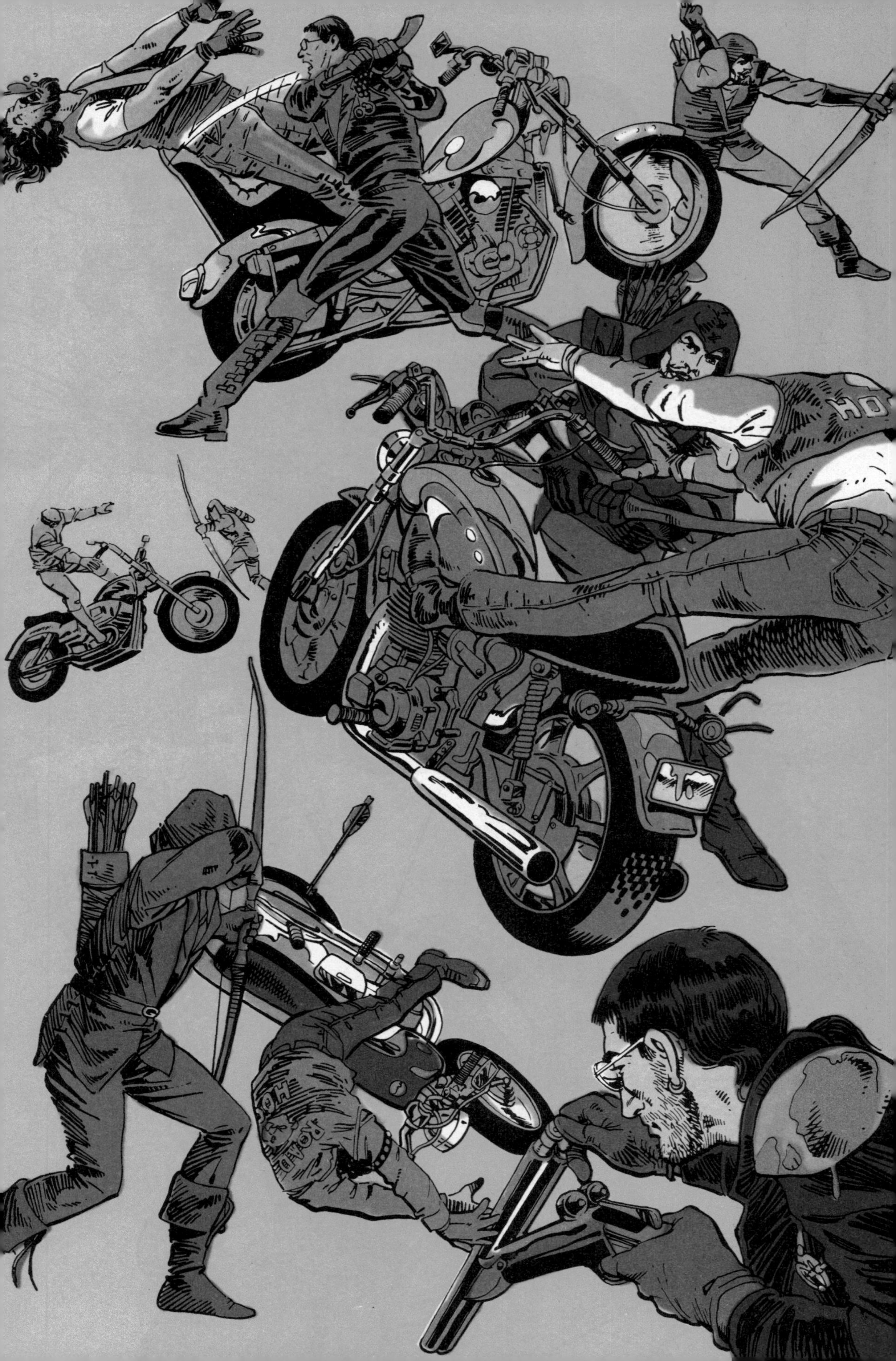

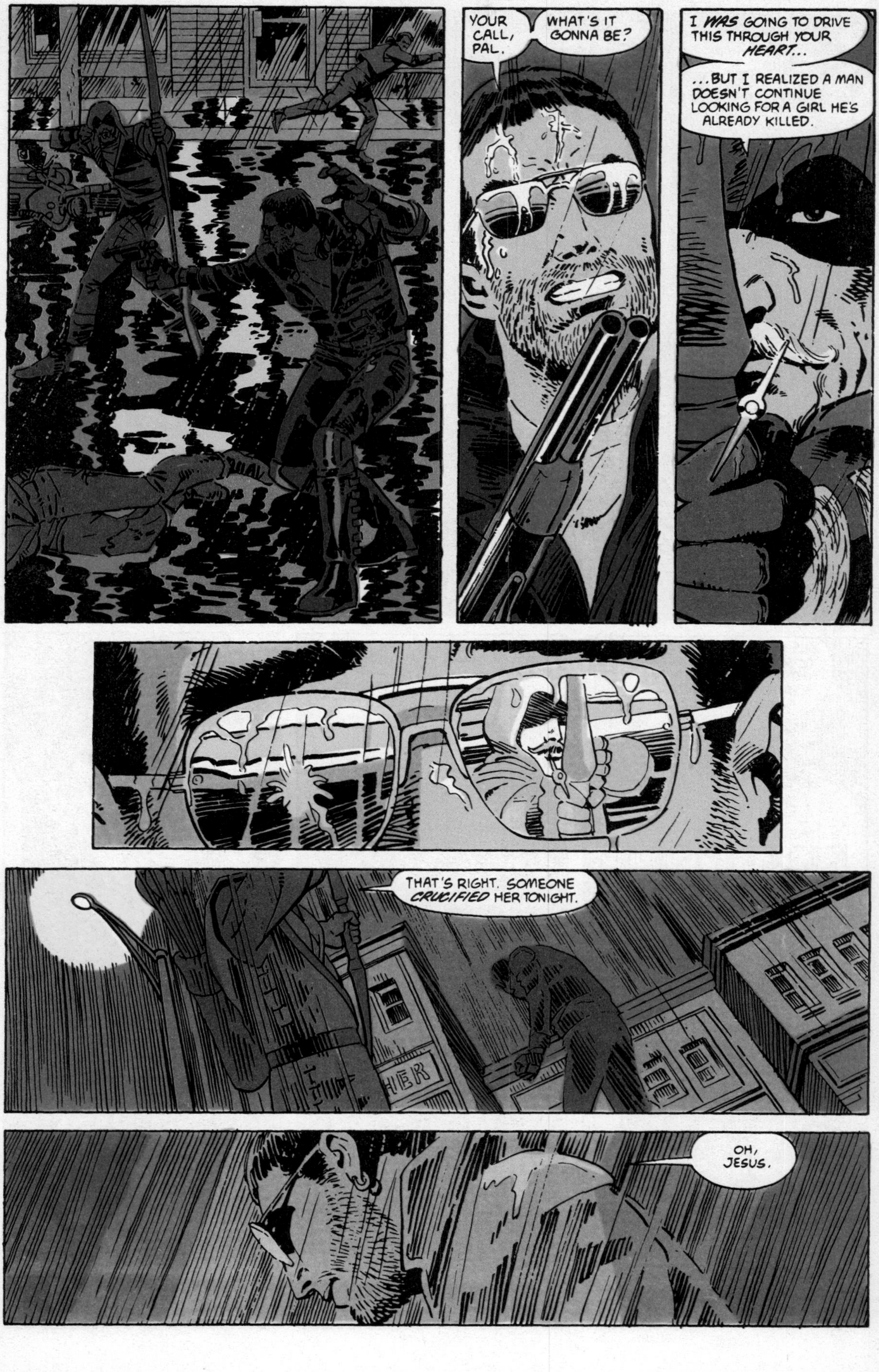

YOUR CALL, PAL.
WHAT'S IT GONNA BE?
I WAS GOING TO DRIVE THIS THROUGH YOUR HEART...
...BUT I REALIZED A MAN DOESN'T CONTINUE LOOKING FOR A GIRL HE'S ALREADY KILLED.
THAT'S RIGHT. SOMEONE CRUCIFIED HER TONIGHT.
OH, JESUS.

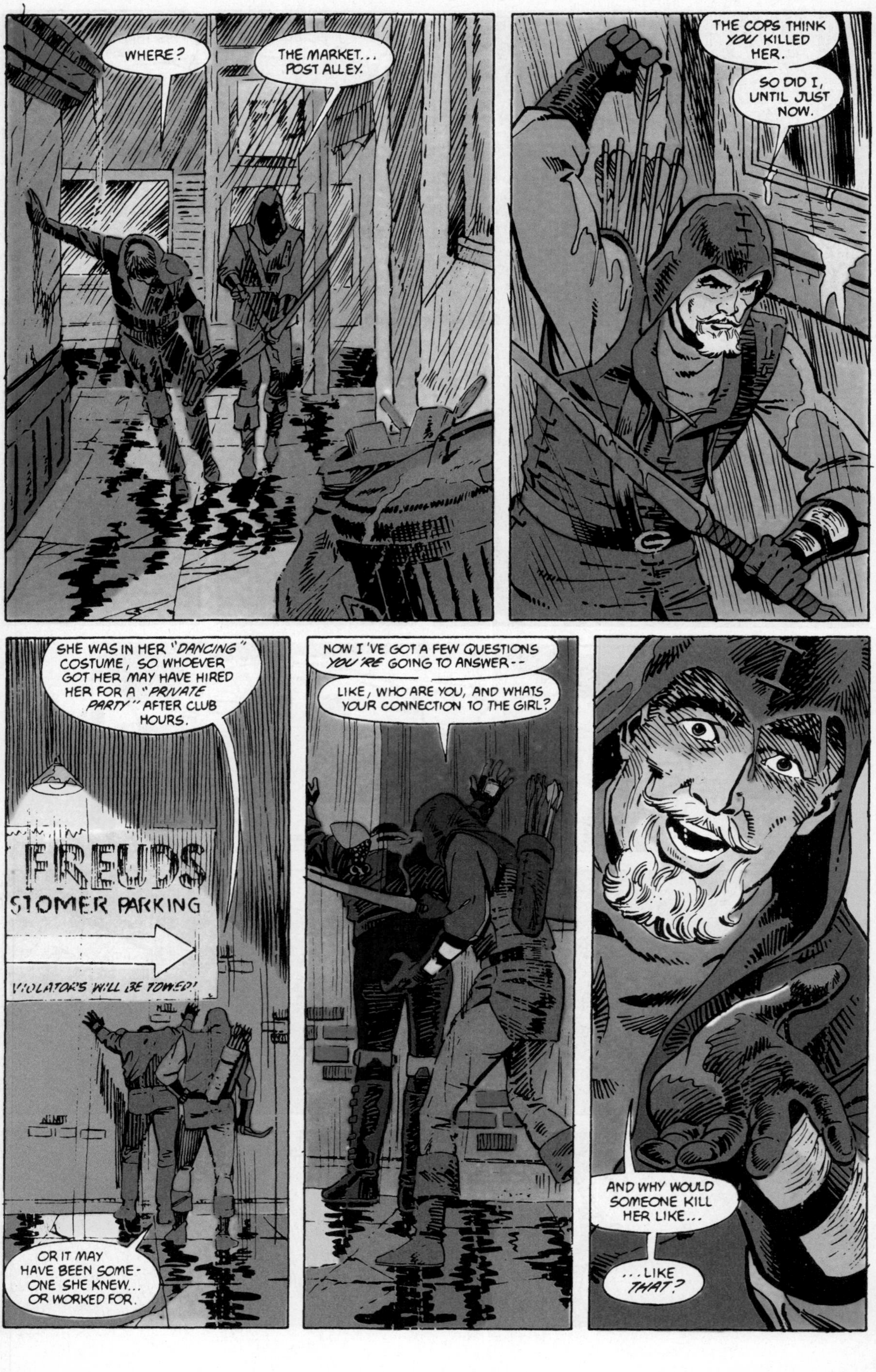

WHERE?
THE MARKET... POST ALLEY.
THE COPS THINK *YOU* KILLED HER.
SO DID I, UNTIL JUST NOW.
SHE WAS IN HER "*DANCING*" COSTUME, SO WHOEVER GOT HER MAY HAVE HIRED HER FOR A "*PRIVATE PARTY*" AFTER CLUB HOURS.
FREUDS
STOMER PARKING
VIOLATOR'S WILL BE TOWED!
OR IT MAY HAVE BEEN SOME-ONE SHE KNEW... OR WORKED FOR.
NOW I'VE GOT A FEW QUESTIONS *YOU'RE* GOING TO ANSWER--
LIKE, WHO ARE YOU, AND WHATS YOUR CONNECTION TO THE GIRL?
AND WHY WOULD SOMEONE KILL HER LIKE...
...LIKE *THAT*?

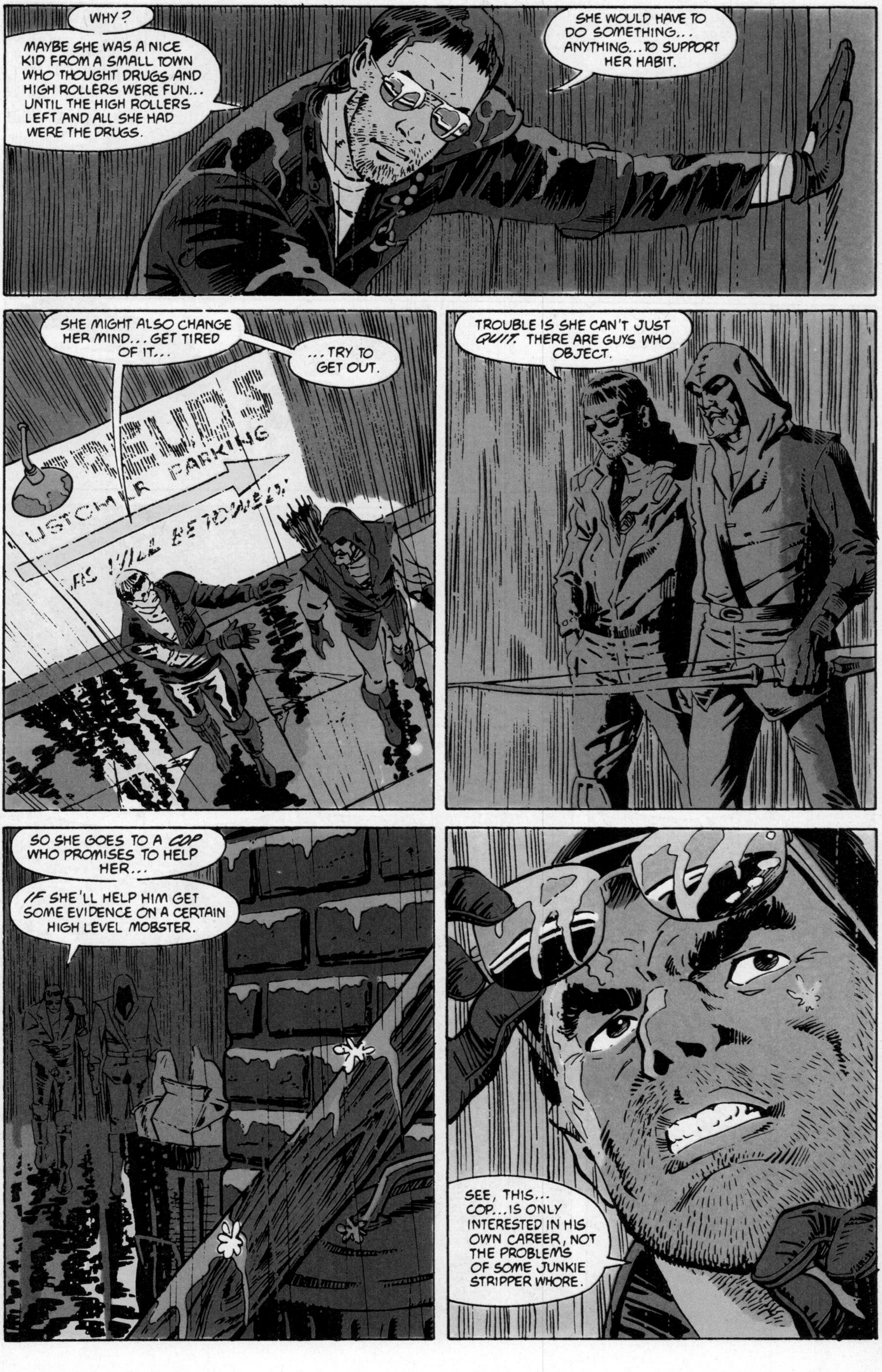
WHY?
MAYBE SHE WAS A NICE KID FROM A SMALL TOWN WHO THOUGHT DRUGS AND HIGH ROLLERS WERE FUN... UNTIL THE HIGH ROLLERS LEFT AND ALL SHE HAD WERE THE DRUGS.
SHE WOULD HAVE TO DO SOMETHING... ANYTHING... TO SUPPORT HER HABIT.
SHE MIGHT ALSO CHANGE HER MIND... GET TIRED OF IT...
...TRY TO GET OUT.
PARKING
TROUBLE IS SHE CAN'T JUST *QUIT*. THERE ARE GUYS WHO OBJECT.
SO SHE GOES TO A *COP* WHO PROMISES TO HELP HER...
IF SHE'LL HELP HIM GET SOME EVIDENCE ON A CERTAIN HIGH LEVEL MOBSTER.
SEE, THIS... COP... IS ONLY INTERESTED IN HIS OWN CAREER, NOT THE PROBLEMS OF SOME JUNKIE STRIPPER WHORE.

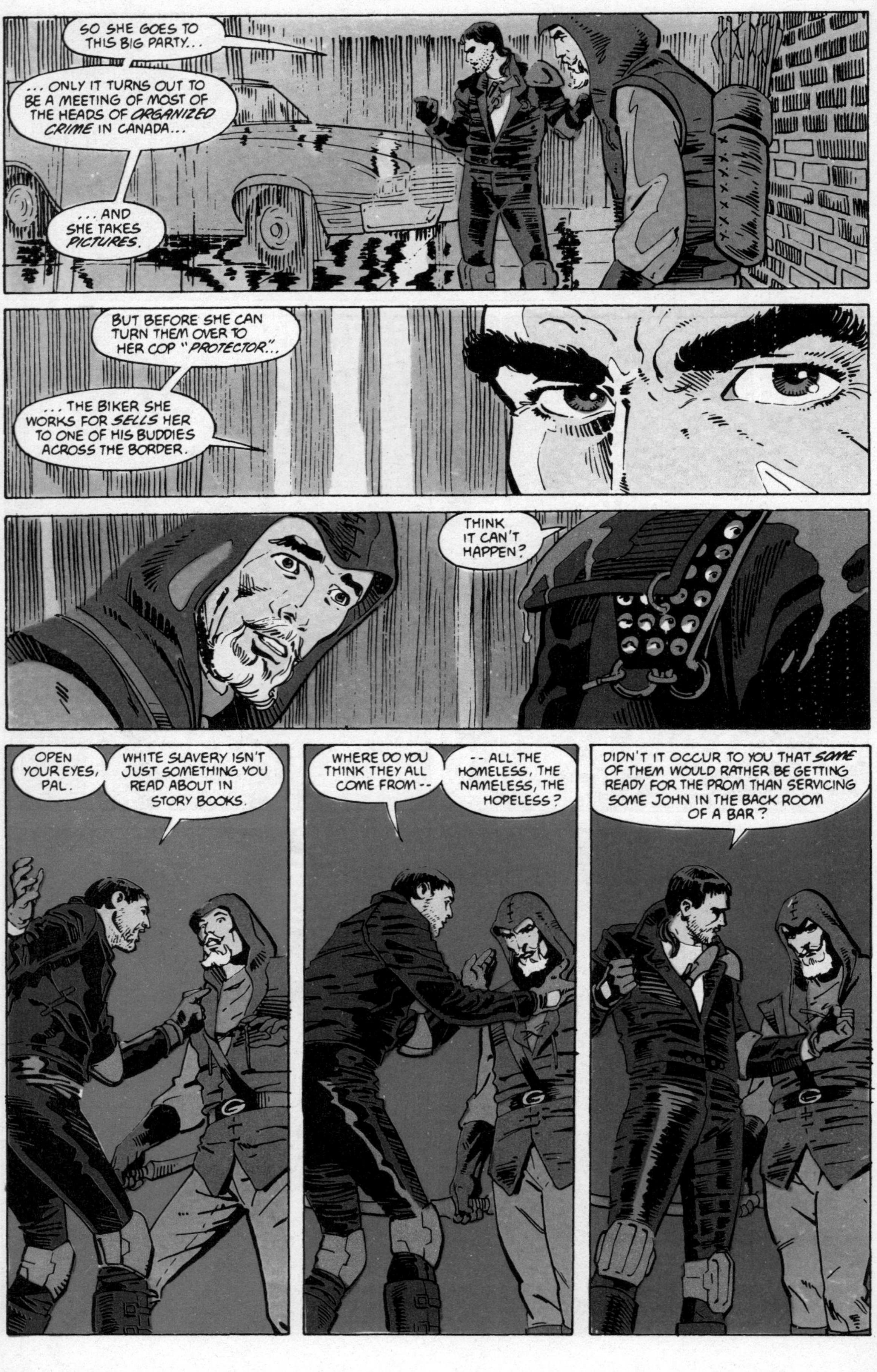
SO SHE GOES TO THIS BIG PARTY...
... ONLY IT TURNS OUT TO BE A MEETING OF MOST OF THE HEADS OF ORGANIZED CRIME IN CANADA...
... AND SHE TAKES PICTURES.
BUT BEFORE SHE CAN TURN THEM OVER TO HER COP "PROTECTOR"...
... THE BIKER SHE WORKS FOR SELLS HER TO ONE OF HIS BUDDIES ACROSS THE BORDER.
THINK IT CAN'T HAPPEN?
OPEN YOUR EYES, PAL.
WHITE SLAVERY ISN'T JUST SOMETHING YOU READ ABOUT IN STORY BOOKS.
WHERE DO YOU THINK THEY ALL COME FROM --
-- ALL THE HOMELESS, THE NAMELESS, THE HOPELESS?
DIDN'T IT OCCUR TO YOU THAT SOME OF THEM WOULD RATHER BE GETTING READY FOR THE PROM THAN SERVICING SOME JOHN IN THE BACK ROOM OF A BAR?

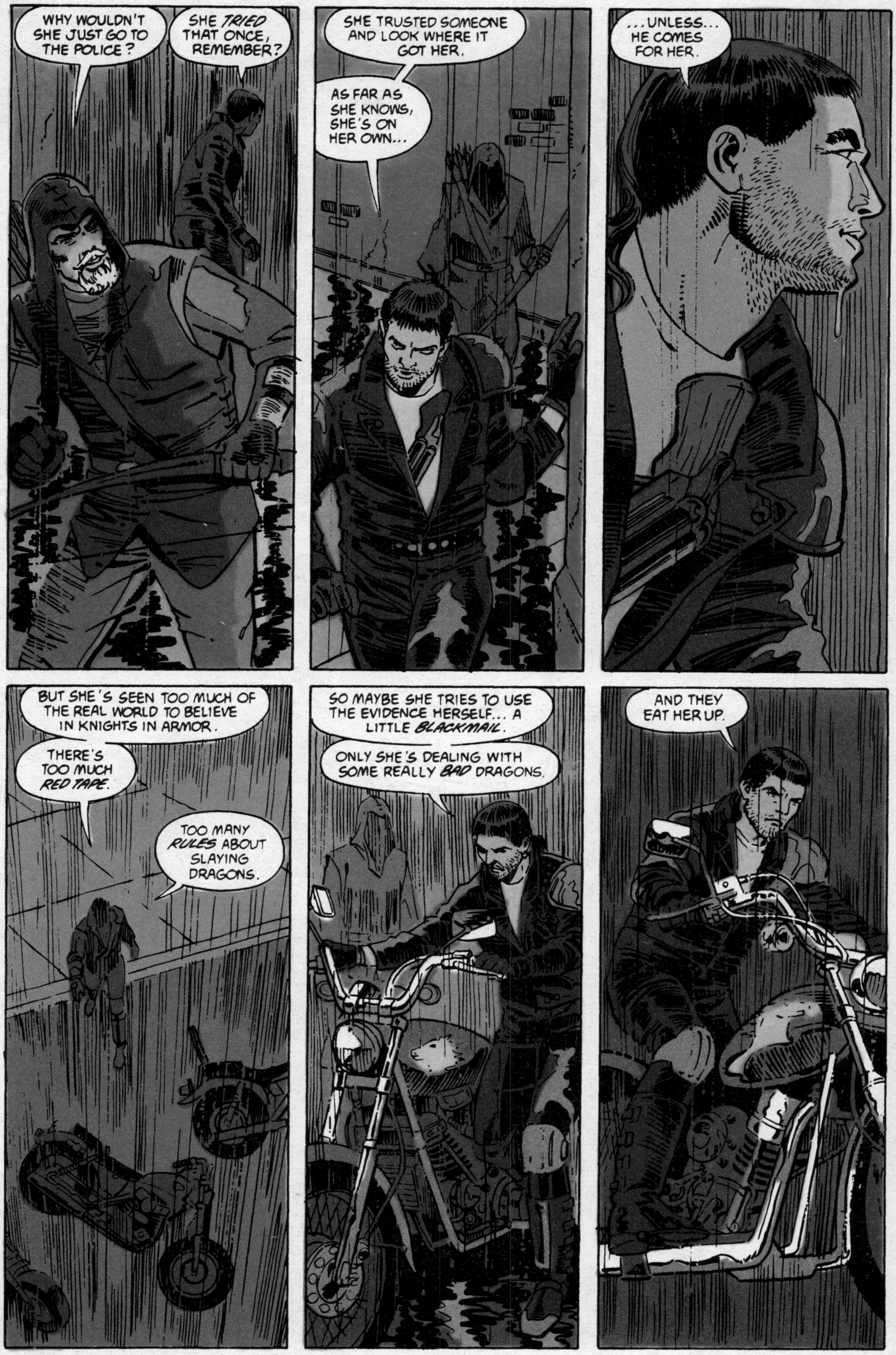

WHY WOULDN'T SHE JUST GO TO THE POLICE?
SHE *TRIED* THAT ONCE, REMEMBER?
SHE TRUSTED SOMEONE AND LOOK WHERE IT GOT HER.
AS FAR AS SHE KNOWS, SHE'S ON HER OWN...
...UNLESS... HE COMES FOR HER.
BUT SHE'S SEEN TOO MUCH OF THE REAL WORLD TO BELIEVE IN KNIGHTS IN ARMOR.
THERE'S TOO MUCH *RED TAPE*.
TOO MANY *RULES* ABOUT SLAYING DRAGONS.
SO MAYBE SHE TRIES TO USE THE EVIDENCE HERSELF... A LITTLE *BLACKMAIL*.
ONLY SHE'S DEALING WITH SOME REALLY *BAD* DRAGONS.
AND THEY EAT HER UP.

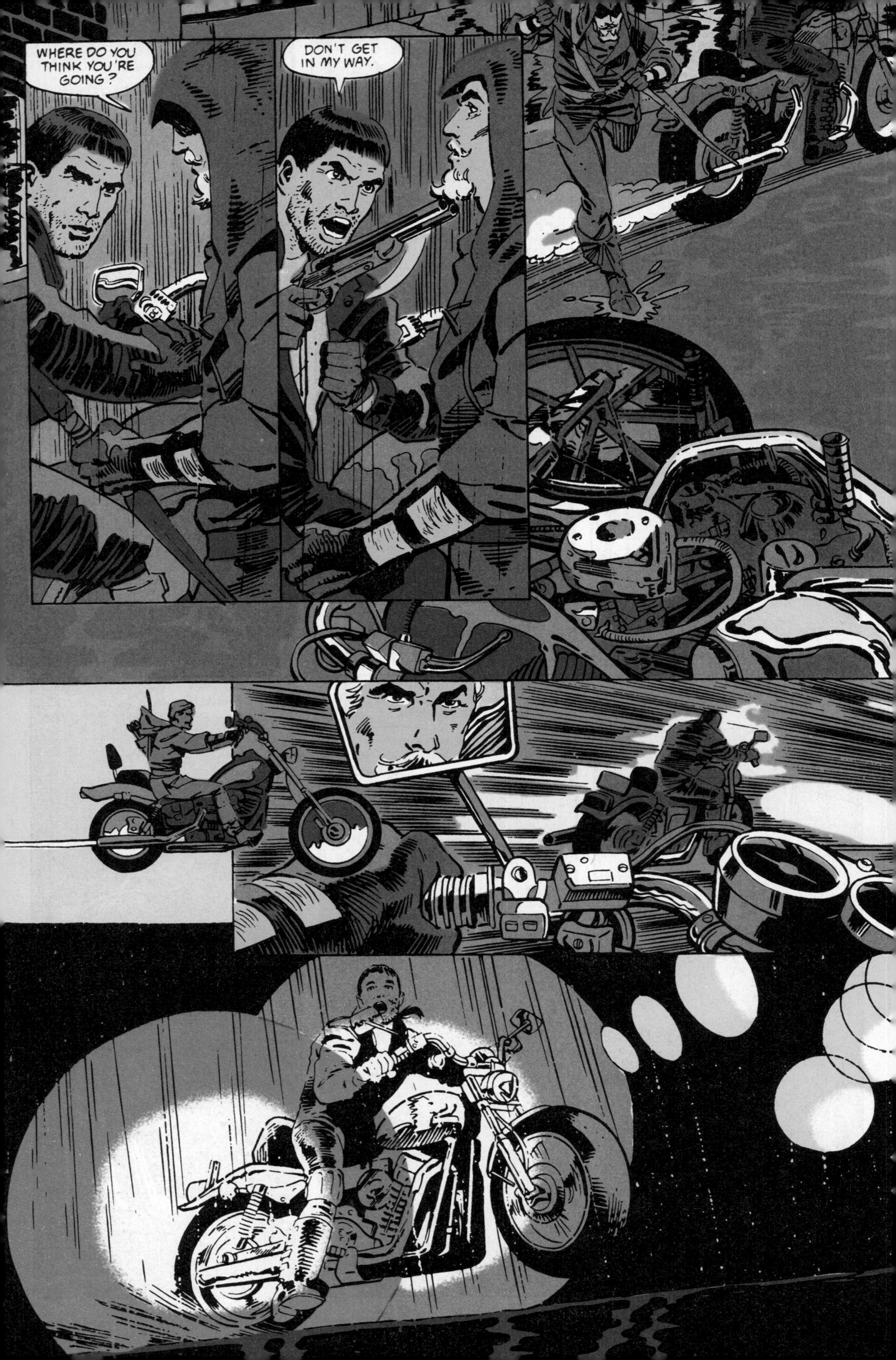
WHERE DO YOU THINK YOU'RE GOING?
DON'T GET IN MY WAY.

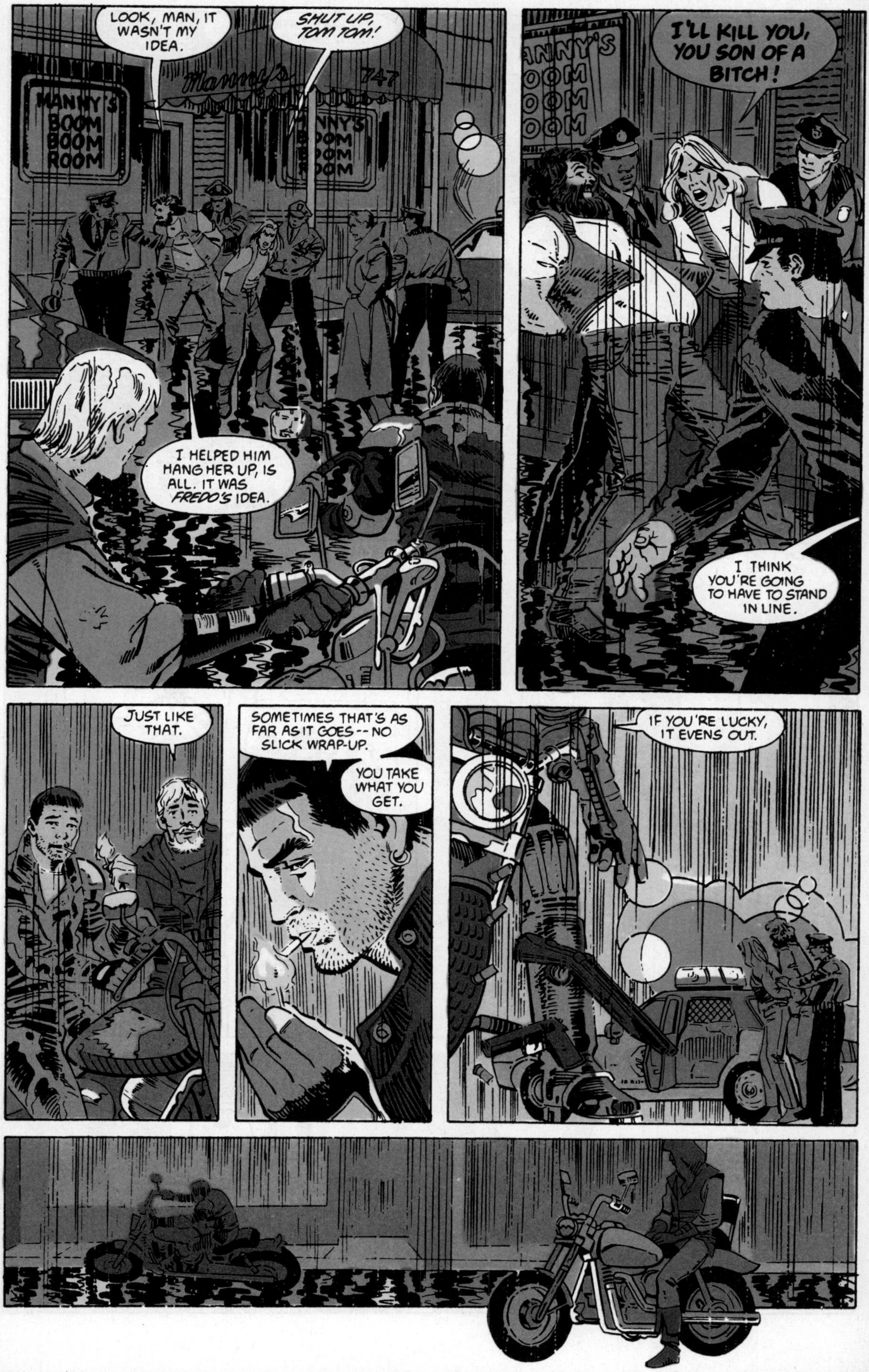
LOOK, MAN, IT WASN'T MY IDEA.
SHUT UP, TOM TOM!
MANNY'S BOOM BOOM ROOM
Manny's 747
MANNY'S BOOM BOOM ROOM
I HELPED HIM HANG HER UP, IS ALL. IT WAS FREDO'S IDEA.
I'LL KILL YOU, YOU SON OF A BITCH!
I THINK YOU'RE GOING TO HAVE TO STAND IN LINE.
JUST LIKE THAT.
SOMETIMES THAT'S AS FAR AS IT GOES -- NO SLICK WRAP-UP.
YOU TAKE WHAT YOU GET.
IF YOU'RE LUCKY, IT EVENS OUT.

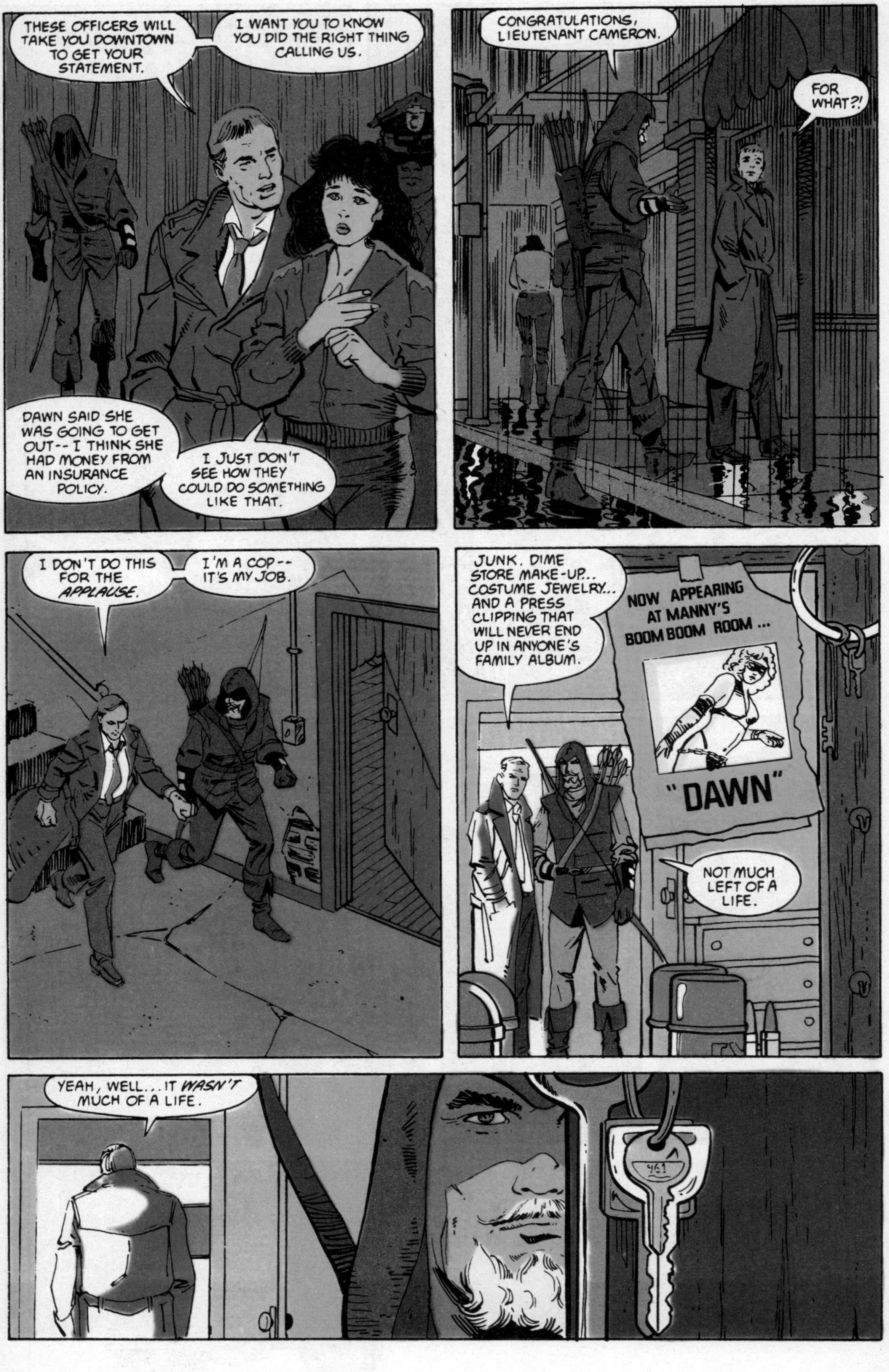
THESE OFFICERS WILL TAKE YOU DOWNTOWN TO GET YOUR STATEMENT.
I WANT YOU TO KNOW YOU DID THE RIGHT THING CALLING US.
DAWN SAID SHE WAS GOING TO GET OUT-- I THINK SHE HAD MONEY FROM AN INSURANCE POLICY.
I JUST DON'T SEE HOW THEY COULD DO SOMETHING LIKE THAT.
CONGRATULATIONS, LIEUTENANT CAMERON.
FOR WHAT?!
I DON'T DO THIS FOR THE *APPLAUSE*.
I'M A COP-- IT'S MY JOB.
JUNK. DIME STORE MAKE-UP... COSTUME JEWELRY... AND A PRESS CLIPPING THAT WILL NEVER END UP IN ANYONE'S FAMILY ALBUM.
NOW APPEARING AT MANNY'S BOOM BOOM ROOM ...
"DAWN"
NOT MUCH LEFT OF A LIFE.
YEAH, WELL... IT *WASN'T* MUCH OF A LIFE.

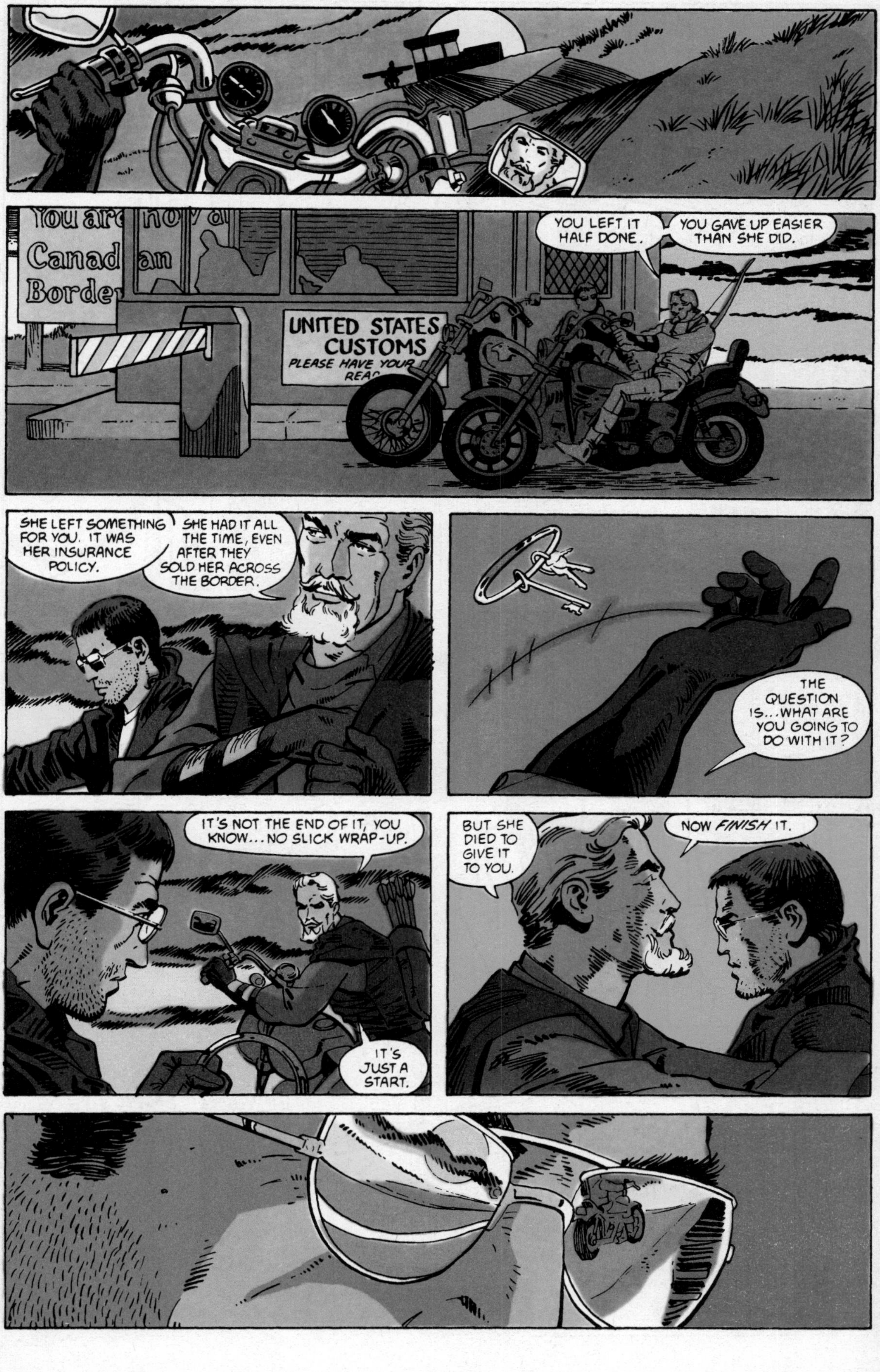
You are now a
Canadian
Border
UNITED STATES CUSTOMS
PLEASE HAVE YOUR
YOU LEFT IT HALF DONE.
YOU GAVE UP EASIER THAN SHE DID.
SHE LEFT SOMETHING FOR YOU. IT WAS HER INSURANCE POLICY.
SHE HAD IT ALL THE TIME, EVEN AFTER THEY SOLD HER ACROSS THE BORDER.
THE QUESTION IS...WHAT ARE YOU GOING TO DO WITH IT?
IT'S NOT THE END OF IT, YOU KNOW... NO SLICK WRAP-UP.
IT'S JUST A START.
BUT SHE DIED TO GIVE IT TO YOU.
NOW *FINISH* IT.

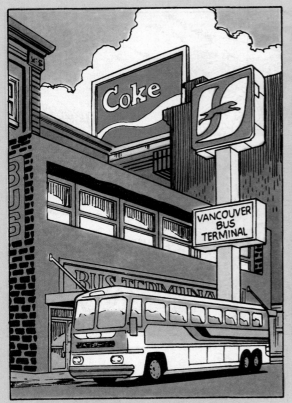

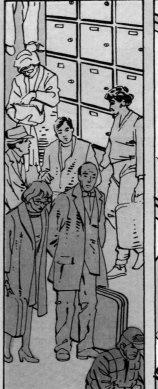

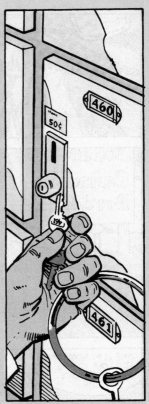

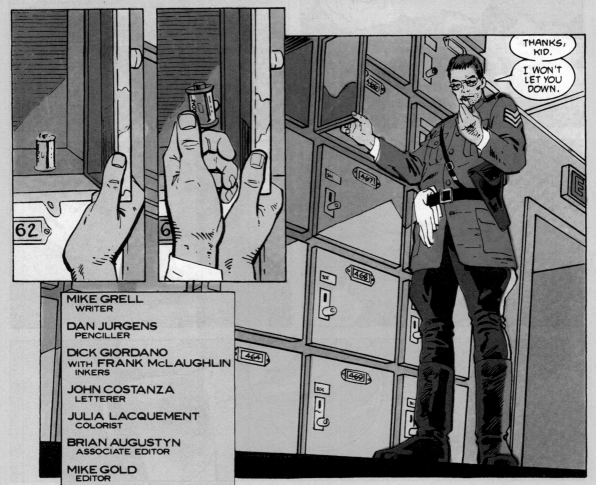

Coke
VANCOUVER BUS TERMINAL
460
50¢
461
62
THANKS, KID.
I WON'T LET YOU DOWN.
467
468
464
469
MIKE GRELL
WRITER
DAN JURGENS
PENCILLER
DICK GIORDANO
WITH FRANK McLAUGHLIN
INKERS
JOHN COSTANZA
LETTERER
JULIA LACQUEMENT
COLORIST
BRIAN AUGUSTYN
ASSOCIATE EDITOR
MIKE GOLD
EDITOR

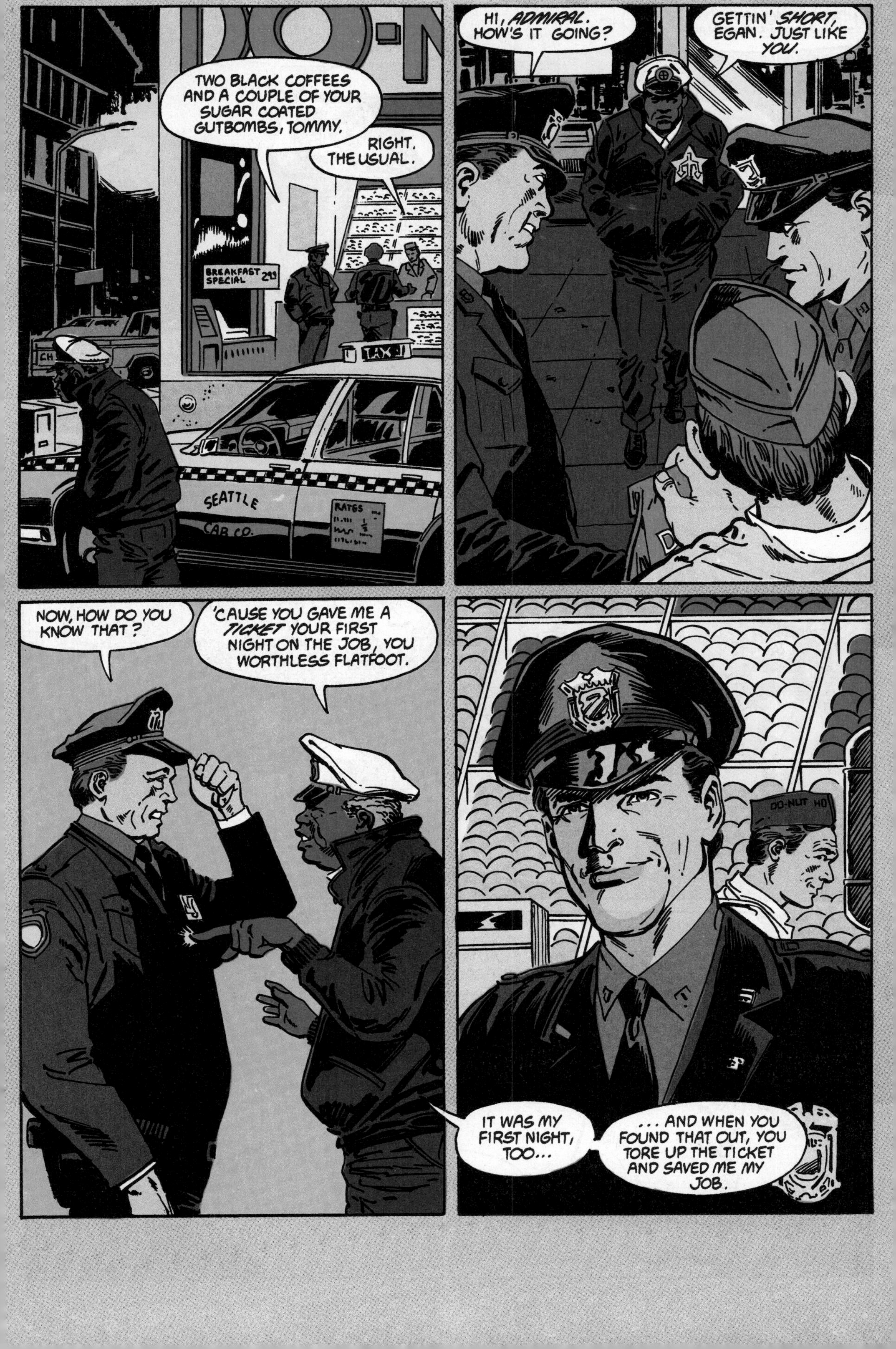
TWO BLACK COFFEES AND A COUPLE OF YOUR SUGAR COATED GUTBOMBS, TOMMY.
RIGHT. THE USUAL.
BREAKFAST SPECIAL 2.99
TAXI
SEATTLE CAB CO.
RATES
HI, ADMIRAL. HOW'S IT GOING?
GETTIN' SHORT, EGAN. JUST LIKE YOU.
NOW, HOW DO YOU KNOW THAT?
'CAUSE YOU GAVE ME A TICKET YOUR FIRST NIGHT ON THE JOB, YOU WORTHLESS FLATFOOT.
DO-NUT HO
IT WAS MY FIRST NIGHT, TOO...
. . . AND WHEN YOU FOUND THAT OUT, YOU TORE UP THE TICKET AND SAVED ME MY JOB.

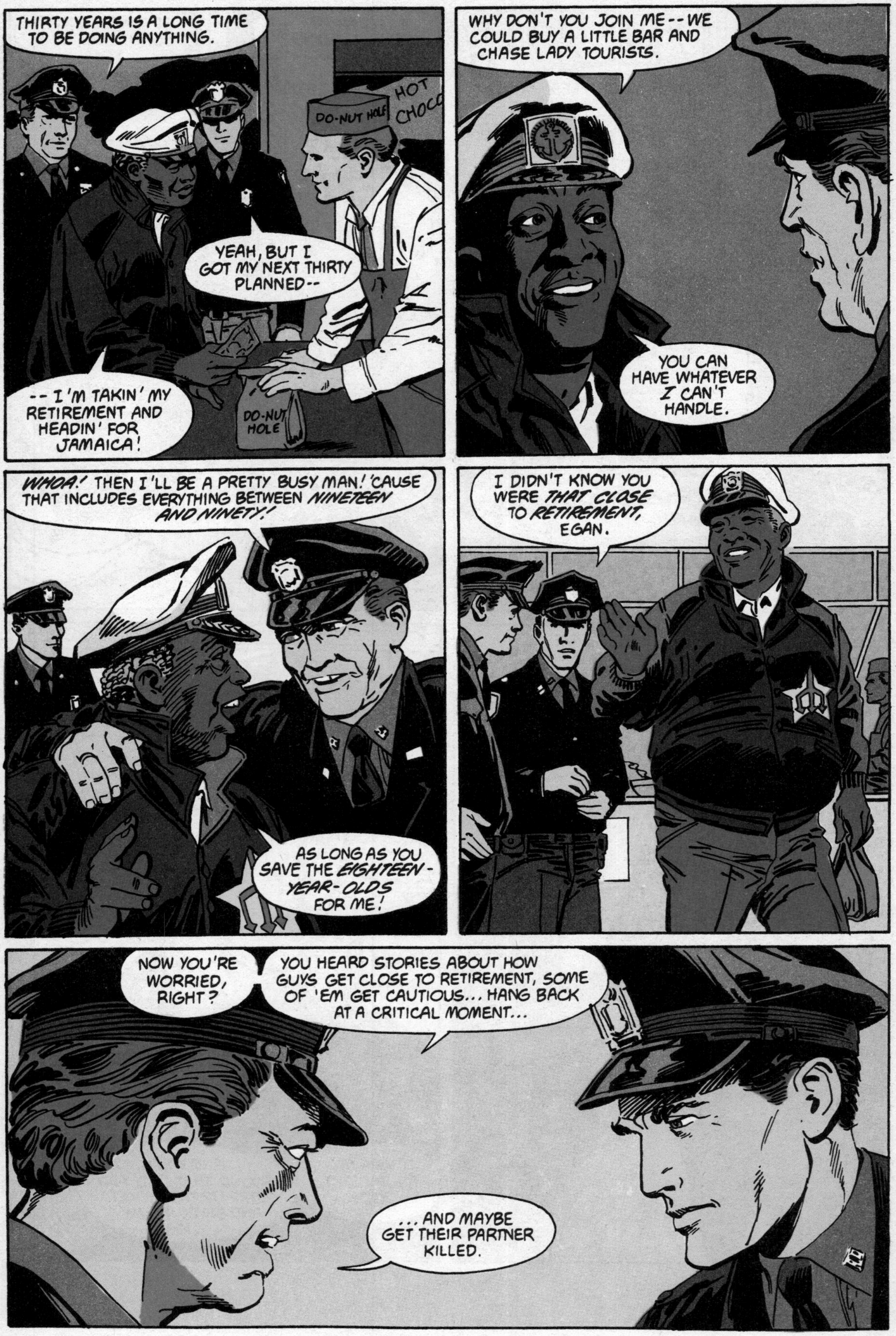
THIRTY YEARS IS A LONG TIME TO BE DOING ANYTHING.
DO-NUT HOLE
HOT CHOCO
YEAH, BUT I GOT MY NEXT THIRTY PLANNED--
-- I'M TAKIN' MY RETIREMENT AND HEADIN' FOR JAMAICA!
DO-NUT HOLE
WHY DON'T YOU JOIN ME -- WE COULD BUY A LITTLE BAR AND CHASE LADY TOURISTS.
YOU CAN HAVE WHATEVER I CAN'T HANDLE.
WHOA! THEN I'LL BE A PRETTY BUSY MAN! 'CAUSE THAT INCLUDES EVERYTHING BETWEEN NINETEEN AND NINETY!
AS LONG AS YOU SAVE THE EIGHTEEN-YEAR-OLDS FOR ME!
I DIDN'T KNOW YOU WERE THAT CLOSE TO RETIREMENT, EGAN.
NOW YOU'RE WORRIED, RIGHT?
YOU HEARD STORIES ABOUT HOW GUYS GET CLOSE TO RETIREMENT, SOME OF 'EM GET CAUTIOUS... HANG BACK AT A CRITICAL MOMENT...
...AND MAYBE GET THEIR PARTNER KILLED.

I'M NOT SAYING THAT, IT'S JUST...

I MEAN... SIX MONTHS... WHY NOT TAKE A *DESK*?

SEE THAT OUT THERE? THAT'S THE *STREETS*.

THAT'S WHERE I'VE BEEN *MOST* OF MY LIFE.

IT'S WHERE I *BELONG*.

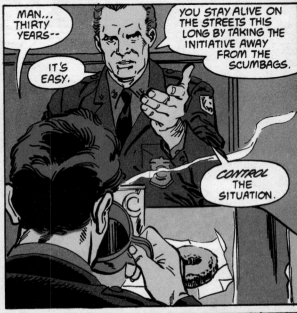

MAN... THIRTY YEARS--

IT'S *EASY*.

YOU STAY ALIVE ON THE STREETS THIS LONG BY TAKING THE INITIATIVE AWAY FROM THE SCUMBAGS.

CONTROL THE SITUATION.

FOR INSTANCE, YOU'RE QUESTIONING A COUPLE OF PUNKS, AND ONE OF THEM PULLS A KNIFE. WHAT DO YOU DO?

I GO TO THE *BATON*.

WRONG!

YOU PULL YOUR *GUN!*

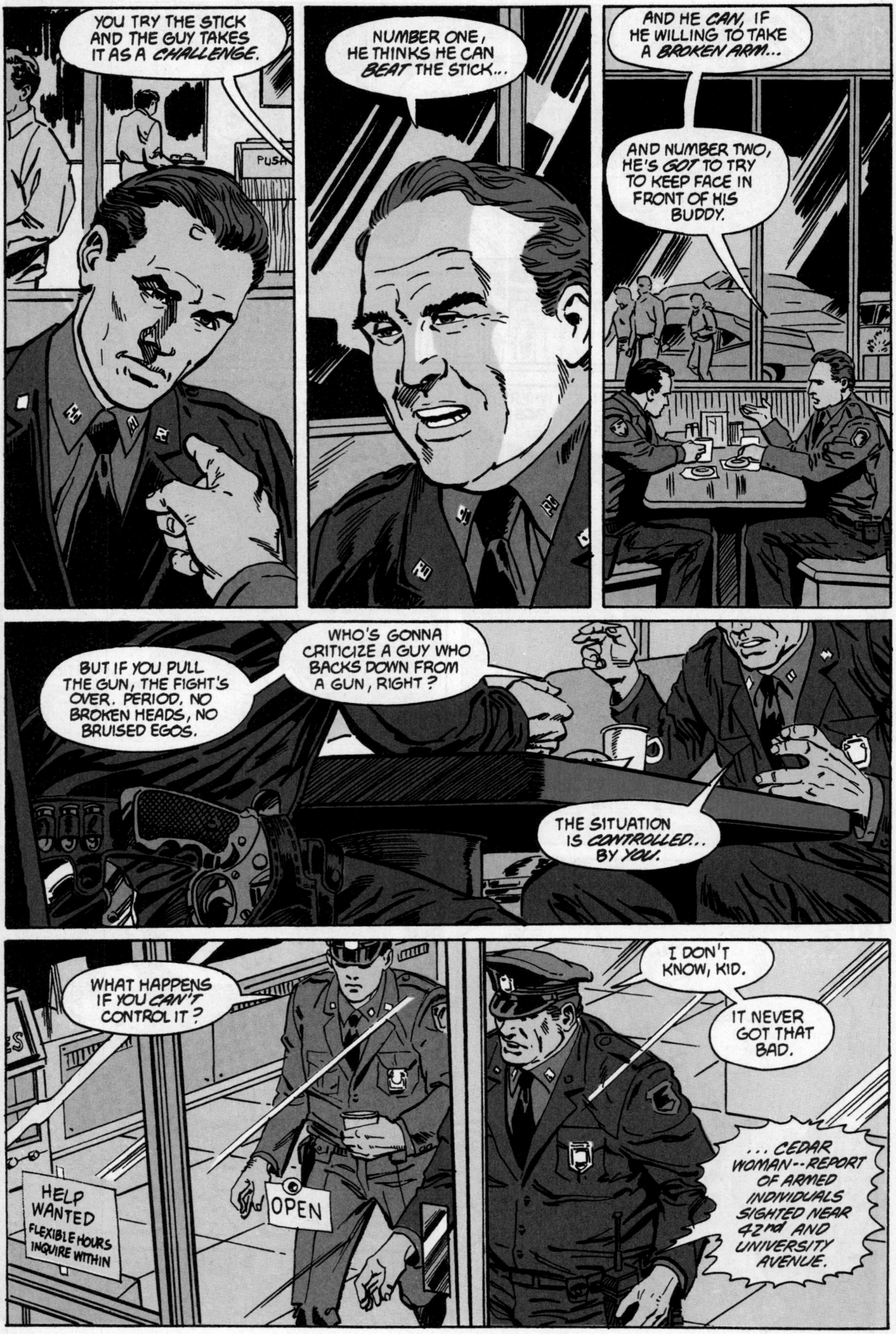
YOU TRY THE STICK AND THE GUY TAKES IT AS A CHALLENGE.
NUMBER ONE, HE THINKS HE CAN BEAT THE STICK...
AND HE CAN, IF HE WILLING TO TAKE A BROKEN ARM...
AND NUMBER TWO, HE'S GOT TO TRY TO KEEP FACE IN FRONT OF HIS BUDDY.
BUT IF YOU PULL THE GUN, THE FIGHT'S OVER. PERIOD. NO BROKEN HEADS, NO BRUISED EGOS.
WHO'S GONNA CRITICIZE A GUY WHO BACKS DOWN FROM A GUN, RIGHT?
THE SITUATION IS CONTROLLED... BY YOU.
WHAT HAPPENS IF YOU CAN'T CONTROL IT?
I DON'T KNOW, KID.
IT NEVER GOT THAT BAD.
...CEDAR WOMAN--REPORT OF ARMED INDIVIDUALS SIGHTED NEAR 42nd AND UNIVERSITY AVENUE.
HELP WANTED
FLEXIBLE HOURS
INQUIRE WITHIN
OPEN
PUSH

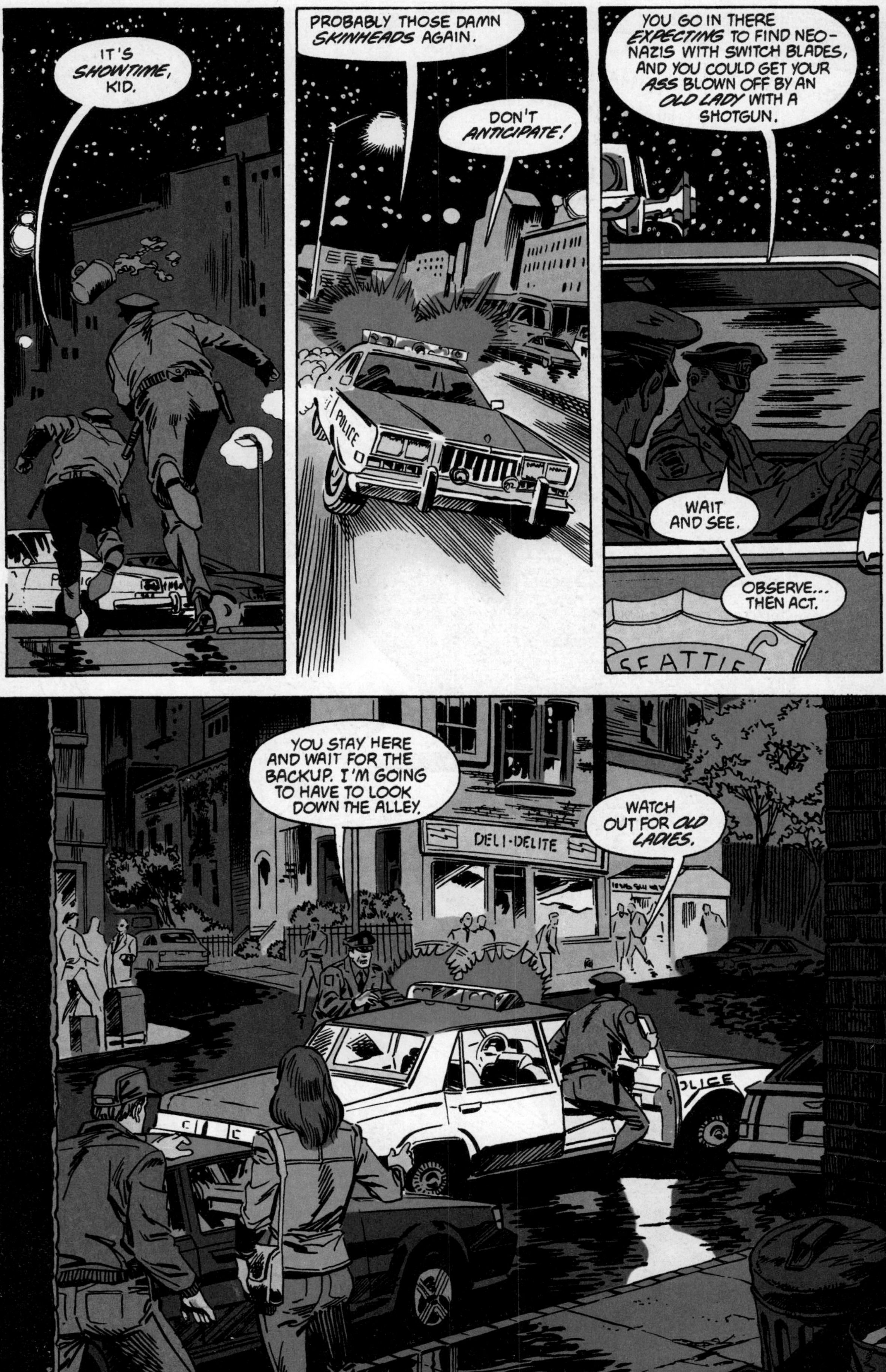

IT'S SHOWTIME, KID.
PROBABLY THOSE DAMN SKINHEADS AGAIN.
DON'T ANTICIPATE!
POLICE
YOU GO IN THERE EXPECTING TO FIND NEO-NAZIS WITH SWITCH BLADES, AND YOU COULD GET YOUR ASS BLOWN OFF BY AN OLD LADY WITH A SHOTGUN.
WAIT AND SEE.
OBSERVE... THEN ACT.
YOU STAY HERE AND WAIT FOR THE BACKUP. I'M GOING TO HAVE TO LOOK DOWN THE ALLEY.
WATCH OUT FOR OLD LADIES.
DELI-DELITE

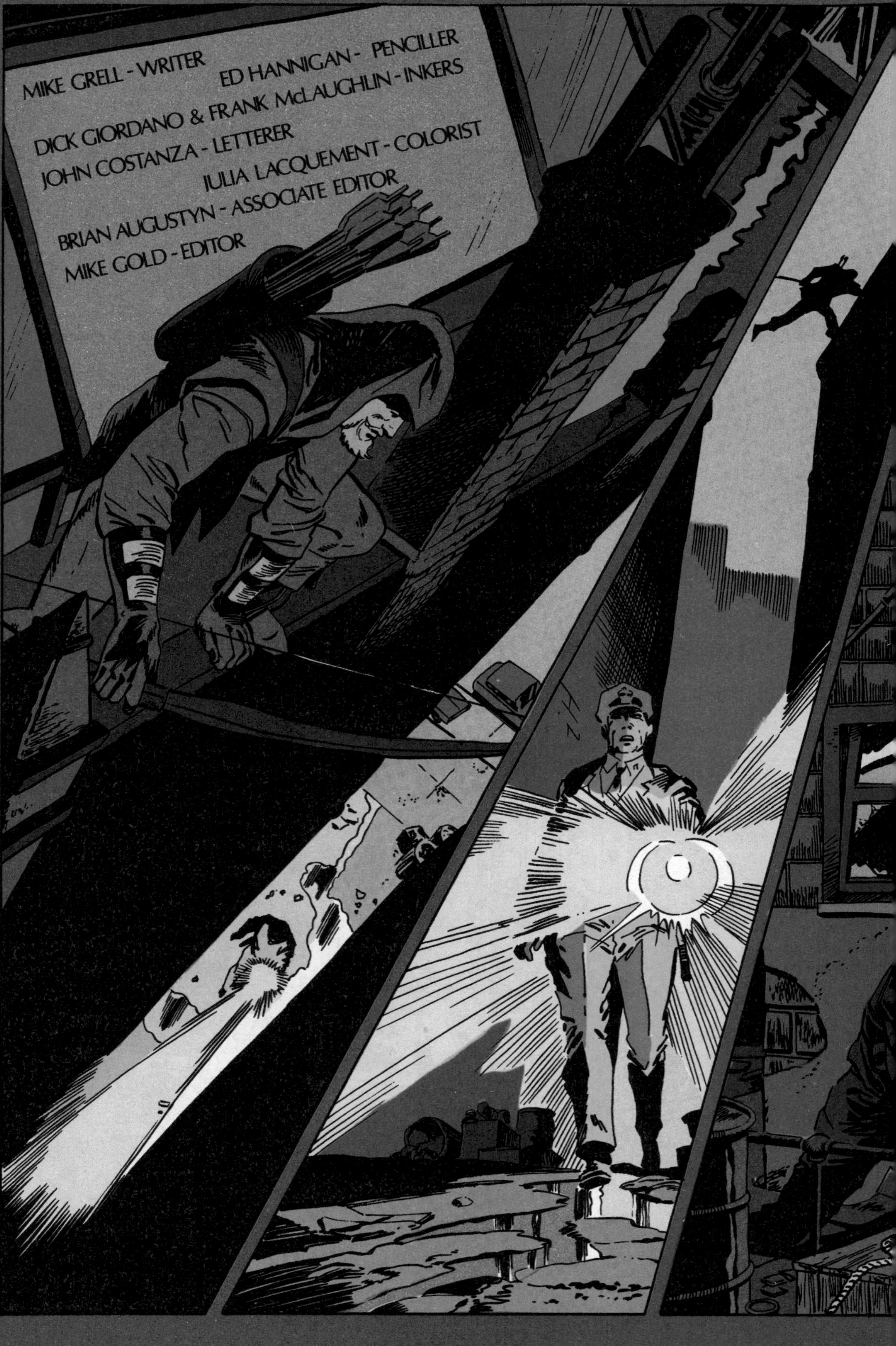

MIKE GRELL - WRITER
ED HANNIGAN - PENCILLER
DICK GIORDANO & FRANK McLAUGHLIN - INKERS
JOHN COSTANZA - LETTERER
JULIA LACQUEMENT - COLORIST
BRIAN AUGUSTYN - ASSOCIATE EDITOR
MIKE GOLD - EDITOR

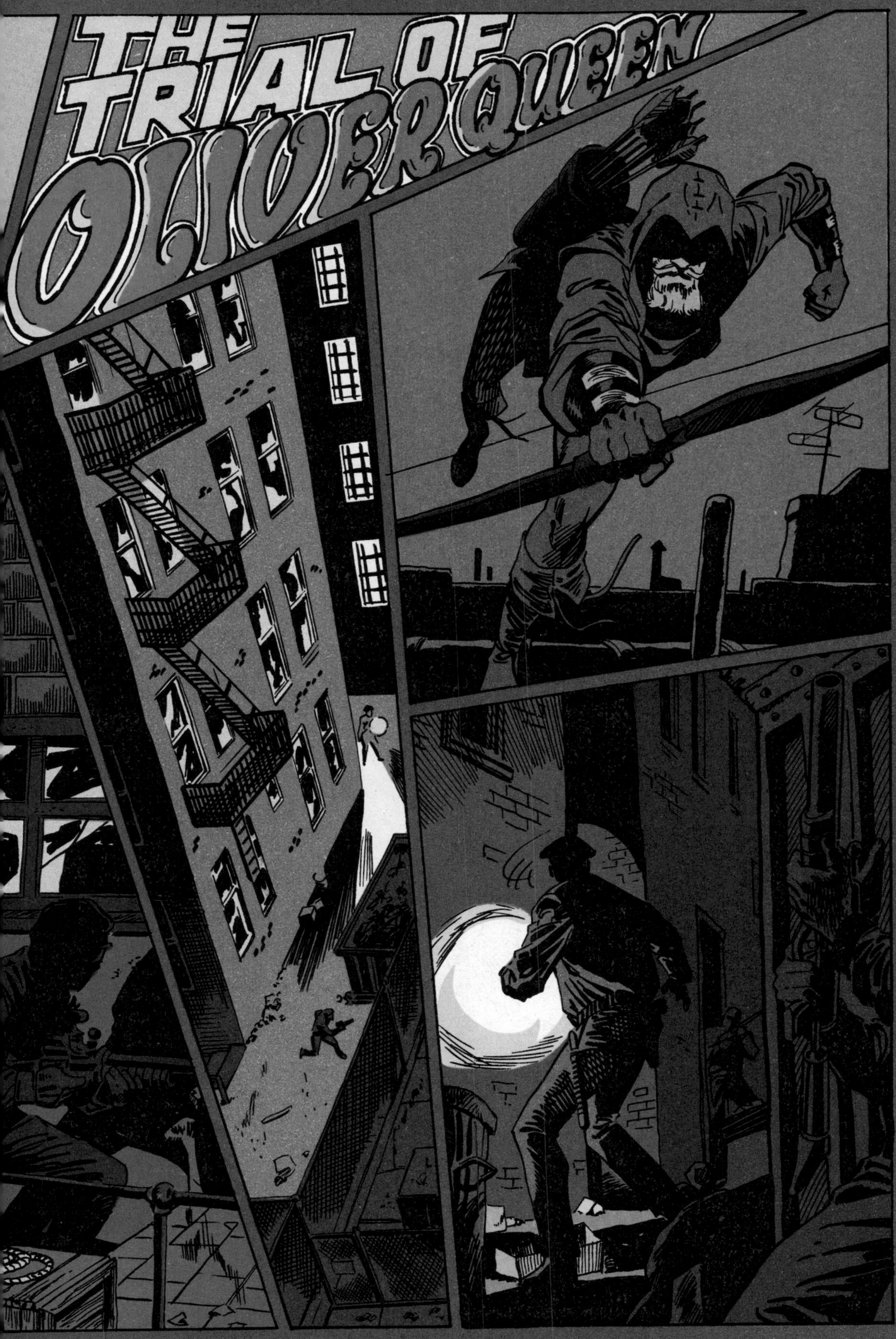
THE TRIAL OF OLIVER QUEEN

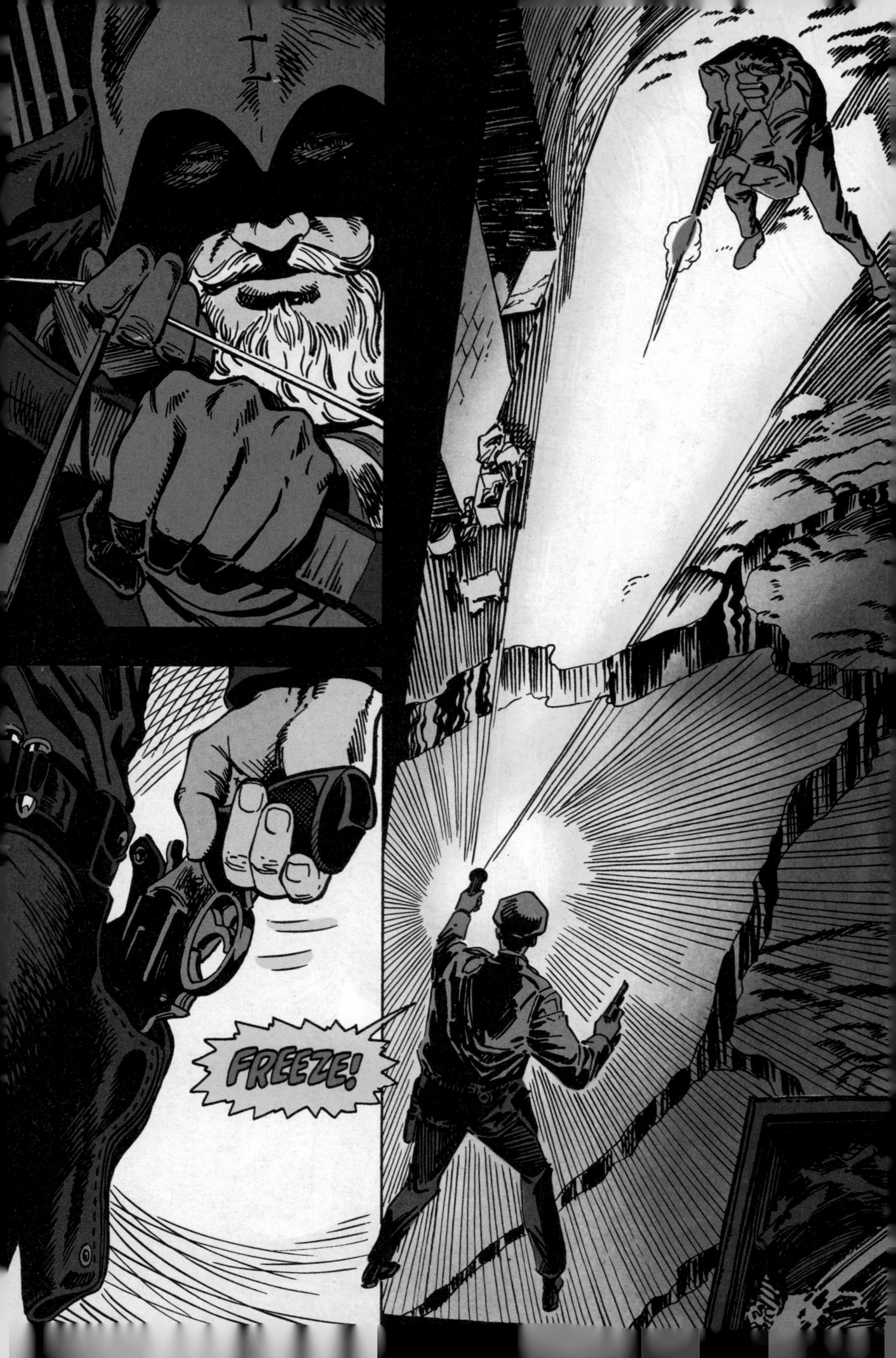
FREEZE!

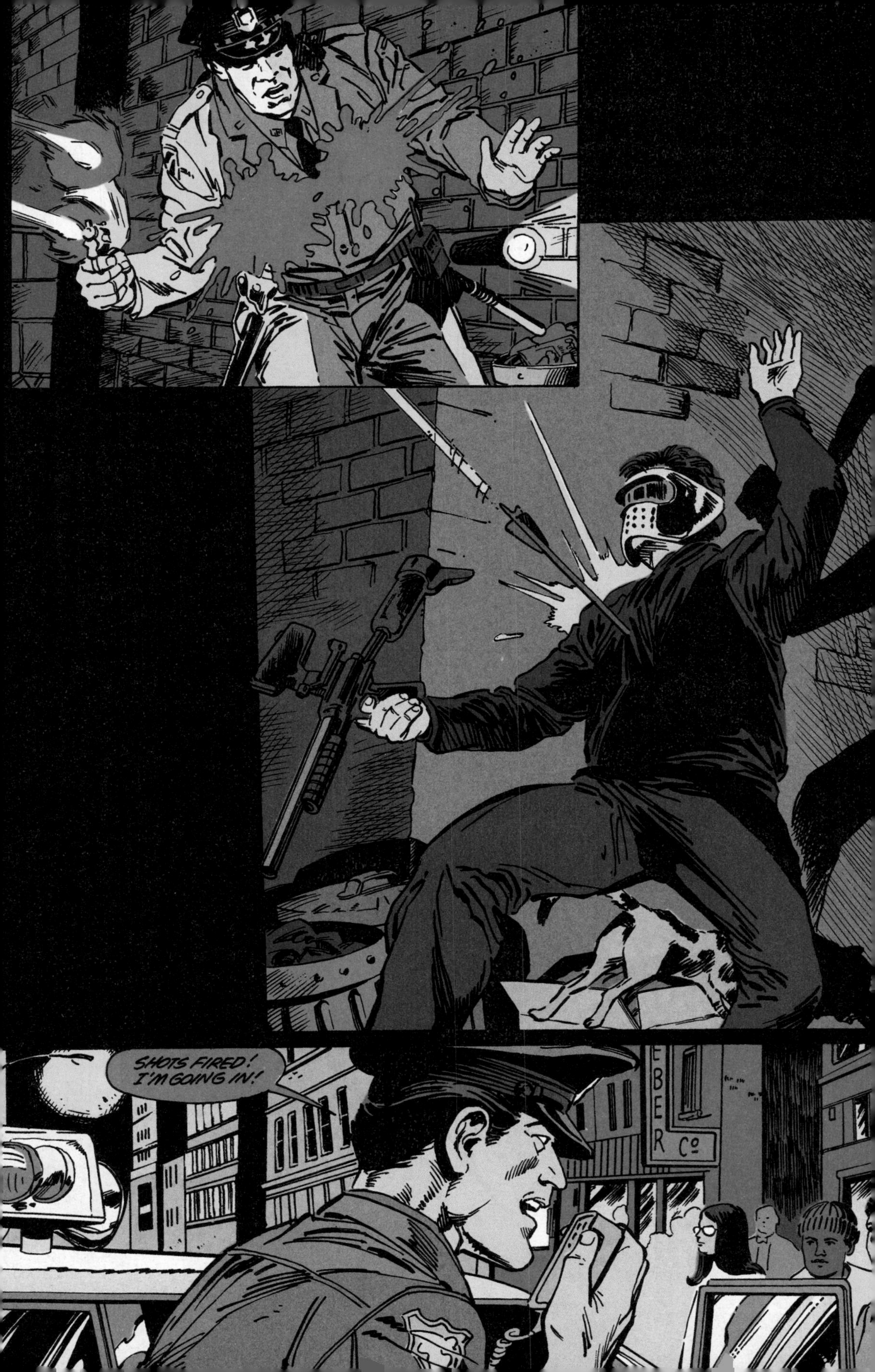
SHOTS FIRED! I'M GOING IN!
EBER
R Co

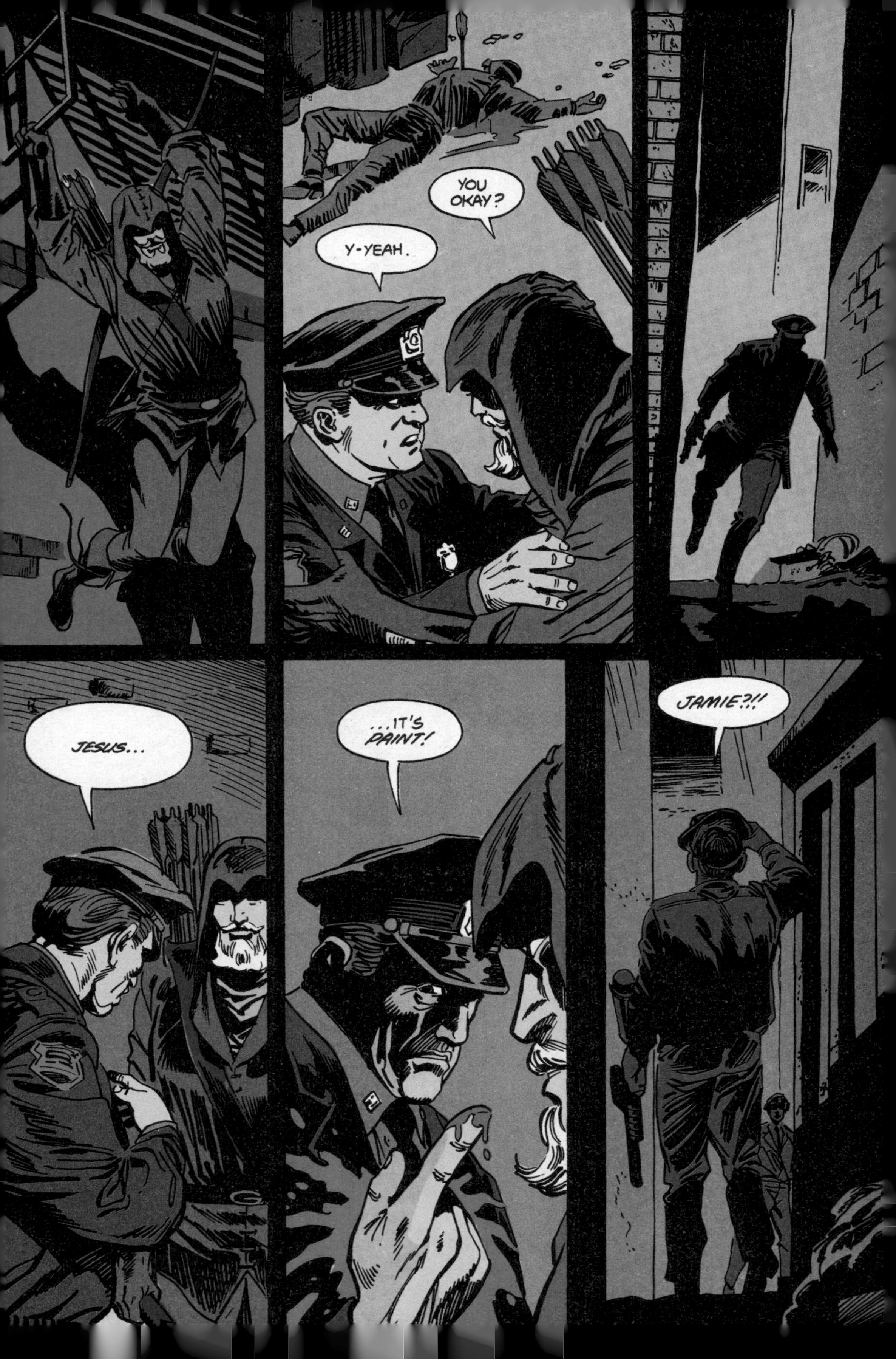
YOU OKAY?
Y-YEAH.
JESUS...
...IT'S PAINT!
JAMIE?!!

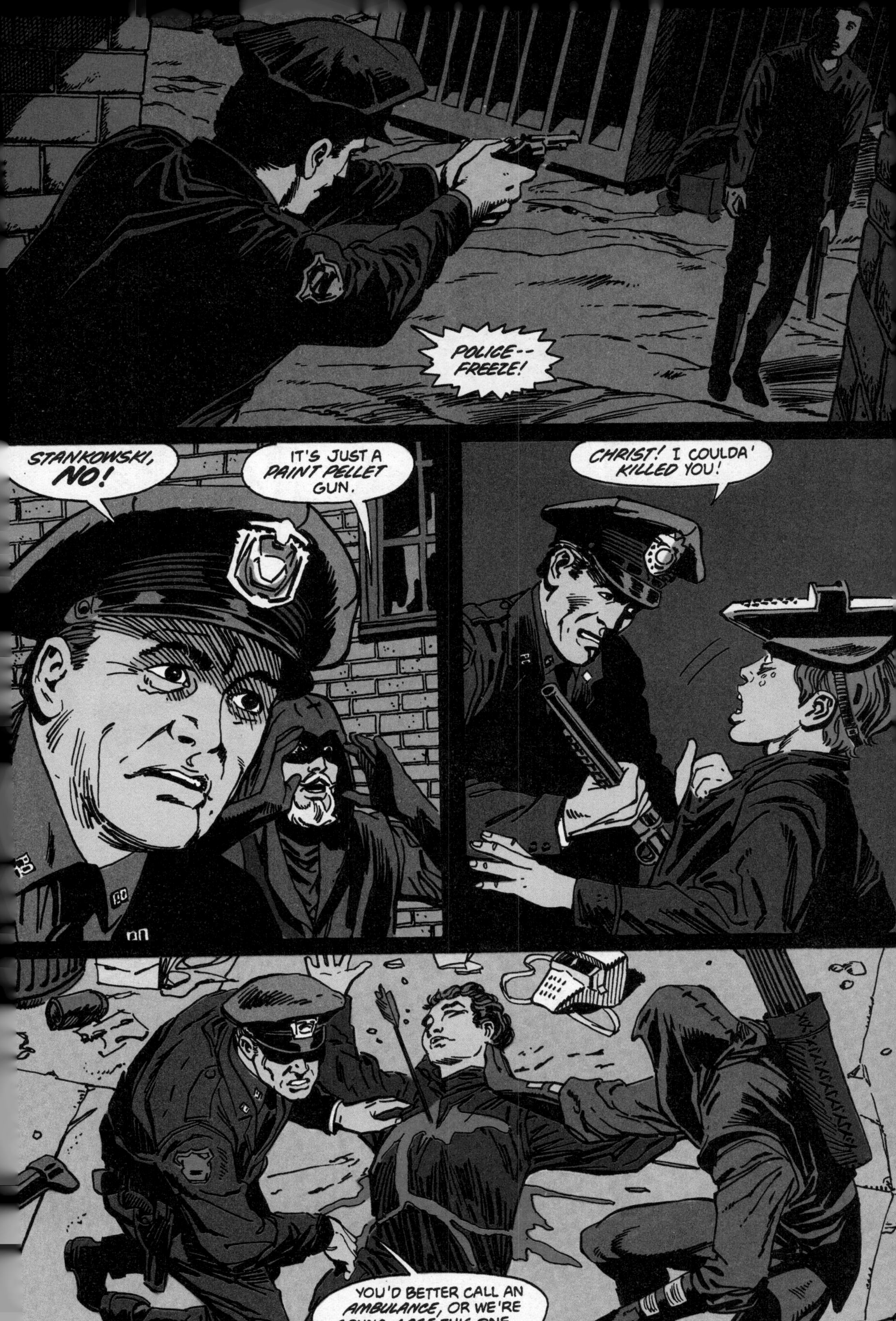
POLICE--
FREEZE!
STANKOWSKI, NO!
IT'S JUST A PAINT PELLET GUN.
CHRIST! I COULDA' KILLED YOU!
YOU'D BETTER CALL AN AMBULANCE, OR WE'RE GONNA LOSE THIS ONE.

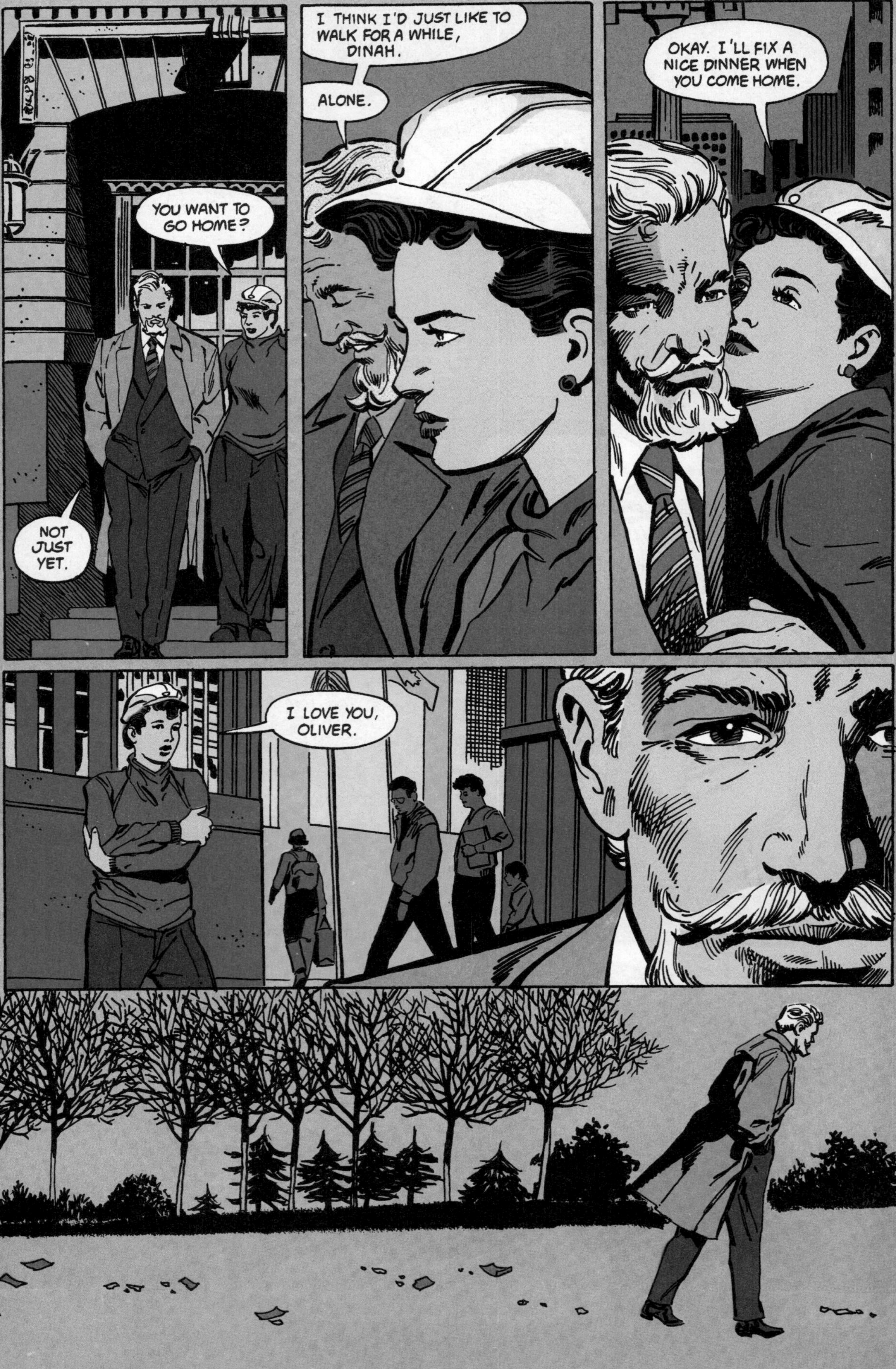
YOU WANT TO GO HOME?
NOT JUST YET.
I THINK I'D JUST LIKE TO WALK FOR A WHILE, DINAH.
ALONE.
OKAY. I'LL FIX A NICE DINNER WHEN YOU COME HOME.
I LOVE YOU, OLIVER.

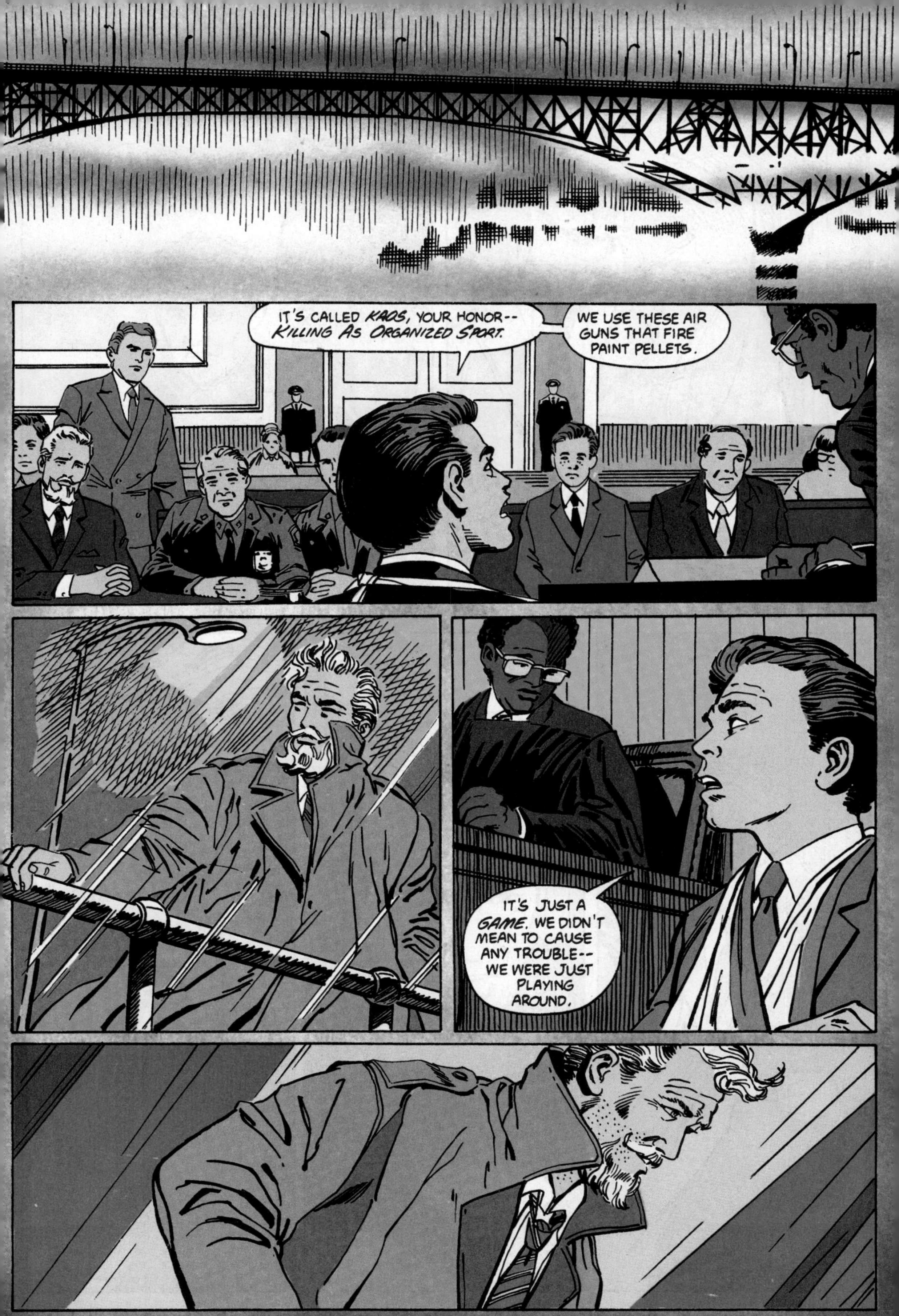
IT'S CALLED KAOS, YOUR HONOR-- KILLING AS ORGANIZED SPORT.
WE USE THESE AIR GUNS THAT FIRE PAINT PELLETS.
IT'S JUST A GAME. WE DIDN'T MEAN TO CAUSE ANY TROUBLE-- WE WERE JUST PLAYING AROUND.

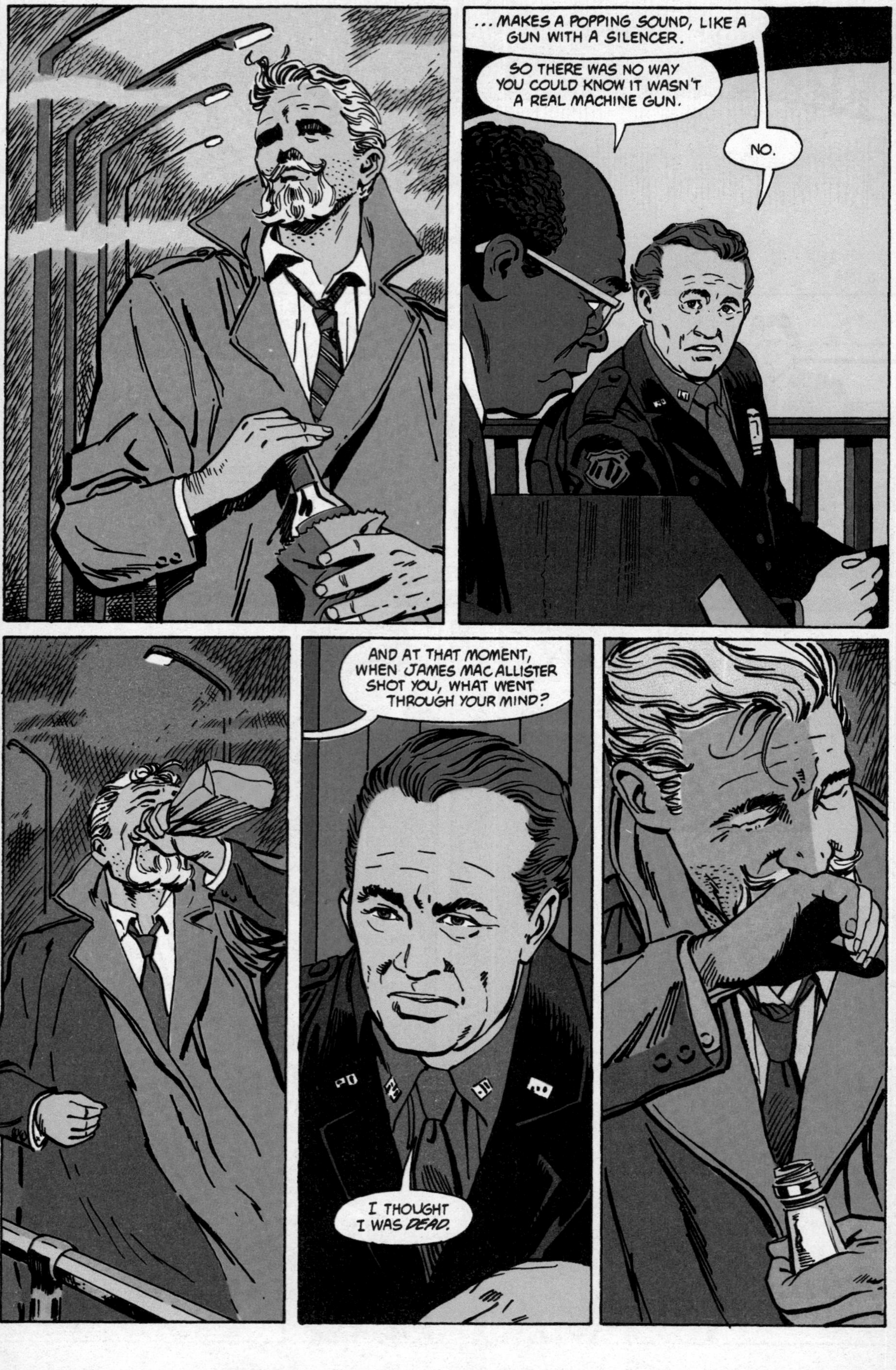
...MAKES A POPPING SOUND, LIKE A GUN WITH A SILENCER.
SO THERE WAS NO WAY YOU COULD KNOW IT WASN'T A REAL MACHINE GUN.
NO.
AND AT THAT MOMENT, WHEN JAMES MAC ALLISTER SHOT YOU, WHAT WENT THROUGH YOUR MIND?
I THOUGHT I WAS DEAD.

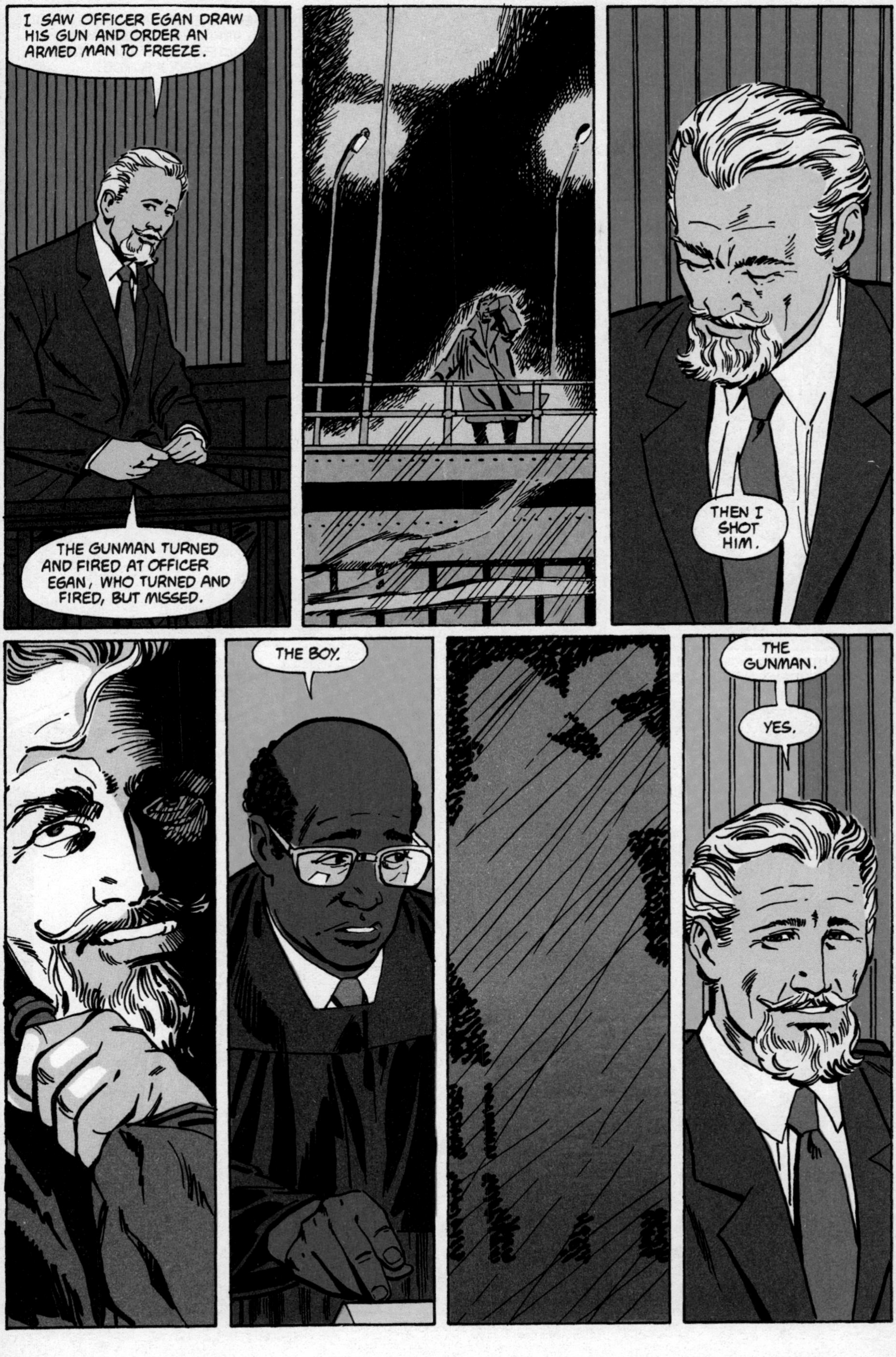
I SAW OFFICER EGAN DRAW HIS GUN AND ORDER AN ARMED MAN TO FREEZE.
THE GUNMAN TURNED AND FIRED AT OFFICER EGAN, WHO TURNED AND FIRED, BUT MISSED.
THEN I SHOT HIM.
THE BOY.
THE GUNMAN.
YES.

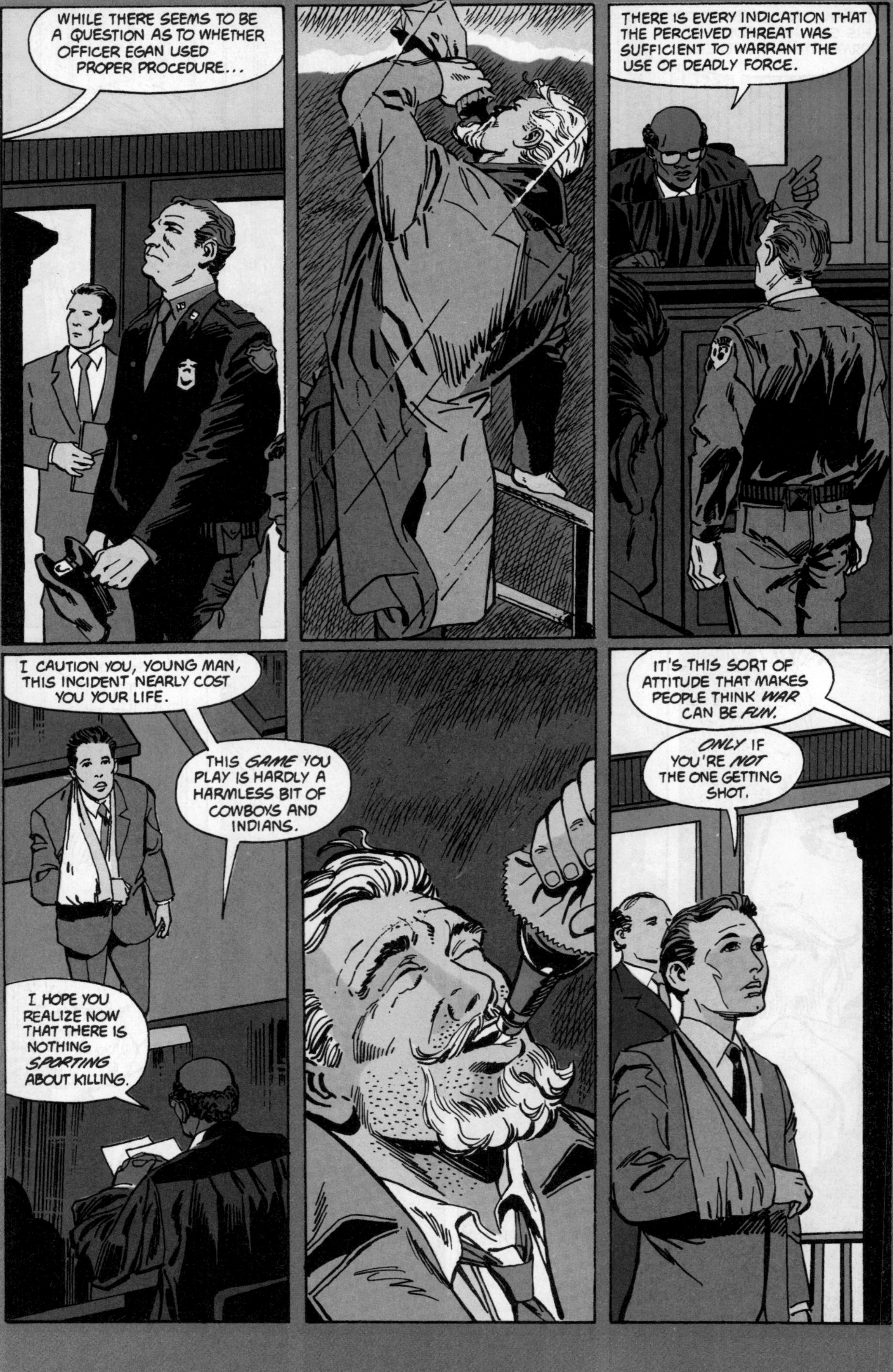
WHILE THERE SEEMS TO BE A QUESTION AS TO WHETHER OFFICER EGAN USED PROPER PROCEDURE...
THERE IS EVERY INDICATION THAT THE PERCEIVED THREAT WAS SUFFICIENT TO WARRANT THE USE OF DEADLY FORCE.
I CAUTION YOU, YOUNG MAN, THIS INCIDENT NEARLY COST YOU YOUR LIFE.
THIS GAME YOU PLAY IS HARDLY A HARMLESS BIT OF COWBOYS AND INDIANS.
I HOPE YOU REALIZE NOW THAT THERE IS NOTHING SPORTING ABOUT KILLING.
IT'S THIS SORT OF ATTITUDE THAT MAKES PEOPLE THINK WAR CAN BE FUN.
ONLY IF YOU'RE NOT THE ONE GETTING SHOT.

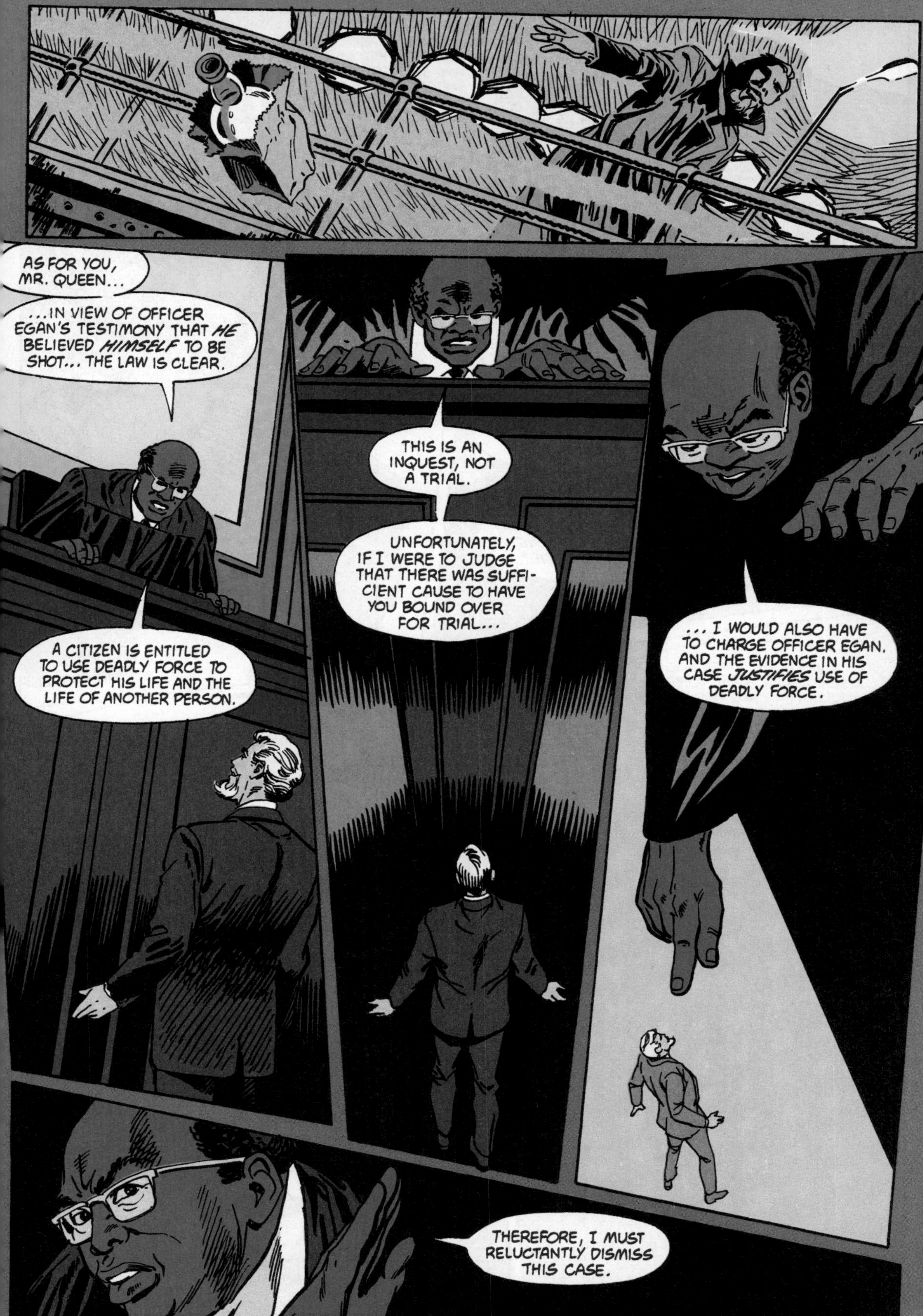
AS FOR YOU, MR. QUEEN...
...IN VIEW OF OFFICER EGAN'S TESTIMONY THAT *HE* BELIEVED *HIMSELF* TO BE SHOT... THE LAW IS CLEAR.
A CITIZEN IS ENTITLED TO USE DEADLY FORCE TO PROTECT HIS LIFE AND THE LIFE OF ANOTHER PERSON.
THIS IS AN INQUEST, NOT A TRIAL.
UNFORTUNATELY, IF I WERE TO JUDGE THAT THERE WAS SUFFICIENT CAUSE TO HAVE YOU BOUND OVER FOR TRIAL...
... I WOULD ALSO HAVE TO CHARGE OFFICER EGAN. AND THE EVIDENCE IN HIS CASE *JUSTIFIES* USE OF DEADLY FORCE.
THEREFORE, I MUST RELUCTANTLY DISMISS THIS CASE.

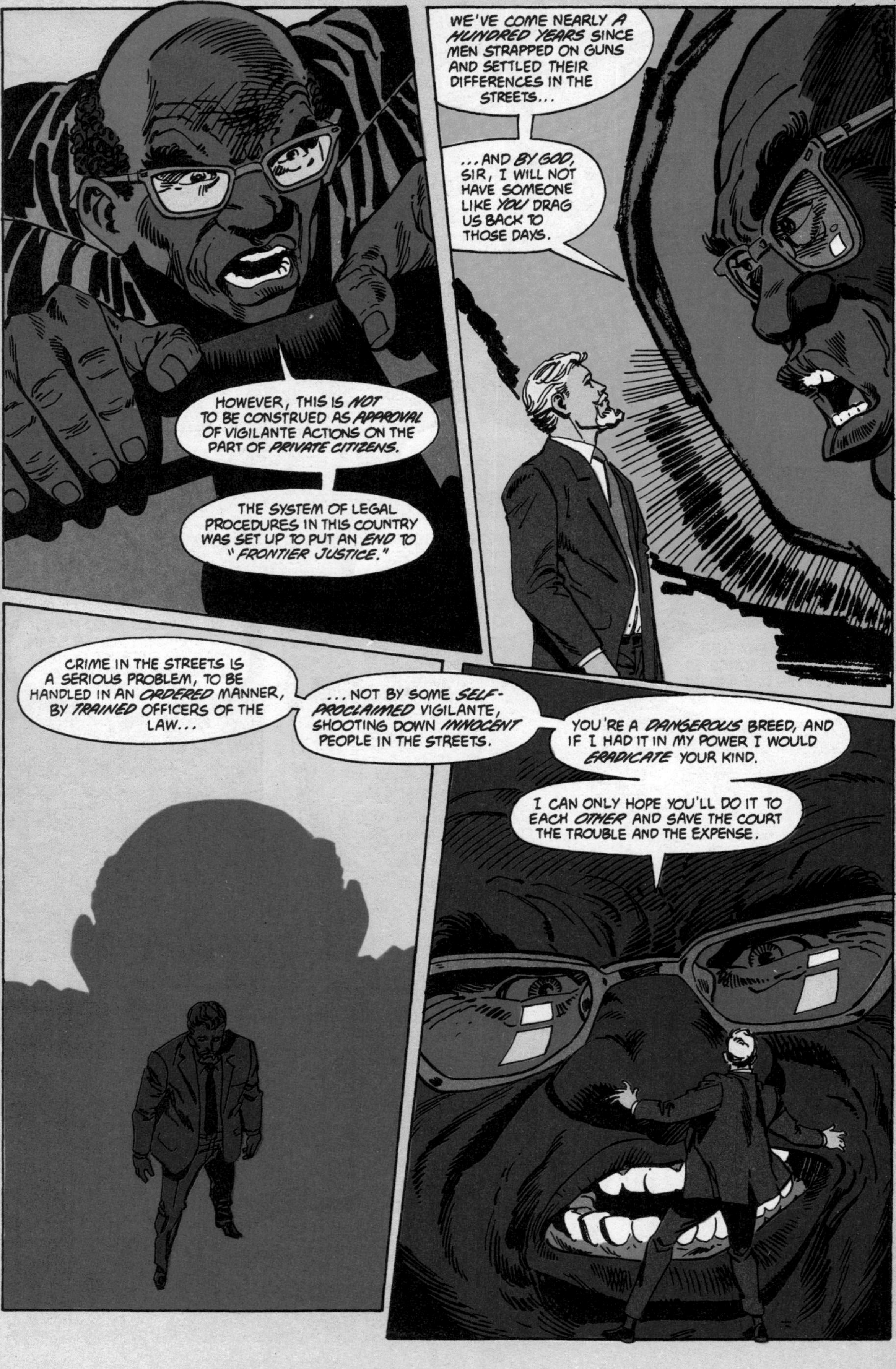
HOWEVER, THIS IS NOT TO BE CONSTRUED AS APPROVAL OF VIGILANTE ACTIONS ON THE PART OF PRIVATE CITIZENS.
THE SYSTEM OF LEGAL PROCEDURES IN THIS COUNTRY WAS SET UP TO PUT AN END TO "FRONTIER JUSTICE."
WE'VE COME NEARLY A HUNDRED YEARS SINCE MEN STRAPPED ON GUNS AND SETTLED THEIR DIFFERENCES IN THE STREETS...
...AND BY GOD, SIR, I WILL NOT HAVE SOMEONE LIKE YOU DRAG US BACK TO THOSE DAYS.
CRIME IN THE STREETS IS A SERIOUS PROBLEM, TO BE HANDLED IN AN ORDERED MANNER, BY TRAINED OFFICERS OF THE LAW...
...NOT BY SOME SELF-PROCLAIMED VIGILANTE, SHOOTING DOWN INNOCENT PEOPLE IN THE STREETS.
YOU'RE A DANGEROUS BREED, AND IF I HAD IT IN MY POWER I WOULD ERADICATE YOUR KIND.
I CAN ONLY HOPE YOU'LL DO IT TO EACH OTHER AND SAVE THE COURT THE TROUBLE AND THE EXPENSE.

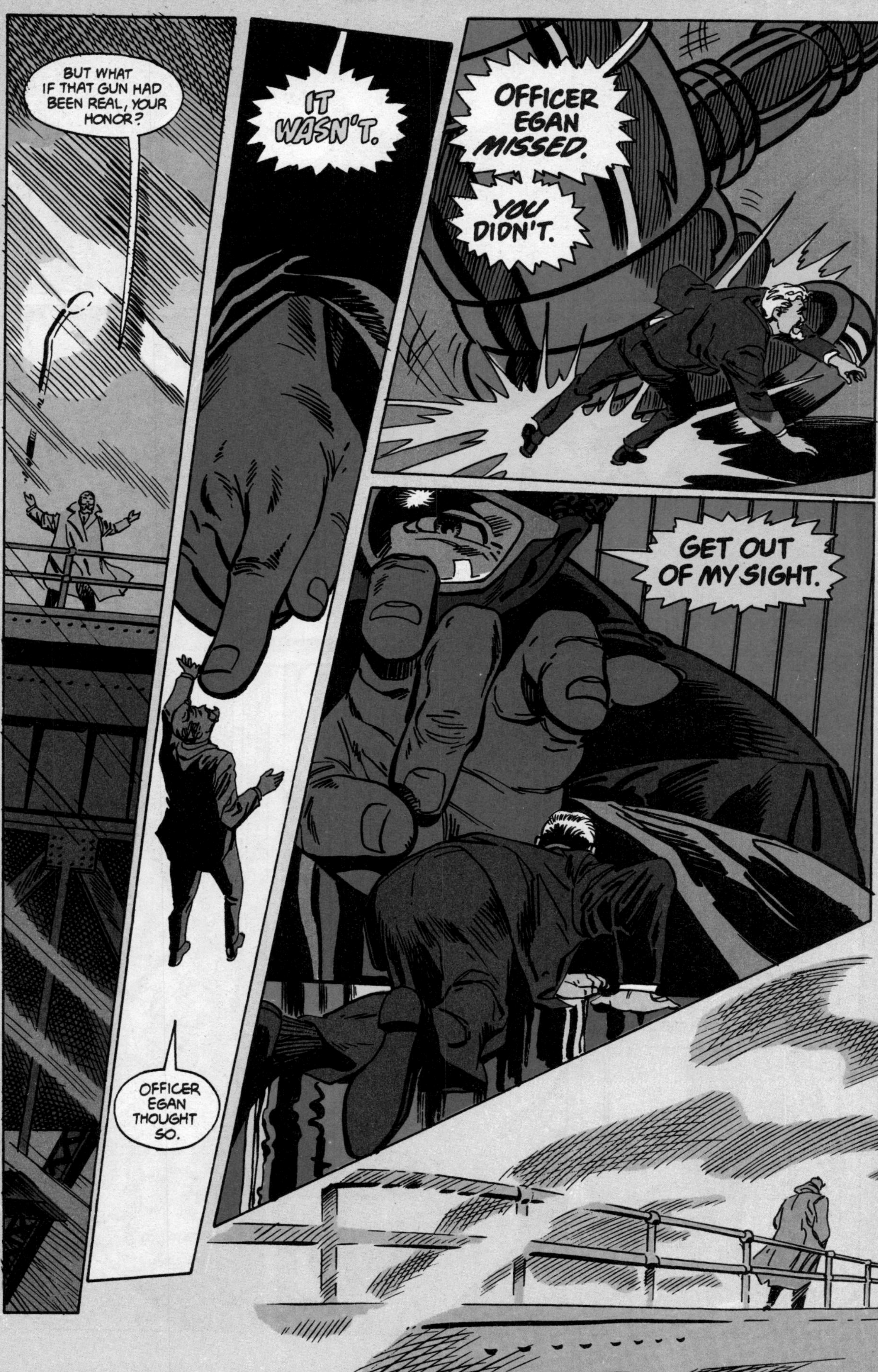
BUT WHAT IF THAT GUN HAD BEEN REAL, YOUR HONOR?
OFFICER EGAN THOUGHT SO.
IT WASN'T.
OFFICER EGAN MISSED.
YOU DIDN'T.
GET OUT OF MY SIGHT.

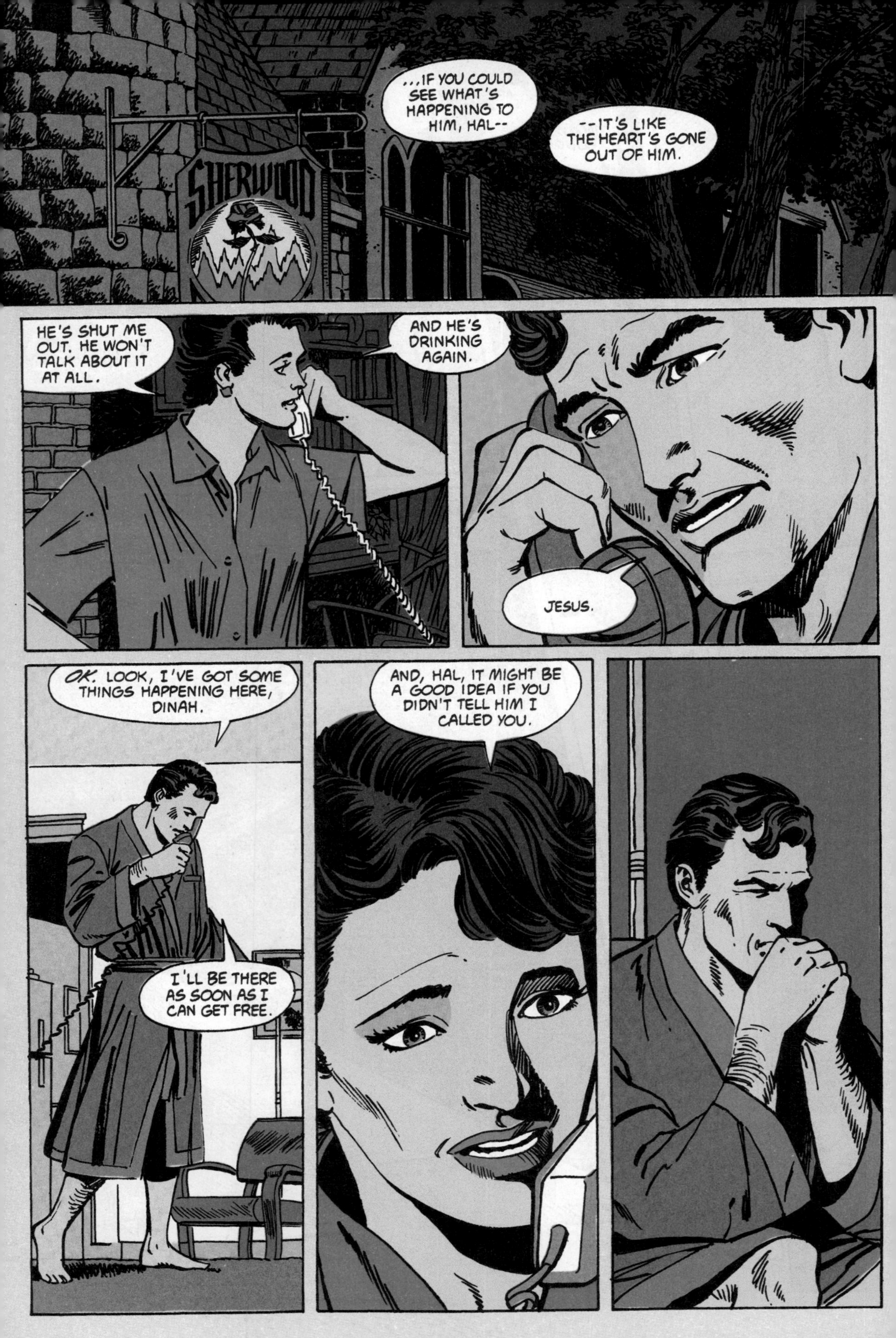
SHERWOOD
...IF YOU COULD SEE WHAT'S HAPPENING TO HIM, HAL--
--IT'S LIKE THE HEART'S GONE OUT OF HIM.
HE'S SHUT ME OUT. HE WON'T TALK ABOUT IT AT ALL.
AND HE'S DRINKING AGAIN.
JESUS.
OK. LOOK, I'VE GOT SOME THINGS HAPPENING HERE, DINAH.
I'LL BE THERE AS SOON AS I CAN GET FREE.
AND, HAL, IT MIGHT BE A GOOD IDEA IF YOU DIDN'T TELL HIM I CALLED YOU.

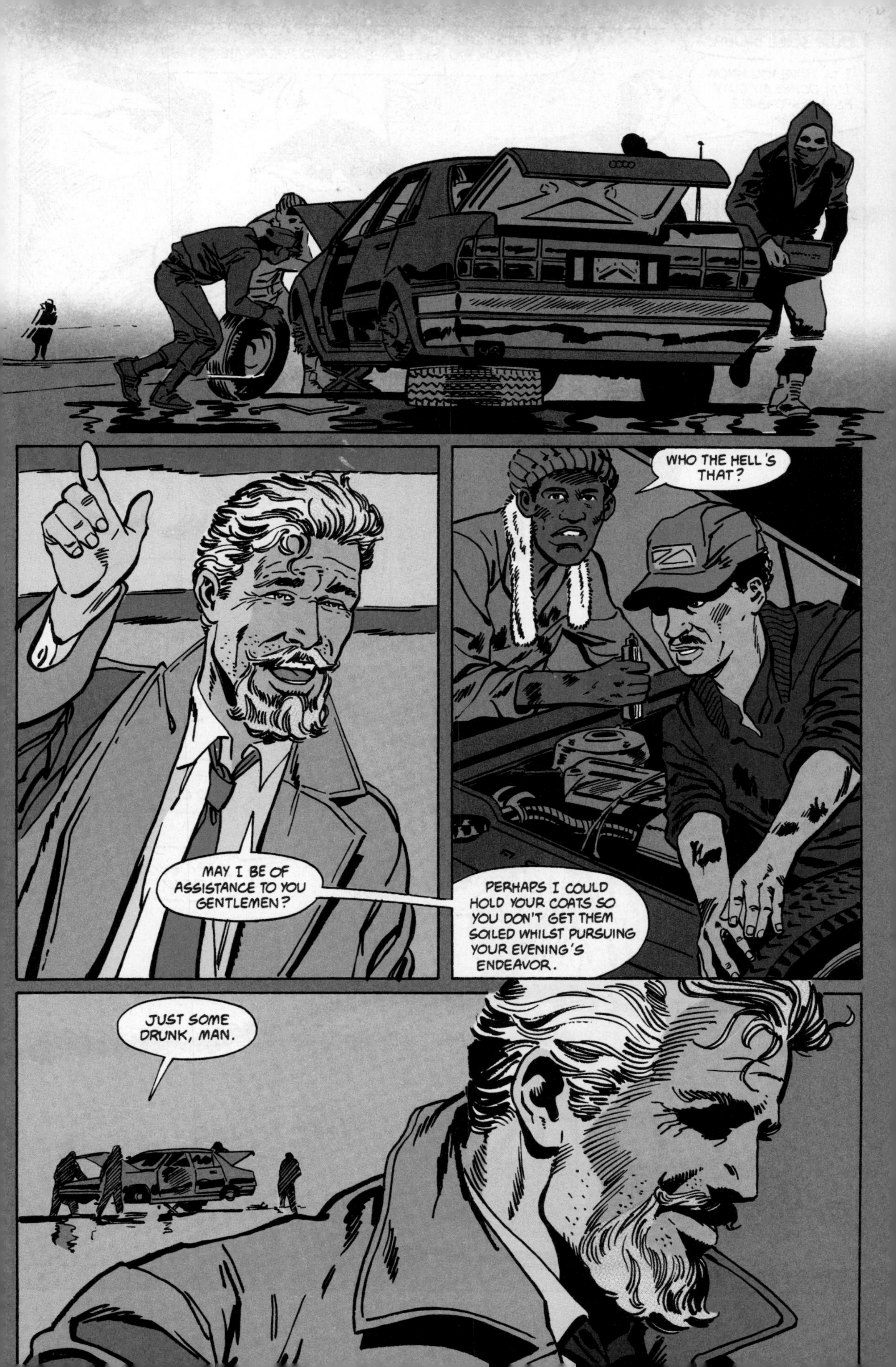
MAY I BE OF ASSISTANCE TO YOU GENTLEMEN?
WHO THE HELL'S THAT?
PERHAPS I COULD HOLD YOUR COATS SO YOU DON'T GET THEM SOILED WHILST PURSUING YOUR EVENING'S ENDEAVOR.
JUST SOME DRUNK, MAN.

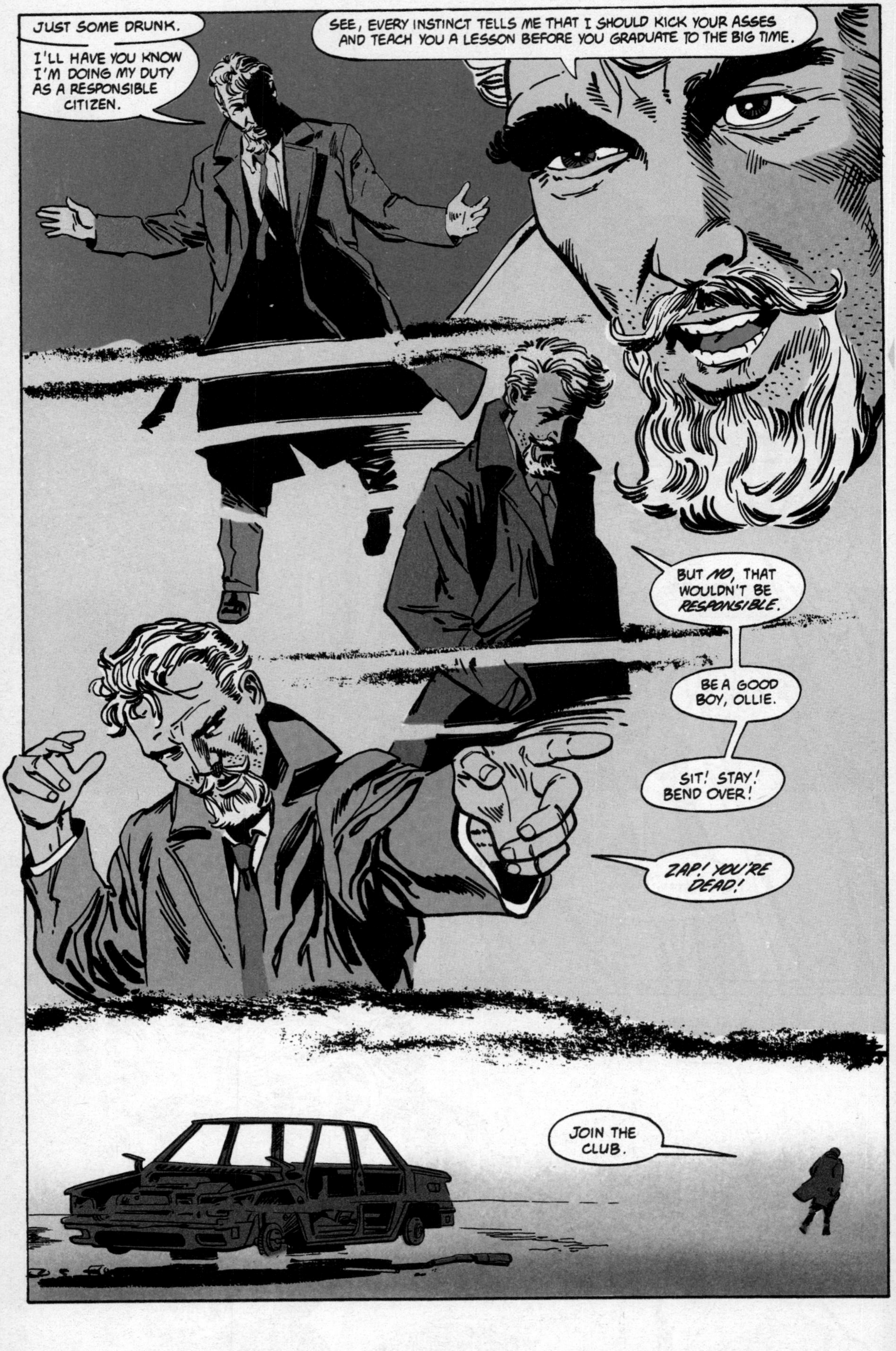
JUST SOME DRUNK.
I'LL HAVE YOU KNOW I'M DOING MY DUTY AS A RESPONSIBLE CITIZEN.
SEE, EVERY INSTINCT TELLS ME THAT I SHOULD KICK YOUR ASSES AND TEACH YOU A LESSON BEFORE YOU GRADUATE TO THE BIG TIME.
BUT NO, THAT WOULDN'T BE RESPONSIBLE.
BE A GOOD BOY, OLLIE.
SIT! STAY! BEND OVER!
ZAP! YOU'RE DEAD!
JOIN THE CLUB.

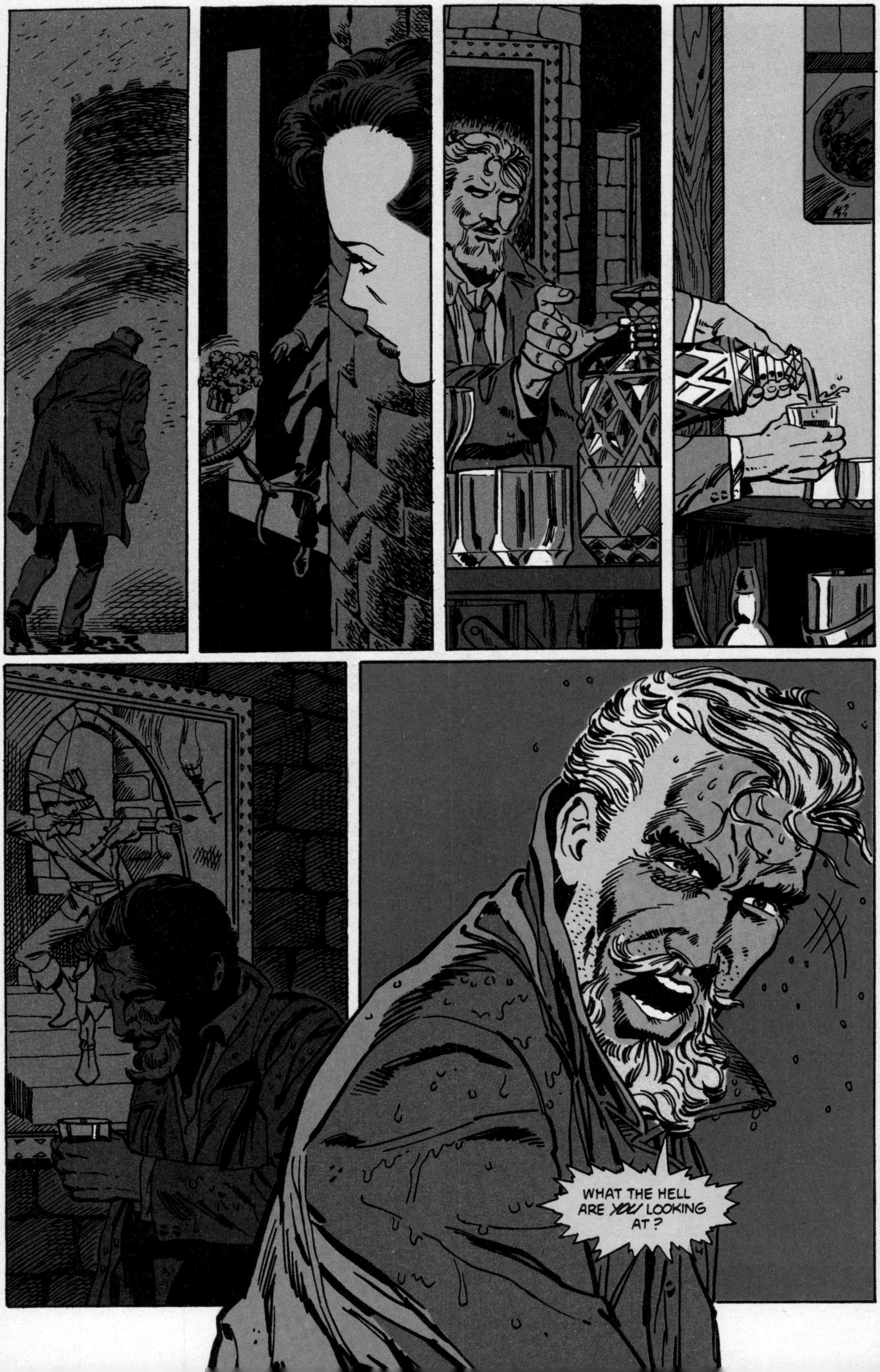
WHAT THE HELL
ARE YOU LOOKING
AT?

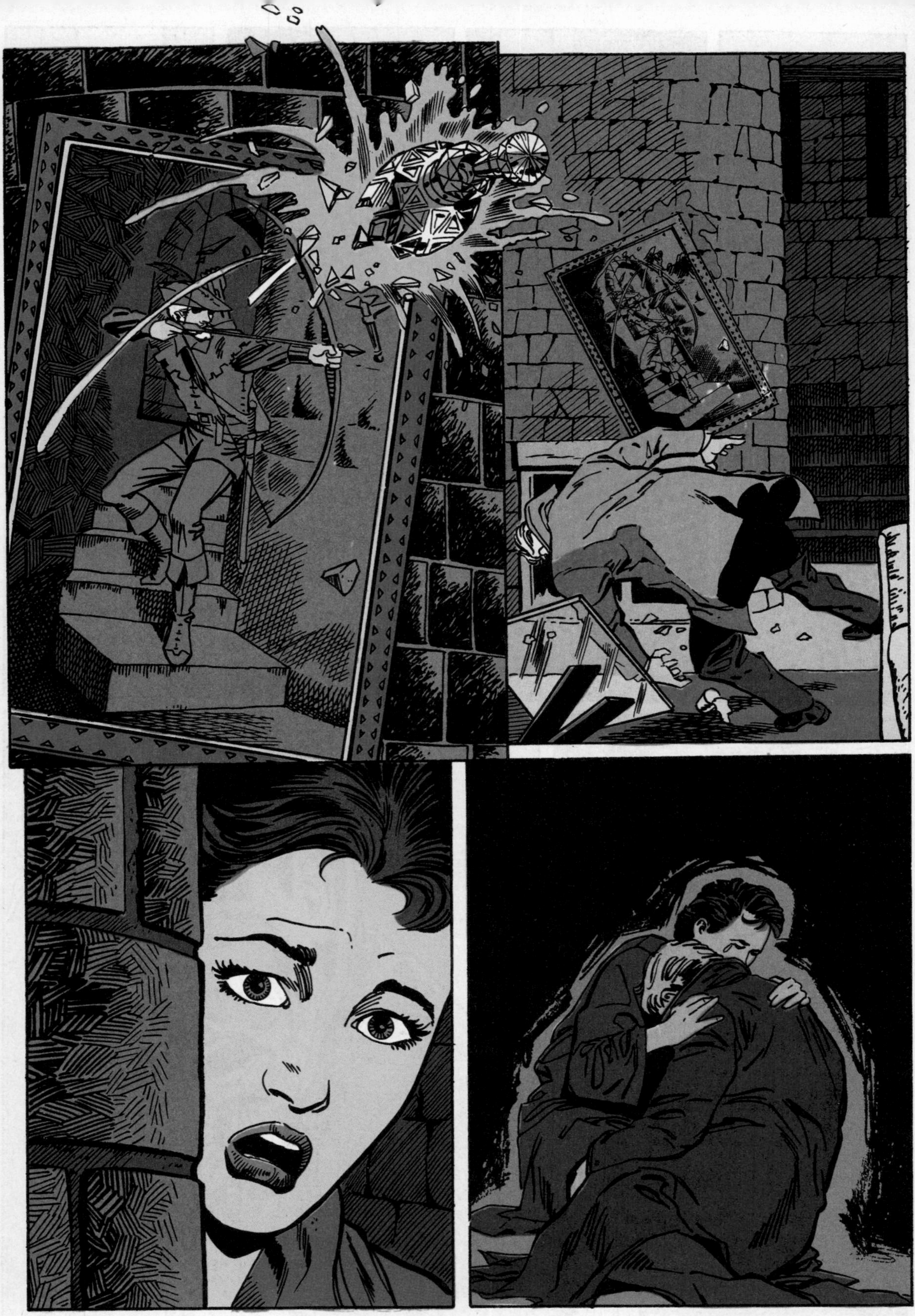

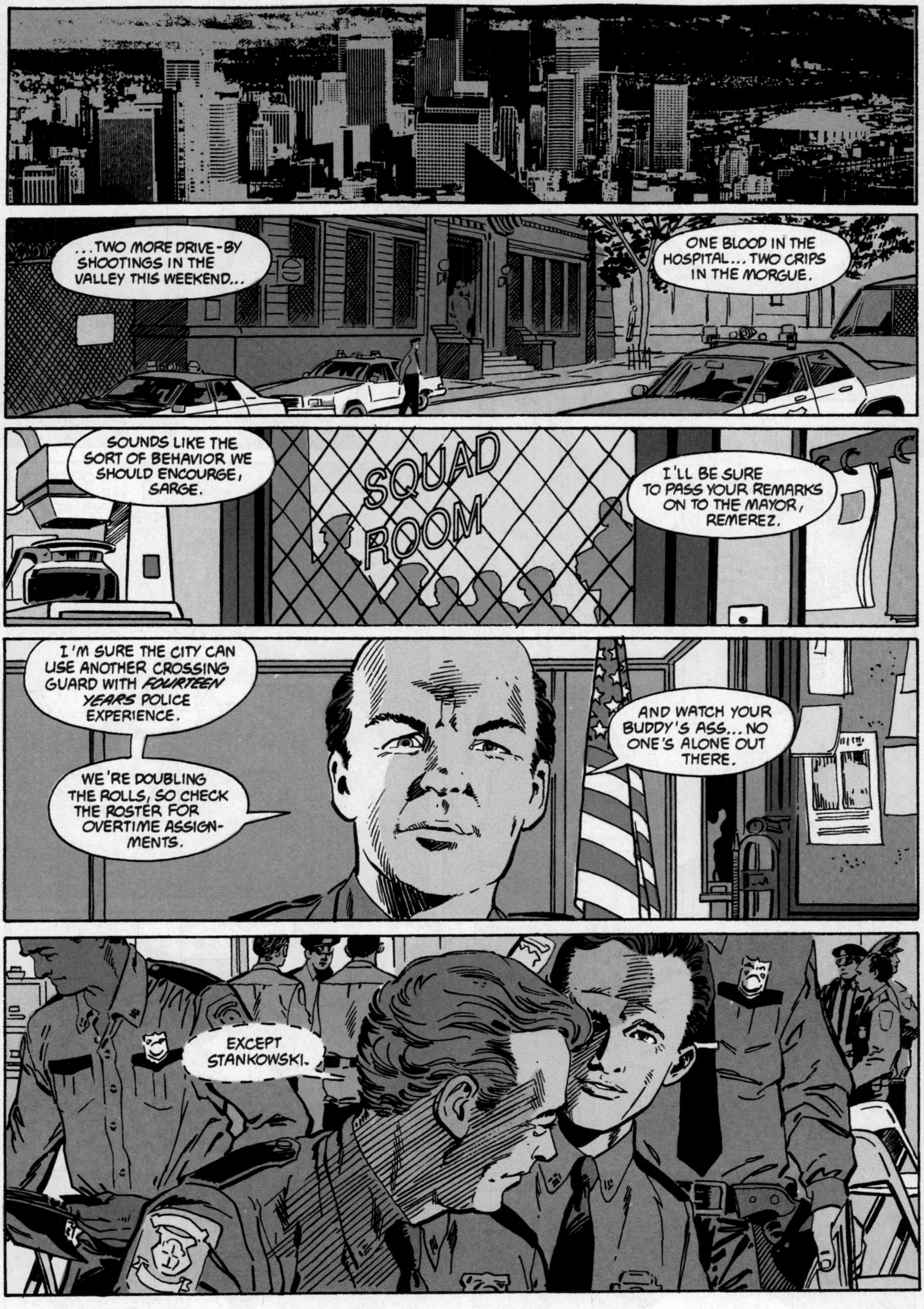
...TWO MORE DRIVE-BY SHOOTINGS IN THE VALLEY THIS WEEKEND...
ONE BLOOD IN THE HOSPITAL... TWO CRIPS IN THE MORGUE.
SOUNDS LIKE THE SORT OF BEHAVIOR WE SHOULD ENCOURGE, SARGE.
SQUAD ROOM
I'LL BE SURE TO PASS YOUR REMARKS ON TO THE MAYOR, REMEREZ.
I'M SURE THE CITY CAN USE ANOTHER CROSSING GUARD WITH *FOURTEEN YEARS* POLICE EXPERIENCE.
WE'RE DOUBLING THE ROLLS, SO CHECK THE ROSTER FOR OVERTIME ASSIGNMENTS.
AND WATCH YOUR BUDDY'S ASS... NO ONE'S ALONE OUT THERE.
EXCEPT STANKOWSKI.

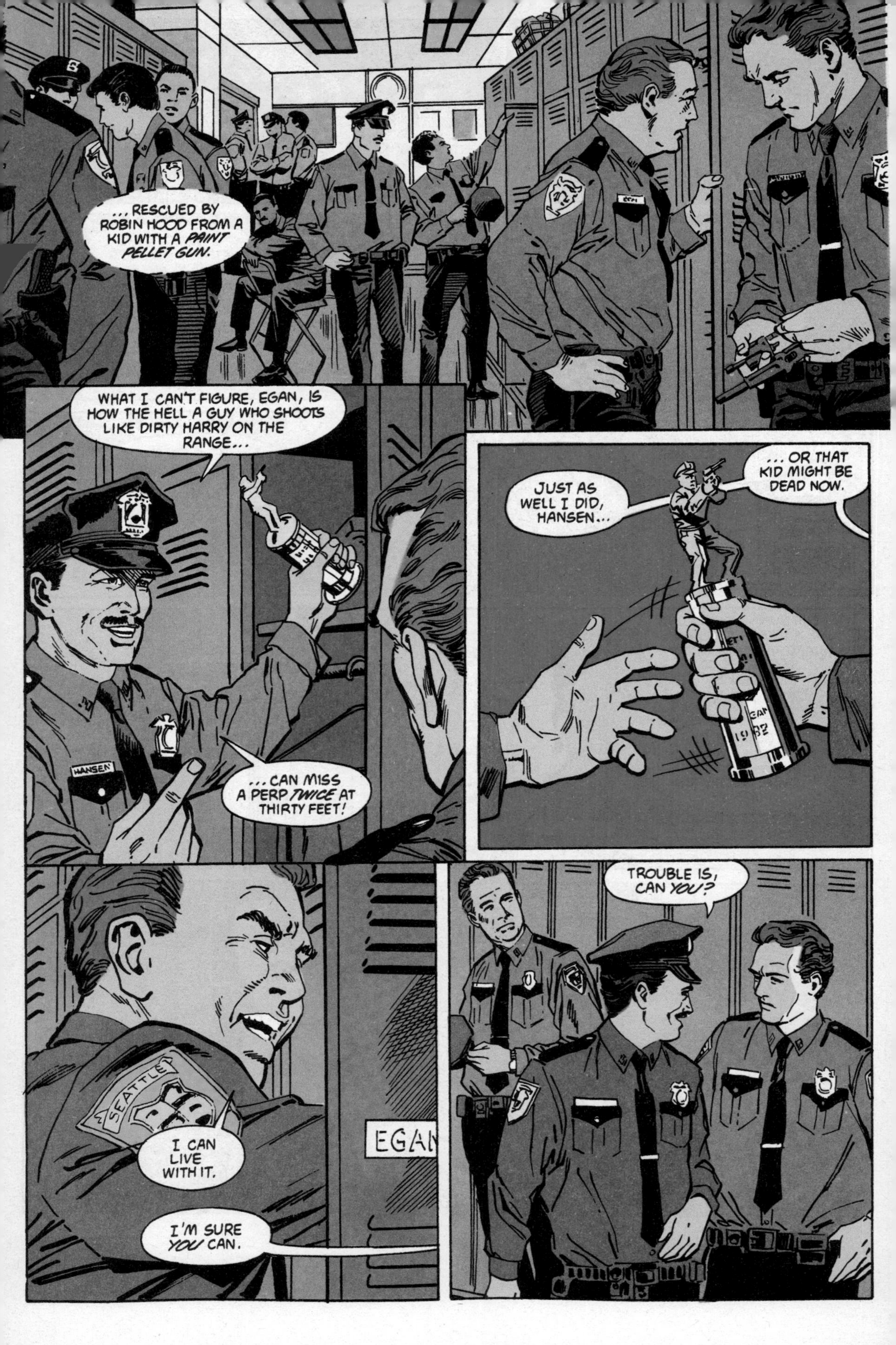
...RESCUED BY ROBIN HOOD FROM A KID WITH A *PAINT PELLET GUN*.
WHAT I CAN'T FIGURE, EGAN, IS HOW THE HELL A GUY WHO SHOOTS LIKE DIRTY HARRY ON THE RANGE...
...CAN MISS A PERP *TWICE* AT THIRTY FEET!
JUST AS WELL I DID, HANSEN...
...OR THAT KID MIGHT BE DEAD NOW.
I CAN LIVE WITH IT.
I'M SURE *YOU* CAN.
EGAN
TROUBLE IS, CAN *YOU*?

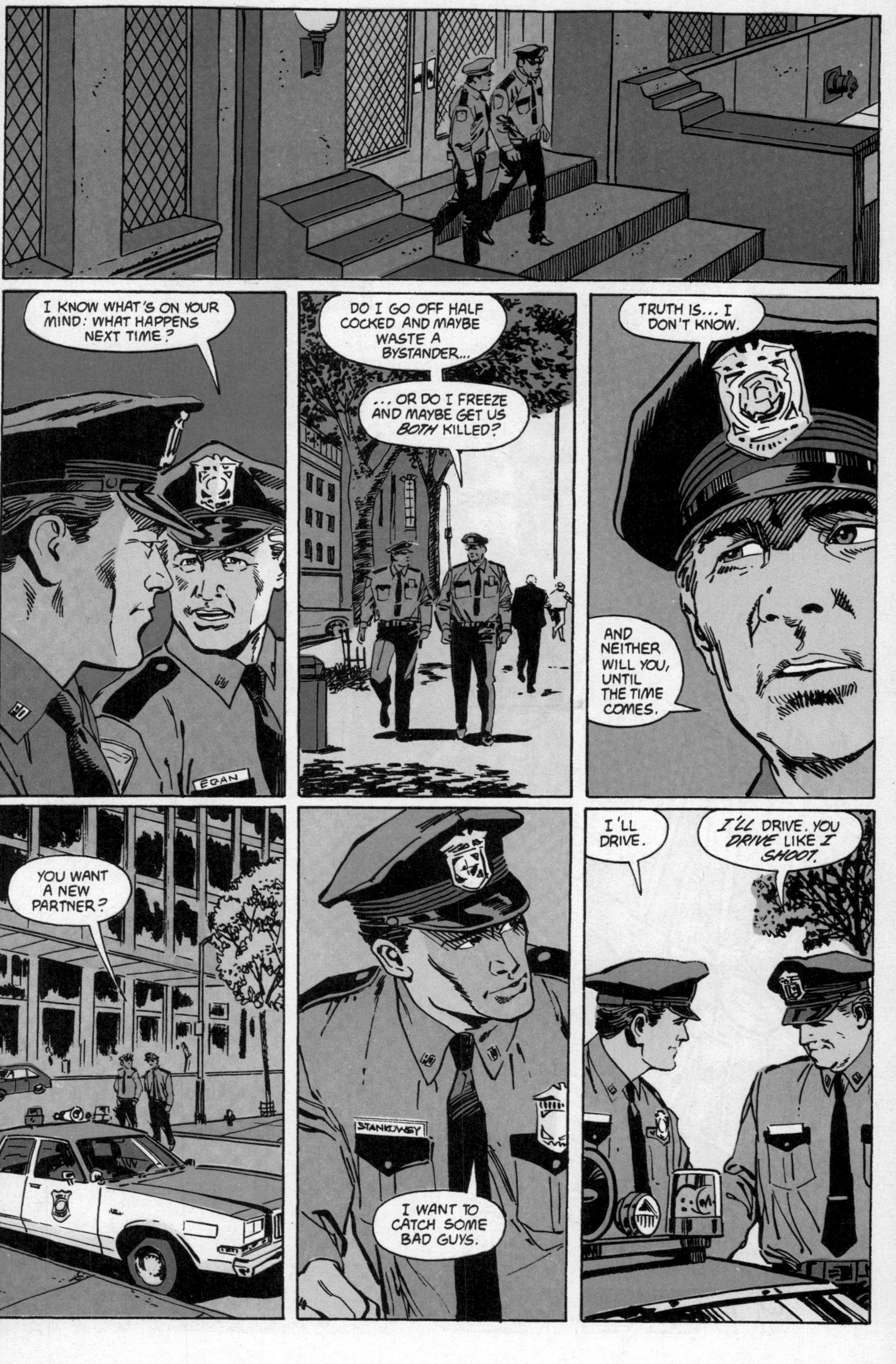
I KNOW WHAT'S ON YOUR MIND: WHAT HAPPENS NEXT TIME?
EGAN
DO I GO OFF HALF COCKED AND MAYBE WASTE A BYSTANDER...
...OR DO I FREEZE AND MAYBE GET US BOTH KILLED?
TRUTH IS... I DON'T KNOW.
AND NEITHER WILL YOU, UNTIL THE TIME COMES.
YOU WANT A NEW PARTNER?
STANKOWSY
I WANT TO CATCH SOME BAD GUYS.
I'LL DRIVE.
I'LL DRIVE. YOU DRIVE LIKE I SHOOT.

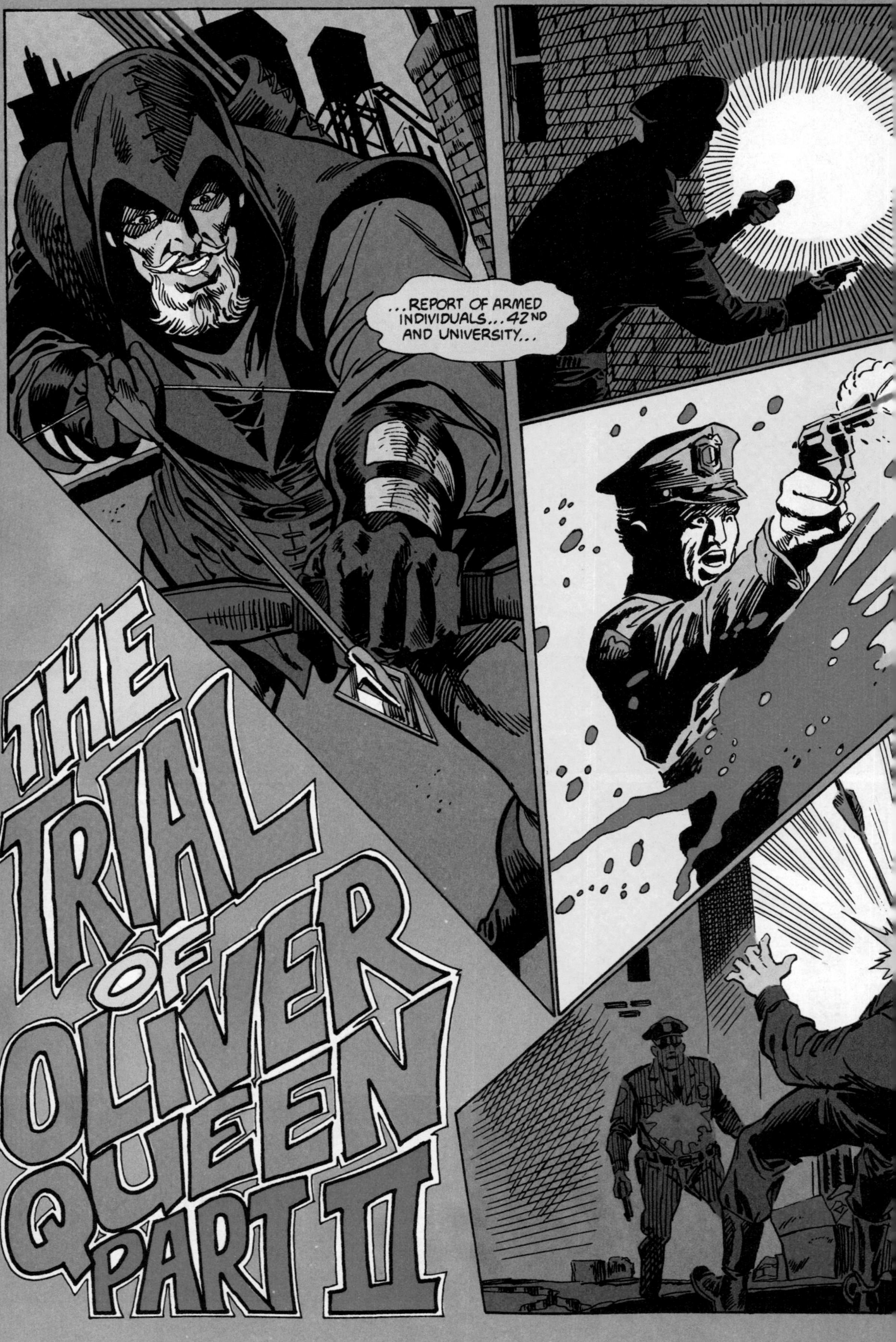
...REPORT OF ARMED INDIVIDUALS...42ND AND UNIVERSITY...
THE TRIAL OF OLIVER QUEEN PART II

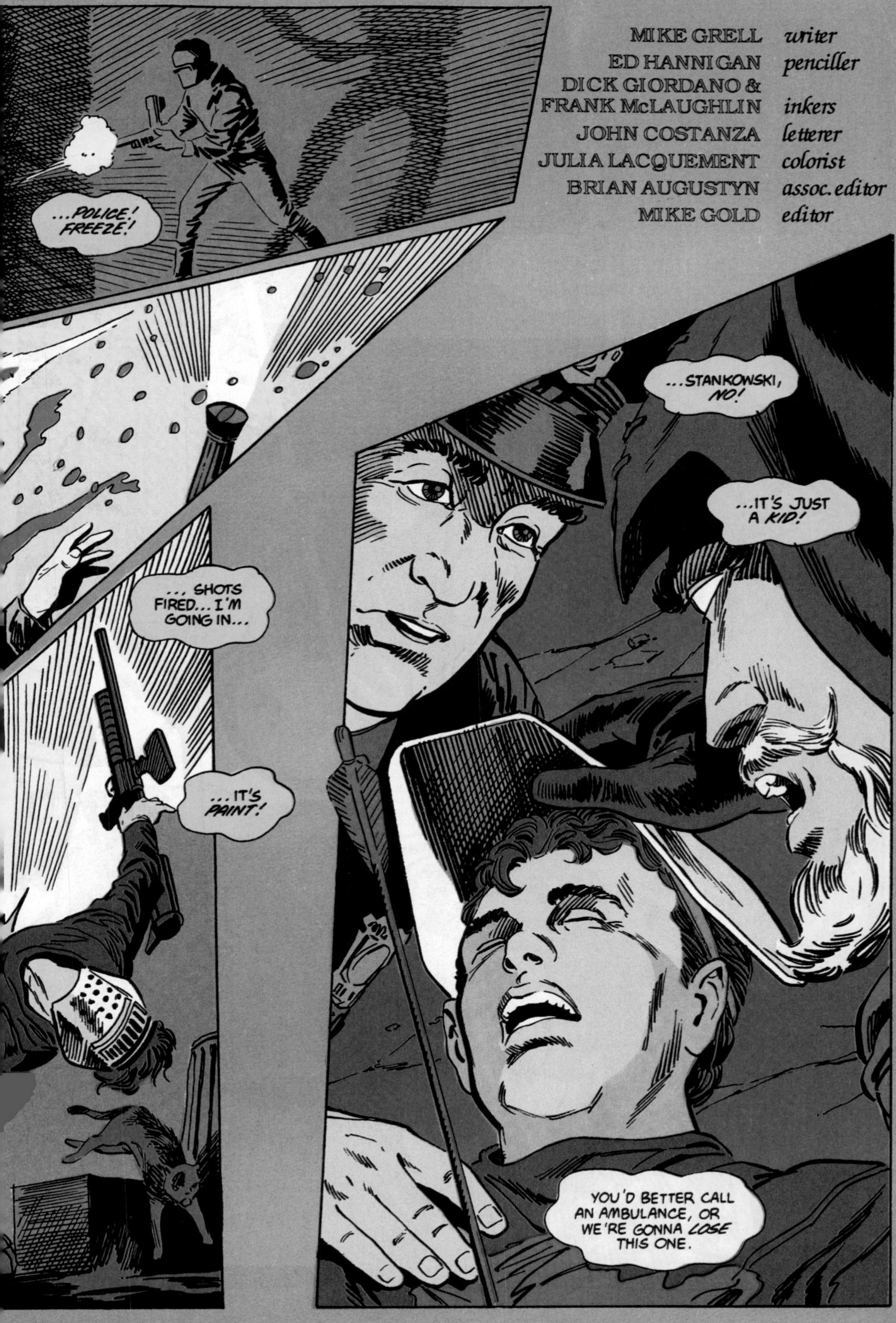
MIKE GRELL writer
ED HANNIGAN penciller
DICK GIORDANO & FRANK McLAUGHLIN inkers
JOHN COSTANZA letterer
JULIA LACQUEMENT colorist
BRIAN AUGUSTYN assoc. editor
MIKE GOLD editor
...POLICE! FREEZE!
..., SHOTS FIRED... I'M GOING IN...
...IT'S PAINT!
...STANKOWSKI, NO!
...IT'S JUST A KID!
YOU'D BETTER CALL AN AMBULANCE, OR WE'RE GONNA LOSE THIS ONE.

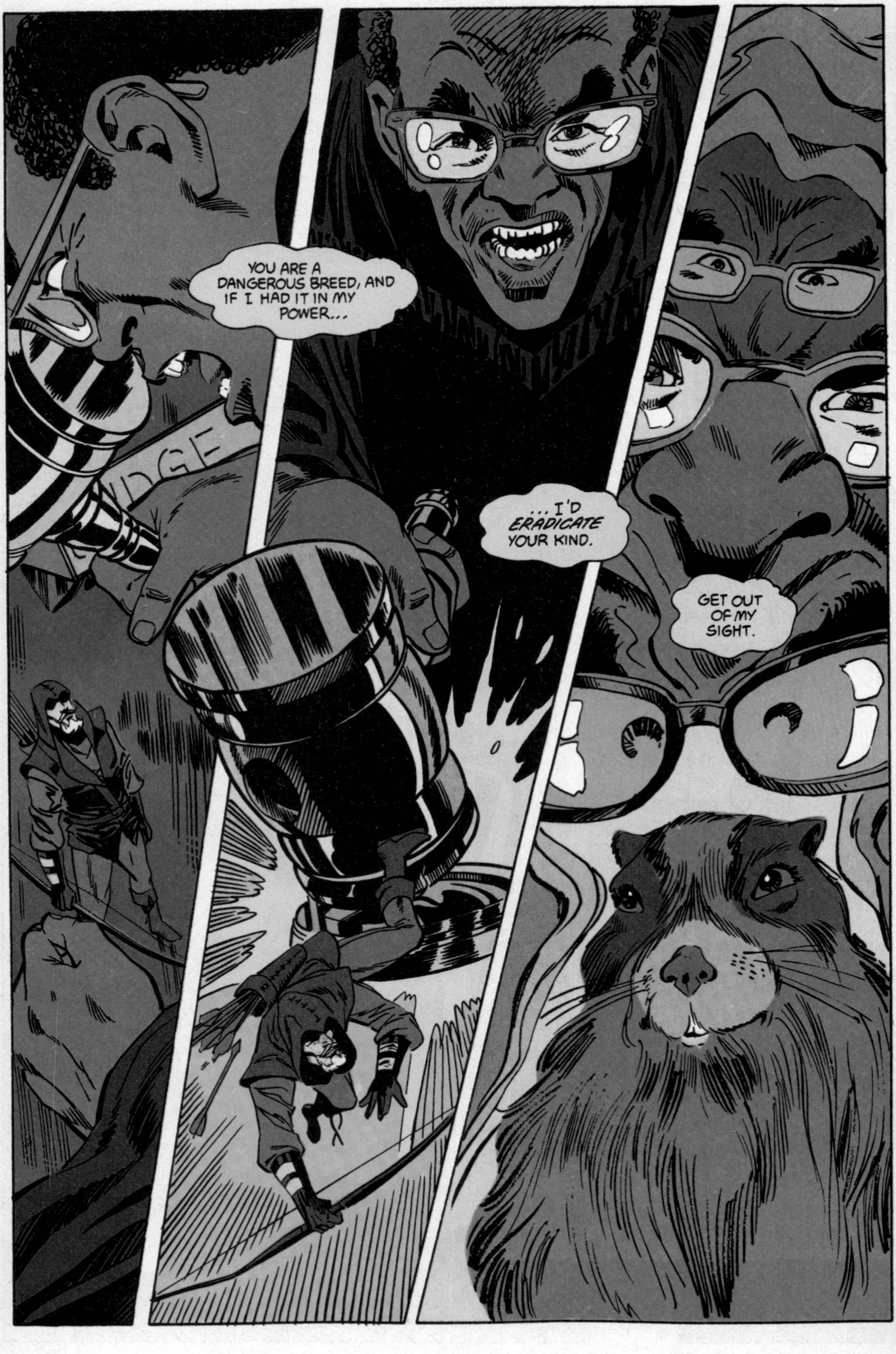

YOU ARE A DANGEROUS BREED, AND IF I HAD IT IN MY POWER...
...I'D *ERADICATE* YOUR KIND.
GET OUT OF MY SIGHT.

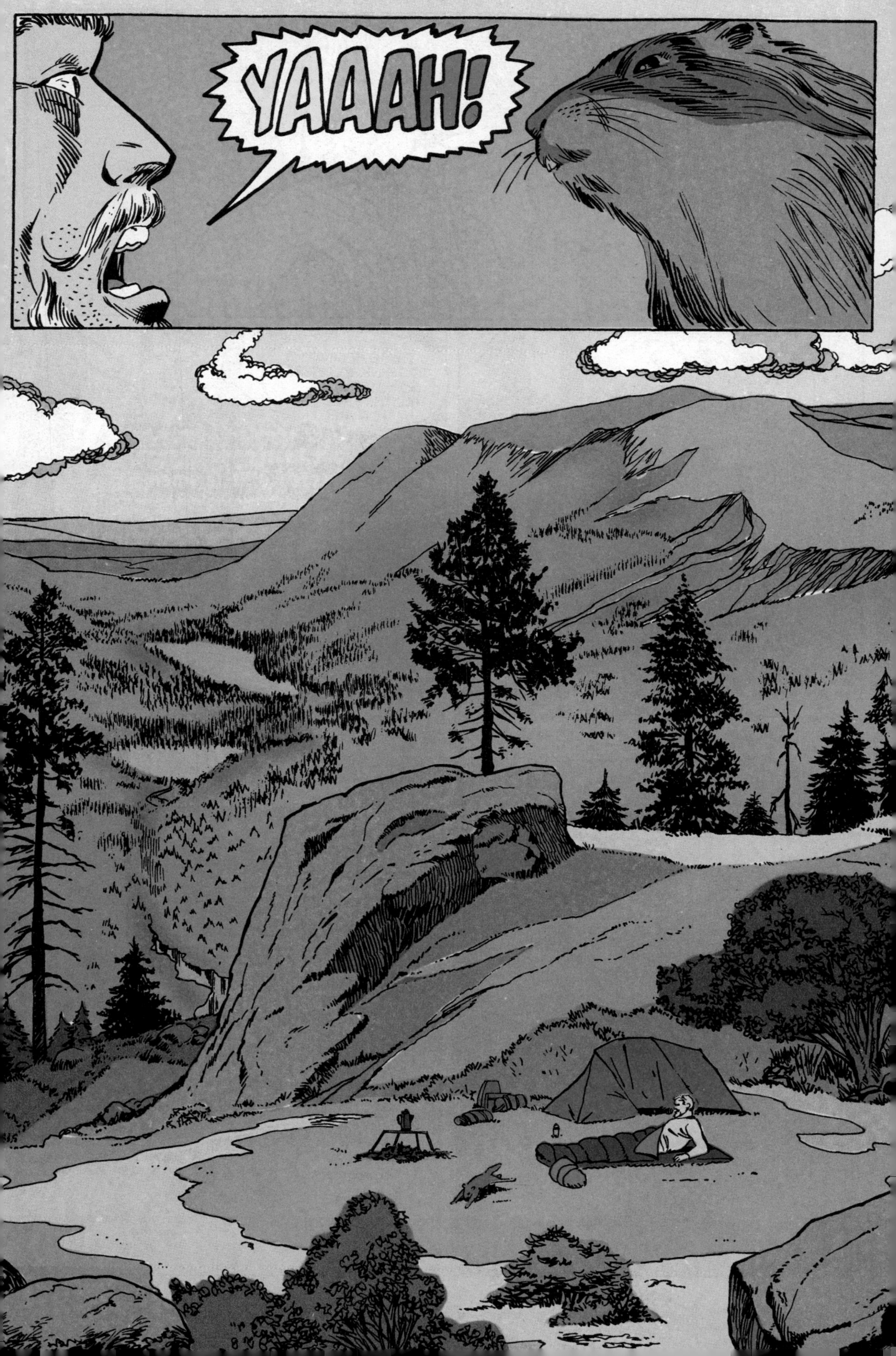
YAAAH!

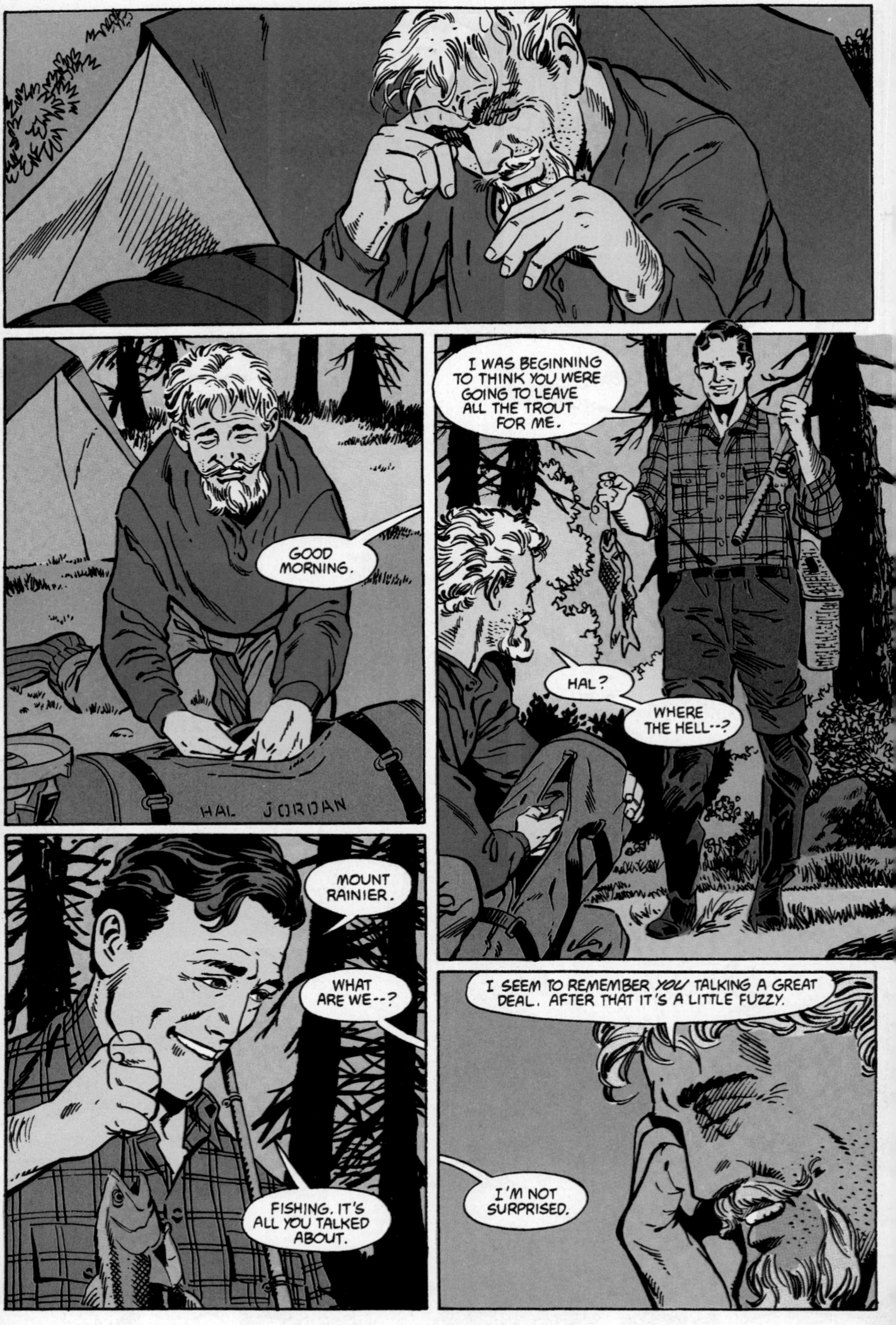
GOOD MORNING.
I WAS BEGINNING TO THINK YOU WERE GOING TO LEAVE ALL THE TROUT FOR ME.
HAL?
WHERE THE HELL--?
HAL JORDAN
MOUNT RAINIER.
WHAT ARE WE--?
FISHING. IT'S ALL YOU TALKED ABOUT.
I SEEM TO REMEMBER *YOU* TALKING A GREAT DEAL. AFTER THAT IT'S A LITTLE FUZZY.
I'M NOT SURPRISED.

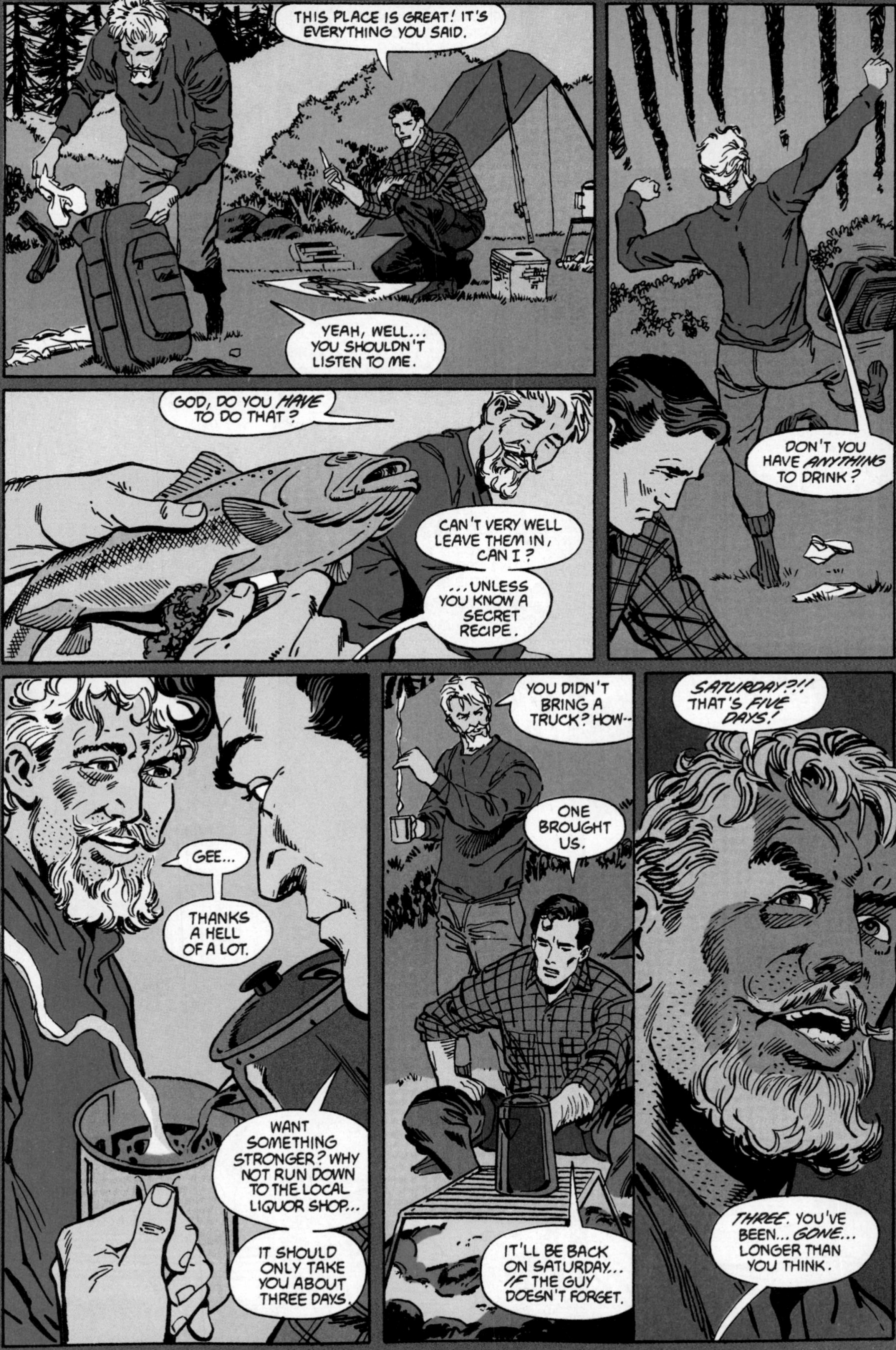
THIS PLACE IS GREAT! IT'S EVERYTHING YOU SAID.
YEAH, WELL... YOU SHOULDN'T LISTEN TO ME.
DON'T YOU HAVE *ANYTHING* TO DRINK?
GOD, DO YOU *HAVE* TO DO THAT?
CAN'T VERY WELL LEAVE THEM IN, CAN I?
...UNLESS YOU KNOW A SECRET RECIPE.
GEE...
THANKS A HELL OF A LOT.
WANT SOMETHING STRONGER? WHY NOT RUN DOWN TO THE LOCAL LIQUOR SHOP...
IT SHOULD ONLY TAKE YOU ABOUT THREE DAYS.
YOU DIDN'T BRING A TRUCK? HOW--
ONE BROUGHT US.
IT'LL BE BACK ON SATURDAY... *IF* THE GUY DOESN'T FORGET.
SATURDAY?!! THAT'S *FIVE DAYS!*
THREE. YOU'VE BEEN... *GONE*... LONGER THAN YOU THINK.

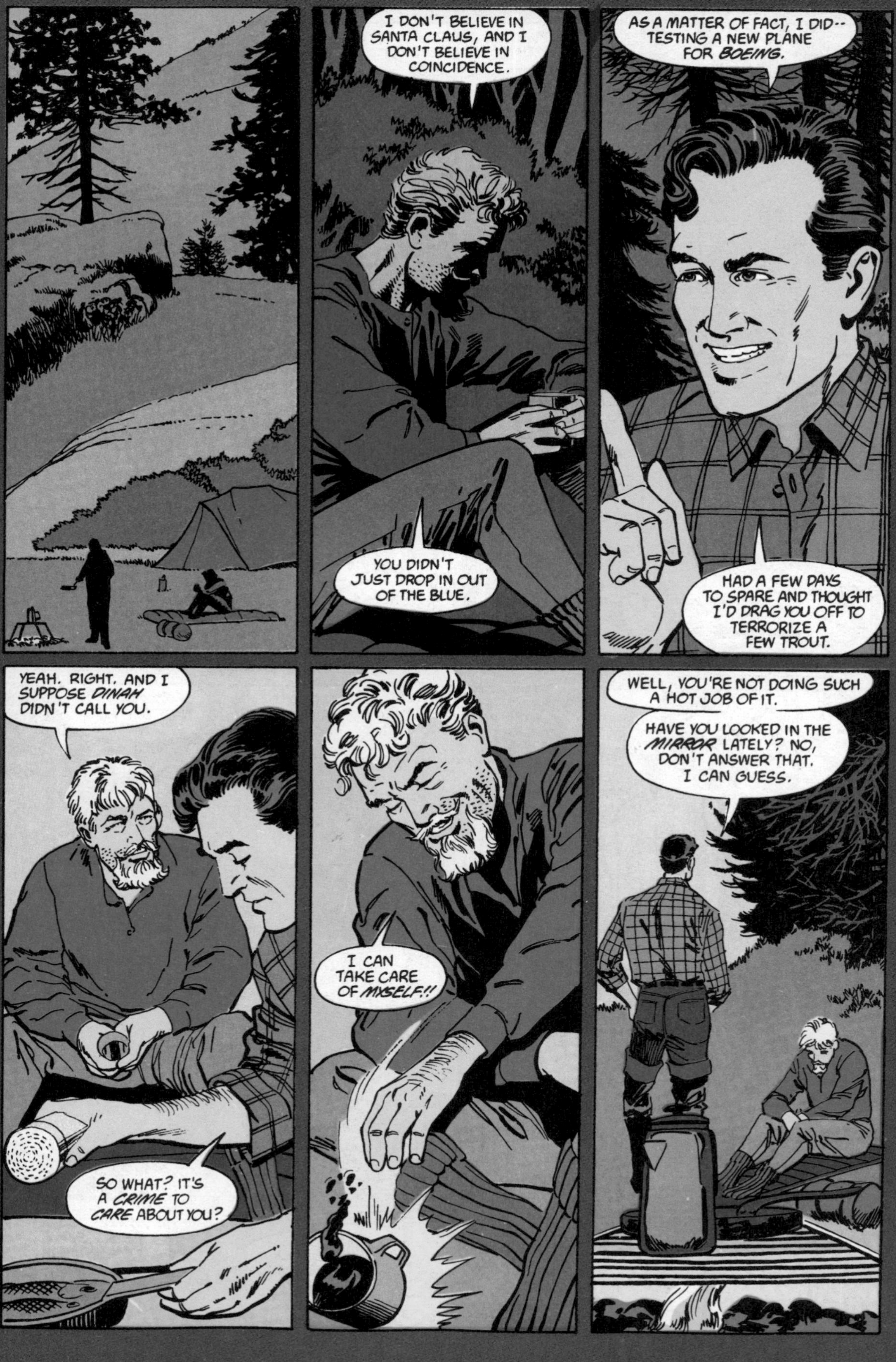
I DON'T BELIEVE IN SANTA CLAUS, AND I DON'T BELIEVE IN COINCIDENCE.
YOU DIDN'T JUST DROP IN OUT OF THE BLUE.
AS A MATTER OF FACT, I DID-- TESTING A NEW PLANE FOR BOEING.
HAD A FEW DAYS TO SPARE AND THOUGHT I'D DRAG YOU OFF TO TERRORIZE A FEW TROUT.
YEAH. RIGHT. AND I SUPPOSE DINAH DIDN'T CALL YOU.
SO WHAT? IT'S A CRIME TO CARE ABOUT YOU?
I CAN TAKE CARE OF MYSELF!!
WELL, YOU'RE NOT DOING SUCH A HOT JOB OF IT.
HAVE YOU LOOKED IN THE MIRROR LATELY? NO, DON'T ANSWER THAT. I CAN GUESS.

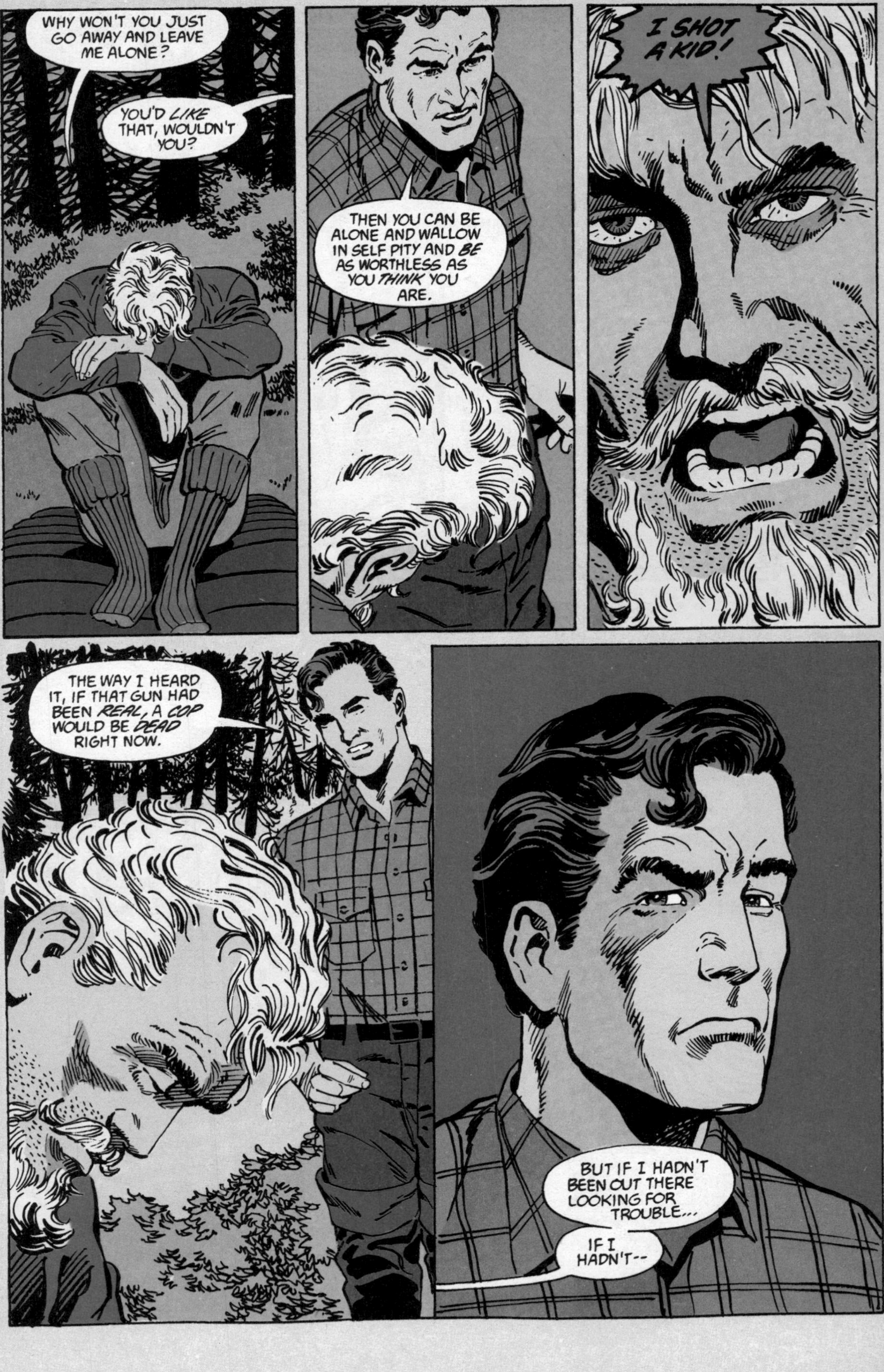
WHY WON'T YOU JUST GO AWAY AND LEAVE ME ALONE?
YOU'D *LIKE* THAT, WOULDN'T YOU?
THEN YOU CAN BE ALONE AND WALLOW IN SELF PITY AND *BE* AS WORTHLESS AS YOU *THINK* YOU ARE.
I SHOT A KID!
THE WAY I HEARD IT, IF THAT GUN HAD BEEN *REAL*, A *COP* WOULD BE *DEAD* RIGHT NOW.
BUT IF I HADN'T BEEN OUT THERE LOOKING FOR TROUBLE...
IF I HADN'T--

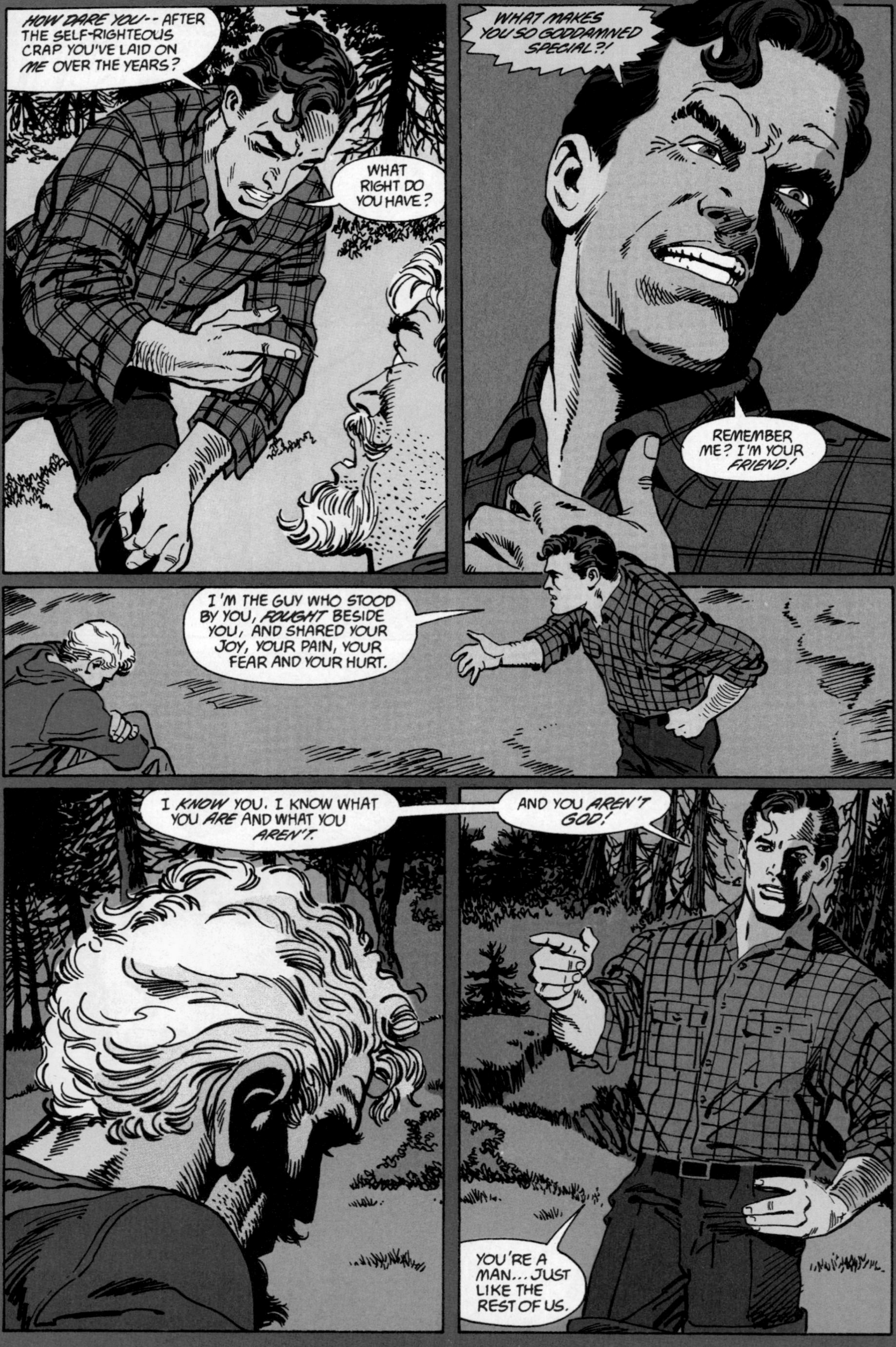
HOW DARE YOU-- AFTER THE SELF-RIGHTEOUS CRAP YOU'VE LAID ON ME OVER THE YEARS?
WHAT RIGHT DO YOU HAVE?
WHAT MAKES YOU SO GODDAMNED SPECIAL?!
REMEMBER ME? I'M YOUR FRIEND!
I'M THE GUY WHO STOOD BY YOU, FOUGHT BESIDE YOU, AND SHARED YOUR JOY, YOUR PAIN, YOUR FEAR AND YOUR HURT.
I KNOW YOU. I KNOW WHAT YOU ARE AND WHAT YOU AREN'T.
AND YOU AREN'T GOD!
YOU'RE A MAN... JUST LIKE THE REST OF US.

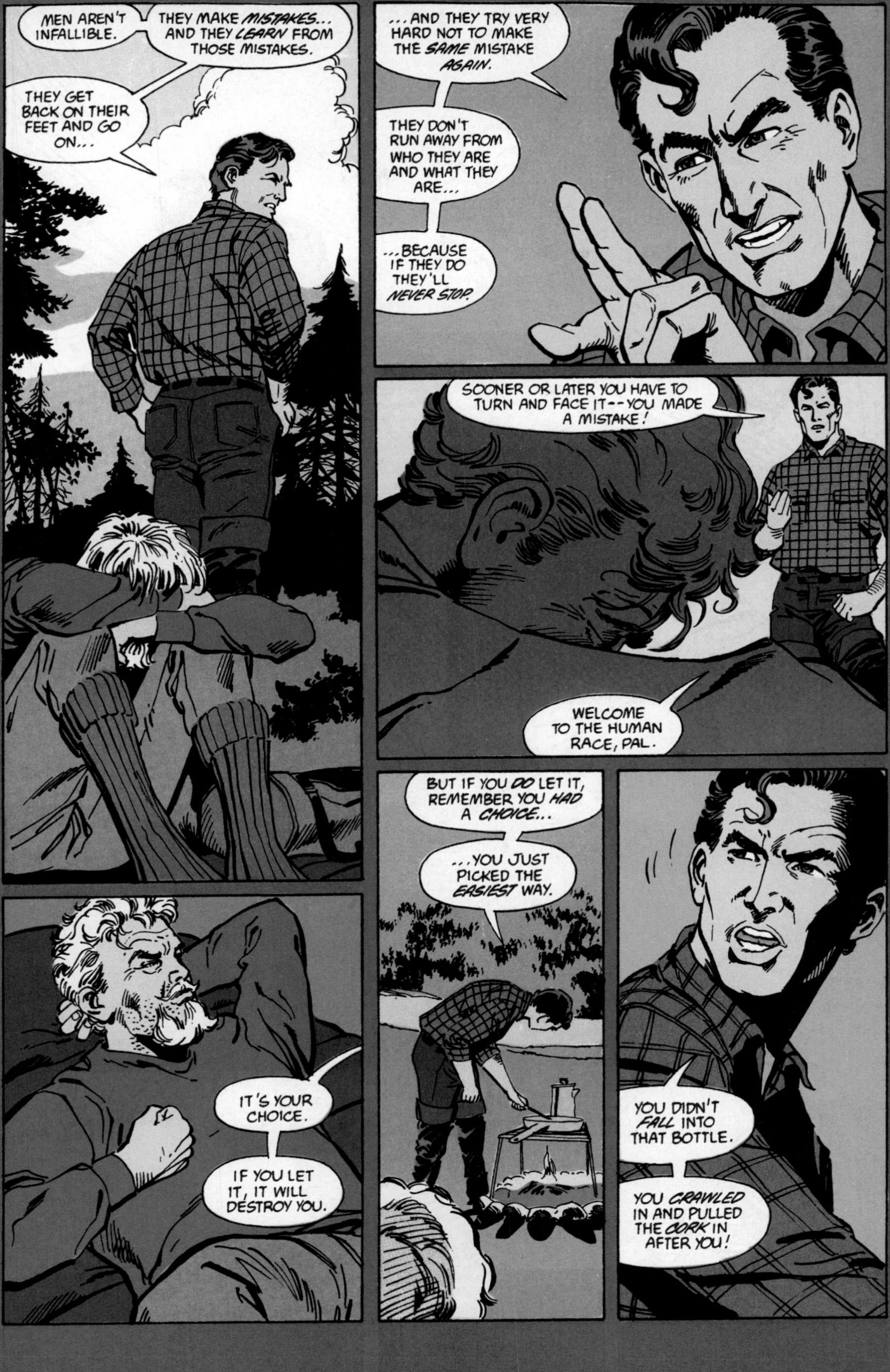
MEN AREN'T INFALLIBLE.
THEY MAKE MISTAKES... AND THEY LEARN FROM THOSE MISTAKES.
THEY GET BACK ON THEIR FEET AND GO ON...
...AND THEY TRY VERY HARD NOT TO MAKE THE SAME MISTAKE AGAIN.
THEY DON'T RUN AWAY FROM WHO THEY ARE AND WHAT THEY ARE...
...BECAUSE IF THEY DO THEY'LL NEVER STOP.
SOONER OR LATER YOU HAVE TO TURN AND FACE IT--YOU MADE A MISTAKE!
WELCOME TO THE HUMAN RACE, PAL.
IT'S YOUR CHOICE.
IF YOU LET IT, IT WILL DESTROY YOU.
BUT IF YOU DO LET IT, REMEMBER YOU HAD A CHOICE...
...YOU JUST PICKED THE EASIEST WAY.
YOU DIDN'T FALL INTO THAT BOTTLE.
YOU CRAWLED IN AND PULLED THE CORK IN AFTER YOU!

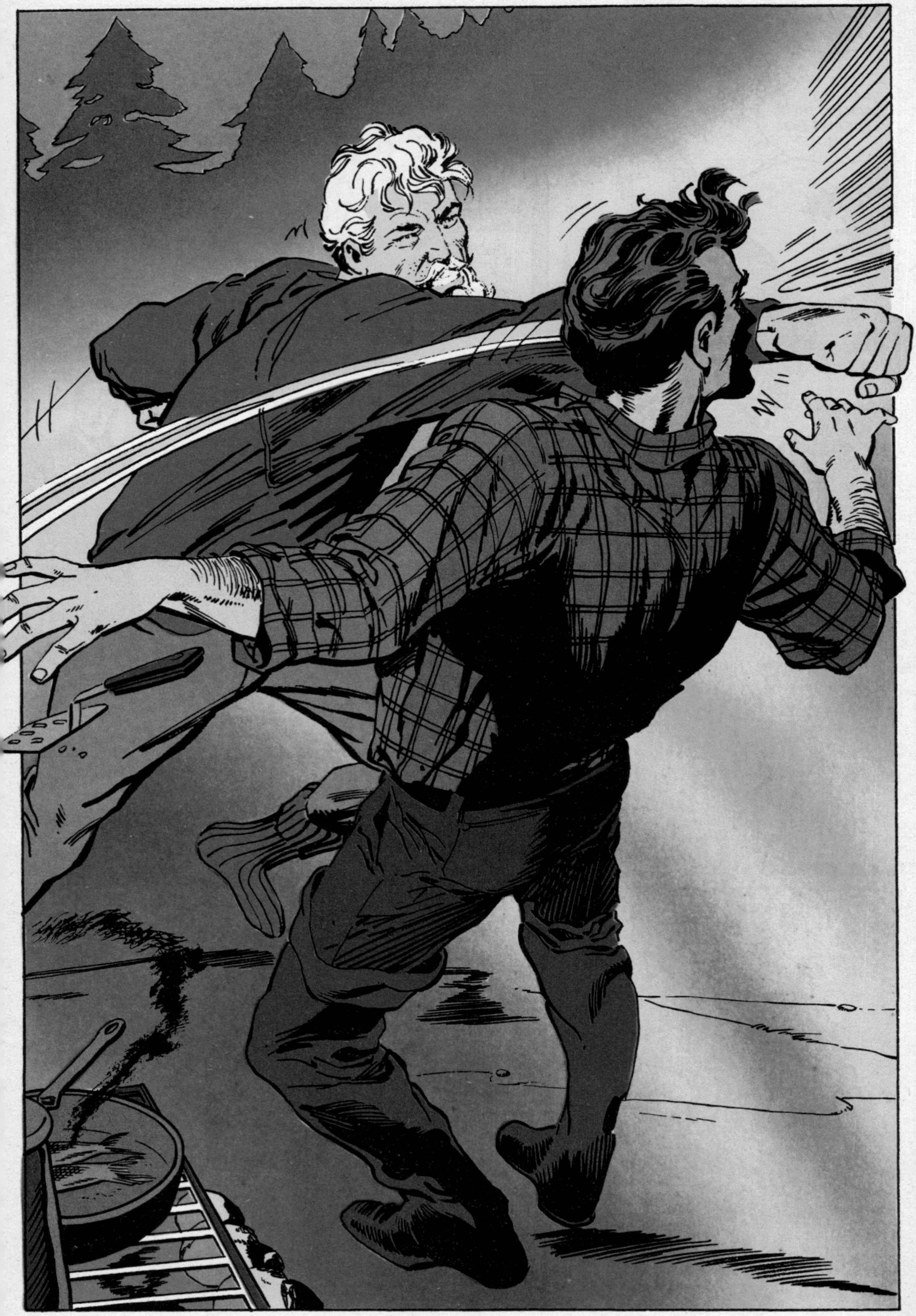

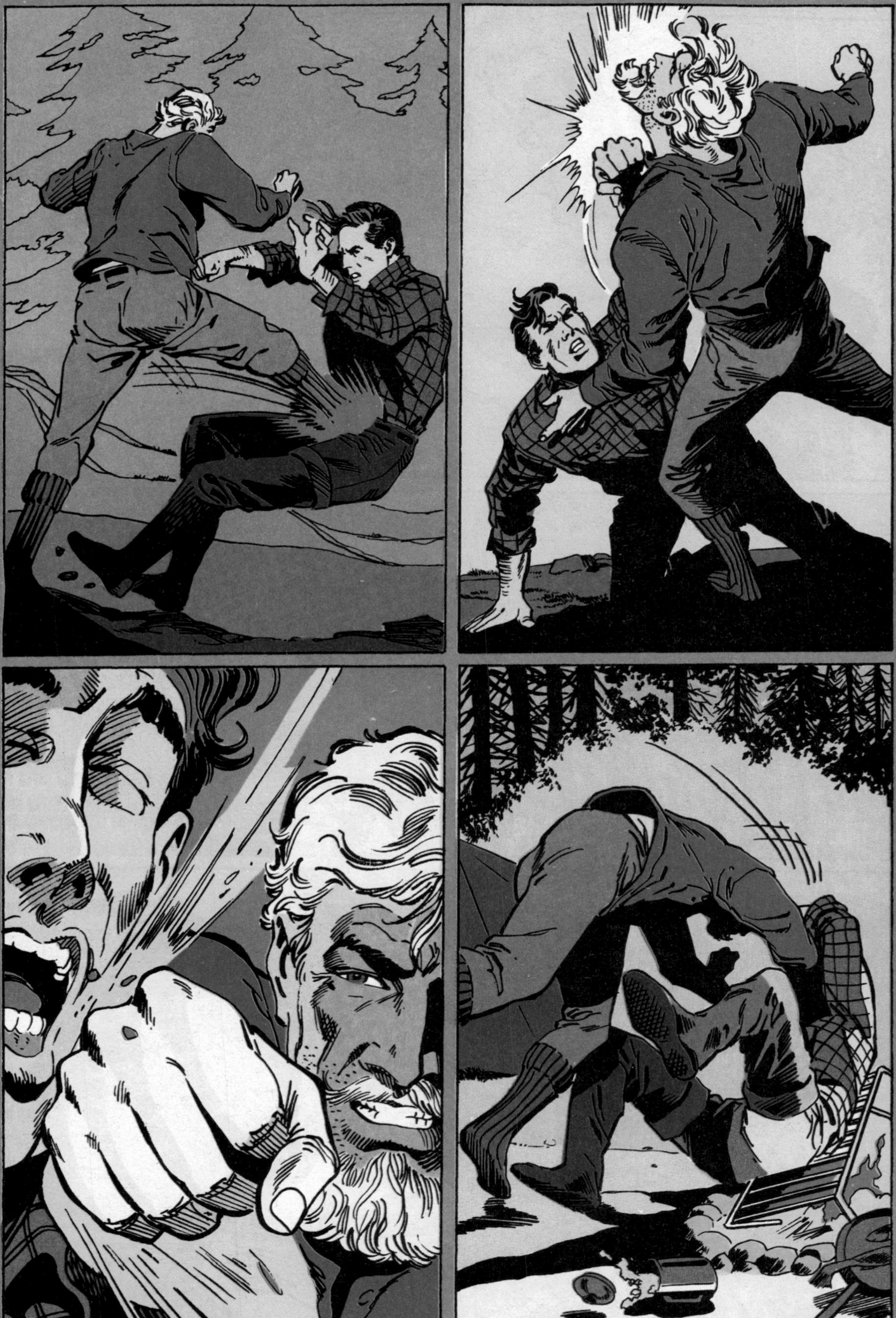

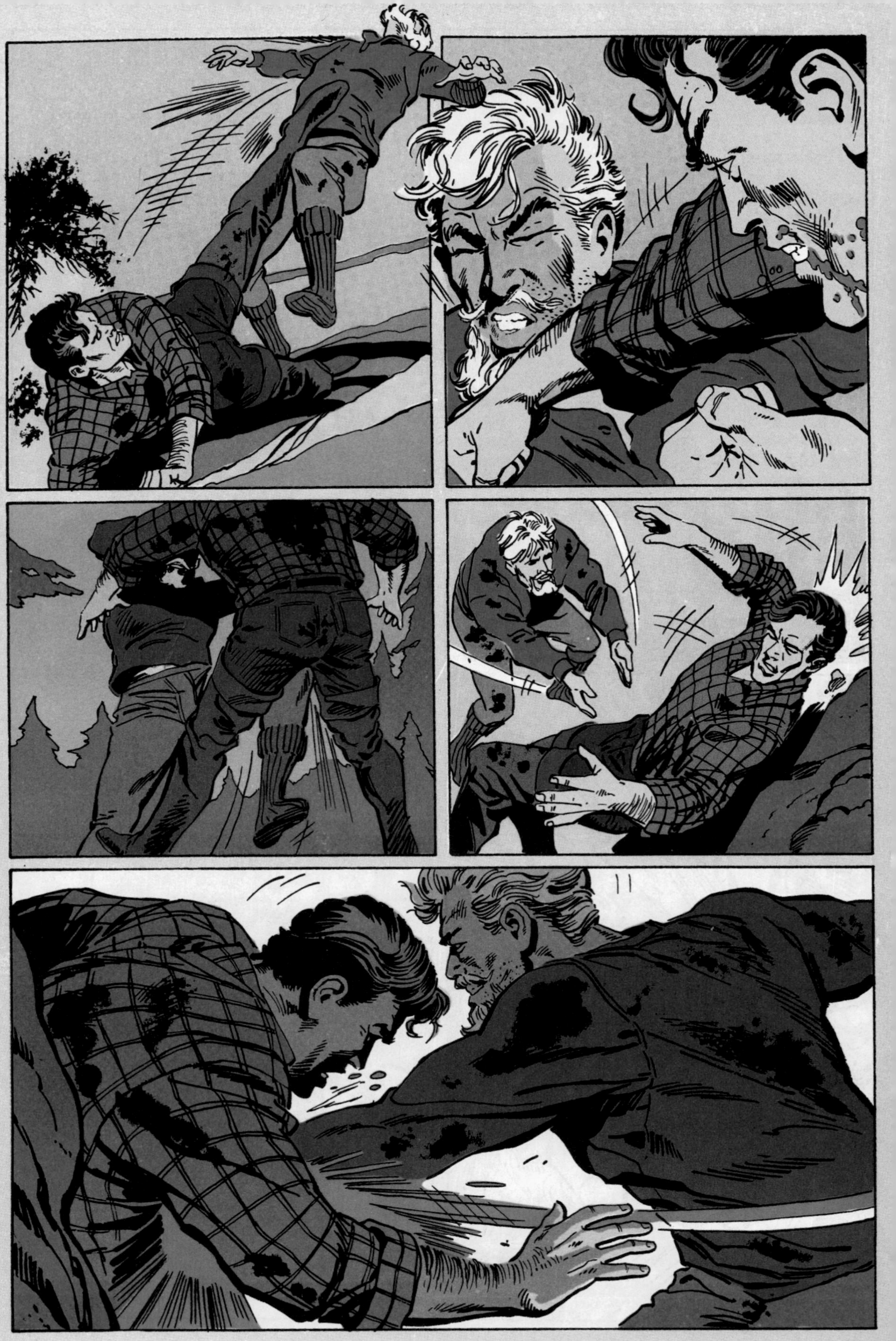

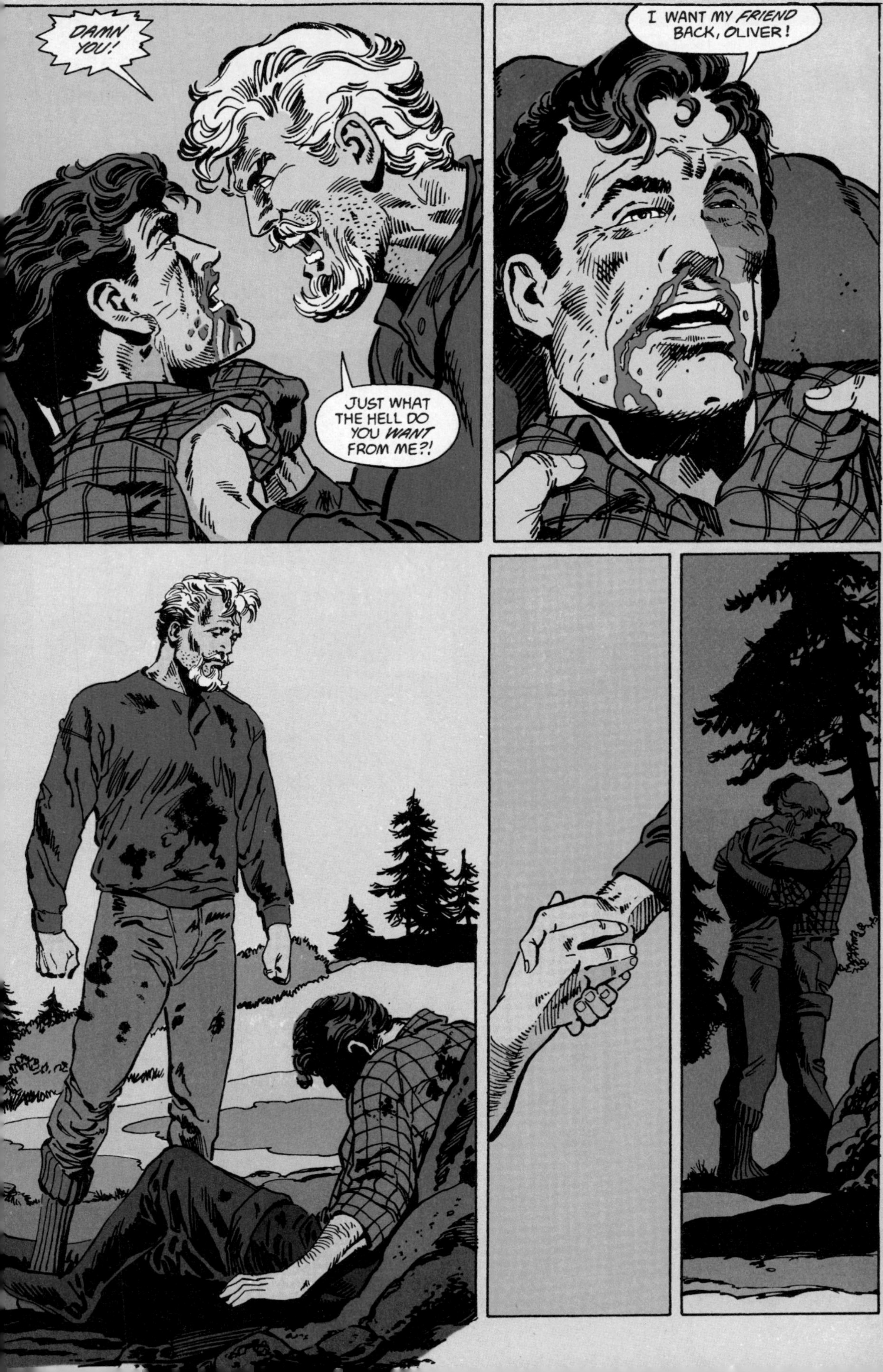
DAMN YOU!
JUST WHAT THE HELL DO YOU WANT FROM ME?!
I WANT MY FRIEND BACK, OLIVER!

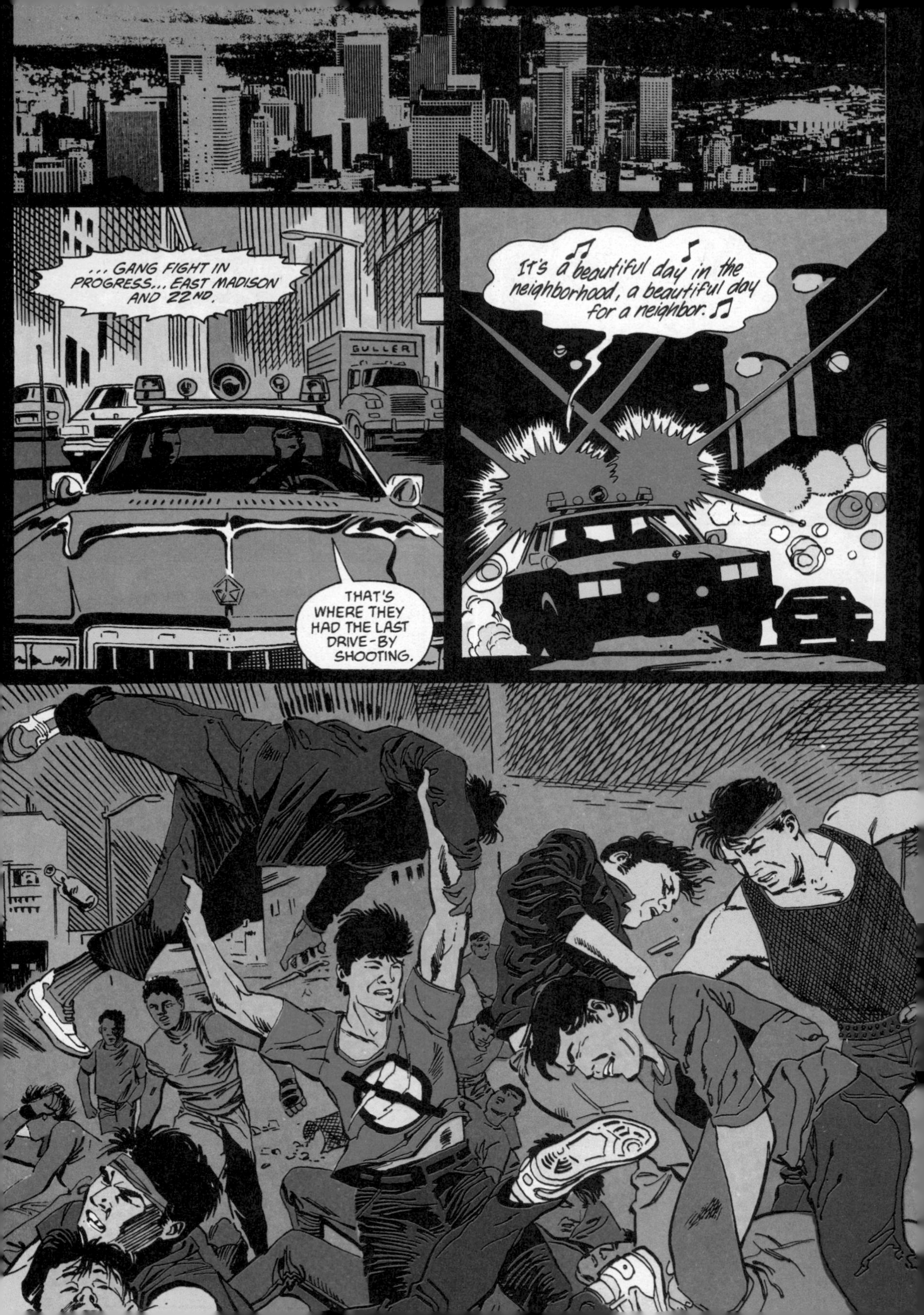

...GANG FIGHT IN PROGRESS...EAST MADISON AND 22ND.
GULLER
THAT'S WHERE THEY HAD THE LAST DRIVE-BY SHOOTING.
♫ It's a beautiful day in the neighborhood, a beautiful day for a neighbor. ♫

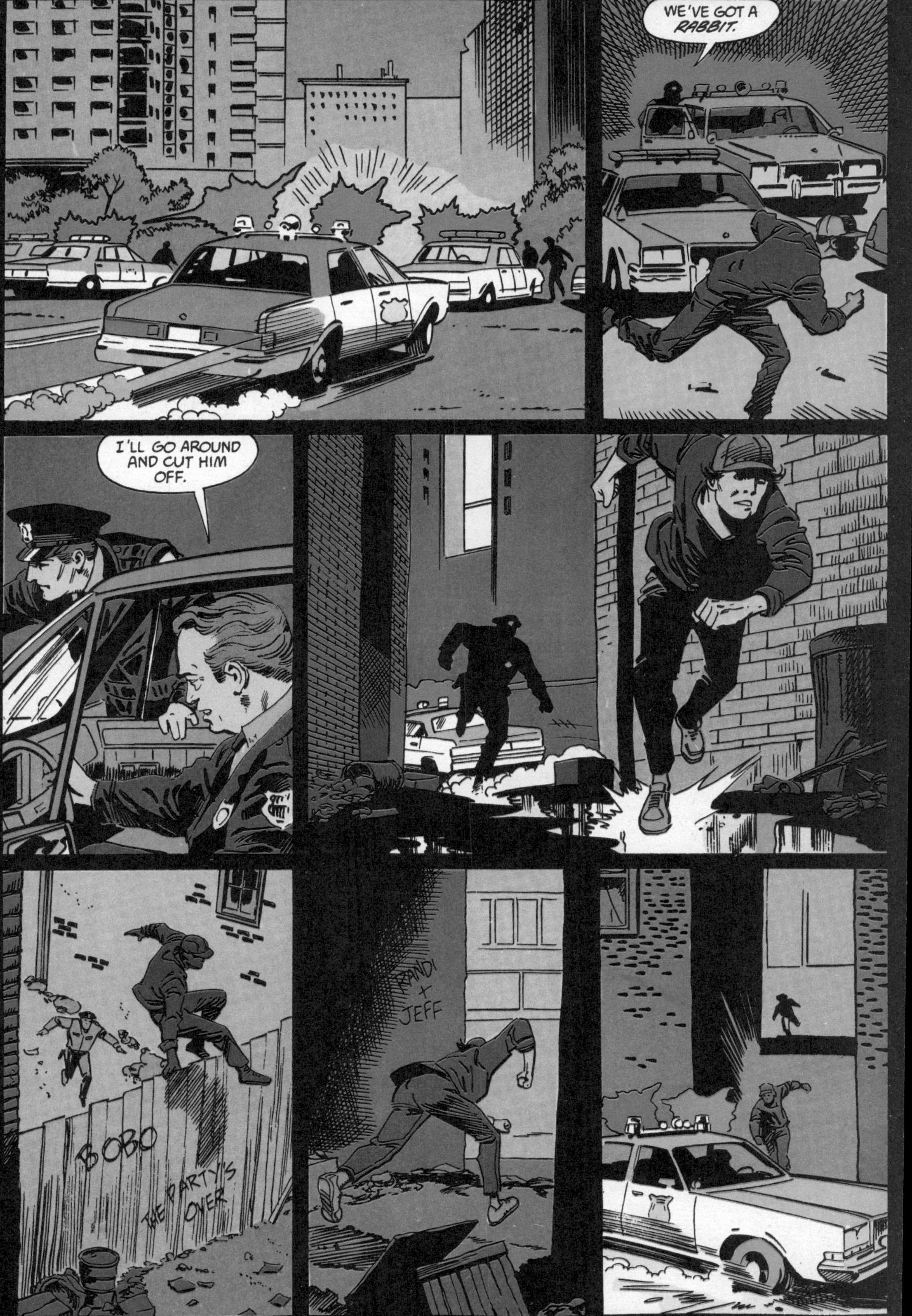
WE'VE GOT A RABBIT.
I'LL GO AROUND AND CUT HIM OFF.
RANDI + JEFF
BOBO
THE PARTY'S OVER

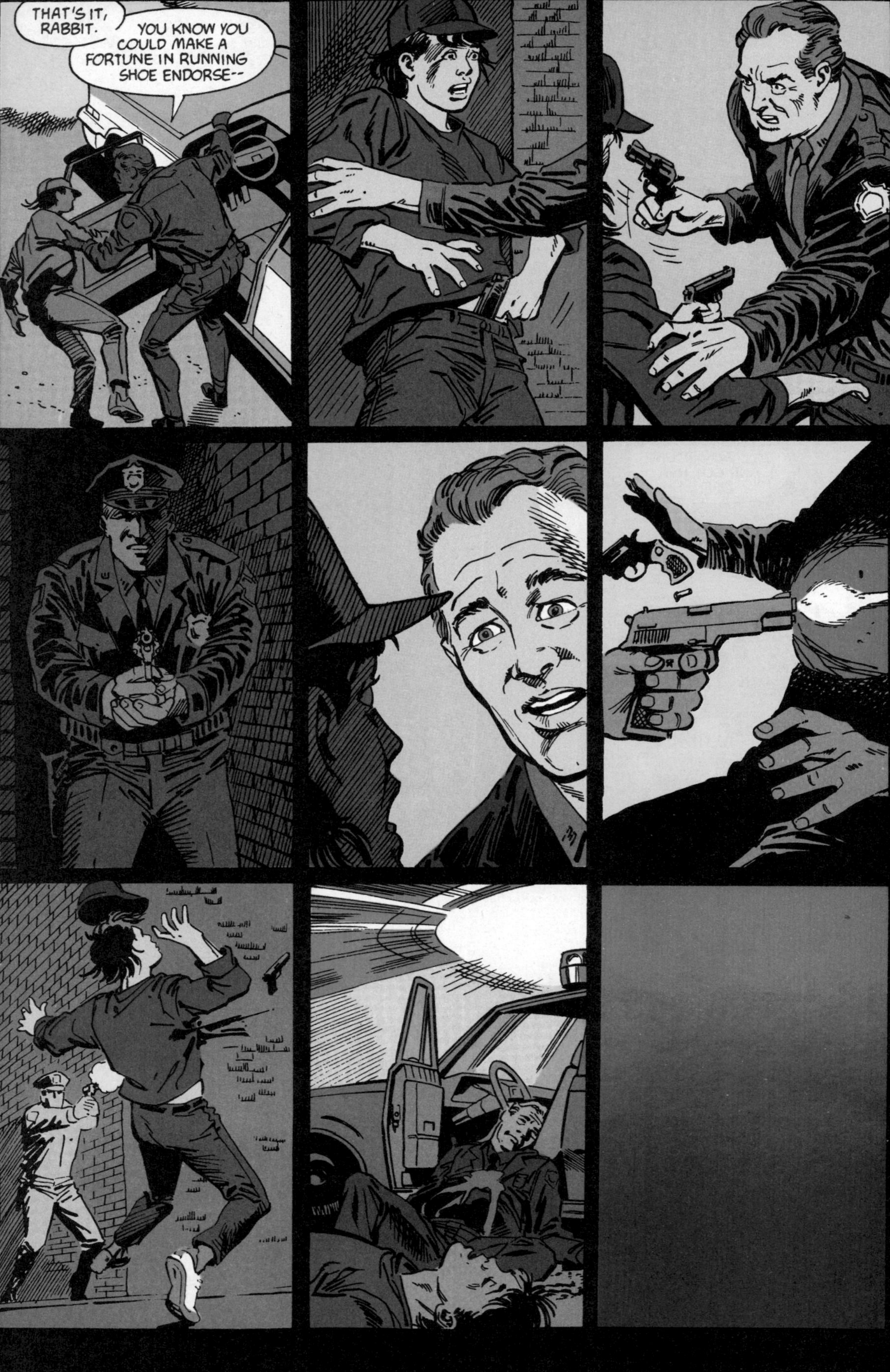
THAT'S IT, RABBIT.
YOU KNOW YOU COULD MAKE A FORTUNE IN RUNNING SHOE ENDORSE--

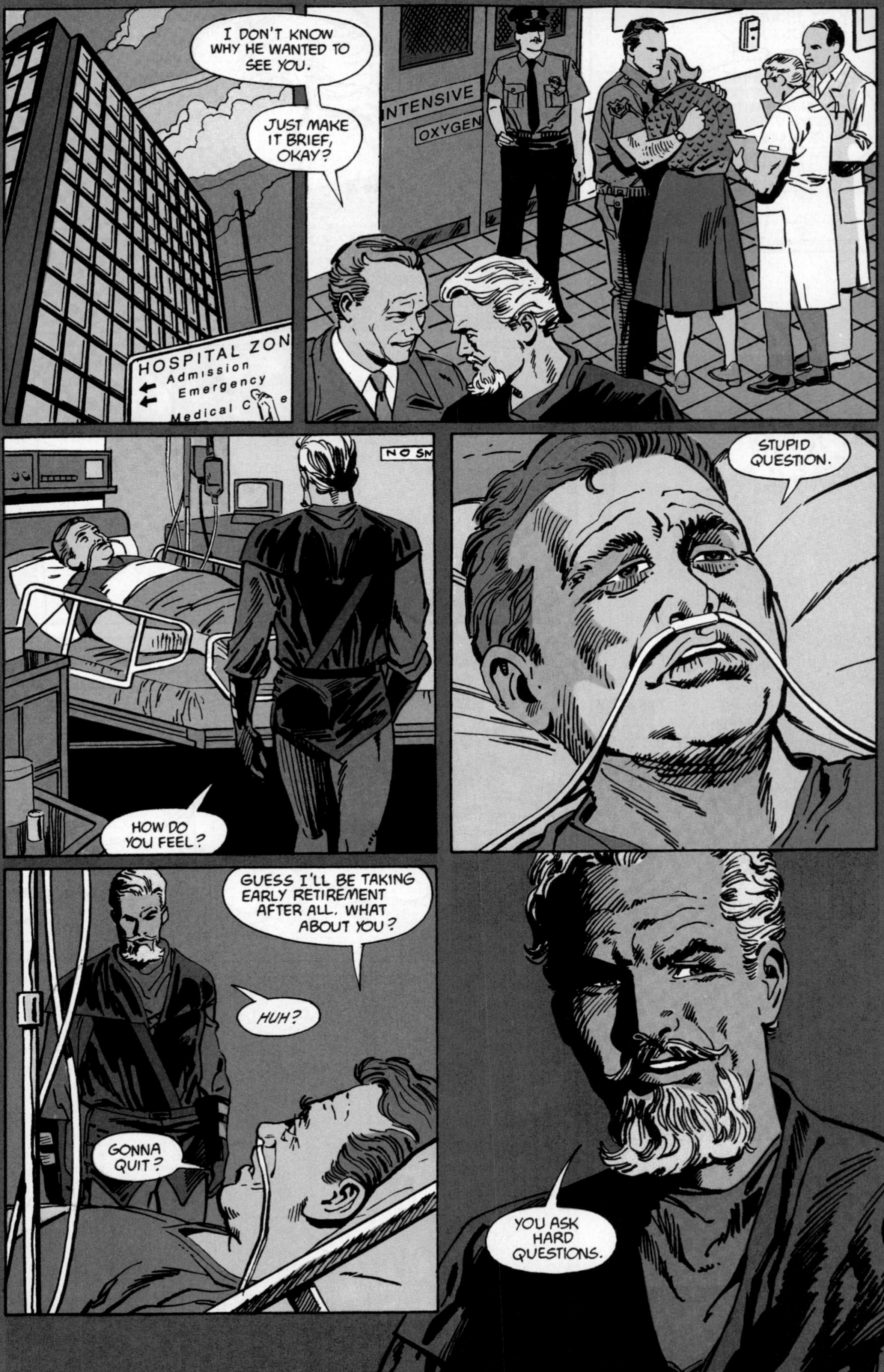
I DON'T KNOW WHY HE WANTED TO SEE YOU.
JUST MAKE IT BRIEF, OKAY?
HOSPITAL ZON
Admission
Emergency
Medical C e
INTENSIVE
OXYGEN
NO SM
HOW DO YOU FEEL?
STUPID QUESTION.
GUESS I'LL BE TAKING EARLY RETIREMENT AFTER ALL. WHAT ABOUT YOU?
HUH?
GONNA QUIT?
YOU ASK HARD QUESTIONS.

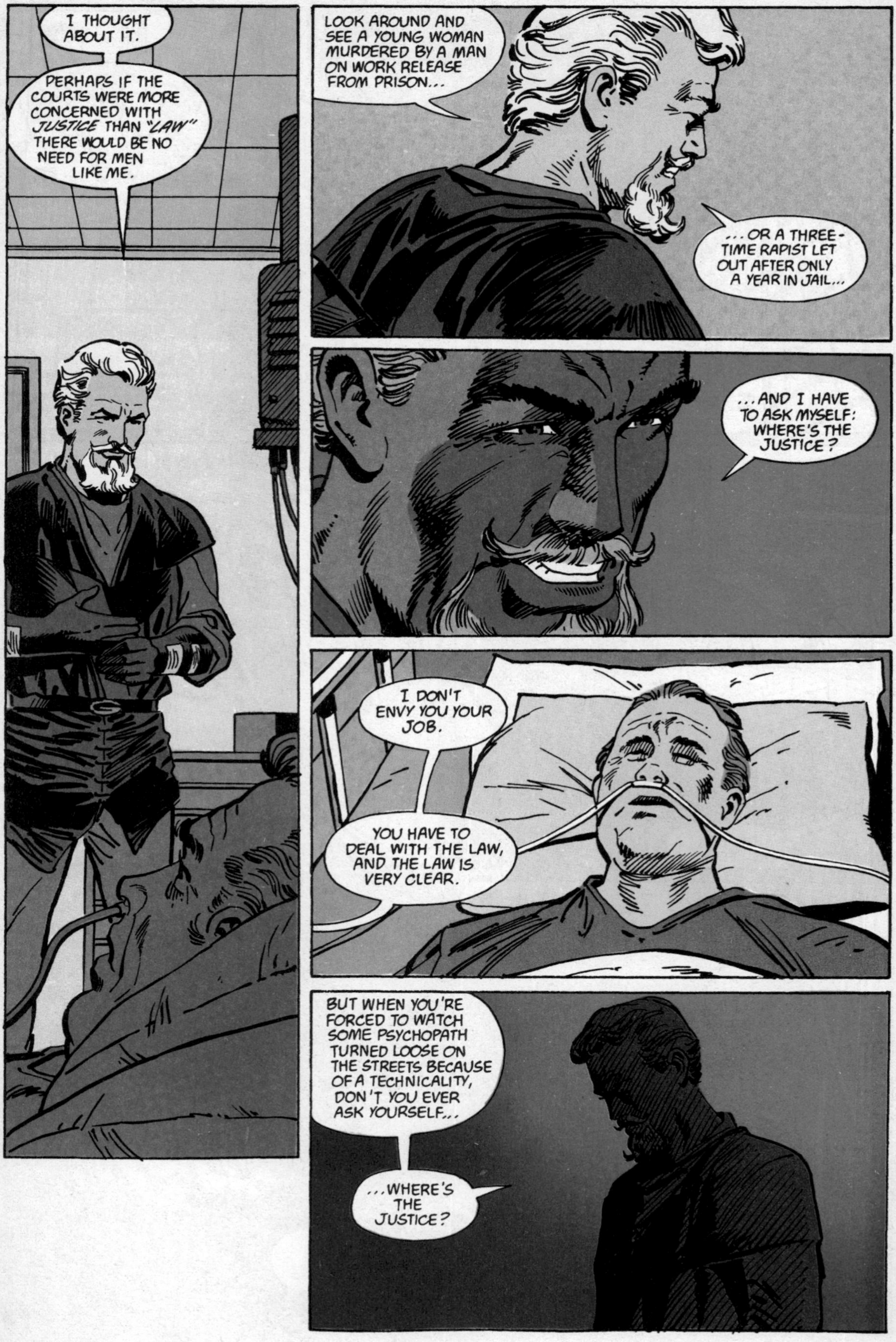
I THOUGHT ABOUT IT.
PERHAPS IF THE COURTS WERE MORE CONCERNED WITH *JUSTICE* THAN "*LAW*" THERE WOULD BE NO NEED FOR MEN LIKE ME.
LOOK AROUND AND SEE A YOUNG WOMAN MURDERED BY A MAN ON WORK RELEASE FROM PRISON...
...OR A THREE-TIME RAPIST LET OUT AFTER ONLY A YEAR IN JAIL...
...AND I HAVE TO ASK MYSELF: WHERE'S THE JUSTICE?
I DON'T ENVY YOU YOUR JOB.
YOU HAVE TO DEAL WITH THE LAW, AND THE LAW IS VERY CLEAR.
BUT WHEN YOU'RE FORCED TO WATCH SOME PSYCHOPATH TURNED LOOSE ON THE STREETS BECAUSE OF A TECHNICALITY, DON'T YOU EVER ASK YOURSELF...
...WHERE'S THE JUSTICE?

I'LL ADMIT, I STARTED DOING THIS FOR *FUN.*

BUT THAT WAS A LONG TIME AGO WHEN THINGS WERE A LOT SIMPLER.

NOW WE'VE GOT *KIDS* ON THE STREET WHO *KILL* FOR *POCKET CHANGE.*

WHEN SOME SCUMBAG BEATS AN EIGHTY YEAR OLD WOMAN FOR HER SOCIAL SECURITY CHECK...

...AND THE COURT CAN'T TOUCH HIM BECAUSE HE'S A JUVENILE WHO'S BACK ON THE STREET IN SIXTY DAYS, A LOT OF PEOPLE WANT TO KNOW...

WHERE'S THE JUSTICE?

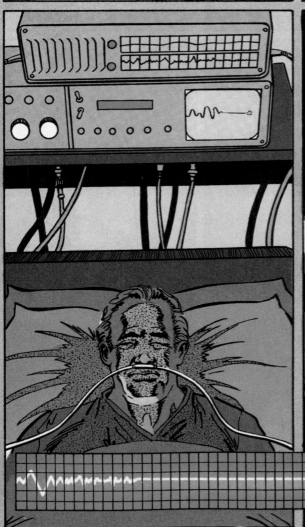

FOR PEOPLE LIKE THAT...

...THE ANSWER IS PEOPLE LIKE ME.

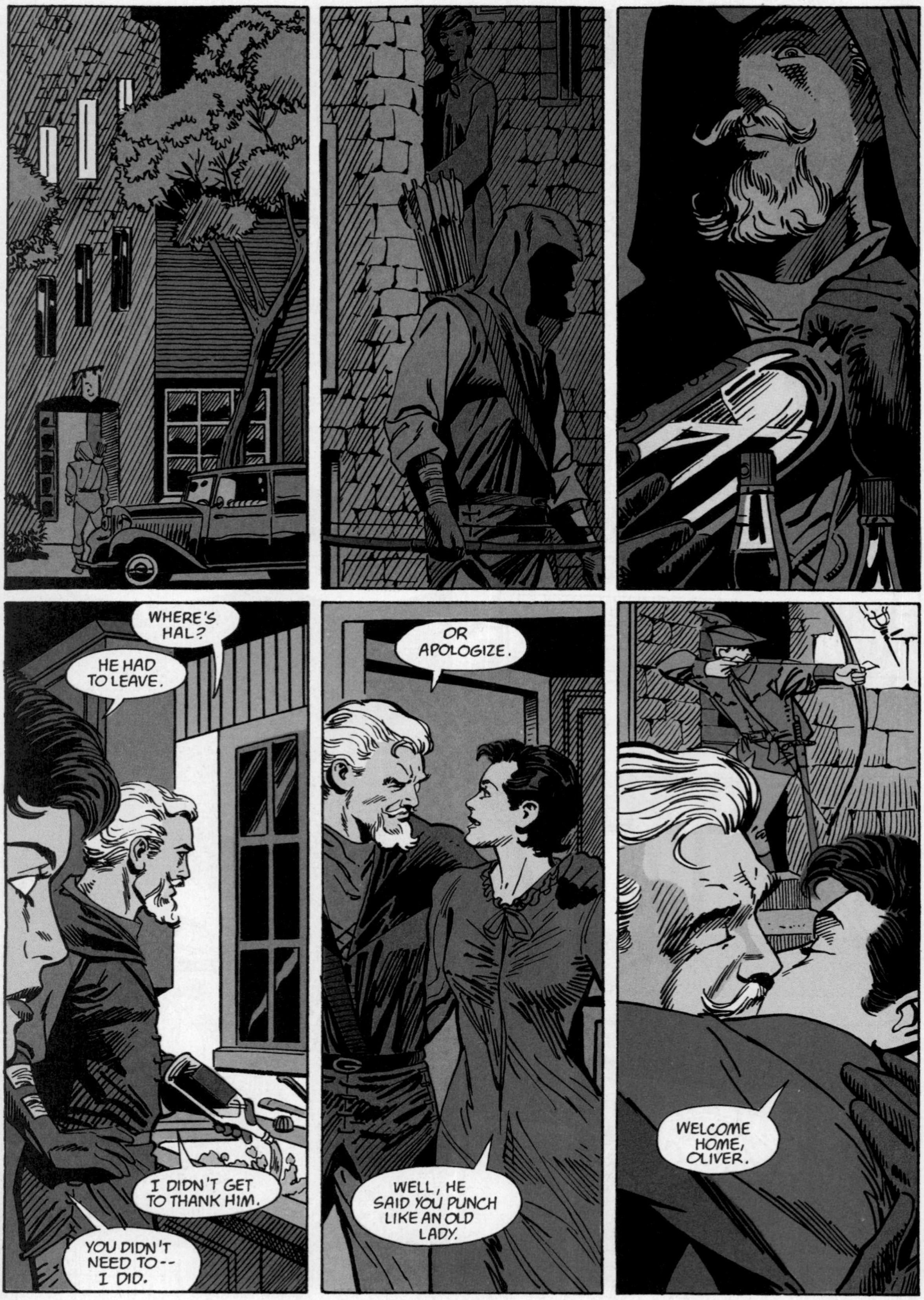
WHERE'S HAL?
HE HAD TO LEAVE.
I DIDN'T GET TO THANK HIM.
YOU DIDN'T NEED TO-- I DID.
OR APOLOGIZE.
WELL, HE SAID YOU PUNCH LIKE AN OLD LADY.
WELCOME HOME, OLIVER.

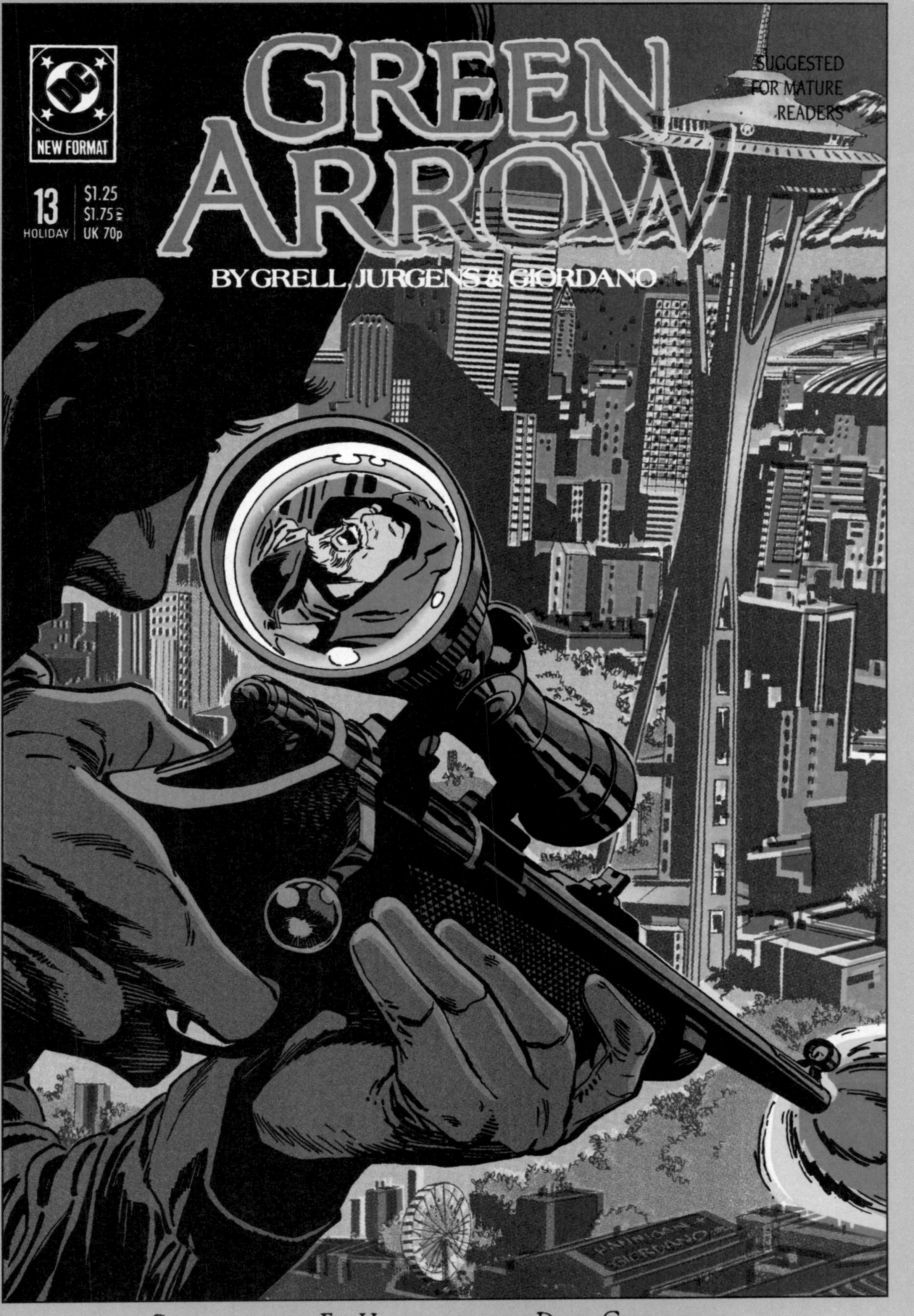
GREEN ARROW
NEW FORMAT
13
HOLIDAY
$1.25
$1.75
UK 70p
SUGGESTED FOR MATURE READERS
BY GRELL, JURGENS & GIORDANO

Cover art by Ed Hannigan and Dick Giordano

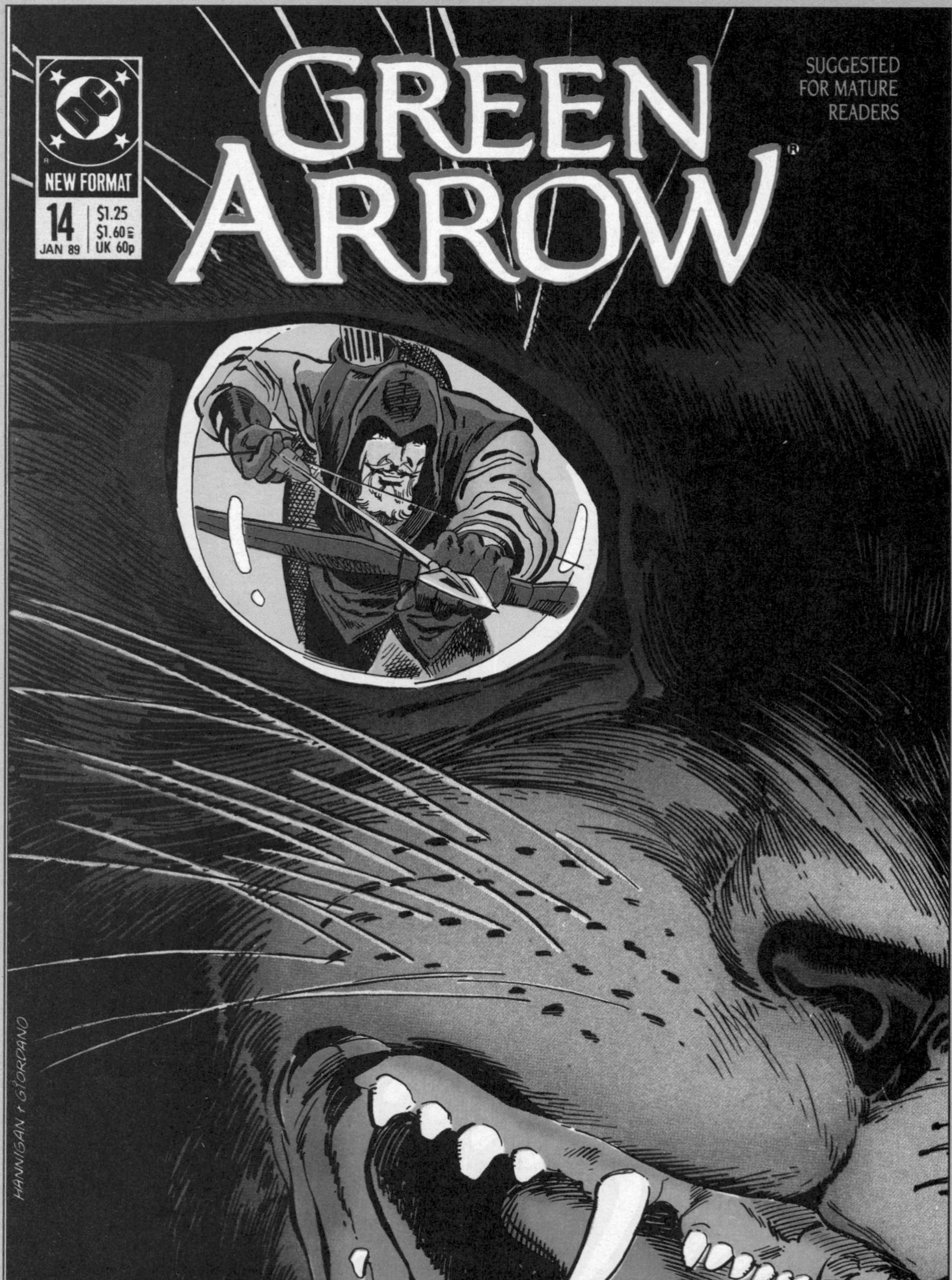
GREEN ARROW
SUGGESTED FOR MATURE READERS
DC
NEW FORMAT
14
JAN 89
$1.25
$1.60
UK 60p
HANNIGAN + GIORDANO
BY GRELL, JURGENS & GIORDANO

Cover art by Ed Hannigan and Dick Giordano

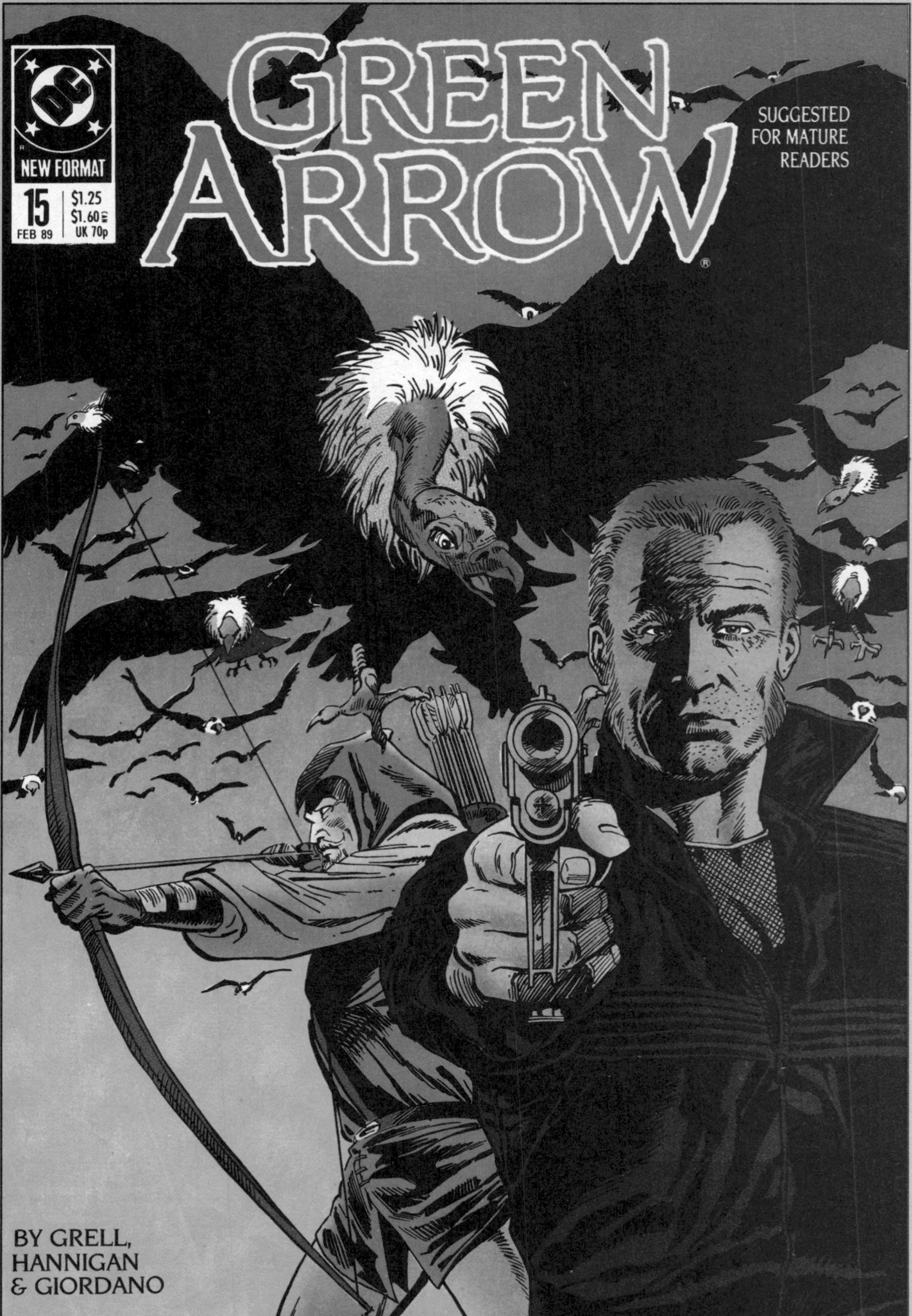

NEW FORMAT
15
FEB 89
$1.25
$1.60
UK 70p
GREEN ARROW
SUGGESTED FOR MATURE READERS
BY GRELL, HANNIGAN & GIORDANO

Cover art by Ed Hannigan and Dick Giordano

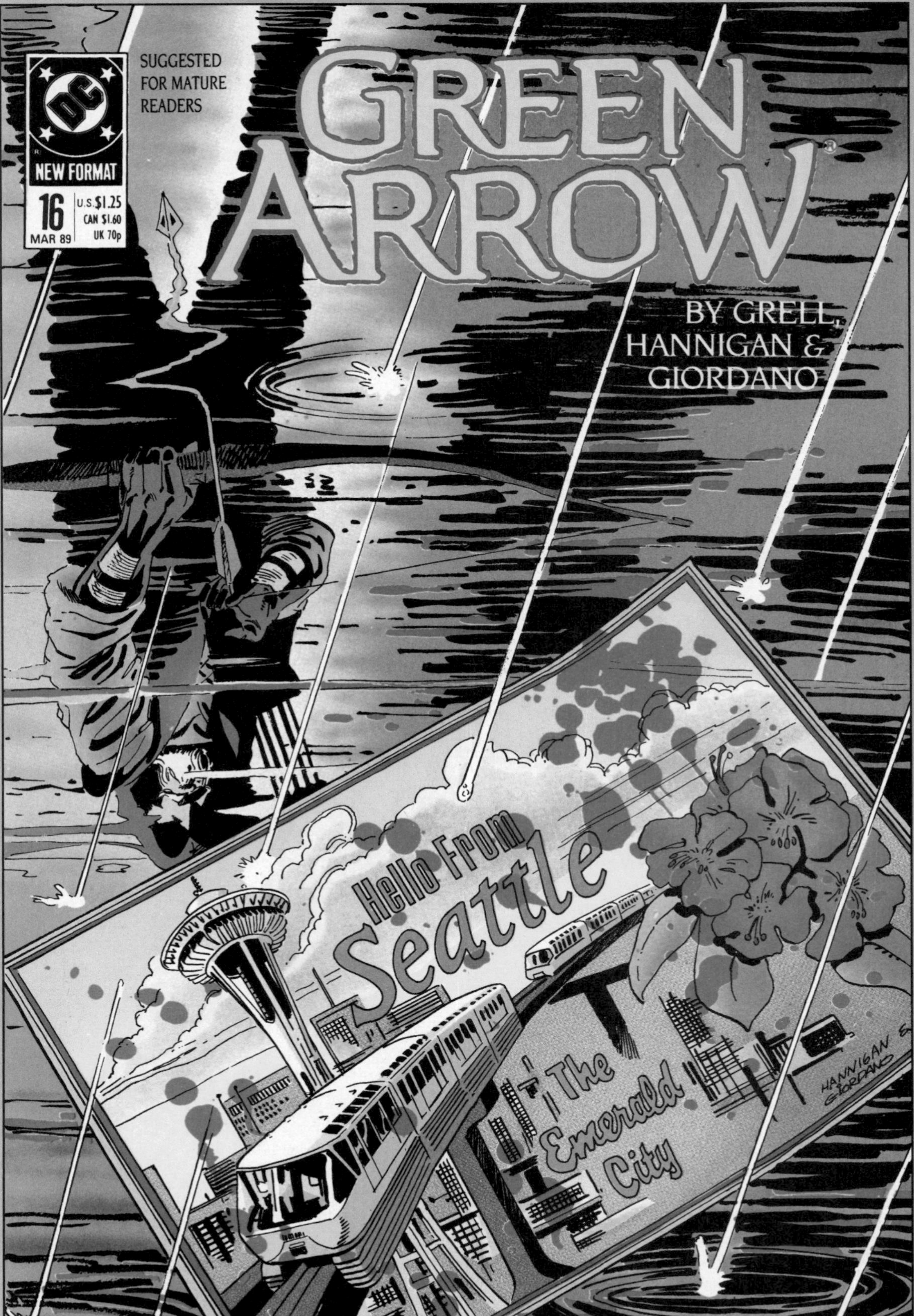
SUGGESTED
FOR MATURE
READERS
NEW FORMAT
16
MAR 89
U.S. $1.25
CAN $1.60
UK 70p
GREEN ARROW
BY GRELL,
HANNIGAN &
GIORDANO
Hello From
Seattle
The
Emerald
City
HANNIGAN &
GIORDANO

Cover art by Ed Hannigan and Dick Giordano

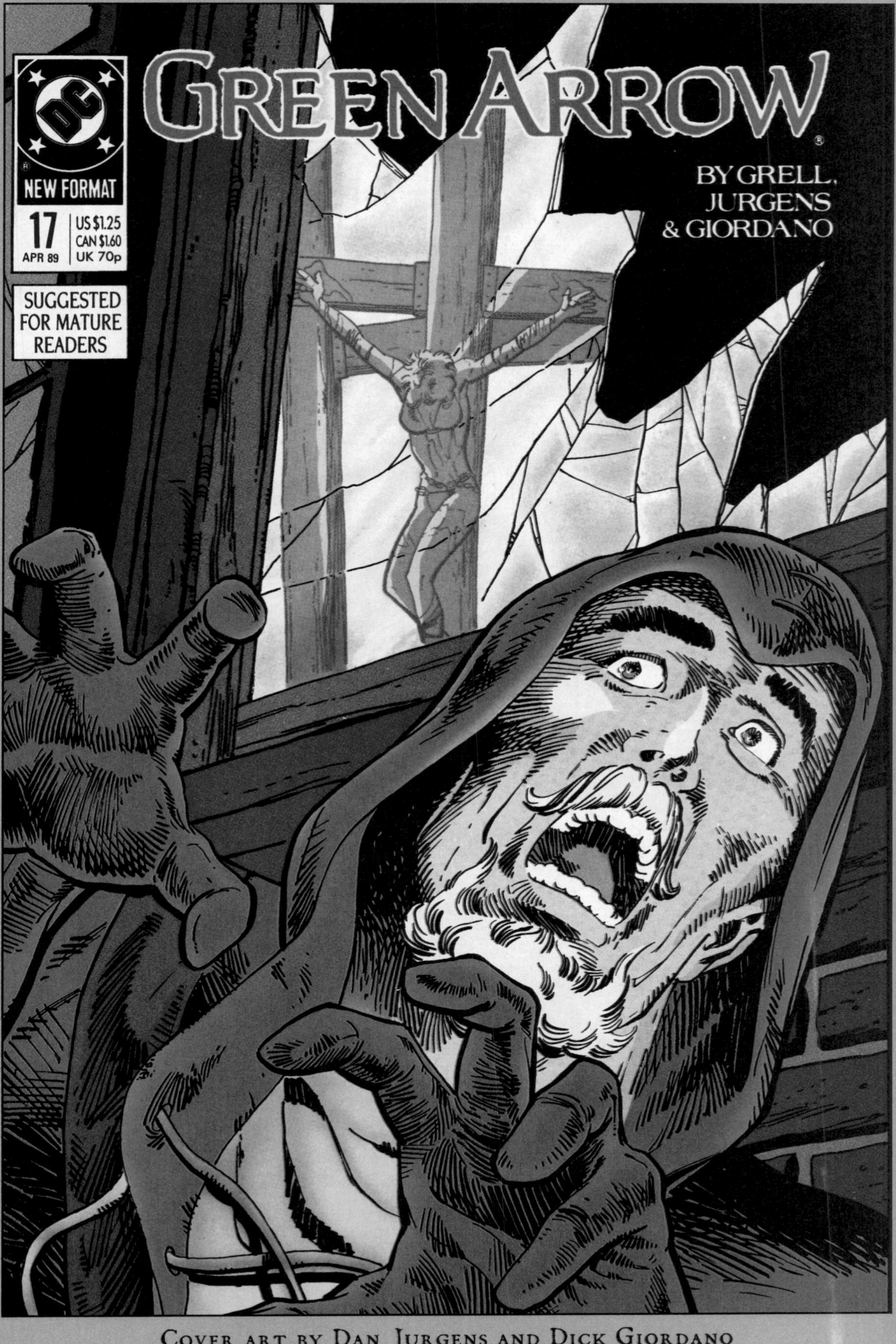

GREEN ARROW
NEW FORMAT
17
APR 89
US $1.25
CAN $1.60
UK 70p
SUGGESTED FOR MATURE READERS
BY GRELL, JURGENS & GIORDANO

Cover art by Dan Jurgens and Dick Giordano

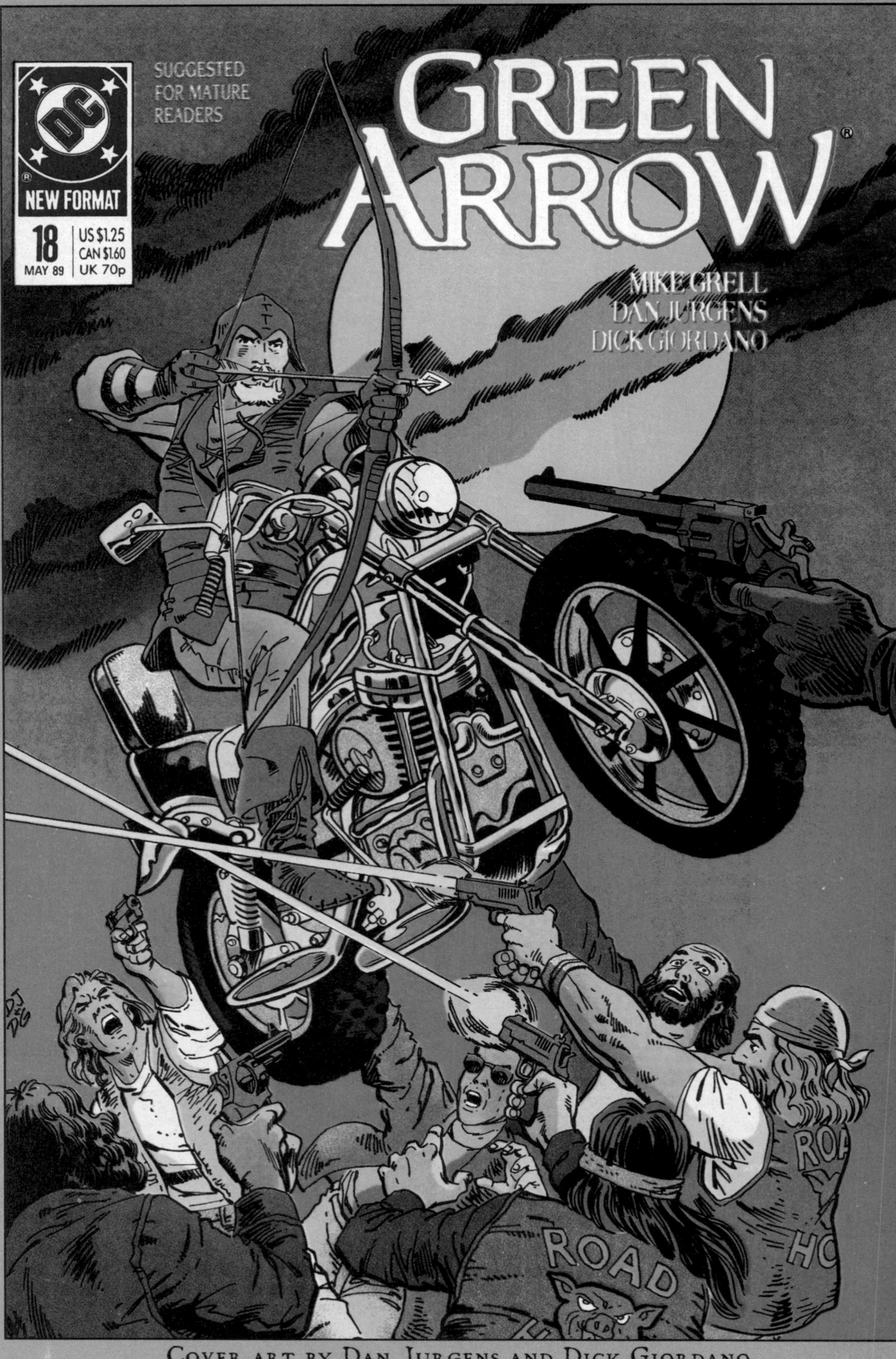
SUGGESTED
FOR MATURE
READERS
DC
NEW FORMAT
18
MAY 89
US $1.25
CAN $1.60
UK 70p
GREEN
ARROW
MIKE GRELL
DAN JURGENS
DICK GIORDANO
DJ
DG
ROAD
ROA
HO

Cover art by Dan Jurgens and Dick Giordano

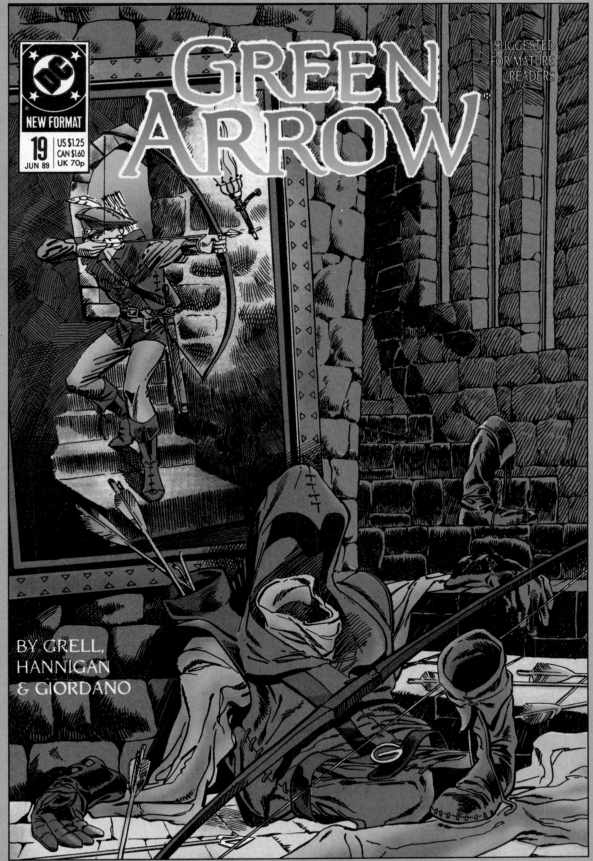

Cover art by Ed Hannigan and Dick Giordano

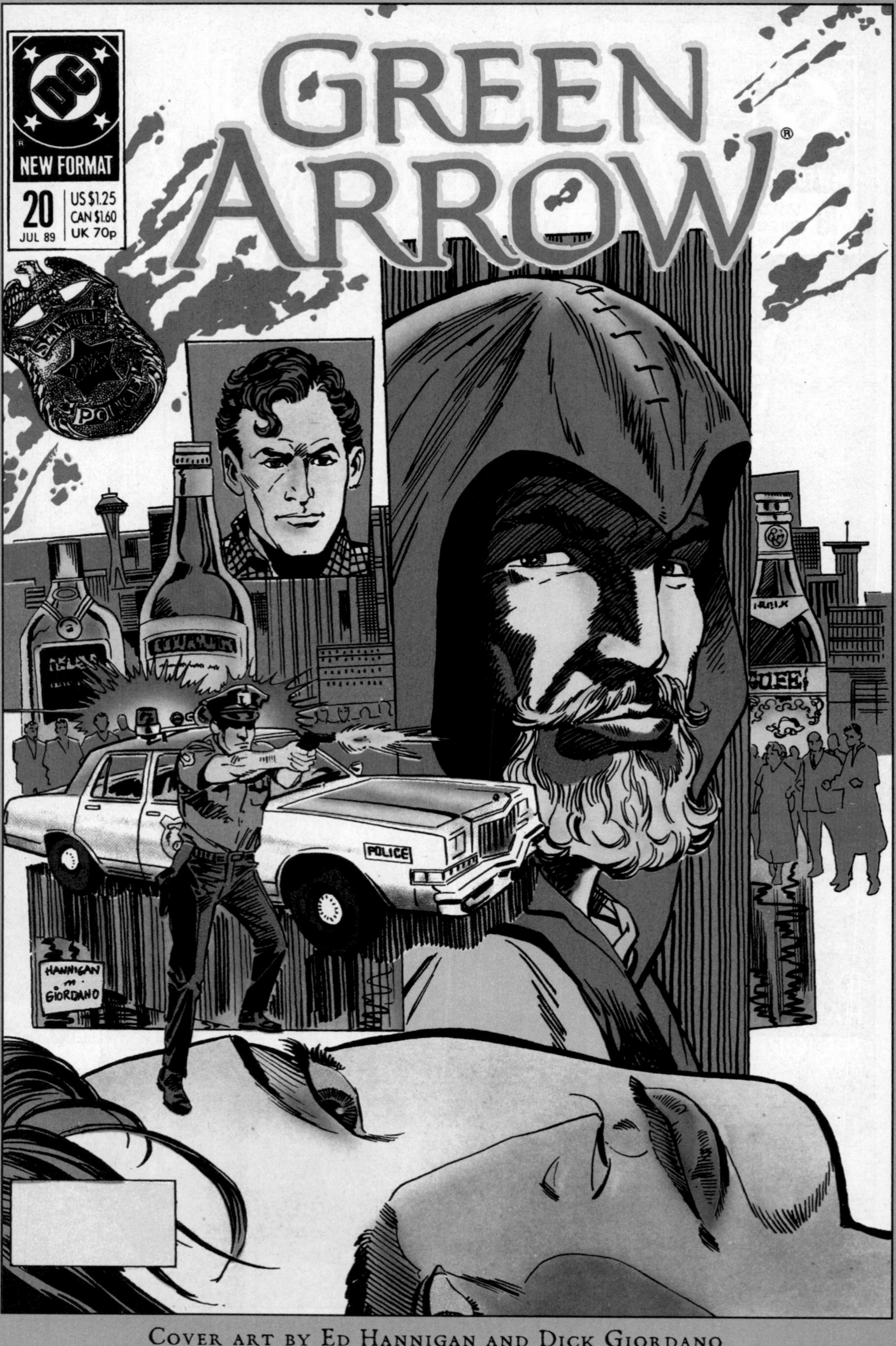
GREEN ARROW
NEW FORMAT
20
JUL 89
US $1.25
CAN $1.60
UK 70p
POLICE
HANNIGAN
GIORDANO

Cover art by Ed Hannigan and Dick Giordano